READING HEBREW LITERATURE

READING HEBREW LITERATURE

CRITICAL DISCUSSIONS OF SIX MODERN TEXTS

ALAN MINTZ, EDITOR

BRANDEIS UNIVERSITY PRESS

Published by University Press of New England
Hanover and London

Published by University Press of New England, Hanover, NH 03755
© 2003 by Brandeis University Press
All rights reserved
Printed in the United States of America   5 4 3 2 1
Book design by Dean Bornstein

The Hebrew appendix was typeset by Dror Magal at Meged Translation and
Type Setting Services, Israel.

Library of Congress Cataloging-in-Publication Data
Reading Hebrew literature : critical discussions of six modern
texts / edited by Alan L. Mintz.
p. cm. — (The Tauber Institute for the Study of European
Jewry series)
Includes bibliographical references.
ISBN 1-58465-195-4 (cloth) — ISBN 1-58465-200-4 (paperback)
1. Hebrew literature, Modern—20th century—History and criticism. 2. Israeli literature—History and criticism. 3. Hebrew literature, Modern—20th century—Translations into English. 4. Israeli
literature—Translations into English. I. Mintz, Alan L.
II. Series.
PJ5020.R39 2002
892.4'09006—dc21
2002010155

Yisrael Gutman, Ezra Mendelsohn, Jehuda Reinharz, and Chone Shmeruk, editors, 1989
The Jews of Poland Between Two World Wars

Avraham Barkai, 1989
From Boycott to Annihilation: The Economic Struggle of German Jews, 1933–1943

Alexander Altmann, 1991
The Meaning of Jewish Existence: Theological Essays 1930–1939

Magdalena Opalski and Israel Bartal, 1992
Poles and Jews: A Failed Brotherhood

Richard Breitman, 1992
The Architect of Genocide: Himmler and the Final Solution

George L. Mosse, 1993
Confronting the Nation: Jewish and Western Nationalism

Daniel Carpi, 1994
Between Mussolini and Hitler: The Jews and the Italian Authorities in France and Tunisia

Walter Laqueur and Richard Breitman, 1994
Breaking the Silence: The German Who Exposed the Final Solution

Ismar Schorsch, 1994
From Text to Context: The Turn to History in Modern Judaism

Jacob Katz, 1995
With My Own Eyes: The Autobiography of an Historian

Gideon Shimoni, 1995
The Zionist Ideology

Moshe Prywes and Haim Chertok, 1996
Prisoner of Hope

János Nyiri, 1997
Battlefields and Playgrounds

Alan Mintz, editor, 1997
The Boom in Contemporary Israeli Fiction

Samuel Bak, paintings
Lawrence L. Langer, essay and commentary, 1997
Landscapes of Jewish Experience

Jeffrey Shandler and Beth S. Wenger, editors, 1997
Encounters with the "Holy Land": Place, Past and Future in American Jewish Culture

Simon Rawidowicz, 1998
State of Israel, Diaspora, and Jewish Continuity: Essays on the "Ever-Dying People"

Jacob Katz, 1998
A House Divided: Orthodoxy and Schism in Nineteenth-Century Central European Jewry

Elisheva Carlebach, John M. Efron, and David N. Myers, editors, 1998
Jewish History and Jewish Memory: Essays in Honor of Yosef Hayim Yerushalmi

Shmuel Almog, Jehuda Reinharz, and Anita Shapira, editors, 1998
Zionism and Religion

Ben Halpern and Jehuda Reinharz, 2000
Zionism and the Creation of a New Society

Walter Laqueur, 2001
Generation Exodus: The Fate of Young Jewish Refugees from Nazi Germany

Yigal Schwartz, 2001
Aharon Appelfeld: From Individual Lament to Tribal Eternity

Renée Poznanski, 2001
Jews in France during World War II

ChaeRan Y. Freeze, 2002
Jewish Marriage and Divorce in Imperial Russia

Mark A. Raider and Miriam B. Raider-Roth, 2002
The Plough Woman: Records of the Pioneer Women of Palestine

Ezra Mendelsohn, 2002
Painting a People: Maurycy Gottlieb and Jewish Art

Alan Mintz, 2002
Reading Hebrew Literature: Critical Discussions of Six Modern Texts

Haim Be'er, 2002
The Pure Element of Time

Yehudit Hendel, 2002
Small Change: A Collection of Stories

Contents

Acknowledgments   xi

Introduction by Alan Mintz   1

I. "The Red Heifer" by M. J. Berdyczewski   21
(translation by William Cutter)
William Cutter   29
Anne Golomb Hoffman   38
Avner Holtzman   52

II. *To the Sun* by Saul Tchernichowsky   64
(translation by Robert Alter)
Aminadav A. Dykman   73
Arnold J. Band   81
Robert Alter   92

III. "The Sense of Smell" by S. Y. Agnon   102
(translation by Arthur Green)
Naomi Sokoloff   109
David G. Roskies   118
Alan Mintz   126

IV. "Man's House" by U. Z. Greenberg   135
(translation by Harold Schimmel)
Lewis Glinert   138
Dan Laor   146
Hannan Hever   154

V. "Bridal Veil" by Amalia Kahana-Carmon   158
(translation by Raya and Nimrod Jones)

Nancy E. Berg   176
Gilead Morahg   185
Hannah Naveh   195

VI. "Hovering at a Low Altitude" by Dahlia Ravikovitch   210
(translation by Chana Bloch and Ariel Bloch)

Barbara Mann   213
Nili R. Scharf Gold   221
Chana Kronfeld   232

Contributors   246
Bibliographical Note   250
Appendix: Hebrew Texts
I. "The Red Heifer" by M. J. Berdyczewski   A3
II. *To the Sun* by Saul Tchernichowsky   A10
III. "The Sense of Smell" by S. Y. Agnon   A18
IV. "Man's House" by U. Z. Greenberg   A23
V. "Bridal Veil" by Amalia Kahana-Carmon   A25
VI. "Hovering at a Low Altitude" by Dahlia Ravikovitch   A37

Acknowledgments

A profound debt of gratitude is owed Sylvia Fuks Fried, director of the Tauber Institute and the Jacob and Libby Goodman Institute for the Study of Zionism and Israel at Brandeis University, for her vision and unfailing good sense. Miriam Hoffman of the Tauber Institute and Lisa Sacks and Michael P. Burton of the University Press of New England are to be thanked for bringing their expertise and abundant good will to the realization of this complex and multiauthored volume.

This publication is made possible in part through the generous support of Beverly Baker and the Morris and Beverly Baker Foundation, the Rosemary E. Krensky Fund for Continuing Studies on the America–Holy Land Relationship, and the Joseph H. and Belle R. Braun Chair in Modern Hebrew Literature at Brandeis University.

READING HEBREW LITERATURE

INTRODUCTION

Alan Mintz

[1]

MODERN HEBREW LITERATURE is typically taught in American universities in departments of Middle Eastern languages and cultures, and this would seem to be the most natural of arrangements because contemporary Hebrew literature is produced in the Middle East and in a language that is a Semitic tongue like Arabic. Yet this location, despite whatever administrative logic or convenience it might have, conceals a tortuous provenance that is far more intriguing than would first appear to be the case. The beginnings of the new Hebrew literature, according to most accounts, actually go back to Germany in the eighteenth century when Jewish intellectuals sought to participate in the Enlightenment by writing poetry, philosophy, and social criticism in the revived classical language of Jewish Scripture. In the nineteenth century, the center of Hebrew writing moved east to Poland, Lithuania, and Galicia, where Hebrew became the main medium for an ambitious program to modernize Jewish society. The centerpiece of this program was the creation of a modern Hebrew belles-lettres in which the ancient language would be used not for religious instruction and scholarly communication but for the purposes of social critique, moral uplift, and beauty for its own sake. Throughout the century, the literary system of modern Hebrew was filled in genre by genre: first, lyric poetry and social satire; and then, novels, epics, and autobiographies.

All this literary activity took place in an era before Zionism and visions of settling the Land of Israel quickened the Jewish imagination and became a significant ideological formation—and certainly long before anyone had thought seriously about actually speaking Hebrew as an everyday language of practical communication. It is, of course, these forces that eventually led to the creation of Israeli literature; but it is important to point out that this was a prolonged process, and a geographically dispersed one at that. It was at the very end of the century that Hebrew took off as a serious modern literature poised between Romanticism and modernism. This moment of flowering was brought about by two forces. One was, indeed, the rise of

Jewish nationalism, in which the idea of a Jewish national language went hand in hand with the idea of a Jewish national homeland. Of these fundamental planks of nationalism, language and territory, the former proved the much easier and quicker to implement. The other force was the spiritual crisis of East European Jewish youth. Raised in the piety and scholarship of the study house and the synagogue, these young people came of age after the metaphysical coherence of this culture had unraveled and before a new, secular and nationalist order had been established. For this generation—we are, again, speaking of the turn of the century—writing in Hebrew was not part of an ideological program but rather an attempt at a desperate solution to the unbearable pain of religious and cultural orphanhood. The vast and reticulated resources of the religious tradition that had collapsed upon them were utilized—often ironically and subversively—to explore the vicissitudes of experience in the world after faith. It was this existential exigency that drove writers to a level of imaginative complexity and invention that turned Hebrew into a serious modern literature.

The destruction and cultural repression brought on by the Russian Revolution and World War I broke up the center of Hebrew literature in Eastern Europe. By the late 1920s, to be sure, most of the writers, the publishing houses, and the literary journals had managed to relocate themselves to Tel Aviv or Jerusalem. But the decade-long sojourn along the way proved fateful. Displaced from the East and sojourning in Berlin, Paris, and other European cultural centers, Hebrew writers encountered the avant-garde of European literature and brought Symbolism and Expressionism with them on their way to Palestine. Then there were those who did not come. Although modern Hebrew was always linked to Zionism and settlement in Palestine, it also had a life of its own as a national idea and a cultural praxis. In such newly independent countries as Poland, Latvia, and Lithuania, Hebrew formed the basis for a network of independent Jewish schools (the Tarbuth schools); on the staffs of these schools, as well as working independently, were scores of Hebrew poets and essayists. Some of them and their students managed to emigrate to Palestine; others, together with Hebrew writers in Vienna, Paris, and elsewhere, were not so lucky.

And then there was America. Among the millions of Jews who came to America from Eastern Europe during the period of mass immigration, there were those who, inspired by the writings of Ahad Ha'am and other nationalist thinkers, believed that Hebrew could serve as a medium for cultural revival in the diaspora. In contrast to Yiddish, for the proponents of Hebrew it was never a mass vision. The prospect of Hebrew culture in America was always conceived of as a matter of high culture and as an endeavor of cultural elites. In New York during World War I, it did not seem a lunatic notion. The war had exiled Zionist leaders from Palestine, and some of the most prominent (Ben-Gurion, Ben-Zvi, and Ben-Yehuda among them) were living at this time in America. The Soviet Union had shut down organs of Jewish self-expression, and Hebrew cultural activity in Central and Western Europe was frozen. As a land of economic security and relative freedom from persecution, America recommended itself as a refuge for Hebrew culture, at the very least, and perhaps even as a vigorous secondary center once the Jewish institutions of the Yishuv were restored.

Although the leaders of the Yishuv returned to Palestine after the war, the vision of a Hebrew culture in America remained. Between the two world wars, literary journals were published; a Hebrew daily newspaper was founded; a network of Hebrew colleges, which roughly paralleled the Tarbuth schools in Europe, sprang up; Hebrew became the dominant ethos of Jewish education; and, most important, dozens of poets, novelists, dramatists, and essayists produced serious literature in Hebrew. For a host of reasons having to do mostly with the enormous force of Americanization, America never succeeded in becoming a major center for Hebrew literature. Some of the strongest writers, such as Shimon Halkin and Israel Efros, eventually emigrated to Israel and took part in the flourishing literary culture there. Others, including E. E. Lisitzky, Gabriel Preil, and Reuven Wallenrod, stayed on as part of a dwindling colony of Hebrew writers who could count on more readers abroad than on native ground.

The waning of Hebraist institutions in America coincided with the establishment of the State of Israel, and this intersection had a profound effect upon the study of Hebrew literature in America, which is the subject and occasion of this volume. After the destruction of European Jewry, which engendered in American Jews a mixture of shame, denial, and grief, the victory of Israel over the Arab armies in 1948 elicited a cathartic outpouring of support and identification from American Jews. The existence of Israel affected American Jews in many ways, and among them was the perception of Hebrew. If Hebrew was once taken as the banner of a parochial nationalist movement and as one ideological claimant among many in Jewish life, Hebrew now attained the status of the official language of a sovereign state. In the university, Hebrew's new position as a modern "foreign language" connected with its long-standing status under the sign of Orientalism as an ancient or classical Semitic tongue. With the spread of ethnic studies programs in the 1960s, Hebrew language instruction spread to many leading universities. Hebrew was taught as a modern language of the Middle East; instruction in Hebrew stressed speaking, writing, understanding, and reading, that is, all the skills of a modern spoken language.

The acceptance of Hebrew as a language in American universities led to a growth of interest in Hebrew as a literature. If creative and original Hebrew writing has not flourished on these shores in recent decades, the critical study of modern Hebrew literature has developed and reached a level of considerable sophistication and critical clarity, a judgment that I hope readers will be convinced of on the basis of the contributions to the present volume. This achievement has been the result of two rather disparate factors: nationalist enthusiasm and literary method. Before the 1960s, there was virtually no Hebrew literature taught in the universities; it was only in the Hebrew colleges that it existed as a subject. The teachers who taught it were more enthusiasts than literary scholars or critics. The whole conception of what it meant to write about literature was caught between the dry positivism of literary history and the impressionism of appreciative literary journalism. Yet if method was in short supply, enthusiasm was not. By enthusiasm, I do not mean a jejune and superficial boosterism but rather a profoundly embroiled connection to Hebrew literature as a fateful national enterprise. For these men—and they were mostly men—Hebrew literature mattered not only because it was beautiful but because it was the chief medium in which the great dilemmas of the Jewish nation and the Jewish individual were being wrestled with.

The rigor came from elsewhere. Scholars such as Arnold Band and Robert Alter acquired their attachment to Hebrew literature in the Hebrew colleges—the Boston Hebrew Teachers College in Band's case, and the Teachers Institute of the Jewish Theological Seminary in Alter's. They took this connection with them when they embarked upon graduate studies in comparative literature at Harvard and drank deeply from the critical currents that flowed there and in the literature departments of other great universities: New Criticism, genre theory, existentialism, and serious literary biography. Especially influential was the vocabulary of New Criticism, whose key terms included irony and metaphor, tenor and vehicle, persona and implied author, form and value, showing and telling. This new regime of reading, with its battery of precision tools, gave students a way to rationalize their enthusiasm and give an account of how a text produces its meaning. It was a way of reading that could be applied, and was applied, with great profit to Hebrew literature.

The immersion in the new literary criticism also had an effect on how the canon of modern Hebrew literature was shaped in America. For example, in the case of the two great poets of the Revival period at the turn of the century, Saul Tchernichowsky and Chaim Nachman Bialik, it was their epic poems on national themes that had captured the minds of earlier readers. But for these new students of Hebrew literature, who had read widely in modernist European poetry and its explication through the New Critical tools, it was the more introspective and imagistic lyric poetry of these same poets that deserved to be foregrounded as the best work of the period. This is not to say that similar revisions of the canon were not taking place at the same time in Israel, which remained the preeminent center of Hebrew literary studies. Yet the intellectual influences were different, stemming more from Russian formalism and German comparative literature, and these in turn affected the works that critics and scholars chose to teach, write about, and have republished. There was, to be sure, considerable cross-fertilization; Dan Miron studied in New York, Gershon Shaked in Zurich, Arnold Band in Jerusalem. But there is no denying that there remained a definite American voice in Hebrew literary studies whose accents were traceable to the distinctive conventions of Anglo-American criticism.

In the decades that followed—the seventies, eighties, and nineties—the study of Hebrew literature here was roiled and energized by the same strong currents that animated literary studies in American universities generally: poststructuralism, feminist criticism and gender studies, psychoanalysis, deconstruction, poetics, postcolonialist theory, film theory. It was a time, and continues to be a time, of enormous ferment, controversy, and dispersion. The enterprise of literary theory, which had long been a respected but abstruse undertaking, suddenly came to the forefront of literary studies. Rather than mining theoretical insights as a reward for prolonged engagement in practical criticism and scholarship, "doing theory" became a privileged and glamorous endeavor unto itself. The stance of the interpreter toward the literature he or she studied changed as well. This stance had long been characterized by appreciation and respect for the artistic achievement of great works of literature. In urging a hermeneutics of suspicion, deconstruction began with the assumption that all literary works are rent by internal contradictions and self-subversions that make artistic coherence illusory. Another fundamental change lay in the removal of the partition between political ideology and literary study. The practitioners of the older criticism had always had politics, which could be inferred from their critical writings; yet there remained an ideal of disinterested scholarship. For practitioners of postcolonial theory and certain varieties of feminist criticism, however, the proposition was turned around. Explicit ideological commitment became the motor that drove all acts of engagement with specific works of literature.

Hebrew literary studies were not, to be sure, at the forefront of these trends. There exists a lag—I think, all in all, a salubrious lag—between Jewish studies and the cutting edge of work in the humanities, and this delay sometimes allows for the kind of shakeout in the market of critical ideas that distinguishes enduring developments from fashionable ones. All things considered, however, the study of modern Hebrew literature can be said to reflect the polyphony of voices that characterizes the general study of literature in America today.

[2]

It is against this background that the present project was conceived. It represents an effort to bring this polyphony of voices into dialogue around a body of mutually esteemed texts. Three pairs of texts, one poetry and one prose in each case, were selected from three periods of modern Hebrew literature, and three readers were invited to offer an interpretive introduction to each of the six texts. The goal of this exercise was not to create an artificial harmony by eliding the intellectual and ideological differences among different readers. Rather than avoiding these differences, it was, in fact, the intention to exploit them by making use of the differential insights offered by each approach to illuminate aspects of a common object of investigation.

This volume is the second stage of a colloquium that took place at Brandeis University in June 1999. Unlike most collections of conference papers, the essays in this book were not simply expansions of presentations made at the colloquium. At the meeting, each of the eighteen participants was asked to prepare a brief interpretive introduction to one of the six texts. After these introductions—there were three for each of the six texts— the greater amount of time was spent discussing the texts themselves, not the presentations. After spending several hours on each text, the participants returned home with the charge of writing a short essay on their assigned text. While it was expected that the essays would be an expansion of the brief oral remarks made at the colloquium, it was equally expected that the writing would be affected by the give-and-take that took place while the participants faced one another around the seminar table.

The design of the colloquium (and the book based on it) is a response, in part, to a set of dissatisfactions about the state of academic communication. At most conferences, a scholar gets up to read a paper, takes a few questions if there is time, and then sits down to make way for the next presenter. The usual format of the twenty- to thirty-minute paper is too short for the adequate presentation of a coherent argument and too long for an audience to give sustained attention to an oral presentation. Even if the paper is given a polite reception, the scholar is left with the empty feeling of having intensively prepared and presented a serious statement on a subject deeply important to him or her, only to receive little or no substantive feedback or attention. Academic exchanges in such settings have come to resemble a kind of contest in which the scholar's performance contributes more to the enhancement or erosion of his or her reputation than to the enlarging of the body of knowledge.

Our response to this situation has been to place the text at the center and to let a community of discourse grow up around it. Placing the text at the center means that the goal of critical statement is to illuminate the text itself—that particular story or that particular poem—rather than using it as an instance or illustration in a larger theoretical or ideological argument. This does not mean that theoretical insights do not emerge from the discussion, but they arise *on the way* to the text and as a result of the encounter with it. The possibility of community arises because the illuminating of the text is the common purpose of the participants in the discourse and also because the inherent value of the text as a source of illumination is the common point of departure. The theoretical and ideological stances of the participants may be divergent and even antagonistic; but if the text is held in common at the center, it is likely that the discourse surrounding it will be marked by the kind of civility that has been in short supply in literary studies in recent decades.

It is not special pleading, I think, to see in this notion of text-centeredness the hovering spirit of classical Jewish learning. It has long been acknowledged that, despite the modernity and secularizing message of modern literature, the close methods with which it has been studied owe a great deal both to the exegesis of Scripture in the Protestant tradition as well as to the rise of modern Bible scholarship. How much more so in the case of Jewish studies and Hebrew literature, in which the shift from the study of classical texts in the study house to the study of modern texts in the university has often taken place in little more than a generation. That this proximity is at times a mixed blessing needs no elaboration. Yet this classical patrimony has served the study of modern Hebrew literature in two signal ways. First, the aura of the text—and by text, I mean the serious modern artwork—has been maintained in the face of efforts to make texts into either lumpen discourse or the tools of cultural elites. Second, the modern text, like its classical precursor, has been conceived of from the outset as a rich nexus of intertextual allusions and overdetermined meanings.

If the text indeed creates community, then one is entitled to ask which of those texts gets to be placed at the center and who those are who are invited to sit around the table. The scheme for selecting the texts for this project was based on considerations of historical period, genre, gender, and practicality. Texts were chosen from the three central historical phases of the development of modern Hebrew literature: the Teḥiyyah, or Revival period (1881–1919), the Moderna period (1920–1947), and the State period (1948 to the present). (As in the case of literary history generally, there are many ways to periodize and classify; this division served simply as a guideline for distributing the texts over a broad historical range, and we have been flexible with these heuristic boundaries. For instance, in the case of Uri Zvi Greenberg, a preeminent poet of the Moderna period between the two world wars, we chose a postwar poem.) When it came to genre, we decided to divide the texts evenly between poetry and short fiction (as opposed to drama, autobiography, the novel, and the essay) simply because of the inherent importance of these kinds of writing and because of the ready expertise of the participants in writing about them. There was a deliberate choice made to select women writers from the latest of the three periods. Writing by women is among the best in Israel in recent decades, and its inclusion requires no special justification. But because it is a scarce phenomenon in earlier periods, we made a point of picking only women writers in the contemporary period. Finally, we kept to short works so that they could be referred to conveniently during the course of the face-to-face discussions and so that they could be included in the published volume.

It is harder to explain the choice of these six particular texts by these six particular writers. There is certainly nothing outré or provocative about the figures of Berdyczewski, Tchernichowsky, Agnon, Uri Zvi Greenberg,

Amalia Kahana-Carmon, and Dahlia Ravikovitch. All serious students would regard them as part of the core of Hebrew literature with secure status in its "canon." Yet at the same time, there are other writers who have often dominated critical attention as well as popular interest. In the Revival period, for example, there are Chaim Nachman Bialik and Yosef Chaim Brenner; in the Moderna period, there are Avraham Shlonsky and Natan Alterman; and in the State period, there are Yehuda Amichai, Amos Oz, and A. B. Yehoshua. Works by these authors, and by a number of others, would also have provided a rewarding set of platforms for critical deliberations. In the end, however, we decided for a set of writers who are a little less well known, especially in America, and for a set of texts that would be opened up to the reader with the help of the critical essays that accompany them. The writers were not chosen, it should be noted in passing, as a group, and they were not chosen to make an argument for a coherent parallel or countertradition. Many considerations surround the choice of the particular stories and poems, and they would be of interest largely to professionals in the field. But in a happy sense, these considerations are not immensely consequential, because the point of this project has not been to pick the six best of anything but to set out an array of rich and intriguing occasions for critical interaction. Within the repertoire of modern Hebrew literature, there are fortunately very many texts that could perform that function.

Finally, a word about the identity of the interpreters who have been gathered around the table at which these texts have been placed at the center. They represent the authorities on Hebrew literature working at American universities, together with a sprinkling of counterparts from Israeli universities. It is by no means an exhaustive list; some important people in the field could not participate because of scheduling conflicts. The disproportionate ratio of Americans to Israelis was part of the original plan of the project, which was entitled "Reading Israel in America." Hebrew literature is now essentially the cultural product of Israeli society, and we wanted to examine what difference it makes to teach and study this literature in North America rather than in the country in which it is being produced. (Great Hebrew literature, as was pointed out above, was, of course, produced in Eastern Europe before the Israeli period, and it has understandably been appropriated by Israeli writing as its direct patrimony.) Hence the question of reading Israel in America: Does the position of the interpreter here—who has been trained in American universities, who teaches American students, and who writes in English for American publications, whether academic or popular—make a difference in what one sees in a text and even in which texts one sees as important?

The answer is obviously in the affirmative, but it was not, in the end, a question that the participants in this project chose to take up. Although the conception of the colloquium and its very title invited hermeneutical self-awareness on these matters, it was an invitation that was declined by implicit omission. The reasons for this, I think, are several. The novelty of the setting, in which the literary text was placed at the center of intellectual deliberations, created the primary focus and did not allow much room for a reflexive dimension. Also, the putative boundary lines between the American interpreters and the Israeli interpreters turned out to be blurred. A number of the "American" participants, so called because of their established careers in American universities, grew up in Israel, served in the military there, and pursued their undergraduate studies in Israeli universities. Among the Israelis, all have spent study leaves in America, and one received his doctorate from an American university. While the Israelis tend to publish in Hebrew in Israel and the Americans in English in America, almost all have occasionally done the reverse, and all follow one another's work in both Hebrew and English. Although in the past, the two academic communities have been influenced by different schools of literary theory, as was outlined above, in recent years there has been a kind of globalization of literary studies in which geographical distinctions have become less significant.

All things considered, there nevertheless remain significant differences, especially concerning the vastly different audiences served by the two scholarly communities. In this bipolar cultural situation in general and in this gathering of essays in particular, there is much unexplored material for rewarding analysis. As a participant myself, however, it is not my place on this occasion to undertake this job of analysis and to probe into what was unsaid in our deliberations. Yet the issue remains important and fascinating; it is to be hoped that the challenge will be taken up by other minds or at other times and that the essays in this volume will provide fruitful material for analysis.

[3]

Of the great classic Hebrew writers from the turn of the century, Saul Tchernichowsky (1875–1943) was surely the most worldly. The literature of the age was dominated by figures like Chaim Nachman Bialik, who were raised in an intense regime of religious belief and practice and came of age in the study house and the yeshiva; their writing dramatizes the vertiginous break with the tradition, and their style is suffused with ironic allusions to the rabbinic learning of their youth. Tchernichowsky, on the other hand, though raised by pious parents in the Russian countryside, studied Russian literature and European culture from an early age, in addition to mastering the Hebrew Bible and the new Hebrew literature of the nineteenth century. Trained as a physician, Tchernichowsky practiced medicine, wrote late-Romantic verse in Hebrew, and translated into Hebrew works from an astonishing range of languages, including the entire *Iliad* and *Odyssey*.

To the Sun, the work of Tchernichowsky's chosen for discussion here, impresses on many levels. It is an example of the exotic poetic genre of the corona: a cycle of fifteen sonnets whose final sonnet is made up of the first lines of the previous fourteen. The Hebrew style is breathtakingly rich in its lexical and syntactic complexity. The range of cultural materials comprehended by the poem is similarly breathtaking: biblical narratives, Canaanite myths, Egyptian hieroglyphs, Druid runes, botany, cosmology, atomic energy, and more. It is astonishing to consider the fact that such a virtuoso artwork could be created at a time when virtually no one (yet) spoke the language in which it was written. The complex accomplishment of *To the Sun* testifies both to the breakthrough in Hebrew literature at the turn of the century and to the century-long development of modern Hebrew verse that preceded it, as well as to the strata of biblical and medieval Hebrew laid down in the more distant past.

More than any other text in this volume, *To the Sun* has presented a challenge to translation. The allusiveness and concision of the language, the exalted romantic stylistic register, the elaborate poetic conventions of the sonnet and the corona, and the intricacy of the rhymes make it nearly impossible to create an equivalent English poem that preserves some of these features and does not sound like an artificial and ridiculous construction. Robert Alter has therefore chosen to produce a translation of *To the Sun* that makes it possible for the English reader to follow the sense of the poem and feel something of its intense pathos without being distracted by a separate poetic edifice that is overwrought and, in the end, not quite English.[1] To compensate the English reader for this inevitable loss, Alter devotes his essay to an explication of "how" the poem means in the original Hebrew. By stressing the "original" Hebrew, Alter reminds us that the way Hebrew was pronounced by Tchernichowsky's generation in Eastern Europe differed markedly from the way Hebrew is pronounced in Israel today; and he explores the subtlety and power with which Tchernichowsky deploys rhyme to convey meaning. In his essay, Arnold Band has taken responsibility for the difficult task of producing a reading of the cycle as a whole against the background of historical and cultural issues that engaged Tchernichowsky's imagination. Band discerns a movement from an auto-biographical exploration of the poet's problematic relationship to the sun in the first half of the cycle to a wider set of reflections on nature and history as embodiments of solar power in the second half, with a climax reached in the fifteenth sonnet, which is a "paean to the wonders of atomic energy." Aminadav Dykman's comparatist approach seeks to situate Tchernichowsky's sonnet cycle within the currents of Russian Symbolist poetry at the beginning of the century. He delineates what is owed to the coronae written by such contemporaries as Viacheslav Ivanov, Valerii Bryusov, and Maximilian Voloshin, as well as indicating the ways in which Tchernichowsky sought to break with this poetic tradition.

Like Tchernichowsky, Micha Josef Berdyczewski (1865–1921) is one of the eminences of the Revival period. In his youth, he was the spokesman for the younger intellectuals who, in the face of Ahad Ha'am's conservatism, espoused the stance of Nietzschean revolt and called for a "transvaluation" of Jewish culture and society. As a young man, he became a pioneer in the fictional exploration of individual subjectivity and of the tormented inner world of young men and women who, as was the case with Berdyczewski himself, had left the world of faith and learning in which they had been raised and plunged headlong into the world of Western university studies. As an older man, Berdyczewski, who had obtained a doctorate in philosophy from a Swiss university, devoted himself to scholarly, antiquarian, ethnographic, and anthological studies. All these efforts were aimed at identifying and championing what he regarded as a suppressed countertradition within Jewish civilization that privileged the vitalistic forces of body and spirit over the rabbinic call for sublimation and obedience to norms.

Berdyczewski's short story "The Red Heifer" is located precisely at the fulcrum between these two conceptions of Judaism. The regime of normative social regulation is represented by the frame story, in which the narrator describes the cow and its proprietary owner, the fate of disqualified ritual slaughterers, and, at the end, the punishments that befell the orgiastic butchers. It is in the enclosed narrative describing the sanguinary dismembering of the cow and the exultation in its blood that the suppressed vitalism bursts through. "The Red Heifer" was written in 1905, and, in his essay, Avner Holtzman takes the story and its date of composition as marking a crucial boundary point in Berdyczewski's career. The story enacts the moment of Berdyczewski's withdrawal from the enterprise of writing fiction. He is no longer interested, according to Holtzman, in the individual self and its reticulations; his concern—really, his sense of dread—now focuses on the Jews as a collective. The narrator is anonymous and flat as a character, and the butchers are represented as a largely undifferentiated body of humanity. For Anne Golomb Hoffman, it is, in fact, the body and bodiliness that stand at the center of the story. Reading through the lens of gender, Hoffman provocatively asserts that there is no cow in the story, or rather that the cow exists only as a figure for a body invested with the desires and aggressions of those surrounding it. The story dramatizes a critical moment in modern Jewish culture in which the previously stable oppositions of Jew/Gentile and male/female are decisively put into play. William Cutter attempts to characterize the knotty issue of Berdyczewski's attitude toward the theft and slaughter of the cow. He argues that rather than admiring the dark forces that lie beneath the surface of human behavior, Berdyczewski is deconstructing the idealization of the shtetl, and this critique places him in a long tradition in Jewish literature. Reflecting on the reception of Berdyczewski's stories among his students, Cutter opines that the breakdown of community in American society and its tolerance for individual expression and deviance have robbed these narratives of their natural audience.

In one thing, S. Y. Agnon (1888–1970) differed from other major Hebrew writers: for him alone, the religious life of Polish Jewry remained the imaginative ground of his fiction. Agnon was raised in comfortable and pious circumstances in Galicia toward the end of the Hapsburg Empire. He left his parents' home in 1907 to settle in Palestine, and after five years in the heady atmosphere of young Zionist pioneers, he left for an eleven-year sojourn in Germany, where he absorbed European literature and studied the world of German-speaking Germany. In the 1920s, he settled permanently in Jerusalem and continued work on a growing corpus of short stories and novels that engaged issues of modernity using the full resources of the Jewish classical tradition. In 1966 he shared the Nobel Prize in literature with Nelly Sachs.

"A Sense of Smell" is not a short story in the conventional modernist sense of the term; rather, it adopts the conventions of earlier eras. It purports to be an account of a scholarly controversy to which are appended various disquisitions concerning the Hebrew language and the reasons for composing stories in it. Characteristic of Agnon's work as a whole is the presence in the story of an autobiographical narrator; here it is a Hebrew writer whose authoritative use of the Hebrew language is challenged by a carping scholar. Along the way to relating the story of his vindication, the narrator, who presents himself as pious and unerringly devoted to the holy books, offers an apologia for his vocation as a fiction writer.

The translatability of such a text as this, with its nuanced and multivalent allusions to classical sources, is the issue explored by Naomi Sokoloff. Considering the teaching of "A Sense of Smell" in English translation to American students, Sokoloff examines a number of critical thematic references in the text that are playfully subversive in the ears of the Hebrew reader— an admittedly literate Hebrew reader—but must seem unremarkable when encountered in translation. It follows from this argument that the Agnon text in translation can achieve aesthetic self-sufficiency only with the accompaniment of critical exegesis. Taking the Hebrew text on its own terms, David Roskies uses the concepts of the Soviet theorist Mikhail Bakhtin to depict Agnon as the master of the "double-voiced utterance," in which the language of collective past and the language of modernity are brought into dialogue. The narrator's antagonist, who quibbles over the correct use of a verb, represents a real threat because the kind of strictures that he proposes would constrict the glorious fluidity of Hebrew and thereby hamstring its power to negotiate between the ancient and the actual. Agnon can be compared to the Soviet Yiddish writer Der Nister in his commitment to the artistic and national enterprise of "creative betrayal," which Roskies defines as the subversion of tradition so that it can be recovered and deployed by the modern sensibility.

My own contribution focuses on the story's autobiographical persona. It is easy enough to succumb to the invitation to identify the author Agnon with the religious writer who narrates the story in his own voice. Yet the alert reader will notice how anti-intellectual and simplistic is the narrator's piety and how narcissistic is his placement of himself at the center of this mock-heroic battle of the books. This is not to say that in "The Sense of Smell" the praise of Hebrew is insincere or that the narrator is not the recipient of providential promptings both in his dream life and in his textual study. But the fact that the narrator's self-presentation is laced with irony means that in order to become proper readers of Agnon we must appreciate, like Agnon himself, the shifting contradictions of being both a modern artist and a religious Jew.

The poetic selection from Hebrew literature between the two world wars is taken from the works of Uri Zvi Greenberg (1894–1981). Considered by many to be the greatest Hebrew poet of the twentieth century, Greenberg cast himself as a defiant antagonist of the mainstream of poetic practice associated with Avraham Shlonsky and Natan Alterman. They emerged from the milieu of Russian literature and were deeply influenced by French and Russian Symbolism; Greenberg, like Agnon, emerged from the Galician provinces of the Hapsburg Empire and was shaped by German Expressionism. Shlonsky and Alterman were closely identified with the secular Zionist socialist leadership of the Yishuv, the Jewish settlement in Palestine, whereas Greenberg was committed to the apocalyptic politics of the Revisionists, which envisioned bloody conflicts with the British and the Arabs on the way to a redemptive Jewish kingdom. The greatest difference lay in the way the poetry looked and sounded. For Shlonsky and Alterman, the well-wrought poem was based on neoclassical wit and the subtle mystical properties of language. For Greenberg, the poem screams out the anguished inner state of the soul in long declamatory lines in massive blocks of utterance.

The strong effects of Greenberg's poetry cannot be sustained unmodulated. The prophetic, declamatory intensity is, in fact, alternated throughout Greenberg's work with poems of lyric stillness and introspection. This is especially true of Greenberg's magisterial book of Holocaust poetry, *The Streets of the River*; here, between the great cycles of poems excoriating the gentile perpetrators and conjuring up visions of Jewish vindication, are haunting poems of lyric self-exposure. "Man's House," the poem chosen for analysis here, belongs to this quieter strain. Written in the late 1940s, the poem contrasts the categories of homeland and exile. Man's liberation from the city and his belated return to his village at evening time become charged and ambiguous in the aftermath of the destruction of the East European prototype for the village.

The most available reading of the poem, argues Hannan Hever, places it within the national Zionist narrative that privileges the healing and holistic homeland over the alienating and dispiriting diaspora. Yet this hierarchy is called into question by the very perfection with which the poem invests the conception of the homeland. It is so organic and totalized an ideal that it becomes, by nature, incapable of attainment and fulfillment.

The longing for homeland, rather than homeland itself, is what remains real; and because the diaspora is the ground upon which this longing is enacted, it is the diaspora, in Hever's reading, that ironically ends up being the necessary condition for man's existence. For Dan Laor, in contrast, it is the opposition between village and city that organizes the poem rather than the opposition between Zion and diaspora. Laor traces Greenberg's antipathy to urban life throughout his poetic career into the period after the war and during the early years of the state. The village in the poem is a version of Eden to which modern man impossibly yearns to affect a belated return.

Lewis Glinert is less interested in the poem's ideological inversion than in its ontological introversion, that is, the poem's journey inward from history to being. Using the tools of stylistic and linguistic analysis, as well as an attentive ear to the many allusions to classical Jewish literature, Glinert marks the stations in this journey according to the gathering meaning of the poem's title: "Beito shel adam" (Man's house/home). What begins as a statement about human (*adam*) dwellings quickly proceeds to a consideration of the primordial Adam and his Edenic habitation, and finally, in a gesture to the alphabet mysticism of the Zohar, to an argument for the identity of *bayit* ("house") with the Hebrew letter *bet*, thus retranslating the title as "Adam's bet."

What Gershon Shaked has called the new wave in Israeli fiction marks a creative resurgence of modernism in the 1960s and 1970s and includes such authors as Amos Oz, A. B. Yehoshua, Aharon Appelfeld, and Amalia Kahana-Carmon. Thematically, this is a development that moves in several different directions. Oz and Yehoshua explore the resistance of the human heart to rational and utopian schemes of socialist Zionism and the new society it created. Appelfeld explores the world of Holocaust survivors and the assimilatory denial of European Jews on the eve of destruction. The inner world of women's experience is the subject of Amalia Kahana-Carmon's (b. 1930) writing, and this choice perforce makes her fictional world different from that of her male contemporaries. Her women exist outside or adjacent to the fierce dialectic of Zionist history and the postures of evasion or rejection in which men are caught. For Kahana-Carmon, as with her precursor Virginia Woolf, subjectivity dissolves into a succession of moments of perception that expand and contract in an irregular rhythm. Very little happens by way of external plot, and the shape of the fiction is created by the interconnections among the reticulated metaphors in

Kahana-Carmon's rich and exotic literary language. Because of the difficulty of the language and the author's concerns about the reliability of translation, very little of Kahana-Carmon's fiction has appeared in English.

Fortunately, two of Kahana-Carmon's best stories, both of them girls' coming-of-age narratives, have been translated into English. The protagonist of "Ne'ima Sasson Writes Poetry" is a young woman who is about to graduate from a religious high school for girls; through her unrequited crush on a male teacher, she learns to turn her disappointment into word and image and thus prepare herself for her vocation as artist. Shoshana, the protagonist of "Bridal Veil," the story analyzed in this volume, is somewhat younger and betrays no writerly ambitions, yet she, too, in the course of the narrative undergoes a critical initiation into the mysteries of adult life. Shoshana is the daughter of a distant and indifferent father and an overburdened mother, and on a nighttime intercity bus trip she accepts the overtures of a good-looking UN soldier. Although they have no language in common, they manage to communicate and negotiate their momentary attachment to each other. As Shoshana returns to her home at dawn, it is clear that a step toward selfhood has been taken.

Invoking the Meir Wieseltier poem that is the story's epigraph, Gilead Morahg sees Shoshana as embarked on a quest to make use of her own meager resources to meet the basic human needs denied her by her neglectful parents. Although the reader is led to expect a narrative of violation and male aggression when Shoshana meets the soldier, the plot actually moves in another direction that confirms her tentative steps toward autonomy. Because "Bridal Veil" has been published three times in three different settings (1968, 1977, 1996), Hannah Naveh argues that the story's meaning has been shaped and reshaped by its author, even though the text itself has remained unchanged. The first appearance of "Bridal Veil" as a separately published short story stressed the quest for true love; when the story later appeared as the first of three stories in a fictional triptych, emphasis shifted to themes of abandonment and substitution; and in its final placement— so far—at the beginning of a composite novella, the story admits of a stress on the possibility of maintaining individual selfhood within the love bond. Coming at the text from another angle, Nancy Berg locates the story's drama in its tightly woven networks of images and metaphors as well as in the very grammatical organization of its sentences. The high ratio of nouns to verbs and the passive mood of the scant stock of verbs, for example, convey Shoshana's essential inaction. Her sense of foreignness is communicated through a pattern of metaphors that compare persons to inanimate objects. Berg's darker reading of the story is based on what she points to as a sinister potential that is released at the lexical level of the text's figurative language.

Female childhood deprivation provides a strong link between the fiction of Amalia Kahana-Carmon and the poetry of Dahlia Ravikovitch (b. 1930), from whose work our final text is chosen. Although Ravikovitch's poetry began to address political themes directly around the time of the war in Lebanon in the early 1980s, until then her verse, like Kahana-Carmon's fiction, described interior experience that was not opposed to the great Zionist narrative but decidedly parallel to it. Ravikovitch's early poetry dealt forthrightly with autobiographical themes of childhood abandonment, fantasies of escape from constrained adulthood, and the subjugation of the female will. But this engagement was always carried out through means of indirection, and often by setting up a finely wrought parabolic or figurative counterpart to the raw emotional extremity.

At the center of Ravikovitch's 1982 poem "Hovering at a Low Altitude" stands a poor shepherd girl in the mountainous reaches of the Middle East who is about to be victimized by an anonymous male assailant. The last day of her life is observed from nearby by the female speaker of the poem, who hovers like a helicopter close to the ground. Although the poem was written and submitted for publication before the invasion of Lebanon, Barbara Mann takes the poem as emblematizing a crucial turn in Ravikovitch's verse toward engagement with public issues and even as being a "self-incriminating reflection upon a poetic self that she was partly responsible for creating." Mann invokes the debates within Hebrew literary circles from the 1940s onward about the defensibility of writing love and nature poetry during times of public trauma. In the volume in which the poem is collected, the particular placement of the poem between poems of love and poems of war indicates an ambivalent medial stance that is represented by the notion of hovering. Chana Kronfeld further sees the poem as emblematic of a turn not in Ravikovitch's poetry alone but in Israeli verse as a whole. "Hovering at a Low Altitude," in her reading, is an examination of the dilemma of witnessing and a caustic critique of "Tel Aviv cool" and the disengagement from human suffering. Nili Scharf Gold takes issue with the sufficiency and inevitability of a political reading of the poem. Attending closely to the poem's imagery and its biblical allusions, Gold argues for a more self-contained reading of the poem within the thematics of childhood trauma. Rather than seeing the shepherd girl as separate in identity and fate from the speaker who observes her, Gold suggests that the poem may be read as a "reworked reconstruction by an adult of her own childhood experience." The speaker's hovering position presents the emergence of a new option in Ravikovitch's poetry between "flying high" (escape) and "touching fire" (being in a place of danger).

[4]

Taken together, these essays illustrate how good reading is a combination of knowledge and surprise. A reader never comes upon a new text wholly innocent. All bearers of culture—and how much more so professors of literature!—bring their previous learning, assumptions, and expertise with them when they approach a new piece of literature; and it is natural—such is the urge to make sense of things—that they will seek to absorb the new text into the critical schemes that they have already developed. Rather than being a heavy-handed act of appropriation, this is, in fact, the way that most knowledge is purchased. By viewing a poem or story through the lens of a critical theory such as gender studies or by placing it within the literary career of the author, we discover dimensions of meaning that would never be accessible if we came at the text simply "on its own."

That said, how dreary it would be if we were always illustrating and refining the ideas and methods we already have in hand! The drama of reading occurs when we encounter resistance in a text that might otherwise be supposed to fit snugly into our ready ideas and methods. This is the element of surprise and, sometimes, of difficulty, too. The honest reader will take this mixture of discomfort and pleasure as a challenge to account for the otherness of the text and its elements of strangeness or "ungram-maticality." Sometimes the result will be an adjustment, even a revision, of the reader's overall assumptions.

At their best, then, these essays are just such an exercise. Inviting several critics to read the same text adds other dimensions. Reading any given set of three essays highlights differences among points of departure, critical terms, and intellectual habits. At the same time, there is a kind of trian-gulation that takes place; this is a process through which the identity of the text emerges more clearly as it is illuminated from different directions. To be sure, there is no closure here, no exhaustion of possible meanings and approaches; what is illustrated is a model for reading as a collective, open process.

In conclusion, one hopes that this volume will succeed as an advertisement for the pleasures and benefits of reading modern Hebrew literature. The six texts commented on are but a tiny sampling of the riches of this literature. The creative reaches of the nineteenth century were not even represented; and in the two decades since the latest texts included here, there has been an enormous outpouring of wonderful Hebrew fiction and poetry. These studies should also suggest what is distinctive about Hebrew literature among other modern literatures: the close, dialectical proximity of modern experience to traditional belief as embodied in complex and ironic allusions to biblical and classical sources. There is also a great deal to be learned from Hebrew literature about the transformation of Jewish society and individual experience in the modern age. Although it is not the sole burden of literary texts to convey this kind of knowledge, Hebrew literature remains the best source for an understanding of the impact of historical change on the lived lives of modern Jews and Israelis. And then there is the spectacle of Hebrew itself: an ancient language that, rather than remaining ancient, became a flexible and vivid idiom for creating beauty in our time as well.

Note

1. For an attempt at a poetic rendering, see Shlomo J. Kahn's translation of *To the Sun* in Eisig Silberschlag, *Saul Tchernichowsky: Poet of Revolt* (Ithaca, N.Y.: Cornell University Press, 1968), 142–50.

[I]

THE RED HEIFER

Micha Josef Berdyczewski

TRANSLATED BY WILLIAM CUTTER

THIS IS A STORY about a red heifer and something that happened not long ago in a little town near Horan, where a certain rabbi lived. I, the storyteller, was not present and did not witness these things myself, but I did hear about them from reliable people. The story is definitely unsettling, and at times I thought it best to cover it up. But when all was said and done, I decided to write it up for others to read.

Our generation, after all, is destined to die out, and the next generation will not know its ancestors and how they lived in the diaspora. Now, if one wants to find out about how that life really was, let him know about it, its lights as well as its shadows. Let us know that although we were Jews, we were also just "flesh and blood," with all that the term suggests.

There was a ritual slaughterer in the town of Dashia who was qualified and was about to become apprentice to the ritual slaughterer in another city; but he was eventually found to be ineligible, so that he could not become a ritual slaughterer, after all. Instead of becoming a teacher or Torah reader or prayer leader or just a laborer without a particular craft, or a *luftmentsch* or a storekeeper, he chose a vocation that was close to slaughtering, even though it was, in terms of social class or religious standing in Jewish life, a long way from it. Put another way, this man had really wanted to attain the pious office of ritual slaughterer, but he had to become a simple butcher in the Jewish street and open up a simple butcher shop. He abandoned his studies and his uniform and the holy laws and prohibitions of ritual slaughter and became a butcher like any other butcher, a profane man standing all day in his shop, dressing the carcasses and the slaughtered lambs on pegs, stripping them of their skin, extracting the proper veins and selling the meat by the pound.

21

And not only that. He took religious matters lightly and wasn't fastidious when it came to Jewish law, in the way of most butchers who were not exactly the most observant. Not to wash our dirty laundry in public, it must be said that they sometimes inadvertently sold nonkosher meat as kosher for the simple reason that unqualified meat in towns like this, where there are more Jews than there are villagers who eat pork, was about half the price; while the kosher meat, because of tax and duty and other such things, was certainly not free and its price might be twice that of nonkosher meat. While these butchers may be punished for this in hell, any Jew with a family needs to find a way to make some profit here on earth. It is well known, moreover, that butchers love to eat and drink and provide three meals a day for their families and not restrict themselves to modest or purely spiritual sustenance, as do Torah scholars and pious people.

All butchering has an element of cruelty in the blow to an animal's throat or when its limbs are cut off, even if the animal is slaughtered properly. Just yesterday a goat may have been grazing in the pasture, the lamb hurrying along to its fold, and today their blood is drained, their breath extinguished, and they are hanging upside down on a pole. Blood, which is life, is now on the hands and fingers of the butcher. It is the butchers who assist the ritual slaughterers, preparing the cow or the bull while the slaughterer's knife is being sharpened. The ritual slaughterer remains pious, for religion and its sacred commandments protect him and his life, and the crueler aspects of this business are left to the butcher and his destiny. Butchers are plenty strong, and when, for example, a disturbance breaks out in town, they are called upon to be the roughnecks. All the spiritual folks fear these physical butchers because they are bullies, and it is best not to anger them, for they can be merciless.

But there is something good about all this. The Jewish people is a weak and timid people, fearful of the slightest provocation; and whenever there have been pogroms against Jews, a hundred might flee from one drunken peasant and passively submit to broken windows and vandalized households. But the butchers learned to fight back and to arm themselves with clubs and axes when the times called for it. Something like this happened once at Easter during a brief interregnum, a full generation before the Jews had learned how to stand up for themselves. Is it any wonder that they called themselves the vanguard of Israel's heroes?

The Torah treats the thief, or *ganav*, more stringently than the robber, or *gazlan*, because the *gazlan* treats all people equally, whereas the *ganav* does not. And to be precise about it, when you are dealing with butchers, you are dealing with two opposites. When these heroes, who are afraid of nothing, do steal a bull or a cow, they do it secretly and without the owners knowing, or they have others do it for them. One can see this as a way of making a living rather than as an act of theft. In the butcher business, when you slaughter a cow or a bull and actually pay for the animal directly, it costs five times as much as an animal for which you haven't paid. Perhaps a bull wandered off and was abducted and turned over to the butchers, or perhaps there had once been fifty cows in a pen and now only forty-nine remain, a number that is still plenty from the owner's point of view. Reckon how many things can go wrong with the slaughter of a cow: sometimes the ritual slaughterer will do damage at the moment of killing, sometimes a lung can be punctured, or damage may occur regarding any one of the eighteen prohibitions. Dashia was a poor city, and often Jews couldn't pay for their meat. Meat that isn't soaked within three days becomes unfit, and in the summer it spoils. How could a butcher survive without some little benefits on the side?

You may say that this is forbidden, that a Jew ought not to do this. Yet do not all social dealings and commercial transactions involve a bit of deception and cheating? There is no essential difference, except that when it comes to business, this is not just a manner of speaking. And it surely won't stop those who do it from wearing the garb of the pious folks who pray in the choice seats in the synagogue. The other ones, that is to say, the butchers and their ilk, don't get reckoned among the pious and have to pray at their own house of worship, the synagogue of the morning watch instead of at the main synagogue in town. The householders have holy excuses and pious terms for the drink that they have in the morning after prayers, as they do for all the gross physical things they do. The butchers down their brew without apology and don't need a death in the family or a holiday to justify having a glass. While I know that the butchers are not saints and I don't want to make too many claims on their behalf, I would not have called them scoundrels were it not for this one thing that happened. It was plain evil! Who among us can pronounce that word in all its bitter meanings? People want to live and they do have uncontrollable urges in their bellies, which do not have silken linings and which can be very insistent.

And here is how it happened: in Dashia there lived a man named Reuven, an average fellow who didn't stand out; and who knows if he would even have been known in Dashia were it not for his cows?

Most of the citizens of Dashia, if they had means at all, kept cows that gave enough milk so that they didn't have to buy it. Reuven always had the best cow in the city. In this he was successful, and this he understood. He knew how to take care of his cows, to fatten them up and to make them look like the healthy cows in Pharaoh's dream. Reuven was not above feeding his cow from his own food and drawing her water himself. The shed was always kept clean, and he watched out so that no accidents would happen. His entire life was devoted to taking care of his cow, and that is what he was known for.

The people of Dashia are city types without much knowledge of nature; but when a cow or a goat gives milk to its owner, some contact with nature occurs. In every corner of the city, people know the local cows and goats; and when the larger or the more delicate animals return from grazing, all the residents look at each cow and goat and express their opinions about what they're worth and the price of their milk. Each household loves its animals, and men walk with their cow or their goat as if they were walking with a friend. And why not? Animals, after all, are living things who get hungry and need that hunger satisfied; they have sad feelings and affections and mothers who love and long for them. If you don't know this already, just take a cow or a sheep or a goat home with you, and you will be looking at a living soul.

In those days, Reuven had a ruddy Dutch heifer, the likes of which— for its beauty and soundness and fullness of body—the inhabitants of Dashia had never seen. When she came back from feeding with the flock, her head was held high like a queen's; and the other cows paid her proper respect. She was indeed of a nobler race, as one could see from her strong body, her healthy udders, and her beautiful coat. Reuven was once offered 150 rubles for her, whereas the most any other cow had cost, even the one belonging to a nobleman, was seventy or eighty rubles. How in the world, you might ask, did Reuven even come to possess a cow like that, given that he was not rich? But the citizens weren't so amazed, since people had come to expect good fortune from Reuven when it came to cows. This fellow's cow simply had to be the most wonderful in and around Dashia, for that is what was written in the book of destiny and that is the way it always was.

And Reuven in those days was as happy as a man whose daughter was going to marry a brilliant Torah scholar; he would gain great delight whenever he heard people praising, glorifying, and exalting his cow. They told wonder stories and spoke in hyperbole as if they were speaking, excuse the comparison, about their rabbi. They even said that the cow yielded four measures of milk at a time. They also said that from the butter alone, left over after they had all the milk they needed, Reuven cleared three rubles per week, and he had thirteen children and fifteen mouths to feed. In short, Reuven's red heifer, who gave birth each spring and whose offspring cost fifteen pieces of silver, gave folks a lot to talk about when they were sitting in the synagogue.

Dashia enjoyed its good fortune over the excellent heifer who could crown even one of the great cities on God's earth. And ineffective were all the incantations of the jealous women who practiced witchcraft and schemed to stop up her milk. Neither Satan nor his minions could do anything against such a grand creature, for God had created her.

But amazingly, all that meant nothing on the day of reckoning. The time came when the heifer's destiny was sealed even though she was the source of life for an entire family and the noblest part of the city's fabric. Were she to die in the fullness of her years, or be felled by a plague or even die a simple death, we would certainly be sad, but we would be resigned. Extinction comes to human beings as well, after all. The house that a person labors to build may burn down; and who can stop a city from being destroyed when enemies attack? When tragedy happens in the course of life, who can complain? Or, if it was said that Reuven had gone crazy, or that the heifer had ceased giving birth for a period and thus had been sold for ritual slaughter, and was found kosher, and had her skin removed and her veins extracted, and was sold for rich flesh for someone's Sabbath table, sweet to the palate when fried or boiled, we might nod our heads in assent at the destiny of the milk-giving heifer. That would be in accordance with the order of things and the way of the world: things like that happen in life. But in the case of Reuven's heifer, a murder was committed, an awful murder as bad as the ambush of a human being. This happened in a way that was not in the natural order of things, or at least in a way that we expect to happen among Jews.

There was a drought, and the price of meat rose. It was very hard to make a living in Dashia, and even butchers who most always could make a go of it were struggling. Disputes broke out, and there were hostilities, as one might expect. Reuven, a peaceful man by nature, took part in those disputes, and the butchers opposed him. One can't explain all the reasons for what happened afterward, but I will tell the reader anyway, one by one.

And I am not judging here, just telling the story, but others will come and judge, and they will expound and clarify the course of events.

It was the heifer's fate to be taken from her owner by a group of butchers. Many had their eyes on her when she returned from grazing, and she had no idea what was going to befall her. The group gathered to conspire in the house of the slaughterer.

It happened on a Saturday night at the end of summer. Reuven and his household were sitting at twilight and enjoying their heifer. His youngest were patting her, the older were praising her. The eldest daughter got up and took some fodder and gave her a nice ladle of water. Suddenly, the heifer let out a piercing moan, and everyone trembled because they didn't know what had happened. Winter would come and darken the hearts of Jews when they realized that there was no firewood or warm clothing for their nakedness. Their deeds must have been wanting, and that is why they had no sustenance.

It was midnight. Everyone was resting, and no light shone in any window. They were dreaming deeply in the gloomy night, because on the morrow the breadless day would begin again . . . Yet one butcher pierced that darkness and sneaked into Reuven's pen, where the heifer was standing. There was no lock on the door, and only a thick rope attached the heifer's leg to a tree. The prowler cut that rope with a sharp knife and took the heifer by her horns, leading her out a narrow pathway, while the heifer followed in astonishment.

And, hush! The man and the animal stood at the door of the large cellar of Shoel the Butcher, where everyone had gathered. Two of them faced the heifer and pulled her while she involuntarily wagged her tail. They abruptly pulled her into the cellar, leading the reluctant animal as she held back and forcing her to do what she feared to do.

Now the heifer stood below, agitated. Seven of the men got up to receive her, dressed in aprons and furs like peasants, with faces aflame. Each man had drunk a little glass to get his strength up, and the little candles shining in the dark made the scene seem like hell. They surrounded the calf and fondled her.

Suddenly, one of the butchers got up like a lion and tried to cast the heifer to the ground, but her legs were like iron. Some others came as reinforcements and struggled mightily with her, but she dug her hooves into the ground while her eyes raged. The heifer got up as if to gore and banged her head against the wall until the cellar shook. One of the butchers crawled under her belly and secured her hind legs with a thick rope. He did it also to her forelegs. All of them got up and girded themselves and climbed upon her back and pushed her. She fell and let out a mighty groan as she tried to sever the ropes. But her attackers grabbed her with a vengeance that no one had seen before. Outside, rain began to fall on the roof and the wind howled. Sweat the size of beans fell from the butchers' foreheads from their efforts; and they looked at one another like strangers and took off their clothes and rolled up their sleeves as if ready for a fight. What pent-up feelings sought release!

One of the butchers, himself a ritual slaughterer, stood up calmly and sharpened the old blade; he took it out and rubbed its point with his fingernails. Once again, the butchers leaned on the back of the heifer. Some took hold of her thick legs below and above, and two especially strong men twisted her head with incredible might. It was as if doom filled the air, an awful decree of the end of days, and suddenly the butcher who was a slaughterer took up his blade and ran it back and forth across her delicate neck. The heifer let out an awesome earth-shattering groan and blood poured out like a fountain, spreading in a great arc and shining in the midst of the light from the lamp that hung from the ceiling. The blood kept flowing, splattering on the roof and walls, on the ground and on the trousers of the men and on their hands and faces. The heifer struggled with her remaining strength, shuddering while the ground became a river of blood. The murderers put her off to the side, and after an hour her ruddy soul departed and she died. Man conquers beast!

Then another of the butchers took a sharp knife and plunged it into the belly of the heifer so that the innards came out, and then others tore off her skin. They did this with a pent-up power and compressed emotion they had never known.

The animal was stripped. The men began to divide her into pieces, cutting off her head and her legs. One butcher couldn't restrain himself. He took the fat liver and put it on the hot coals that had been placed in the corner. When the blood reached the flames, everyone ate it without proper salting and with ravenous hunger, licking their fingers eagerly. A large bottle of brew was ready, so they ate and drank until they satisfied their lust. They were like priests of Ba'al when the sacrifice was on the altar. But this did not happen at Beth El or at Dan; it happened in the Jewish city of Dashia, not at the time when the ten tribes were exiled from the Northern Kingdom, but in the year 1884.

The second watch passed, and the rains poured while the wind raged. They divided the heifer ten ways, each man putting his portion in a sack. Each carried his share on his shoulders and then repaired to his shop in the dark of night in order to hide the spoil. The city slept, and the people dreamed while dogs barked and the skies were gloomy with rain. No one knew what had transpired!

In their haste, the butchers forgot to close the cellar door, and so the dogs came and licked up the blood. In the morning, folks saw that Reuven's heifer had been stolen and they searched for her. Within an hour, they found her ruddy coat still wet. The matter frightened them, and everyone who heard about it was shocked. In Reuven's house, there was moaning and deep grief.

From the time of Dashia's founding, there had never been such a terrible day. Men wandered around aimlessly outside, women came together whispering and talking. It was as if there had been an eclipse of the moon in the midst of an eclipse of the sun, and everyone looked at one another as if the world had been turned into Job's Valley of the Ghosts. To slay an animal in the middle of her life is an awful thing.

And as for what happened to the butchers who took part in the murder of the animal, the various quarrels and court trials and their punishment— both by man and God—if I would tell all these in detail, they would take up much space. In brief, however, everyone who had a hand in doing in that red heifer experienced bad things in his family life, as if a curse had been cast on him and his house, without leaving any remnant. But all these things are written in the history of Dashia and its chronicles.

The reader can find out more there.

William Cutter

THIS TRANSLATION OF "The Red Heifer" is an opportunity to experience the work of Micha Josef Berdyczewski in somewhat contemporary language and with the benefit of renewed interest in the author's oeuvre, especially within Israeli scholarship. Berdyczewski was a polymath intellectual and an enigmatic author, essayist, and anthologizer who played a key role in early-nineteenth-century European Jewish life, but who spoke from the margins of the public activity on which he had so much influence. Much discussion continues about the particular place of his vitalistic ideology and his appreciation for the "lived life" of Jews as over against Judaism's normative and essentialist trends. A corollary of this appreciation highlights his enthusiasm for the darker forces in human experience, and it is those darker forces that lead us to reckon with this dramatized representation of a supposedly actual event.

In this story Berdyczewski's narrator exposes a town and its habits to readers who he asserts might have been incredulous, or who might forget the relevance of that place or its habits. Berdyczewski's narrator thus takes on a role that Berdyczewski, the author, occupied in the nearly forty years of his productive career: the anthologizer and collector—without apology—of the behaviors of his people.[1] The story he tells—once the frame is set—is about a tiny community of poor Jews in which a group of violent men appropriate the beloved animal of one of the simpler members of the community for greedy and violent purposes.

In his article "Shniut" (Secondary-ness) of 1903, Berdyczewski wrote that the past is a "cultural inheritance that is relevant for the present; we bring it forth into our current context and make a new creature out of it."[2] "The Red Heifer" is a fictionalized version of the act of making such a new creature. The Red Heifer begins its career in biblical lore (Num. 19:1f.) in a complicated ritual that can be summarized for our purposes here as "purifying the impure" and making the pure impure in a complex ritual choreography. The rabbinic extension of the basic paradigm occupies pages of discussion and legislation in the Mishnah, tractate Parah.

Berdyczewski's passion for retrieval is important background to reading this story about a certain Jewish community at a specific time in modern

history. The degree to which Dashia is meant to be representative or syn-
ecdochic is, of course, one of the interesting problematics of this kind of
story. Our narrator claims that he is describing actual events and preserving
these events for those whose historical memories would otherwise fade.
Readers have differed as to whether his straightforward "descriptions" and
recording of legends represent an advocacy, or a kind of dash of critical
cold water in the face of idealizations. I will argue that Berdyczewski's skepticism about idealizations is a driving feature of this story.

Discovering Berdyczewski's take on the world he left behind is rewarding
even if modern literary sensibilities might be unsatisfied on purely aesthetic
grounds. Part of our response to the story is influenced by our interest in
a past that has been delivered through history and inflected by nostalgia
and the self-interest of positive description, even as we bring to our reading
the tools of modernity and postmodernity. The author's response to that
world is certainly influenced by his access to Nietzschean tropes—old material to us, but fresh for him—and an interest in the subterranean motives
of human beings. The notion of smoldering, subdued passion beneath the
placid surface is common in world literature, but the use of that theme
within Jewish post-Enlightenment literature is noteworthy as a mark in the
shift in attitudes about what constitutes Jewish reality. In Jewish terms,
Berdyczewski's appreciation of the underside of life is still appealing to
many readers: those who view shtetl romanticization with irony or those
who are suspicious of straightforward normative appreciations of Jewish
values and haloed perspectives. This may have been especially true a generation or two ago, as intellectuals smarting from the clash between modernity and tradition resisted the prevailing positive descriptions of Jewish
life and values. Thus, while it has been customary to read Berdyczewski in
light of his passion for the vitality of simple common folk and in light of
his attraction to the buried past in Jewish folklore, and while we know of
his rejection of Ahad Ha'am's historically inflected formulas, these attitudes
do not lead to a specific conclusion about the values that he does embrace.[3]
His own fully constructed worldview was never completed, and his failure
to design a clear-cut worldview may have helped preserve the sense of
intimidation he created within many people. I often think of him as a *vieux
terrible*.[4]

Intellectuals always appreciate skeptics, of course, but we have gained
even more tools with which to understand our own darker impulses to
debunk expressions of simple value. Although Berdyczewski did proclaim

a Nietzschean revolt against rabbinical ethics, as David Biale has noted, and although he did argue for a nationalist return to nature and to elemental strength in place of bookish learning, he was neither pure Nietzschean nor anti-bookish.[5] For the original Berdyczewski audience, the primary tension was between power and intellection, eros and authority. For a contemporary reader, the distinction might be between normative behavior and acknowledgment of the forces that work against that behavior, or the eros and violence that lie beneath bourgeois propriety. More distant yet from Horen and Dashia than the original ideal reader of this story, we may be closer to a certain kind of Berdyczewski ideal, since we bear newer tools even more closely honed to Berdyczewski's sense of exegesis. We are now free to ask in a more detached way: What kind of story is "The Red Heifer," irrespective of what we know about the man who invented this portrait? Is it a story of particular codes? Of the failure of a system of norms when stacked up against human passions? Is there a feminist case here? Is it the story about a village or about a narrator? Finally, is our own tendency to challenge romantic visions of shtetl life influencing our understanding of this narrator?

Whichever it is, the narrator presents his story as a literary retrieval of a lived situation. Like so many tales of the early twentieth century, "The Red Heifer" is two stories in one, in which the framing convention may be more important than it appears. In the frame the narrator shifts his view as he develops from opening to conclusion—not in the usual sense, however. He does not undergo psychological or moral growth; there is no dynamism in who he is, and he comes to no new personal insight. The "change" occurs in how he presents his point of view about the story within. He has begun by suggesting an innocent impulse to report and even to preserve, a motive that presumably either sets him up as an advocate for the world he is going to describe or as a purely empirical recorder. ("Now, if one wants to find out about how that life really was, let him know about it, its lights as well as its shadows . . .") But by the end, he reveals that he has tricked us; his tale preserves a world with plenty of shadows, and it is a cruel world, best put behind us if we privilege civilizing impulses.

But as we move beyond the opening frame, we visit a village in the Pale of Settlement where a lot of stock characters carry on their simple lives. The narrator suggests that the experience in this village was typical among Jews of small villages, and that this is why the story must be preserved.

Daily life in the village seems unperturbed, but the potential for disruption is present. Class distinctions exist, harsh even when described with humor (who gets to drink what after morning prayers); a culture of thugs has been created, perhaps made necessary by the presence of hostile forces, but behaving more as thugs than as protectors. Economic pressures are ever present, and not just in the emergency of this story's moment. Witchcraft and spiritual adversary are taken for granted. The generalized picture of the town is told through a particular family that is poor, like so many other Jewish families in the area, with the exceptional fact that Reuven, the family's father, has a good eye for cattle. Reuven's family has an irenic attitude toward the world, which will be shattered by story's end. Neither their poverty nor their good fortune is described in any detail, and there is little individuation or character development within the family members. The behavior of Dashia's citizens is indicated in genre portraits: proud facial expressions, sitting contentedly with their animal, stroking the animal's ruddy skin, feeding it with water and fodder. Even the cow is a cartoon, as she struts like a queen at the head of a file of personified animals. The narrator personifies the animals, and the villagers do the same. ("Each household loves its animals, and men walk with their cow or their goat as if they were walking with a friend.")

The only dramatic shift in one of the town's provincial characters is that Reuven acts against type when a drought strikes and he must join in the dispute among the desperate and greedy. The most vividly individualized characteristics among the citizens of Dashia are greed, passion, and cruelty, and they are ascribed to the roughneck butchers who eventually and inevitably appropriate the cow for their vulgar purposes. I suggest that while those vulgar purposes may have been titillating to the author and may even have some allure for his narrator, they are not moral desiderata.

Reuven's red heifer isn't just any cow. It is a "Red Heifer," whose place in Jewish lore is as central as that of his animal cousin, the "Only Kid," of the Passover Haggadah. The depiction of the heifer covers chapters in the halakhic material concerning the proper procedures for sin offerings and purification. Although Berdyczewski loved the aggadic spirit that fostered the Only Kid, and resisted the halakhah that fostered the Red Heifer, here he converted the complex system of meanings associated with the halakhic heifer into the aggadic form traditionally associated with the kid. But he surely was enchanted by the strange mystical authority of the Bible's Red Heifer. One has to assume that the ideal reader is expected to know the paradoxical quality of the Red Heifer: that it purifies what is impure and renders impure what is pure. While the full allegorical reading of the cow of the Mishnah would deflect from the narrated events, the central aspect of the biblical material is necessary background to the overall irony of this element within the story: priests function to purify the very community that the heifer has the ability to contaminate. This modest concurrence of meanings between our story and the original biblical concept is a crucial part of the story's symbolic energy.

Berdyczewski was often attracted to the possibility that something could be one thing and its opposite at the same time. It is in this turn of his mind that we find the most satisfactory understanding of this story. He understood and his narrator understands that forces of evil have a contract with forces of good: that thugs save nice guys, and that contamination lurks in the background of even the most benevolent of situations. Contamination intensifies the move of this story from its simple function of recording to the narrating of grievous results for Dashia.

The narrator's perspective represents the preferred vantage point from which to view the brutality and sadness inherent within Dashia, Anytown, in the Pale of Settlement. Its economic base is shattered so that the drought tests its fragility even further. It does not pass the test. Thug-like butchers are an essential part of the community's security, and in order to make a living the merchants must fiddle with weights and measures (another vital reversal of Jewish norms). They, too, can be the opposite of what they ought to be.

Berdyczewski's abiding attachment to the subterranean realities of Jewish life has been noted by most scholars, especially recently Hamutal Bar-Yosef, Gershon Shaked, Nurit Govrin, and Menachem Brinker.[6] The question is whether that attachment determines our conclusions about an underlying point of view of the story, its author, or its narrator.

In my reading Berdyczewski's affectionate and even hopeful introduction is a deceptive gesture that heightens the story's irony. It is a story of negative nostalgia, or, perhaps to borrow Arnold Band's famous phrase, of nostalgia and nightmare,[7] insofar as it records this brutal incident within an environment made inevitable by those social and economic conditions that were strangling an entire Eastern European Jewish world.

Throughout his essays, implicitly in his anthologizing and obliquely through his stories, one can discern Berdyczewski's preference for flesh-and-blood people, as opposed to notions of an essential "Jewish" quality.

Indeed, all references in "The Red Heifer" to physical life, to the reality with which flesh-and-blood people must cope, occasion a smile of recognition at the debunking of romanticization of Jewish life in the shtetl. Notions about punishment in the world to come ("While these butchers may be punished in hell . . .") echo formulas in the Jewish code of law that, in some cases, assign punishment to a deferred time when no one can prove it anyway, and that are part of the tradition of idealization that Berdyczewski rejected. Citing these ideas was his narrator's way of further mocking the religious community's theodicy and sense of justice.

Berdyczewski cautioned about idealizations in his essays on the Jewish people and culture. In his essay "On the Question of Culture" of 1903, he asks Jews to look into their own history to see how far they were from being an ethical light to the world. The debunker in him is evident in a more direct fashion in such essays, but he seems to be at work in this story as well. Thus when our narrator adopts the stance: "I am going to tell you how life really was . . ." it seems that we are being exposed to an ironic subversion of the tradition of idealizations. Thus the narrator, as a character within the story, may delight in the real and brutal, but because it is real and brutal and not because it represents preferred moral practice. No doubt many of the hasidic masters whom Berdyczewski idealized[8] understood the importance of the brutal reality and the power of the pent-up subversive forces within human beings. Tools of modern psychology have helped readers in the post-Berdyczewski period understand the presence of a dark side to the surface politesse of middle-class society; and no less true it is that Berdyczewski's tools enabled him to comprehend the dark side against the social surfaces that he witnessed: the simple village, the bucolic love of animals, religious piety, and godly talk. He had Nietzsche for ideological skepticism and a Durkheim-like perspective to explain communal behavior.

Berdyczewski's attack on his idealized shtetl occurs near the end of this story in the simile about the prophets of Ba'al. Our narrator reminds us that this episode happened only recently in his readers' modernity, even though it would have been less surprising had it occurred in a primitive time. The narrator has thus created a negative simile ("this did not happen at Beth El or Dan; it happened in . . . Dashia, not at the time when the ten tribes were exiled . . . but in the year 1884.") that reminds one of the orgiastic qualities latent in the ancient world. Thus Jewish "values" are preserved here, but not in the way that we normally use that idea. I will give you Jewish values, if you wish, but you can be certain that they are closer to the values of Tchernichowsky's God of the ancient desert ("In the Presence of Apollo") or to David Frischmann's sarcasms about our biblical tradition ("Tales of the Wilderness") than to the God of order and social organization.

Berdyczewski often argued that occult and vital elements were looking for an opportunity to burst forth and emerge from the underground, where they had been forced by Jewish tradition to disappear. That is why he penned his numerous descriptions of transgression with a profound understanding of the soul of the sinner. Sin means impulse, flesh and blood and *élan vital*. That, however, is only part of what made Berdyczewski such an original. Alan Mintz brings this vitality to bear when dealing with Berdyczewski's attention to the erotic side of his young heroes,[9] and others have attached Berdyczewski's vitalism to the sheer "size," the broadness and grossness of human behavior. In no case, however, is it clear that Berdyczewski had an uncomplicated attachment to the brutalization of people. The full context of the story before us is a quartet of stories named "Shadow and Light," in each of which one sees a rounding out of the complexities within the small Jewish town.

Thus, I read this story and others like it as a vindication of Berdyczewski's case against idealization rather than as a case for specific ethical behavior that grows from the dark and vigorous forces that lie submerged just below the surface of human experience and expression of value. But it is the idealizations that Berdyczewski repudiates, and consequences of plot support that repudiation. That de-idealization has been part of a tradition within Yiddish and Hebrew literature since the end of the Haskalah.

Berdyczewski fostered much of my own reading in Hebrew literature, because his characters went through the struggle of the private person against the communal polity and suffered the erotic surge within a culture that repressed that surge. A spate of stories in this tradition have included writers from several corners of the tradition of Jewish writing (along with writers of other cultures, obviously). In American letters, Henry Roth, Saul Bellow, Bernard Malamud, and Philip Roth join with the more Jewishly grounded Cynthia Ozick in fascination with the subterranean without being advocates of the bizarre and wicked behavior they often delight in describing. We might suggest, by analogy, that Berdyczewski's erotic stories call attention to the passions and longings of the sexual self, though he would not have applauded rape; and similarly, his stories that tell of the deeper passions of gluttony are part of an antic view whose excesses remind us of the cant in piety more than the value on which a society ought to be built.

Avner Holtzman has noted that the Berdyczewski of "The Red Heifer" may be representative of Berdyczewski, but what constitutes that representation remains the necessary object of our scrutiny. He, like any secular intellectual unfettered by codes and easy legalistic solutions, groped toward a resolution of the Jewish condition in existential terms. These terms had to include for him an appreciation of the impossibility of codes. Indeed, he does seem here to see the evil in the very thing that attracted him, or to be attracted to the very thing that he knows is evil. As such, he was very much a modern man suited to the later twentieth century. But Berdyczewski's manipulation of these forces as some kind of desideratum would have wound up idealizing one set of qualities while having rejected the idealization of another.

The translation of this story into English seems most timely. One finds our popular culture today intrigued by alien and occult forces and mysterious results, and by the curious need to appropriate what is not one's own. If one senses the hypocrisy that fosters idealizations that are of little value, one may find that "The Red Heifer" is an emblem of mock folklore. The story, written a bit woodenly, to tell the truth, holds up on several levels. The author's stories share the revelation of the reality behind the manifest experience and argue for the notion that things are precisely the opposite of what one might expect. That is the universal in this story, grounded in a mysterious biblical mythology, and surfacing still in idealized villages or the sanctum of the White House oval office. That is the cause for celebration in revisiting the work of a forgotten world that itself tries to revisit another world that might have been forgotten, or recalled in the misunderstood and simple nostalgia of simple folks invested in the project of idealization. Harking back in Berdyczewski, then, may bring one to the realization that the very foundation of Jewish values is burdened with the same brutality as the more recent environment of the Eastern Europe that the narrator is retrieving. From any current perspective, "the good old days" may start out to seem better, but when you tell the story, the truth is always there that pent-up brutal forces are waiting to erupt at the slightest provocation. These forces can forge good or evil results, depending upon how they are deployed. And that is the way of the Red Heifer.

Notes

1. See, most recently, Ziporah Kagan, "Homo Anthologicus: M. J. Berdyczewski and the Anthological Genre," *Prooftexts* 19, no. 1 (January 1999): 41–57.

2. "Shniut," in *Kol ma'amarei M. Y. Bin-Gorion* [Essays of M. Y. Bin-Gorion], (Tel Aviv: Devir, 1952), 63.

3. See Adam Rubin, "Hayim Nachman Bialik, Hebrew Culture and the Creation of Jewish National Identity" (Ph.D. diss., University of California at Los Angeles, 1999).

4. On this subject, see Holtzman, ed., *Boded bema'ravo* (a collection of essays by Berdyczewski contemporaries) (Holon, Israel: Devora and Emanuel House, 1998).

5. David Biale, *Eros and the Jews* (New York: Basic Books, 1992), 157, 165, 169, 171–72. Nietzschean strains in Berdyczewski have been discussed by almost everyone who has written about him. For a recent helpful essay, see Zafrirah Din, "Abstract Judaism and Jews in Reality in Berdyczewski's Thought" [Hebrew], in *Ginzei Micha Yosef*, vol. 4 (Holon, Israel: Devora and Emanuel House, 1990).

6. This has, in fact, been the conventional view of Berdyczewski's thought. But it has a far more nuanced position than one might assume from the summary consideration of Berdyczewski's point of view; it makes him a unique figure in the development of national Jewish consciousness. Notice Nurit Govrin's comment in her article "Berdyczewski as a Guide to the Second Aliyah": "From this strange fire come all those yearnings that impregnate everything that lives within us and fills us with the resonance of life. The righteous and the contemplative are, in general, only reincarnation of the wicked. . . . Berdyczewski himself did not draw the final and practical conclusions from such views. He did not develop them into a system of thought that leads to a certain way of life. But those who read his articles and stories did so." In *Alienation and Regeneration* (Tel Aviv: MOD Books, 1989), p. 45.

7. Arnold Band, *Nostalgia and Nightmare.* (Berkeley: University of California Press, 1968).

8. Berdyczewski's fascination with Hasidism ranged widely. His essays on the subject are found in his collected works: "On the Appreciation of Hasidism" [Hebrew], in *Kol ma'amarei*, 3–9. See Shmuel Werses, *Sippur veshorsho* (Stories and their origins). (Ramat Gan: Masad, 1971), 104–18. Werses is also preparing a further study of the subject, and I am preparing translations of the original essays on Hasidism. For an understanding of Berdyczewski's origins in Hasidism (and indeed for any feature of his biography), see Avner Holtzman, *El haker'a shebalev* [Toward a tear in the heart]. (Jerusalem: Mossad Bialik, 1995).

9. Alan Mintz, *Banished from Their Father's Table: Loss of Faith and Hebrew Autobiography.* (Bloomington: Indiana University Press, 1989).

Anne Golomb Hoffman

THERE IS NO COW in this story.[1] The cow is a figure of the "body," and thus there is no cow in the sense that there is no "body"—no one entity that exists in any simple fashion, as stable, bounded, and knowable. The body can be glimpsed through the desires of those who are in proximity to it, a proximity that evokes responses of desire and aggression. Thus the cow exists insofar as it is an object invested with the desires of those around it. We can study and come to know the field of forces within which it is to be found. What, then, is the role of the cow in Berdyczewski's story? The cow is the vehicle through which desires and aggressions find expression and a historical crisis acquires representation. A text comes into being.

Avner Holtzman tells us that Berdyczewski turned away from fiction in 1905, toward research into the history and texts of the Jewish people, in a move that positioned him more as ethnographer of the Jews than as their storyteller.[2] "The Red Heifer" can be read as a gesture toward capturing the history of a "Judaism" that had hitherto gone unrecorded. It is less a tale of human subjects who act intentionally than it is a brief narrative portrait of human beings *Mibein hatslalim* (from among the shadows) and *Mehe'avar hakarov* (from the recent past) as the titles of the collections in which it is found suggest. The story gives us human beings, lived by their desires, poised at the intersection of change, change of which they are unaware.

Berdyczewski's story brings into speech the crisis of a historical moment. Ethnographically, the text offers itself as an "utterance," a verbal production that belongs to a larger cultural context. Why dwell on the text as utterance? Because the story asks us to. Might this tale be told? Berdyczewski's narrator asks hesitantly, thus bringing to the fore his doubts about the propriety of his subject. Worrying aloud that he may offend his readers, our narrator tells us he is transcribing events that might be better off hidden. Berdyczewski's text is thus a very self-conscious narrative performance, exaggeratedly conscious of its own linguistic expression. All this fussing creates in the reader an impression of instability in the rules of storytelling and the norms that determine what may be told. The elaborate dance of approach and avoidance that our first-person narrator carries out in relation to his subject matter allows the writer Berdyczewski to underscore the historical shift that is, in fact, his real interest.

The historical shift that the story enacts is both trivial and momentous. How can this be so? "The Red Heifer" takes up actions carried out by men in relation to the red cow, a valued object, prized for its beauty and its milk, that is subject first to adoration and then to violence. Large meanings attach to seemingly trivial acts: the narrative takes shape through a shift in the relationship of men to the body that is the cow. In this succession of behaviors, actions, and desires, we may discern a choreography of men's movements that suggests shifting paradigms of masculinity. I shall explore the dynamics of these movements and shifting relationships and will conclude by suggesting some of the historical contexts in which they acquire meaning.

French psychoanalyst Jacques Lacan offers a way of understanding historical change in light of our relationship to signifiers, the words that name us, designate bodies, and position us in relation to those bodies. He writes that "the slightest alteration in the relation between man and the signifier ... changes the whole course of history by modifying the moorings that anchor his being."[3] "History" can be understood here as both individual and collective, private and public. And "a change in the relation between man and the signifier"? Something like what we glimpse here, in the shift from the highly ritualized role of *shohet uvodek* (ritual slaughterer) to the brute force of the *katsav* (butcher): a shift in terms that produces abruptly a drastic shift in relation to a body. Out of a set of contingent relationships to the body, Berdyczewski fashions a story.

Lacan's comment on the relationship of man to the signifier may remind us of the process through which one enters culture and becomes an individual subject, possessed of social identity and position. To become a "subject" means to acquire subjectivity and agency, the capacity to speak and act within the cultural order. But while the acquisition of language produces a speaking subject who is able to express desire, this achievement comes at the cost of any simple notion of fulfillment. The cost of entry into language is alienation, a split within the self. Language may allow for the expression of desire, but the words are never simply one's own, nor is there ever a perfect match between word and thing, or need, desire, and demand. Acquisition of the status of "subject" can only occur through subordination to cultural authority, represented by the name of the father, and concomitant loss of an imagined omnipotence. Linking issues of culture and the body through the unconscious, Lacan follows Freud in accounting for the priority of culture over the individual. The subject comes into being, forever divided against itself in the very splitting that constitutes its formation. Following Freud, Lacan names this split "castration" and understands gender difference in terms of the position that the subject assumes in relation to that originary loss, through which entry into culture occurs. Gender difference can thus be formulated in terms of a relationship to the signifier. Language and the processes of signification shape what we know of the body and of ourselves.[4] What we know as masculine and feminine can be understood as differing positions in relation to the body and the primal inscription of castration.

Acknowledging the relation to the body, Lacan observes that "desire is inscribed on the basis of a corporal contingency," and I suggest that, in reading Berdyczewski's story, we think of the red cow as "corporal contingency" embodied.[5] More than it is a portrait of the cow as such, this story portrays conflicting relationships to a body—an emblematic body that is lovingly cared for and just as suddenly attacked, dismembered, and consumed. One could see this story as consisting of interchangeable parts that offer the reader opportunities for combination and recombination on several levels of experience. It can be read in terms of individual development, but can also be approached in terms of larger, collective models of experience.

On the level of individual prehistory, the abrupt shift from pleasurable absorption in the body to brute dismemberment may resonate with echoes of the incoherence of bodily experience in early life. Freud remarks that the first ego is a bodily ego. He thus draws our attention to the formation of a rudimentary sense of self out of opposing experiences of the body whole and the body in fragments. Body whole: the coherence of body parts into an imagined whole that yields a working sense of identity and produces the coherence of a knowable self. Body in parts: that imaginary coherence produced out of a fragmented disarray of body parts and sensations that Lacan likens to a painting by Hieronymus Bosch.[6] "The Red Heifer" locates itself in the tension between those opposing, yet mutually implicated, experiences. The story thus tells us ourselves: it addresses embodiment, the body as a sealed container and the violent disruption of that container.

Yet it does so without ever really letting us know what it is doing. Deadpan, the narrator pursues his mundane agenda. An unspecified impropriety in a *shohet*'s methods of ritual slaughter brings about the cancellation of his certification as a ritual slaughterer. From ritual slaughterer, he becomes a *katsav*, a simple butcher, a hacker of flesh. The shift from *shoḥet* to *katsav*, a shift in signifiers, exposes the relationship to the body that those signifiers regulate.

In a world shaped by language, we are made aware at the outset of the politics of location. The incident is described as occurring in a small town. *Be'ir ketanah semukhah lehoran, mekom moshav rabbi eḥad* ("in a small town near Horan, where a certain rabbi lived"). Is this "rabbi" a hasidic rebbe? What does it mean to live at a slight but distinct distance from the rebbe? Mapping a social world regulated by Jewish law, the narrator goes on to contrast the positions of *shoḥet* and *katsav*; with great precision, he locates the work of the *katsav*, the simple butcher, as closer in nature to the work of ritual slaughter, but remote from the "social and religious position" that ritual slaughter occupies in Jewish life.

From *shoḥet* to *katsav*, the shift in terms that identify social role through a relation to the body thus opens an ambiguous space in which the story unfolds. This is Lacan's change in moorings, a change in relation to the signifier.

Do we possess the capacity to look? the story asks us. The narrator worries out loud whether he should cover up unseemly events or write them out and in so doing, expose them to our sight, as he says, *le'eineinu*. The very act of telling is poised between concealing and revealing, as the narrator questions what can be seen and what can be told. Writing to give historical place to those of whom he speaks, he opens with a bold claim. These men are both *benei basar vedam* ("men of flesh and blood") and *yehudim* (Jews), he tells us, setting up a pair of attributes in opposition to each other, each with its own force and direction, one toward the flesh, the other in an ostensibly more spiritual direction. That exaggerated opposition organizes the narrator's mode of address to the reader.

The narrator wavers between the poles of the opposition he has set up, at times reluctantly admiring, even excusing the lawless violence of the *katsavim*. Ultimately, he summons up all his moralizing resources in order to lay claim to closure: he tells us, at the very end, of the evil consequences that came to every one of those who participated in the violent assault on the cow. But his ostentatious claims fail to convince. Indeed, such anxious efforts to reinstall authority draw attention all the more to its absence. We might remind ourselves here of the minimal requirements for a story: an initial equilibrium, disruption of that equilibrium, and the establishment of a new equilibrium. "The Red Heifer" fulfills those conditions, as the narrator takes care to remind us, but it does so uneasily. Inevitably, we feel a gap between the claim to closure and the pungent resistance of the story to the form of narrative.[7]

The narrator serves as a vehicle through which to explore ambivalent attitudes to body and action. Maintaining his position as shocked observer, he relays what he has heard, insisting that it not be lost. Underscoring his scribal function, the narrator uses the biblical phrase *keri uketiv* to designate his inclusion of the incident into the communal record.[8] Writing in Hebrew, moreover, Berdyczewski can count on his readers' acquaintance with the biblical phrase *The Red Heifer* that forms the story's title, referring us to the red heifer of Numbers 19, an important component in the ritual life of the people. Strikingly, however, no one in the story—neither the narrator nor the characters—ever refers to the cow with this verbal tag. The title resonates solely as a communication between author and reader. In using such a famous phrase, Berdyczewski effectively tells readers that we already know this "ruddy heifer." She is always already there, constructed for us through biblical and rabbinic texts. There are no virgin readers here. And so, too, there is no simple "cow." To use so overloaded a verbal tag as *The Red Heifer* is to acknowledge the web of significations in which "she" participates.

Indeed, the biblical and rabbinic contexts of the phrase *The Red Heifer* heighten the play of ambiguities around Berdyczewski's cow. From the passage in Numbers 19, we know that the body of the cow—its blood and, once it is burned, its ashes—constitutes a ritual substance that both purifies and renders impure those who come into contact with it.[9] The ashes of the red cow play a central role in the ritual of purification; however, anyone who has had contact with the cow becomes impure and must undergo purification. The masculine discourse of biblical and rabbinic tradition raises suggestive ambiguities that surround the very question of activity, or what it means to be an active male subject in relation to a body that is identified or coded as feminine. Insofar as this mix of biblical and rabbinic significations reverberates for Berdyczewski's readers, it helps to underscore an ambiguous mix of Jewish historical positions. Who are you and where in Jewish history, this story seems to ask, as it explores an array of positions defined through relationship to the red cow.

Consider the spectrum of behaviors that unfold. We have, first of all, the narrator's detached piety and anxiously sustained propriety. At the same time, the narrator describes the cow as *ra'vah lekhol ro'ehah* (a sight to behold for all who gaze at her), phrasing that positions the cow as a spectacle of the body.[10] And indeed, the story depicts worship of the flesh on all sides. Reuven and his family sit around the "queen" cow and stroke and feed her. Women are jealous of her. And then there are the *katsavim*, who carry out the equivalence of a gang rape, where the blood-splattered cellar walls testify to the fierce joy of their animal spirits.[11]

The story deals in oppositions, antitheses, and transgressions. Setting off the claims of Jewish spirituality against the blunt edge of embodiment, the narrator contrasts *ha'am haruhani* (the spiritual nation) to *hakatsavim hagufaniyim* (the fleshly butchers). Similarly, a reference to an unearthly piety—*me'ein yir'at shamayim* (a kind of fear of the heavens)—finds its counterpart in the simple designation *hanut shel basar* (a meat store). This contrast is elaborated in the reference to *halimudim* (studies), on the one hand, and *adam megusham ha'omeid kol hayom bahanut . . . vemokher et habasar* (a fleshy man who stands in a store all day, selling meat), on the other. *Limudim* (studies) thus bumps up against *basar* (meat). This pronounced opposition appears to shape the plot and to reach a marked climax in two long descriptive paragraphs that elaborate the contrast between the proper slaughter of a cow, as opposed to the murder of the red cow.

Here, however, we must draw ourselves up short in the realization that there are no actual *shohatim* (ritual slaughterers) in the present tense of the story. In his detailed description of a proper slaughter, the narrator is dwelling nostalgically on a vision of the past. His eloquent description of the *shohet* is put forward as an account of what *should* have happened. We can wonder whether it is precisely this temporal distance that allows for an idealization of the work of ritual slaughter by distancing it from the actuality of the physical body. The description of what a proper ritual slaughter would have been can be read as the elaboration of a sentiment of nostalgia for a more decorous relation to the body.

In his own history, Berdyczewski, we know, was drawn toward a Nietzschean responsiveness to the instinctual. We are reminded of this in "The Red Heifer" when the *katsavim* are likened to *kohanei ba'al* (priests of Ba'al), phrasing that brings to mind the violence of primitive sacrifice and implies a contrast to the priest-ridden attenuated laws of ritual slaughter.[12] From this angle, the *katsavim* recover connection to elemental forces in a tale of masculine action unbound. The marked absence of the rebbe with which the story opens acquires further significance once we see that the story concerns the band of "brothers"—the *katsavim*—who act out of greed and desire, enjoying the taste of blood, as they take for themselves what the paternal authority of the law has denied them. At the point of description, even the narrator appears to join gleefully in the orgy of violence, as he itemizes the limbs that are hacked off and comments on the "cruelty" that is involved. Thus while the narrator may claim to uphold the opposition between ritual slaughter and the brute violence of the *katsavim*, he is, in fact, the vehicle for its transgression. His ostensible propriety masks his connection to the activities that he tells us about. In fact, Berdyczewski might be said to stage the narrator's performance so that we cannot fail to notice these shifting and contradictory positions.

"The Red Heifer" belongs to what Avner Holtzman identifies as a fertile period in Berdyczewski's life, between 1904 and 1907, when he shifted his energies from Hebrew and Yiddish literature to absorption in ancient Jewish texts and to the production of anthologies with more of an ethnographic and historical focus.[13] M. J. Berdyczewski's own appearance on the literary scene changed the face of Hebrew literature. In his choice of subject and narrative mode, he defied Ahad Ha'am, who advocated leaving aesthetics to European belles-lettres and employing Hebrew literature as an instrument for the betterment of the Jewish people. Challenging Ahad Ha'am's conception of the literary, Berdyczewski uses the short story to give emphatic expression to conflict without pressure to resolution. Ambiguities are not there to be resolved, but rather to be understood as forces that shape a historical/narrative moment.

Holtzman notes the influence of Berdyczewski on *dor hasofrim*, the rising generation of writers that included Gnessin, Shofman, and Brenner.[14] Holtzman's account of their intoxication upon meeting Berdyczewski makes me think of the homoerotic intoxication of the *katsavim* in "The Red Heifer." Drawn together as a band of brothers, the *katsavim* are intoxicated with the immediacy of touch, the blood of the *The Red Heifer*. They bathe in her blood, roast her liver, and devour it half raw. The young writers whom Holtzman describes revel similarly in the immediacy of sensation to which Berdyczewski gives them access and that he himself appears to have embodied for them. He is their cow: to be violated and consumed. Of the response of these writers, Holtzman says: "The expressions of these outpourings of soul were translated into concepts [conventions] of literary influence."[15] We have here suggestions of an enactment of the creative process in all its violence through a time of change: creative process as a violent disruption of existing boundaries. The tensions of literary production inform this narrative in a way that expresses something of the encounter between Berdyczewski and his contemporaries, as Holtzman tells it.[16] The tale itself enacts something of the violent shift that is its subject. Its failure to secure adequate or convincing closure thus testifies to historical change.

In light of the terrain that he explores, we might find a place for Berdyczewski among the social theorists of the late nineteenth and early twentieth centuries, men who were engaged by questions of mass psychology, in particular by the behavior of men in groups. We can think here of Nietzsche, as well as Gustave LeBon, the nineteenth-century positivist whose work on the sociology of crowds Freud cites, and even of Freud himself, drawn as he was to examine crowd behavior and to interpret the instinctual impulses of the mob who act as one, rebelling against the primal father. From *The Genealogy of Morals* to *Totem and Taboo* and on to "The Red Heifer," the writing of each of these men carries the inscription of struggle, conveying at once an attraction to and a recoil from the lawlessness of the crowd.[17] No one is above the fray. Thus, Berdyczewski's story italicizes its own terms, exaggerating the opposition between the cow's owner, Reuven, and the *katsavim* to ensure that we do not miss it, heightening that opposition to the point of parody—parody of the writer's preoccupations and the issues of the age. In so self-conscious a narrator, who oscillates between horror at and admiration for the violence of the *katsavim*, Berdyczewski parodies his own Nietzschean infatuations. Every impulse is overwritten.

Furthermore, there's no distinction between surface and depth in this tale. The narrator's self-proclaimed function is to witness, which is enough, in fact, because there is only the surface of actions here. Unlike the complex composite of opposing impulses that we find in Berdyczewski's more psychological fiction, this is no story of inner exploration. "The Red Heifer" consists of one-dimensional characters, positions, really, no one of which is ever developed beyond that flatness of a single attribute or set of actions.[18] In this fictional universe, consisting simply of externalized forces, the narrative remains stubbornly opaque in its refusal to supply motivations to character and action. A more interpretive narrator might have exercised more of a capacity to absorb and process events within a frame of values. But this story is about the dislodging of just such an interpretive frame.

The story catches the "system" in a moment of change. It's a non-starter of a story about a red cow, which ends up giving us in its entirety (but in no one of its parts alone) the inner dynamics of a historical moment.

For contemporary readers, it is this very opacity that makes of the text a mirror in which we may glimpse ourselves. The killing of the cow as a violent act stands for a historical trauma that cannot be represented directly. Its power might be understood in terms of a capacity to evoke in the reader vague stirrings of events barely recalled, if at all. The "historical" trauma to which I refer can be understood in the context of individual prehistory. If this story is about nothing, it is a "nothing" so evocative that the reader cannot help but be drawn into filling in, unawares, events and scenes that he or she can never fully see.

Something other than what we see acquires representation here, or perhaps it is that each of us supplies our own reading, unawares. We can "read" the cow as an excess of body—as body multiplied, magnified, and italicized. In the shift from public adoration to the "rape" and "murder," what violence is recalled? Berdyczewski's imagination embraces the mythic and the historical, as Holtzman notes, but it does so in a manner that includes a *mythos*, in the Aristotelian sense of plot, whose component actions evoke a primitive drama of body and self. That *mythos* engages an experience of body that is never fully available to consciousness, an experience, moreover, of a body that is phantasmatic, rather than biological.[19] Each of us as readers may bring to our reading some embedded sense of body, violence, and law, ingredients of a narrative that can never be told directly, the originary violence of our entry into culture.

Unreflective, a dumb beast, but beautiful, the cow constitutes the field of desire. Characters—or, more accurately, groups of characters—in the story constitute themselves in relation to the cow. As a figure of the body, in all its attractions and dangers of contamination, the cow is the axis around which the story turns. As such, the red cow opens up a semantic space that is organized into meaning by the activities that go on in relation to it, on it, and through it.[20] The cow as a bodily envelope is penetrated in an orgy of sexualized violence made possible by a shift in the order of signification of which Berdyczewski takes great care to remind us.

Read thus, the story offers a parable of a shift in the formation of the male subject. In the cultural alignment of gender, the realm of the body belongs to the domain of femininity. Attaching high stakes to this tale of a cow that falls subject to sexual violence, Berdyczewski accounts for masculinity as a position taken in relation to a body. At its most stereotypical, normative masculinity rests on a fiction of presence and self-sufficiency that denies the splitting of the subject. The sense of loss and lack that accrue in the process of becoming a subject are instead displaced onto a female other, who is seen as deficient, or "castrated." Conventions of masculinity are thus predicated on a denial of lack and a displacement of castration onto the feminine. In a splitting that is simultaneously denied, the cow is both the rupture and the defense against the rupture. It embodies—or allows for an enactment of—the contradictions through which a gendered self comes into being.

I am working with an understanding of "gender" as the classification of difference in terms of a relation to the body. It is not (identical with) the body, but is rather a mode of experience, a relation to the body, whose determinants are fixed and unavailable to consciousness. This conception of gender can be extended into the historical context in which the story was written, where we come upon the paradoxes of Jewish gender in Europe at the turn of the last century. Cast as the other of the European male, Jewish masculinity had long carried an association to the feminine: iconography of menstruating Jewish men can be found in the European Middle Ages. Over the course of the nineteenth century, newly pathologized and politicized conceptions of gender developed, including, for example, the degeneracy of the Jewish male that served as contrast to his Aryan counterpart. (This embedded stereotype of a feminized Jewish male led Freud to explain antisemitism as the product of the castration anxiety felt by Gentiles at the Jewish practice of circumcision.) Gender was enlisted in service of the political projects of racial and nationalist thought.[21] Thus, a history of Jewish male feminization makes itself felt in Berdyczewski's story, where it shapes a relationship to the cow on the model of identification.

At the same time, however, Berdyczewski's story also registers indications of an encounter with newly embodied conceptions of masculinity that oppose any identification with the feminine. Giving context to the simple violence of the *katsavim*, the narrator refers to the rise of Jewish self-protection societies, mobilized to defend Jewish communities against the predations of gentile violence. This can be read as a nod to a historical dilemma—a crisis of action that invokes the very terms of masculinity. Similarly, Berdyczewski's Nietzscheanism must be read in terms of shifting identifications between active and passive, aggressor and victim. We might think here of Bialik's cry in "On the Slaughter": "Executioner! Here's the neck—come and butcher me! Behead me like a dog—you have the arm with the ax."²² Bialik's poetic outcry evokes the feminized passivity of the victim, even as it rebels against the historical demarcation of Jewish martyrdom. Berdyczewski's story, then, views a crisis of Jewish life through the lens of a relationship to the body: cataclysmic shifts and a concomitant crisis in narrative.

In terms of the expression of a literary shift, this story belongs to what Robert Alter refers to as Berdyczewski's "revisionist vitalism" and the effort of Berdyczewski, Gnessin, and their contemporaries to create "on Central and Eastern European soil . . . an authentically European Hebrew fiction."²³ Berdyczewski's story links the psyche to history, as it tells its tale of appetite and restraint, violence and law, a dance in relation to a phantasmatic body.

David Biale describes the dilemma of turn-of-the-century intellectuals in terms of a mix of erotic passivity and the drive for political power, conflicts that form part of what he refers to as "the politics of modernization."²⁴ Historically, that shift can be attributed generally to the impact of the Haskalah and the rebellion against normative Jewish law, as well as to a response to outbreaks of violence against Jews. Almost in cartoon form, "The Red Heifer" renders visible the crude dynamics of that "politics." The story highlights a web of significations, male/female, Jew/Gentile, shohet/katsav, but these seeming pairs of opposites resist assignment to assigned places at the opposing poles of masculine and feminine. Or rather, the opposing poles remain stable, and the grouping of actual historical subjects shifts in their lineup.

Throwaway anecdote of a small-town scandal that it is, "The Red Heifer" marks a shift that can be understood as a repositioning of the male subject. Who is male, the story asks, and who is female? The answers are contradictory, in a manner that reflects the underlying shift, without resolving it. The force of that shift makes available to readers in its time and in our own the reverberations of those primal scenes/dramas through which we are gendered and positioned in culture. Gender is produced and reproduced in violent scenes of desire and aggression in which subject and object mingle and an immobilized viewer finds multiple positions vicariously, as active or passive, male or female.²⁵

Berdyczewski's brief story allows for an apparent range of positions that are defined in terms of relationship to the body. But while the butchers may lay claim to the violence of a stereotype of male power to which

European Jews, historically, had little access, this tale of a contested masculinity does not omit the "fact" of castration, even in the very enactment
of that violence. In effect, the story relinquishes neither the identification
of the Jew with the bloody victim, nor with the aggressor. If the cow is the
body, it embodies not only the relation of men to a female body, but to
their own bodies, their own experience of embodiment.

Fiction becomes the realm of play. Berdyczewski's story gives expression
to impulses, identifications, and positions in a macabre dance of relationship to the body. Where is masculinity to be located? Out of these scenes
of adoration and violence, what identity constitutes itself as "masculine"?
Against this shifting historical ground, we become viewers of a spectacle, a
grotesque enactment of the Jewish negotiation with modernity, played out
in a theater of the body.

Notes

1. I adapt here Lacan's provocative formulation, to the effect that "Woman does
not exist." See "God and Woman's Jouissance" and "A Love Letter," in *The Seminar
of Jacques Lacan: On Feminine Sexuality: The Limits of Love and Knowledge, Book
XX: Encore 1972–73*, ed. Jacques-Alain Miller, trans. Bruce Fink (New York and
London: Norton, 1998).

2. See Holtzman's essay in this volume.

3. Jacques Lacan, "The Agency of the Letter in the Unconscious, or Reason since
Freud," in *Écrits: A Selection*, trans. Alan Sheridan (New York and London: Norton,
1977), 174.

4. I would like to acknowledge the struggles in which we engage to express our
own experience, even as I draw attention to the impact of existing modes of signification.

5. See Lacan, *Encore*, 93.

6. "This fragmented body . . . usually manifests itself in dreams when the movement of the analysis encounters a certain level of aggressive disintegration in the
individual. It then appears in the form of disjointed limbs, or of those organs
represented in exoscopy, growing wings and taking up arms for intestinal perse-
cutions—the very same that the visionary Hieronymus Bosch has fixed, for all time,
in painting, in their ascent from the fifteenth century to the imaginary zenith of
modern man. . . . Correlatively, the formation of the *I* is symbolized in dreams by
a fortress, or a stadium" (*Écrits:* "The mirror stage," 5).

7. In this sense, historical narrative is a form of allegorisis, as Hayden White
puts it, that is, in the sense that any narrative of events signifies more than it can
say, offering readers an understanding that has reference beyond the specific events

it depicts. Hayden White, "The Question of Narrative in Contemporary Historical Theory," in *The Content of the Form: Narrative Discourse and Historical Representation* (Baltimore: Johns Hopkins University Press, 1987), 45.

8. Yosef Even comments on this double-edged narrative, which speaks condemnation of the *katsavim*, while celebrating the sheer cruelty and violence of their actions. Yosef Even, "The 'Fictional Author' of Berdyczewski's Stories" [Hebrew], in *Micha Josef Berdyczewski: Mivḥar ma'amarei bikoret 'al yetsirato hasifrutit* [M. J. Berdyczewski: A selection of critical essays on his literary writings], ed. Nurit Govrin (Tel Aviv: Am Oved, 1973), 182.

9. As Jacob Milgrom notes in his commentary to the JPS volume devoted to Numbers: "It is the blood of a *hattat*, a purification offering, which is the ritual detergent *par excellence* and which will remove the impurity from those contaminated by contact with corpses" (159). He goes on to observe: "Whereas the ashes of the red cow purify those on whom they are sprinkled, they defile those who do the sprinkling (vv. 19, 21) and, indeed, anyone who handles them (v. 21) and is involved in preparing them (vv. 6–10). This paradox is neatly captured in the rabbinic apothegm: They purify the defiled and defile the pure (PdRK 4:6)" (438). Jacob Milgrom, ed., *The JPS Torah Commentary: Numbers/BaMidbar* (Philadelphia and New York: Jewish Publication Society, 1990).

10. In structure, meaning is a function of position: signification is a product of relations among terms. With the weakening, but not disappearance, of law, the system is destabilized and we are given to glimpse, however indirectly, the shifting relationships within the system. This is Saussure's image of a language state as a chessboard, as read by Lacan.

11. The action of sprinkling before the *ohel mo'ed* (tent of meeting) through which the blood becomes sanctified may remind us, in Berdyczewski's story, of the blood that spatters all over the room in which the butchers are gathered; they are sticky with it.

12. Avner Holtzman, *Hakarat panim: Masot 'al Micha Yosef Berdyczewski* [Recognition: Essays on M. J. Berdyczewski] (Tel Aviv: Reshafim, 1993).

13. See Holtzman's essay, this volume.

14. See Holtzman, *Hakarat panim*, 22–23.

15. *Hakarat panim*, 23.

16. This story can be read as a tour de force of ambivalence and thus the vehicle for what Bakhtin calls an "idea-feeling" or an "idea-force": "Thought, drawn into an event, becomes itself part of the event and takes on that special quality of an 'idea-feeling' or an 'idea-force.'" Mikhail Bakhtin, *Problems of Dostoevsky's Poetics*, ed. and trans. Caryl Emerson (Minneapolis: University of Minnesota Press, 1984), 10.

17. Nietzsche writes: "For these same men who, amongst themselves, are so strictly constrained by custom, worship, ritual, gratitude, and by mutual surveillance and jealousy, who are so resourceful in consideration, tenderness, loyalty, pride, and friendship, when once they step outside their circle become little better than uncaged beasts of prey." *The Birth of Tragedy and the Genealogy of Morals* (trans. Francis Golffing; New York: Doubleday, 1956), 174.

18. Consider the kind of exploration of psychological dynamics that Alan Mintz carries out in his study of turn-of-the-century Hebrew writers. The protagonist of *Urva parah*, for example, merits that attention to inner conflict. *Banished from Their Father's Table: Loss of Faith and Hebrew Autobiography* (Bloomington: Indiana University Press: 1989).

19. Serge Leclaire writes of the "corporeal nature of the object, which is the cause of desire," but situates that "body" between "a hallucinated reality . . . and . . . a substitute object, . . . such as a fetish." *Psychoanalyzing: On the Order of the Unconscious and the Practice of the Letter*, trans. Peggy Kamuf (Stanford, Calif.: Stanford University Press, 1998), 44.

20. The body of the cow is constituted as "semantic space" in the sense that Barthes develops in his study of the narrative uses of the body in *S/Z*. Roland Barthes, *S/Z*, trans. Richard Miller (New York: Hill and Wang, 1974), 61, 65. See *S/Z*, 65 on oppositions and antitheses. Transgression of the opposition leads to catastrophe, "a paradigmatic conflagration." We might think here of the orgiastic frenzy of the *katsavim*.

21. See George Mosse, *The Image of Man: The Creation of Modern Masculinity* (Oxford and New York: Oxford University Press, 1996); Sander Gilman, *The Jew's Body* (New York and London: Routledge, 1991); Daniel Boyarin, *Unheroic Conduct: The Rise of Heterosexuality and the Invention of the Jewish Man* (Berkeley: University of California Press, 1997). See also my essay "Bodies and Borders: The Politics of Gender in Contemporary Israeli Fiction," in *The Boom in Contemporary Israeli Fiction*, ed. Alan Mintz (Hanover, N.H.: University Press of New England, 1997).

22. Chaim Nachman Bialik, "On the Slaughter," in *The Modern Hebrew Poem Itself*, ed. Stanley Burnshaw, T. Carmi, and Ezra Spicehandler (Cambridge: Harvard University Press, 1989), 32–33.

23. Robert Alter, *The Invention of Hebrew Prose: Modern Fiction and the Language of Realism* (Seattle: University of Washington Press 1988), 86, 71.

24. David Biale, *Eros and the Jews: From Biblical Israel to Contemporary America* (New York: Basic Books, 1992), 172. David Biale, *Power and Powerlessness in Jewish History* (New York: Schocken, 1986), 103.

25. In the eyes of French psychoanalyst Serge Leclaire, this is an ongoing process: "The subject is born and reborn solely from a constant disentanglement of body and words, from a perpetually repeatable crossing of the grid of signifiers, from the ghostly, hallucinated reunion with the lost but immediately present object, right there, so very close to us. That object has no image nor any possible representation in the margin of figures and words, in what is forever closing and opening the doors of our body. It is the pulsing of our desire." Serge Leclaire, *A Child Is Being Killed: On Primary Narcissism and the Death Drive*, trans. Marie-Claude Hays (Stanford, Calif.: Stanford University Press, 1998), 53.

Avner Holtzman

[1]

READING "THE RED HEIFER" one instantly feels that he faces what Amos Oz once called "a genuine Berdyczewskian story,"[1] namely, a story that represents the core of Berdyczewski's world and the foundations of his narrative art in the most characteristic and intensive manner. Indeed, all editions of Berdyczewski's writings, even the most selective ones, contain this important story.[2] What makes "The Red Heifer" such a representative, paradigmatic Berdyczewskian work? I would point out three main features that combine to create this impression.

First, the story clearly reflects the essential characteristics of Berdyczewski's narrative fiction because its composition consists of three superimposed layers, representing the three facets of Berdyczewski's thematics. These are the autobiographical perspective, the realistic content, and the mythical infrastructure.[3] The autobiographical layer manifests itself in the short introduction by the first-person narrator. In his opening lines, he defines his spatial and temporal relations with the narrated events and hints at his ambivalent emotions toward them. The realistic or social layer is framed by a general comparative discussion about the relative status of ritual slaughterers and butchers in the historical reality of the shtetl. This discussion serves as an intermediate link between the short introduction and the story itself, leading to the mythical heart of the story—the tale of the Red Heifer. The mythical layer culminates in the expressive description of ancient lust hidden within the group of butchers, erupting during a violent storm of rape, murder, and carnivorous gluttony. The nocturnal ceremony that they perform in the dark cellar is explicitly presented as a reconstruction of pagan ritual.[4]

Second, the story can be interpreted as a concentrated expression of Berdyczewski's moral and national philosophy, which is marked by the Nietzschean phrase *Umwertung aller Werte* (*Shinui 'arakhin*), which he adopted as a slogan for his overall stance in the public arena. The transvaluation of values, according to Berdyczewski, demands to expose the "other side" of the Jews—namely, the earthly, vital instincts suppressed within them for many generations. When these suffocated powers find their way out in his fictional world, they usually burst through illegitimate channels such as crimes and sins against accepted social and moral norms. In this context, we may find special interest in the narrating voice of "The Red Heifer." On the surface, he seems to share the moralistic condemnation of the butchers' crime and the shame they brought on the entire town. "The story is definitely unsettling," he remarks in an understatement. However, he can hardly conceal his deep satisfaction with their orgiastic frenzy. He even admits to it almost openly in a seemingly apologetic paragraph that can serve as a motto for the whole story:

> Our generation, after all, is destined to die out, and the next generation will not know its ancestors and how they lived in the diaspora. Now, if one wants to find out about how that life really was, let him know about it, its lights as well as its shadows. Let us know that although we were Jews, we were also just "flesh and blood," with all that the term suggests.

Third, in the poetic sense, "The Red Heifer" can clearly exemplify Berdyczewski's art of fiction, especially his poetics of language. This poetics consists of bold, condensed intertextual relations with the entire range of Jewish and non-Jewish cultural heritage.[5] "The Red Heifer" interweaves dozens of ancient narratives of crime and sin, sacrifice, atonement, and destruction. Therefore, it will not be an exaggeration to claim that almost every sentence of the story is potentially explosive. The most visible intertext is, of course, the biblical discussion of the Red Heifer (Numbers 19) and its Mishnaic elaboration. At the same time, however, the story echoes other ancient stories of pagan rituals involving sacred animals, from the story of the golden calf to the legends of Dionysian ceremonies. The rich allusive web supports Berdyczewski's overall concepts, which are cyclic and deterministic but at the same time indefinitely pluralistic.

It is possible and even necessary to elaborate on these three aspects, further establishing them with detailed textual evidence. However, developing the discussion in these directions will merely rephrase well-known issues and already resolved questions. Therefore, I would like to take the discussion beyond its known and accepted boundaries, and raise new questions about the story that may produce fresh insights into Berdyczewski's world in general and the meaning of this story in particular.

My preliminary assumption is that the chance to infuse new energy into the study of Berdyczewski's work does not lie in any additional interpretation of one story or another, brilliant as it may be. Furthermore, it will not benefit from any up-to-date presentation of his ideological concepts. I believe that this potential chance lies in an integrative scrutiny of the entire range of his trilingual, multi-generic intellectual activity. Such a scrutiny has to take into account his narrative fiction, essays, anthological collections, and historical research, all linked together as different facets of a unified spiritual process. Therefore, we should start by placing "The Red Heifer" in the exact chronological context of its inception.

[2]

The archival material supplies us with valuable information concerning the genesis of the story. On 3 May 1905, Berdyczewski noted in his diary: "I began a new Hebrew story: Red Heifer."[6] We may assume that the story was completed in a short while, since it was to be published as the sixth story in a cycle of short stories entitled *From the Recent Past*. Its first five stories had been published around that time in the Hebrew daily *Hazefirah*. For reasons unknown, the sixth story was not printed there at the time. It is evident, however, that sometime during 1906 Berdyczewski made corrections in the story, most significantly in its opening lines. The corrected version was finally published, over a year after the composition of the original draft, in a short-lived daily newspaper called *Hayom* that appeared in Warsaw.[7] A copy of the unpublished original manuscript (which was not kept by the author) found its way, quite curiously, to the Berdyczewski archive in Holon over seventy years later.[8]

What was the meaning of the years 1905–6 in Berdyczewski's personal world? What was on his mind and what was the nature of his work when he began "The Red Heifer"? It was indeed a discernible period both in the wider circles of Jewish public and cultural life and in Berdyczewski's personal world. In the Jewish world, it was a period of confusion and crisis: the Zionist movement seemed to have lost its course following the Uganda debate; and there was Herzl's premature death and the dissent of the Territorialist faction in 1905. The revolution in Russia in the same year generated a wave of pogroms, accompanied by deep feelings of destruction, helplessness, and despair. The modest beginnings of the Zionist enterprise in Eretz Israel had not yet been successful. This atmosphere of crisis naturally influenced the literary scene. The political and economic circumstances in the years 1904 to 1907 put an end to all Hebrew daily newspapers in Russia (*Hamelitz, Hazefirah, Hazofeh, Hazeman*), as well as other literary periodicals (including the important monthly *Hashilo'aḥ*, which was temporarily closed between 1905 and 1907). Publishing activity was radically reduced, and the reading public almost disappeared.

For Berdyczewski, this was a period of seclusion and introversion. His intensive involvement in Hebrew and Yiddish literary life diminished gradually, until it almost ceased in 1906. However, his detachment from the public arena was not entirely unwilled by him. From the day he had settled in Breslau in 1902, after many years of wandering, he was set to dedicate his life to the study of ancient Jewish literature and history. Indeed, despite severe financial troubles and other practical difficulties, he managed to make the years 1904–7 the most intensive and fertile period of his literary career. We may even suggest that during those years, he laid the foundations for almost every literary and scholarly enterprise that he was destined to create for the rest of his life.

By 1904, he had completed his book *The Life of Moses*, constituting his own version of the story by rearranging the biblical material in a new order. In the same year, he prepared two other books: an anthology of mishnaic, talmudic, and midrashic proverbs; and a comparative critical edition of *Pirkei avot*. In 1904 and 1905, he composed a broad literary and documentary anthology, concentrating on three of the founding fathers of Hasidism. In 1905, he conceived his initial revolutionary ideas concerning the origins of the people of Israel, later to be materialized in his book *Sinai and Gerizim*. At the same time, he began to plan his comprehensive collections of Jewish folk literature. In 1906, he put in writing his basic assumptions on the history of Hebrew prophetic literature and Oral Law, as well as initial outlines for his studies of ancient Christianity. Around 1907, he collected diverse materials for two more anthologies: on the Samaritans and on the Karaites.

Occupied as he was by his scholarly activities, Berdyczewski did not abandon the literary channel. This was not the center of his activity in those years, and his diary documents his struggle to suppress his "poetical drives." It is noteworthy, however, that in May 1905, the same month in which he wrote "The Red Heifer," he also sketched a detailed plan for the novel *Miriam*, to be fulfilled fifteen years later.[9] At the same time, he composed dozens of short essays (most of which were published years later) on diverse subjects—from Zionism, Hebrew literature, and Jewish history to religious and existential issues, not to mention his vast correspondence and daily diary writing, which also intensified in 1905–6. The overall picture is breathtaking. Evidently, in those three or four years, during which he did not publish any book and reduced his participation in the Jewish press to a minimum, he was producing an overwhelming amount of scholarly and literary works in many disciplines, genres, and subjects and in three languages, adding up to thousands of written pages.

The picture drawn here arouses many questions. What is the meaning of the fervent creativity that swept Berdyczewski between 1904 and 1907? Why was his activity divided into so many channels? Is there a link between the numerous works he wrote and planned at that time? What made him restrain his narrative powers in Hebrew and at the same time create a great number of Yiddish stories? What is the nature of the Hebrew stories that were born at that time despite his self-limitation? Above all, why did Berdyczewski shift the focus of his activity from narrative art and current journalistic essays—fields that he had just conquered—to historical studies and anthological compositions?

Random notes scattered in Berdyczewski's diary may shed light on these issues. "Every day, I sit on the bench to pass judgment on Judaism, and I never see an end to it. [Judaism] constitutes my imaginary world and my concrete pain," he wrote in April 1905.[10] Two years later, he added: "My struggle with Judaism is interwoven in everything I have done so far. It has not ended and it never will."[11]

It is indeed a paradox that Berdyczewski, known for his struggle to welcome European philosophical and aesthetic values into Jewish culture, and who fought against the manifest Judaistic views of Ahad Ha'am, practically remained bound all his life to "the world of Israel," as he called one of his early articles. None of his hundreds of literary essays in Hebrew, Yiddish, and German was dedicated to a non-Jewish figure. His entire narrative writing is rooted in the reality of Jewish life in Eastern Europe or in traditional Jewish sources that he remodeled.

Judaism always was central in his mind, but his attitude toward it and the perspectives through which he examined it changed significantly over the years. The period discussed here—the middle of the first decade of the twentieth century—marks one of the most dramatic of the changes to influence his entire literary route. Only a few years previously, at the outset of the new century, Berdyczewski was struggling to define and establish a modern, secular Jewish identity, enabling individuals to set their own concept of Jewishness and the nature of their commitment to the tradition of their forefathers. Constantly aware of the tragic gap separating his own generation from the world of their ancestors, he was nevertheless full of optimistic energy in his writing. It expressed his belief in the ability of the individual Jew to liberate himself from the burden of heritage and become part of a secular Jewish culture. It was full of confidence in the power of modern Hebrew literature to become the core of this culture, substituting for a lost religious identity. His writing also anticipated positive results of the Zionist experiment in Eretz Israel, despite his severe criticism of the Zionist political establishment.

All these concepts, however, seem to have collapsed within a few short years. In his influential early collections of essays (1899–1900), Berdyczewski had preached for the dominance of the individual Jew over conceptualized Judaism, coining the amazingly radical slogan: "We are Hebrews, worshiping [only] our own hearts." Now he seemed to have retracted from this stance, shifting his interest to Judaism as a historical phenomenon and a system of ideas. The crisis of 1904–7 seems to have awakened his deep pessimistic views toward the chances for Jewish revival, accompanied by bitter visions of destruction and death. Berdyczewski lived under the impression that everything was falling down: East European Jewry was marching toward destruction, the Zionist movement was paralyzed, and modern Hebrew literature was dying. Any active involvement in public life seemed futile to him. All that remained for him was to adapt a contemplative, scholarly perspective toward the Jewish past, to study and document it as a historical object, detached from the issues of actual, concrete Jewish existence.

As a practical conclusion of this view, Berdyczewski turned to deconstruct the concept of Judaism, characterize it, and trace its origins; he did so in every possible genre and method. Thus, his newly born inclination to view individual Jews merely as representatives of a diverse collective entity became the cornerstone for his monumental collections of legends and folktales. The main goal of this enterprise was to expose "the people's soul," preserved and reflected in the anonymous folk literature that originates from oral traditions. Consequently, these collections were meant to create an authentic unified portrait of Jewish life for many generations, different tribes, and changing geographical settings.

Another aspect of his abandonment of contemporary Jewish life is apparent in the essays that he wrote during that period. In contrast to his almost daily comments on actual public affairs, culminating in 1903, he turned after 1904 to a much more distant, panoramic overview of East European Jewry. At the same time, he crystallized his theological concepts into a series of essays removed from any historical reality. That drive to decipher the deepest codes of Judaism is especially manifest in his growing dedication to biblical studies. The most significant outcome of this effort was *Sinai and Gerizim*, a monumental study that strives to trace the crucial moment of inception creating the fateful bond between the Jewish people and its god. "I do not consider myself a creative writer any more," he wrote to his friend F. Lachover in 1913, "but a scholar of religion or Judaism. This core question engages me wherever I go and wherever I have gone, even when I have fled afar from it."[12]

[3]

The overall process described above may also explain the significant changes in Berdyczewski's fictional writing around 1905. From that time on, he abandoned the autobiographical route, no longer depicting the psychological drama of the young Jewish intellectual torn between tradition and the modern world.[13] He was no longer interested in shaping the idiosyncratic mechanism that motivates his hero and differentiates him from his environment. At the same time, he almost lost interest in depicting individual grotesque characters from the shtetl. Instead, he turned to investigate the general forces that shape Jewish existence in its traditional setting. He examined the dynamic interplay inside extended multigenerational families. He described the social and economic communal system, the nature and consequences of living under strict religious law, the archetypal patterns ruling the characters' psyches, and the hidden links between shtetl Jews and the surrounding Ukrainian gentile population.

"The Red Heifer" embodies all the components of this change. The autobiographical narrator retreats to the margins of the story, relinquishing his individual identity and shifting to the first-person plural. He openly identifies himself with the "flesh and blood" collective Jewish entity and commits himself to documenting traditional Jewish life for the sake of future generations. The characters are modeled in a schematic, typological manner, devoid of unique personal characteristics. The plot echoes its condensed biblical structure, turning the story into a strange realization of the ancient law written in the Book of Numbers. The air of the Berdyczewskian shtetl, here and elsewhere, is full of ancient national memories as the miserable East European Jews are constantly compared with their giant biblical ancestors. When the community in the story "The Interval" (1902) is swept into an orgy of dancing, drinking, and adultery, the narrator comments: "A sealed fountain of the ancients' joy of life is now pouring forth and inundating. . . . Give them compensation for the life that they and their fathers have not lived, compensation for all generations and all times."[14] The same happens to the group of butchers in our story who steal the beautiful heifer, slaughter her, and dance ecstatically around her body while biting off pieces of her raw flesh. At this point, the narrator remarks: "But this did not happen at Beth El or at Dan; it happened in the Jewish city of Dashia, not at the time when the ten tribes were exiled from the Northern Kingdom, but in the year 1884."

The dynamic shift from concrete Jews to abstract Judaism is visible even in the minor differences between the 1905 manuscript and the 1906 published version. The manuscript reveals that the story was initially located in a real, well-known historical place—the Ukrainian hasidic town of Savran. However, in the later version, the town was given a symbolic, mysterious name: Dashia. A similar change occurred in the characterization of the ritual slaughterer who became a butcher. This man plays an important role in the plot as the actual slaughterer of the heifer. In the manuscript, he has a private name, Gad, but in the published version his name is eliminated, turning him into an anonymous, representative character. The same tendency toward abstraction and generalization made the author blur other marks of historical context. He omitted, for example, the following sentence describing the town's discussion about the heifer: "And they were worth no less than talks about a new governor or about miraculous deeds by Baron Hirsch and Montefiore." He also omitted the following explanation for the prevailing financial troubles of the town: "The livelihood in Savran was very hard. Because of the great dispute between the rabbi of Savran and the Tsaddik of Talna, the number of travelers was reduced."

The published version includes, on the other hand, words and phrases that enhance the general symbolic meaning of the story. For example, the struggle between the butchers and the heifer contains the following addition: "What happened to them? What pent-up feelings sought release?" The moment of the heifer's death is also charged with symbolic energy, thanks to seemingly minor additions. In the manuscript, we read simply: "Her soul departed and she died"; and in the published version: "Her ruddy soul departed and she died. Man conquers beast!"

If, indeed, Berdyczewski wished the story to express his views of the Jewish condition at the outset of the twentieth century, what is the nature of this message? In other words, what is the meaning of this strange tale, reaching its climax in a horrifying scene of rape, murder, carnivorous orgy, and a bath of blood?

It may be helpful to reflect on the story's protagonist—the Red Heifer. In the biblical context (Numbers 19), it embodies an inexplicable contradiction, representing purity and impurity at the same time. On the one hand, the ashes of the slaughtered heifer were used to purify those who were contaminated by touching dead bodies. On the other hand, we read that everyone involved in its slaughtering becomes impure during the process. The Red Heifer thus purifies the impure and renders impure the pure. This basic paradox relates to the initial pattern that dominates the story, dividing the fictional world into two opposite poles. This world sways between normative Jewish existence and the breach of every accepted moral law. The ritual slaughterers, representing the rule of halakhah, are opposed to the butchers, personifying the direct contact with a primary world of flesh and blood. However, the dividing line between them is very thin, almost invisible. The Red Heifer is opposed to the herd of regular cows. Thus, whereas they metonymically represent the mediocre Jewish community, she is a condensed symbol of beauty, power, sexuality, mystery, and demonization. Standing in the middle of the Jewish town, the heifer serves as a living challenge against accepted social order. Therefore, she is destined to be destroyed, according to the harsh deterministic rules of Berdyczewski's world. In this respect, she parallels the mysterious beautiful girls miraculously emerging from time to time like shining stars in the Berdyczewskian shtetl, but destined to be removed in a tragic, violent manner.[15]

Paradoxically, the ultimate act of fervent lust, entirely fulfilling the "flesh and blood" nature of the butchers, results in the violent removal of its object, the Red Heifer, from the world. The implied author obviously celebrates that moment of deliverance with the butchers, deriving much pleasure from the eruption of pagan instincts in the dark cellar. However, the ecstatic descriptions of slaughter, dance, and the biting off of raw flesh seem to blur the reader's senses as well, delaying comprehension of the full meaning and real consequences of the scene. The concluding paragraphs of the story transform that victorious moment into bitter defeat. Soon after the wonderful moment of redemption is a series of punishments and disasters cast upon the butchers by human and heavenly causes: "Everyone who had a hand in doing in that red heifer experienced bad things in his family life, as if a curse had been cast on him and his house, without leaving any remnant."

What were the butchers punished for? Did they suffer, as the story implies, because of their sin against Reuven, the owner of the Dutch red heifer? Does such a relatively minor crime justify the apocalyptic atmosphere encompassing the town and the feeling of its inhabitants? "It was as if there had been an eclipse of the moon in the midst of an eclipse of the sun, and everyone looked at one another as if the world had been turned into Job's Valley of the Ghosts." We may assume that this atmosphere derives from a deeper source than the trivial felony of stealing a cow in order to sell her flesh. The sense of death that colors the story's ending may hint that slaughtering the Red Heifer is but a symptom of a deeper illness within Jewish society. Berdyczewski seems to suggest that a society that fails to absorb the values embodied in the beautiful Red Heifer has no future. The murder of the heifer should therefore be viewed not as a positive, heroic expression of Jewish yearning for material life, but as the opposite: an act of symbolic separation from the primary powers of life personified in the heifer. The erotic ectasy engulfing the butchers is therefore only a passing spasm, like a last convulsion of a dying man.

One of Berdyczewski's favorite quotations was the last stanza of Y. L. Gordon's obituary poem dedicated to the writer Peretz Smolenskin:

> What is our people and what is its literature?
> A great corpse, a lying giant;
> The entire earth is his burial place
> And his books are the inscription on his gravestone.[16]

"The Red Heifer" has emerged from a similar elegiac state of mind. Since the actual Jewish people seemed to be perishing, all that remained was the urge to mourn it, to document its existence, to preserve its memory, and to study its heritage. These feelings may explain the following bitter lines, written in Berdyczewski's diary only two weeks before he wrote "The Red Heifer": "While for the Jewish people I can foresee only the abyss, . . . some feelings arouse and glimmer within me toward Judaism."[17]

Writing "The Red Heifer" was, no doubt, part of this commemorative tendency, as the narrator explicitly states in his opening lines quoted above. Practically, though, it was interpreted in contrast to the writer's intentions.

For generations of readers, this story was viewed as an expression of belief in the potential powers of earthly life hidden beneath the surface of diasporic meager existence, waiting for their fulfillment. Perhaps now, almost a century after the creation of "The Red Heifer," we may determine that both the author and the readers were proved right. Bearing in mind the depth of catastrophe as well as the miraculous national and cultural revival that the Jewish people has experienced in the past century, we can now identify these two contradictory directions inseparably interwoven in Berdyczewski's story.

Notes

1. Amos Oz, "A Man Is the Sum of His Sins and the Fire Locked in His Bones" [Hebrew], in *Be'or hatekhelet ha'azah* [Under this blazing light] (Tel Aviv: Sifriyat Poalim, 1979), p. 31.

2. See, for example: *Ma'asim shehayu* [Genuine tales] (Tel Aviv: Am Oved, 1945), 166–78; *Micha Yosef Bin-Gorion: Leket umavo me'et Yehudah Ehrlich* [Micha Josef Bin-Gorion: Selection and introduction by Yehudah Ehrlich] (Tel Aviv: Mesilot, 1958), 57–64; *Mivhar sippurim* [Selected stories] (Tel Aviv: Dvir, 1965), 91–100; *Sippurim* [Stories] (Tel Aviv: Dvir, 1980), 149–58.

3. This triple thematic division is commonly agreed upon by Berdyczewski scholars, though it is usually presented not as a simultaneous phenomenon but as a diachronic development from the autobiographical phase to the social one and then to the concluding mythical phase. See, for example: Ortsion Bartana, "The Model of Neo-Romantic Myth" [Hebrew], in *Telushim vahalutsim* [Uprooted and pioneers] (Jerusalem: Dvir, 1983), 91.

4. On the mythical aspects of the story, see Yoav Elstein, "The Transformation of a Myth: A Reading of 'The Red Heifer'" [Hebrew], in *'Iggulim veyosher* [Structures of recurrence in literature] (Tel Aviv: Aleph, 1970), 148–69.

5. On the rich intertextual web in "The Red Heifer," see Herzl and Balfour Hakak, "Myth and Tradition in 'The Red Heifer'" [Hebrew], in *Pirkei Berdyczewski* (Jerusalem: Shalhevet-Yerushalem, 1975), 192–231.

6. Micha Josef Berdyczewski, "Diary Notes, January–November 1905" [Hebrew], trans. from German by Yitzhak Kafkafi, *Ginzei Micha Yosef* 6 (1995): 54.

7. Micha Josef Berdyczewski, "The Red Heifer," *Hayom* (Warsaw) 1, no. 30 (31 August 1906); no. 31 (2 September 1906); no. 33 (4 September 1906). Collected in *Mehe'avar hakarov* [From the recent past] (Warsaw: Hasefer, 1909), 124–33; *Kol sippurei M. J. Berdyczewski* [Complete stories of M. J. Berdyczewski] (Tel Aviv: Am Oved, 1951), 181–84.

8. See Emmanuel Bin-Gorion, "'The Red Heifer': An External Version of the Story's Opening" [Hebrew], *Ginzei Micha Yosef* 1 (1980): 41–43.

9. See "An Outline for the Novel *Miriam*" [Hebrew], in *Kol sippurei M. J. Berdyczewski*, 329–31.

10. Berdyczewski (n. 6 above), 51.

11. Micha Josef Berdyczewski, *Pirkei yoman* [Chapters of a diary], trans. from German by Rachel Bin-Gorion (Tel Aviv: Moreshet Micha Yosef, 1974), 89.

12. Berdyczewski to Lachover, 28 July 1913, *Ginzei Micha Yosef*, Lachover file.

13. The latest story belonging to this group is "Between Hammer and Anvil" [Hebrew] (1903–04). We may also mention "The Stranger" [Hebrew] (1907), in the same context.

14. "The Interval" [Hebrew], in *Kol sippurei M. J. Berdyczewski*, 157. See also Nurit Govrin, "The Sources of the Story 'The Interval' and Their Reshaping" [Hebrew], in *Ma'agalim* [Circles] (Ramat Gan: Masada, 1975), 79–85.

15. See, for example, the stories "Summer and Winter" [Hebrew] (1904) and "In the Valley" [Hebrew] (1909), both belonging to the same phase in Berdyczewski's writing as does "The Red Heifer."

16. Y. L. Gordon, "To the Soul of the Creator of *Hashahar*" in *Kitvei Yehudah Leib Gordon: Shira* [The writings of Yehudah Leib Gordon: Poetry] (Tel Aviv: Dvir, 1950), 306.

17. Berdyczewski (n. 6 above), 52.

[II]

TO THE SUN

Saul Tchernichowsky

ROBERT ALTER

The translation is more or less literal. No attempt has been made to reproduce the rhyme scheme or the meter of the Hebrew sonnets. The text is laid out with line divisions in order to enable readers to imagine how the lines of verse are deployed in the original, though the necessities of literal fidelity often produced arrhythmic lines. Whenever it was feasible to represent the Hebrew with reasonable faithfulness while imparting some rhythmic coherence to the English, I have done so. Divergences from literal translation are minimal, generally dictated by the choice of a more readable or less awkward English approximation of the Hebrew. For example, the Hebrew nir, *which means "plowed field," and which occurs several times, is here represented as the less ungainly "furrow," which, in any case, implies a plowed field. But explanatory paraphrase and loose equivalences have been scrupulously avoided. The pressures of the sonnet form at times led Tchernichowsky to rather knotty formulations, and I have not tried to simplify these.*

[1]

I was to my god like a hyacinth or mallow
   Who has nothing in his world but this sun of his gleaming,
   And an angel raps it: Rise and grow, sproutling, and burst forth
With your song, festive song, in the jagged thorn.

And I sucked the furrow's juice. Like wine it went through me,
   This fragrance of rich soil with its clods, soft clods.
   Did he lack prelate and priest in the great city's temple,
That he brought me to this place and made me his prophet?

Is the sap on cypress-silver less in my eyes
Than your goodly oil, shining gold on the head;
   And the fragrance of pear tree and field that I stored up

Than the powders of Sabean merchants, than my nard and my incense?
    I bow to you in secret, I bend low in reverence,
    And like an ear of golden grain in the heavy standing wheat.

[2]

And like an ear of golden grain in the heavy standing wheat,
    That has shot up in great splendor and flourished to the quick,
    Like this ear of grain hiding in its hollow its secret,
Pledge of everlasting life and flotsam of time past.

Like an ear of grain stolen from the furrow, sucking the countryside's
    breast
    And wet with living nectar, dreaming its glory-dream,
    I, too, did burgeon. But my soul was ever thirsty.
Alas, day chases day. Will I redeem the bill of credit?

My dream has not yet come. From my eyes my path is hidden.
When I turn this way and that, I'm distraught: What's mine, who's
    mine . . .
    Have I come to the border or already crossed it?

Has my father lied to me, not kept his word?
I am a wild blossom, I. And my father is my sun.
    And he summoned me warm rains and decreed me mountain mists.

[3]

And he summoned me warm rains and decreed me mountain mists,
    Twilight of sea-depths, abode of great stillness,
    Crown of fiery cloud incandescent in its casement,
And before it bursts upward, the earth's close is too cramped for it.

And the sundial's too cramped to encompass the limit,
    The sun in the roar of the fiery ocean on its back,
    And legacies immemorial received by father from father
Raptures of the great city's sick, lore of guileless countryfolk,

For me to be the axis of the world that he fashioned,
    Its essence, its utter center, he abounded, treasured up
    For the present and what's to come, for the past that has vanished.

And with the abundance of all charm in the colors he did not shame me.
    And he enriched me abundantly—by his power, which is mighty—
    With symphonies of light and shade, and kohl, and rouge, and
        crimson.

[4]

With symphonies of light and shade, and kohl, and rouge, and crimson,
    Cold crystal's mummies and aquamarine slumberers,
    The brief moment's life of a spark struck off hot
Within heavy-hued alabaster and sepulchered shipwrecks.

And the network of wood-veins in the crosscut of mahogany,
    Trees bloodlogged that spurt up ferocious,
    And hues of near-daybreak and of evening washed in blood
That sloughs off golden treasures and will never be impoverished—

One melody they are, one wondrous lofty song.
    The master of computation, can he solve the enigma?
    Or, student of life's kingdom, can you tell it to me?

Guileless hearts already solved it, and from the innocent heart
    I, too, received it, for my heart did not deceive me.
    I fathomed an age's sorrow, each nation's song bewitched me.

[5]

I fathomed an age's sorrow, each nation's song bewitched me.
    The dream of On's soothsayers inscribed upon a wall,
    This inscription of Druids incised in chalkstone,
Amulet on parchment, magician's song, the poor man's stutter.

And in the writ that gives command to an age and folk before me,
    In the shepherd's incantations, whispered on the sheep-shed's threshold,

In the magus' babbled rapture, when travail has seized him,
In the talismans of China, my curious gaze

Discovers but this prayer, the entreaty of flesh and blood:
  "You who dwell in being's recesses, pray keep for me the blood.
  Quench not your fire that you lit in me in your mercy,

Liquid fire, guarding fire, one spark from your flames!"—
  That's the great total sum, lodged in the bitter heart,
  The voice of the soul wrapped in light, voice of wanderer in foreign
    darkness.

[6]

The voice of the soul wrapped in light, voice of wanderer in foreign
    darkness,
  Clash within me, for I'm not consecrated as I should.
A realm of sheer doubt, doubt of what is certain,
  Encompassed me like a dream in weavings of rapture.

And in the upheavals of the living who cling to each decree
  Piercing decree, undermining the Almighty,
  A shield of innocent faith I donned over my battle-garb
And in the everydayness of each day some little bit stayed with me.

And were it not for the fragrances of that rich crumbly soil,
Stifling heat drifting up with the chaff from the silo,
  The shovel's ring splitting furrow and scythe singing in the grain,

I soaked them up in the village, in that freedom, and I still budding—
Who would have stood by me in straits, in the battle, as my heart
    constricted,
  As I stood between the living and one already dying?

[7]

As I stood between the living and one already dying
  (What a terrible craft!), a sharp scalpel in my hand,

Some would weep for joy, some would curse me roundly,
I soaked up the last light in a dying stranger's pupil.

By the thunder of potent cannons rolling through the meadow,
    By the fire flashing in the pitch-black of my bunker to me only,
    I traced the last line, erased the living from my page,
From a bejeweled threshold thus a precious stone is torn.

And yet in that spark in the guttering eye,
    In the light soaking up light before blanking out forever;
    And yet in that fire-flash burning and shrieking,

In the fire calling to fire that bids disaster and destruction—
    It was you who were in them, this your glory that stunned me;—
    Did I come too soon or was the Rock late who created me?

[8]

Did I come too soon or was the Rock late who created me?
    'Gods' are around me and fill all existence.
    Stars are my gods, I pray to them bewitched
By their faces, light of day and pale moon.

For beside you there is nothing, O sun that has warmed me!
    Sun-children you are to me, the cocoons hanging high,
    Sun-children—the elephant tree, the peel of each garlic,
Avatars of light and heat, the combustible coal.

And all existence becomes a voice of prayer, the prayer of all:
    To you the mother jackals call as they litter their whelps,
    To you the battle trumpet as light breaks in the camp,

The suns in the sphere above as the voice sweeps them up.
    In the chorus of the infinite I'll sing out and not be still:
    In my heart the dew yet lodges that descends on Edom's steppes.

[9]

In my heart the dew yet lodges that descends on Edom's steppes
    And moistens the sand in the desert of God,
    And in my ears lives the song that comes with shadow's coming
And a gentle star glitters to primeval lays,

And primeval night shades existence with its wings,
    And the desert and the night become but one secret,
    And from its tents the assembly of peoples inclines on each mound,
And bows to him in trembling in their fete and their disaster.

And when the nation's skies change above it, the skies of blue,
    When the face of its stars dims above it, and if in the yoke
    Of alien heavens it turns backward and forward,—

Once a month it goes out in mysterious night
    To sanctify the moon, as it sanctified her then
    On the crest of Mount Hor, abode of primeval God.

[10]

On the crest of Mount Hor, abode of primeval God,
    Shining forth in clouds of light giant with law-fire,
    From the brilliance before him Chaldean Bel bowed on the Euphrates,
And the Sphinx's visage went pale in the Nile red in its channel.

In his hand a staff with which El smashes, and stilled
    Is the pride of Zeus, quickener of ivory, and Perun heard his word
        and fled
    To the forest, and the moth met the worm
In the breastplate of Lubian priest, and Wotan's sacred trees their prey.

And when era gives way to era, and the East once more brightens,
    Ethiopia's fetishes quail, shamed are Hurmiz and Kerub
    And the Arabian idols, by the light of the crescent moon.

And yet there's a vision . . . an age then will fashion, like the refiner,
    Its god to come—and we shall worship him in gladness—
For my heart utters song to the sun and Orion.

[11]

For my heart utters song to the sun and Orion—
    Will you bring against me judgment and thrust me to dust,
    If to the god of the vulgar people I pour no libation,
In dances before the people I put no crown on his head?

And in his heavenly temple, stripped of all image and writ,
    In the beauty-of-all-in-all with no cherub does he answer me,
    And with his pedigree-book he comes not to blind my eyes,
In which there's a signature like the law in the bill of a fool.

But if a wave of great sacred ecstasy's gone through you,
    Joyous trembling in the hour of vision's creation,
    In the flood of heart-life taking part in all mystery:

In the pride of your loving true with a virile man's noblesse—
    You've found favor with him, as the gift-garden finds favor,
    When the bean-pod swells and the tree's fruit matures.

[12]

When the bean-pod swells and the tree's fruit matures,
    Weeds, all trespassers of border and fence,
    When they ripen their seed in the heart of the fruit-skin
And light-rays are hidden and stored away filtered.

From them till time's ending, when this earth's
    Climate changes, and its forest fragrance fades,
    With the remnant of structures on poles, rot's survivors,
And in the graves of great princes, in amphoras and jars.

And after thousands of ages, it will come from a cramped mine,
    Will shine forth on tower-heights in the court

Of every convent of fire-worshipers, in pyres where they offered up
    daughters;

And it will burn in the brain of the greatest of geniuses, and in the flesh
    Of the mosquito, which sings, and in an age empty and lacking
    A vanished world's idols, they seized me and I have no escape.

[13]

A vanished world's idols, they seized me and I have no escape!
    The idols of this nation, all who touch it know beauty,
    Loveliness became its wisdom, its wisdom became loveliness,
And it scattered its beauty over Hades and Ocean.

North-sea winds bewitched me from among the trees,
    Telling of the frost that is cloaked in agate pattern,
    And among the sun-shrines of On, in the temple I sought out,
I imagined this spark, that says within me Repeat,—

But this flash is from the East, from Canaan I preserve it,
    Danite icons compelled me, sacred groves filled with trembling,
    Sacred trees, blocks from Tyre, in Ur of the Chaldees did I worship.

Where's the way I must choose, and where is the path?
    Shall I anoint my oil for Yah, or Zeus shall I choose,
    Or the last age's icon in the kingdom of the idol?

[14]

Or the last age's icon in the kingdom of the idol,
    Or the song of strength's dream we'll establish forever.
    And a man's eye will try to find matter's secret,
The fine atom's permutations in gold and in tin.

And from the minerals he will bend and stretch line and path
    To the kingdom of trees and the hidden growing things.
    And a single chain's his: the mushroom among molds,
The green slime on the lake, the almond tree and the elephant's get.

And the secret of heat, electricity and light will be grasped,
    The mystery of magnets, the riddle of barley's granule,
    The vibration of the roused nerve, stretched without hiatus.

And it will become a single secret, the secret of all secrets—the living.
    Then will the song be sung him: this sun of mine's warmed me,
    I was to my god like a hyacinth or mallow.

[15]

I was to my god like a hyacinth or mallow,
    And like an ear of golden grain in the heavy standing wheat;
    And he summoned me warm rains and decreed me mountain mists,
With symphonies of light and shade, and kohl, and rouge, and crimson.

I fathomed an age's sorrow, each nation's song bewitched me,
    The voice of the soul wrapped in light, voice of wanderer in foreign
        darkness,
    As I stood between the living and one already dying,
Did I come too soon or was the Rock late who created me?

In my heart the dew yet lodges that descends on Edom's steppes,
    On the crest of Mount Hor, abode of primeval God,
    For my heart utters song to the sun and Orion.

When the bean-pod swells and the tree's fruit matures,
    A vanished world's idols, they seized me and I have no escape—
    Or the last age's icon in the kingdom of the idol?

Aminadav A. Dykman

ANYONE WHO TOUCHES, however superficially, on such authors as Y. L. Gordon or Brenner knows full well how crucial it is, while examining their work, to take into account the legacy of Central European Romanticism, or that of Dostoevsky; all the more so when one approaches the major Hebrew poets. It is now commonly acknowledged that considering Bialik, Uri Zvi Greenberg, Shlonsky, or Pen in a strictly intra-Hebrew manner, without considering the general context of Russian Symbolism, German Expressionism, or Soviet Futurism, is much too narrow an approach.

Although comparative perspectives were present at the very roots of Hebrew literary scholarship, in the works of Klausner, Shapiro, and Zinberg and were further enhanced in writings of scholars of subsequent generations, in the particular case of Saul Tchernichowsky's literary legacy, it seems that only the tip of the iceberg has been exposed. This is so despite the fact that there is hardly a better candidate for such a comparative examination. The astounding scope of his work, his numerous translations from ten languages (be it directly or obliquely), and his known connections with Russian authors suggest that in his case, such comparative treatment may prove extremely productive. The immense variety of overt and semi-overt allusions to world literature to be found in Tchernichowsky's work offers the comparatist working on Hebrew material a rare treat.

Before I move *in medias res*, I have to state that what concerns me, the effort of revealing the general meaning of *To The Sun*, is not so enticing a task. In spite of the notorious density of these sonnets, which, at times, borders on hermeticism, I feel no particular enigma here, although I can perfectly understand those who do. What interests me is what these sonnets are made of in terms of literary material. To investigate this, I would like to use a simple method proposed by W. H. Auden forty-odd years ago. Reviewing Saint John Perse's *Seamarks*, Auden wrote: "Only the poet himself has the authority to say what his literary influence has been, but a reader may legitimately say, 'to me, the poems of A seem to have a certain kinship with the poems of B, but are totally alien to the poems of C.' " This is precisely what I would like to do here: to point to several poems that seem to have a kinship with Tchernichowsky's sequence of sonnets.

73

The method may be simple, but the execution is not: the number of possible intertextual signals is simply staggering. We have the sun, a number of flowers and plants, and, somewhat later, the entire cosmos, then several deities, some named specifically, and on and on. In view of Tcherni-chowsky's "thirst for world cultures," the area of research is practically unlimited, ranging from the literature of the ancient Near East to all European literatures. Taking into account the poet's biography, however, there is every reason to focus on Russian poetry, which Tchernichowsky knew well and borrowed from in his own poems. Moreover, there is the question of the sonnet form. Tchernichowsky expressed his general poetic concept of this verse form in the celebrated sonnet "To the Hebrew Sonnet" (1920), where we read: "I like the density of the idiom of your rhyme . . . polished, containing fine goods in small parcels . . . but once my thought, the daughter of my musings, is concentrated within you / to what shall I compare you?—Gushes of base metal / conquered by print, now cast solid, filled with melodies. / For you are also like that: embroidered paintings / within form, which is all restriction." These lines are very close to the poetic statement made by the Russian Symbolist Valerii Bryusov in his "Sonnet to Form" (1894). Although the imagery is different, both poets share the same thought about the sonnet being "the stern freezing of volatile thought." This image is the kernel of the second quartet of Bryusov's sonnet: "Thus, the images of traitorous fantasies / which fly, like clouds in the sky, / having been petrified, later live for centuries / within the polished, perfected phrase."

Consider *To the Sun* in formal terms, as a cycle. Many of the critics who wrestled with Tchernichowsky's corona (wreath of sonnets)[1] underlined the rarity and complexity of this sequence form. Generally speaking, this observation is valid. In the rich and long history of the sonnet, the elaborate form of the wreath, with its fourteen linked sonnets and the fifteenth *sonetto magistrale*, is indeed a rare, if not marginal, phenomenon. Like most kinds of *technopaignia* ("games of art," such as figurative poems or palindromes), the corona is challenging and most rewarding, but at the same time tainted with a strong kinship to the odd, the bizarre, and the curious. Yet when one turns to the Russian poets who were Tchernichowsky's contemporaries, this general picture changes radically. In the preface to his *Book of Sonnets* (1923), which includes all his sonnets and sonnet cycles, Tchernichowsky listed several of his Russian contemporaries. "The form of the sonnet," he wrote, "found favor with some of the most important Russian poets of our

time, poets such as Ivan Bunin, Viacheslav Ivanov, Bal'mont, Valerii Bryusov, Igor Severyanin, M. Voloshin, and G. Shengeli."² This is the context
in which I would like to place Tchernichowsky's stunning poem cycle *To
the Sun*. Interestingly enough, half of those whom Tchernichowsky dubbed
"important Russian poets" wrote wreaths of sonnets, and more than one
at that.

Viacheslav Ivanov (1866–1949), a most prolific poet, critic, and classical
scholar, was, like Bryusov, Bal'mont, and others, one of the pillars of Russian Symbolism. His corona of sonnets, which bears no title, is a cycle of
quasi-mystical love poems, dedicated to his wife, the colorful *femme des
lettres* Lidia Zinov'eva-Annibal. On the face of it, there is nothing in this
text that would connect it with Tchernichowsky's corona, except for the
general form. *To the Sun* is anything but a Petrarchan realization of the
genre (i.e., a cycle of love sonnets) and has a well-marked single lyrical
voice, unlike as with the two heroes of Ivanov's corona. Yet every now and
then, one detects in it single lines and half-quartets that do bear a close
resemblance to Tchernichowsky's lines, at least on the general semantic level
and in their tone. A good example is the third sonnet of that corona, where
the two inseparable lovers are described as meteors, and where Ivanov
writes: "And to you, the magicians of the starry night-watch / We are two
interpreters of the secret names / Of him, whose path, having absorbed the
bronze din of time, / Is spread with the sweetness of roses by the shining
aurora." In simpler, nonpoetic words, Ivanov calls himself and his wife
"interpreters of the secret names of the sun." This quatrain has a ring that
resembles sonnet 5 of Tchernichowsky's corona, with its ancient magicians
and their prayer to the sun.

Ivanov's corona, first published in 1910, became part of his most famous
and influential book, *Cor ardens* (The flaming heart). Even a quick glance
at the table of contents of the first part of that volume reveals how central
was the symbol of the sun; various sections bear such titles as "Sun-Heart,"
"The Sun of Emmaus," and "Northern Suns." No less significant, perhaps,
is the fact that the second part of *Cor ardens* revolves around the symbol
of a flower, the rose. The section "Sun-Heart" contains a poem entitled "A
Sun-Psalm," and the poem after it, entitled "The Sun Double" (in the sense
of *Doppelgänger*), concludes with the theme of resurrection: "I, the one who
forgot and was forgotten / Shall one day rise from my grave, / To meet
your light . . . / We shall unite, resurrecting / You within me, and me within
you." Although very different from Tchernichowsky's poems, these lines do

remind one of the theme of resurrection that appears in the twelfth, enigmatic sonnet of *To the Sun*.

Valerii Bryusov, another major name on Tchernichowsky's list, also wrote two coronae of sonnets. From a strict methodological point of view, Bryusov's coronae should be kept out of the account, for the first is a Petrarchan corona that displays no thematic kinship with *To the Sun*, and the other one, although written in 1918, just a year before Tchernichowsky's wreath, could not have come to his attention, as it remained unpublished until 1928. And yet this wreath is worth mentioning together with *To the Sun*, since it displays in a perfect way one of the pivotal traits that Tchernichowsky's wreath shares with Russian Symbolism as a whole, namely, historicism. This corona of Bryusov is a short history of humanity in sonnets: the opening sonnet is entitled "Atlantis," the next is "Babylon," than "Egypt," "Hellas," "Hellenism and Rome," and so on, until World War I. The *sonetto magistrale* declares: "Over the chaos of natural forces / Thought shined for men, as light in the air, / The spirit of man lived by its hope to reveal secrets," and further down, in the tercet: "During all generations it lived / Hidden, the hope to reveal all the secrets of nature, / And all nations moved toward this grand aim." These last lines sound, at least to my ear, very close to Tchernichowsky's description of the "revealing of the secrets of nature" in the thirteenth sonnet of *To the Sun*. As for the general "historical move," that, of course, is one of the main axes of *To the Sun*, as all critics point out. For a historian of literature, Bryusov's corona has a salient organic relation to the famous *Trophées* of the French poet José-María de Heredia (1842–1905), a cycle that is a celebrated model for the history of humanity in sonnets. Indeed, the strong trans-historical vision of *To the Sun* can and should be related to Heredia's collection (some critics have, in fact, mentioned the possibility of such a relationship, although *en passant* only). Bryusov's corona, although unknown to Tchernichowsky, would prove that Heredia and his vision were very much "in the air" around 1919, and not altogether alien to Tchernichowsky.

Let me now go to the last pair of coronae that Russian poetry offers as a candidate for influencing Tchernichowsky, however obliquely. They belong to the poet, critic, and painter Maximilian Voloshin (1877–1932), with whom Tchernichowsky had many things in common, especially a deep love for the Crimean peninsula, which both poets celebrated in numerous poems. Most interestingly, both of Voloshin's coronae bear astronomical titles:

Corona astralis (A wreath of stars, 1909); and *Lunaria* (1913). Both wreaths were published in Voloshin's collection of 1918, *Iverni*.

As in the case of the corona of Ivanov, there is a more than a good chance that Tchernichowsky actually read these cycles of sonnets. Here the kinship is at times stronger, especially in the case of *Corona astralis*, since Voloshin's lyrical heroes are "we poets" at large. The poets are described, in this corona, as the chosen few whose fate it is to be eternal vagabonds in search of some elevated and secret cosmic truth. This, of course, is a motif not so very far from the general stance of the poet of *To the Sun*. Even more interestingly, the sun appears in this cycle in a function directly related to poets. In sonnet 8 of *Corona astralis*, we read: "The giver of Life— Phoebus / Gives the blind ones deep illuminations. / . . . / Night, the great mother . . . Brings its gifts to the chosen one, / He who was thrust into darkness angrily by the sun, / and became the blind toy of the fates." This oxymoronic image has to do with Voloshin's theosophic convictions, which he masterfully developed in both cycles. Compare this image with the opening of Tchernichowsky's sonnet 6: "The voice of the soul wrapped in light, voice of wanderer in foreign darkness, / Clash within me". In sonnet 6 of Voloshin's corona, one reads lines that sound very familiar to anyone who remembers *To the Sun*: "Our bitter spirit grew out of darkness, like grass, / it contains an ancient venom, the poison of tombs. / In our spirit time sleeps, as inside the ancient pyramids." Again, the specific wording here may have nothing in common with Tchernichowsky's sonnets, but the general idea, that a poet's soul possesses some kind of a cosmic memory, is very much present in Tchernichowsky's wreath, especially in sonnet 4.

Let us now go to the third poet on Tchernichowsky's list, Konstantin Bal'mont (1867–1942). This major Russian Symbolist did not write any coronae but has a multitude of texts that can be related to Tchernichowsky's wreath. One of Bal'mont's most famous collections of poems, published in 1903, bore the title *Let Us Be Like the Sun*, and had a motto from Anaxagoras that sounds like a perfect source for the opening lines of Tchernichowsky's corona: "I only came to this world to see the sun." In 1910, Bal'mont published an anthology of poetic adaptations of various ancient hymns from many cultures, under the title *Ancient Echoes*. In the section of Persian hymns, one finds a poem entitled "Ahurmiz," where the ancient god proclaims: "I am Ahurmiz, creator of Darkness, maker of Light . . . It is I who generously put semen in the earth. . . . I wove every vein in every plant . . .

And poured into all creatures *an intoxicating libation of Fire* / Which . . . burns and yet never dies" (italics mine—A.D.). These words are extremely close to the pan-human prayer that Tchernichowsky wove into sonnet 5 of his wreath: "You who dwell in being's recesses, pray keep for me the blood. / Quench not your fire, that you lit in me in your mercy, / Liquid fire, guarding fire, one spark from your flames!"

Even more important, perhaps, is the strong kinship between Bal'mont's celebrated programmatic booklet of 1915, "Poetry as Magic," and sonnet 5 of Tchernichowsky's corona. In both texts, one encounters a historio-anthropological theory concerning the origin of poetry, a theory in which ancient magical incantations occupy a pivotal place. Tchernichowsky writes of "the dream of On's soothsayers inscribed upon a wall" and of "the inscription of Druids" and "in the shepherd's incantations." Compare this with Bal'mont's words: "Listening to the music of all voices of nature, the primitive mind rocks them within itself. It gradually penetrates the patterned polyphony and composes an inner music, which it then expresses through melodious words, tales, magic, and incantation."

I have briefly examined the possible kinships between *To the Sun* and some of the poetic texts of those poets whom Tchernichowsky himself mentioned in his *Book of Sonnets*. If we are to enlarge the field of inquiry so as to include Russian Symbolism and Russian poetry in their entirety, the number of intertextual signals will increase significantly. The following three examples will suggest the broad range of filiation.

One of the thematic axes of Tchernichowsky's corona, which begins to evolve in the opening lines of the first sonnet, is the quasi-mythological notion of being "the sun's son." The same myth, or "mythologem," as Russian critics often dub it, is very much present in the complex of basic themes of early Russian Symbolism. Ivan Konevskoy (1877–1901) elaborated this myth in lines to which those of Tchernichowsky bear great resemblance: "He grew in a half-pagan family / And already as a child thought the laws of nature holy / . . . / Meanwhile the sun poured for him / A wreath of curls."

In sonnet 4 of *To the Sun*, Tchernichowsky relates in great detail his poetic conviction that the entire world of nature is filled with "one melody," known to "guileless hearts" and to him. This idea of "the music of nature" is the theme of one of the most famous single poems in Russian poetry, Fedor Tyutchev's "Pevuchest' est' v morskikh volnakh" (There is melodiousness in the waves of the sea), a poem that was one of the fundamental canonic texts of Russian Symbolism. Here are the first 6 lines (in Dmitri Obolensky's prose rendition): "There is a melody in the waves of the sea, harmony in the clash of the elements, and a harmonious musical rustle passes through the swaying reeds. / There is an untroubled harmony in everything, a full consonance in nature." Interestingly, man himself appears in this poem in his famous Pascalian definition, "the thinking reed." There is, of course, an obvious connection between this and Tchernichowsky's "I was to my God like a hyacinth or mallow."

Finally, I would like to point to a possible intertextual connection between Tchernichowsky's wording in sonnet 3 and the Russian ode of the eighteenth century. In the second quatrain of that sonnet, one reads: "And the sundial's too cramped to encompass the limit, / The sun in the roar of the fiery ocean on its back, / And legacies immemorial received by father from father." To a Russian reader, the image of the "ocean flames" of the sun immediately recalls an identical image in one of the most famous poems of Russian poetry of the eighteenth century, Mikhail Lomonosov's religious ode "Morning Meditation on the Majesty of God" (*utrenee razmyshlenie o bozhiem velichestve*), written in 1743. "If mortals only had the power to soar so high above the earth, come closer to the sun and see it," wrote Lomonosov. "On all sides would there be revealed / An ocean burning for all time" (*togda b so vsekh otkrylsya stran / goryashchii vechno okean*). Except for this salient verbal similarity, there is nothing else in Lomonosov's ode that would put it in any intertextual relationship with Tchernichowsky's wreath. But the identical wording in both texts provides strong evidence of the Russian background of Tchernichowsky's lines. I would go so far as to say that this seemingly trivial identity of images may be even more significant than the other intertextual signals that I have mentioned above, because it looks like a model case of "unconscious quotation" that would prove, better than any other instance could, the Russian orientation of Tchernichowsky's text.

So far, I have used the comparative mode to point out various similarities between *To the Sun* and Russian poetry. To return to Auden's proposal, I strove to show that "the poems of A" had some kinship with "B." But the same comparative method can—and should—also be used to demonstrate the opposite. For whereas Tchernichowsky was oriented, consciously or unconsciously, toward Russian texts, he also made a marked effort to break with poetic tradition. The opening line of his corona may serve as a case in point. "I was to my God like a hyacinth or mallow." For a comparatist, this single line opens a vast field, since poems containing flower imagery or flower symbols are legion. Within European poetic tradition, the hyacinth has a well-defined symbolic meaning, as the flower of death *par excellence*. It is in this symbolic function that the hyacinth appears in Keats, Shelley, and Sidney; for Milton, the hyacinth was "that sanguine flower, inscribed in woe" (*Lycidas*, 106). The hyacinth has a similar sinister function in the rich floral dictionary of French Symbolism, as in Jean-Antoine Nau's (1860–1918) poem of 1897, "Jacinthes": *Jacinthes, fleurs de l'ireel, / Fleur dont le parfum est . . . / Emanation d'un faux ciel!* ("Hyacinths, flowers of the unreal, / a flower whose perfume is . . . an emanation of a false sky!"). Tchernichowsky, of course, uses the hyacinth in a diametrically opposed way, making it a symbol of life. In the same way, Tchernichowsky's use of paganism, so pivotal in this wreath, does resemble the pagan motifs of various Russian Symbolists, but it is given a marked Jewish bent.

One question remains to be considered: What do the kinships that have been demonstrated in these pages prove? Most of all, they help us understand the nature of Tchernichowsky's poetic act. Writing his wreath of sonnets, Tchernichowsky acted as a pioneer, much like the poets of the Haskalah. His wrestling with the complex genre of the corona, in an effort to "import" it into the realm of Hebrew poetry, can be compared with similar earlier efforts in other genres. *Mutatis mutandis*, the relationship between his corona and the Russian poems and wreaths of sonnets that may have inspired him, however obliquely, is akin to the relationship between the ballads of Schiller and Bürger and those of Meir Halevi Letteris (1800–1871) and other poets of his generation. Such a perspective would help to explain the hermetic complexity, sometimes even awkwardness, that marks some of the sonnets of *To the Sun*.

Notes

1. A wreath of sonnets is a special sub-form of the sonnet sequence. A wreath of sonnets consists of fifteen sonnets. The main sonnet (called *sonetto magistrale*) serves as the thematic and architectonic axis of the entire wreath. This sonnet is situated at the close of the wreath. The other fourteen sonnets all have to begin with lines from the *sonetto magistrale*: the first sonnet has to open with the first line, the second with the second line, and so on.

2. Saul Tchernichowsky, *Mahberet hasonetot* (Jerusalem: Dvir, 1922), 18.

Arnold J. Band

SHORTLY AFTER WRITING his sonnet corona *To the Sun* in late summer of 1919, Tchernichowsky formulated his poetics of the sonnet in a sonnet, *El hasonetah ha'ivrit* (To the Hebrew sonnet), also written in Odessa.[1] After discussing in the first quatrain the history of the Hebrew sonnet from the Renaissance on, he details his love of the linguistic compression, the focusing of meaning, the sudden, powerful rhymes, the shifts of thought as brilliant as flashes of lightning. In seeking a proper simile for the concentration of thought in the sonnet, he suggests the pouring of hot iron into blocks of print. What intrigues him in the final tercet is the tension between complex imagery and formal borders, new significance in traditional signs and forms. He sums up this amazing form with the term *kelil*, which could mean "perfection," or "a crown," or "the corona." Recasting a phrase originally used to describe the wondrous attitude of worshipers in the Temple in Jerusalem (note the two terms *tsefufim* and *revahim*), he says of the corona: "Its thoughts are packed, but its utterances are expansive." The corona is a paradoxical tension between thoughts condensed in language, yet expansive in utterance.

This formulation of the sonnet can serve to guide us through a reading of one of the great achievements of modern Hebrew literature, Tchernichowsky's own sonnet corona written in the late summer of 1919 in Odessa, but published in the spring of 1921 in Jerusalem.[2] The publication in 1996 by the Bar Ilan University Press of a volume of interpretive essays on Saul Tchernichowsky's sonnet cycle, *To the Sun*, confirms the poem's status as one of the classics of modern Hebrew literature.[3] The essays range from Josef Klausner's pioneering attempt in 1921 to explain what he correctly believes to be a great, but difficult, poem, to Boaz Arpali's analysis in 1994 of the tensions between the classic form and the romantic impulses of the poem. These two articles reveal in their very titles two radically opposed readings of the poem. Klausner calls his article "Shemesh hasifrut ha'ivrit" (The sun of Hebrew literature), while Arpali's article bears the title "Tom vi'ydia bikhlil hasonetot *Lashemesh*" (Innocence and knowledge in the corona sonnet *To the Sun*).

Clearly, the very existence of this considerable body of interpretive literature spanning over seventy years and several literary generations in one of the most tumultuous centuries in the history of Hebrew literature must affect our reading. One cannot simply approach the cycle with a New Critical close reading that ignores either the history of the poem or its interpretations. Specifically, after reading the articles of Luz or Arpali, the two most meticulous analyses of *To the Sun*, one cannot avoid considerations of the relations between this cycle and other, primarily earlier, poems of Tchernichowsky. The issues raised by three generations of critics force us to a host of questions of imagery, language, and context generated by this complicated sonnet cycle.

How, for instance, can one avoid notice of the date of composition— Odessa, August–September 1919—appended to the poem? Tchernichowsky originally came to Odessa as an adolescent in 1890, studied in two commercial gymnasia there, and traveled abroad in 1899 to study medicine in Heidelberg. After several years of practice (1903–6) in Lausanne, he returned to the Ukraine in 1906 to practice medicine and write poetry. He experienced the upheavals of the time: the chaos after the abortive revolution of 1905; the disintegration of civil order during the disastrous years of World War I, in which he served as an army doctor in Minsk; the Russian Revolution of 1917; and the civil war in which he again served as an army doctor, mostly in Odessa. By the time he wrote this sonnet cycle, he was an accomplished poet in his forties who had witnessed much. These troubling events might have affected his poetry directly or indirectly—or not at all; the reader, nevertheless, should not approach the text ignorant of them. We shall suggest, toward the end of this essay, a plausible nexus between this cycle and the turbulent times in which it was written.

By the time he wrote *To the Sun*, Tchernichowsky was one of the best-known modern Hebrew poets, eclipsed in fame only by Bialik. He had earned a reputation as a master of poetic forms and a provocative iconoclast. His "Lenokhaḥ pesel Apollo" (Facing the statue of Apollo), for instance, published as early as 1901, attracted attention for its exuberant vitalism conveyed by his adoration of Apollo and his rejection of traditional Jewish religious practices. *To the Sun*, a massive cycle of complex, sensual poetry, ostensibly an ode to the sun, the source of all energy in many of his previous poems, must therefore be read in the context of his previous poetry. Zvi Luz, in fact, argues that this sonnet cycle is one of the three great "poetic summaries" that Tchernichowsky wrote in his life, containing all the "ideational, historiosophical, national, existential, and aesthetic motifs" of the poet, and of the three, *To the Sun* is the most "torn between contradictory tendancies."[4] Arpali attributes much of this tension to the fact that *To the Sun* is both a sonnet corona and a romantic poem like Wordsworth's "Prelude," a meditation on the development of the spirit.

Focusing on the expressive self of the poet is, in fact, a productive strategy for interpreting *To the Sun*, even though the poem purports to be an ode to the sun. The poetic self is prominent not only in the direct statements in the poet's voice, but also in the intricate imagery that is either a simile of the self, a metaphor for the self, or is observed and internalized by the self. Unlike the uninhibited youthful exuberance of a lyric poem like "Lenokhah pesel Apollo," *To the Sun* is self-reflective and chastened. The poet reflects upon his experiences and how they have shaped his imagination. In fact, it is helpful to regard the repeated apostrophe less as an ode to a divinity than as an aesthetic organizing device: by addressing the sun, the ultimate source of energy, the poet can fuse together many aspects of his experience and identity.

This fusion is never complete. The cycle, in fact, is really a brilliant series of poetic investigations of the poet's relationship to his childhood, to his memories of his exuberant delight in nature, and to his wide reading in cultural and natural history. It is shot through with poignant questions:

Sonnet 2: ". . . What's mine, who's mine . . .
    Have I come to the border or already crossed it?"
Sonnet 2: "Has my father lied to me, not kept his word?"
Sonnet 7: "Did I come too soon or was the Rock late who created me?"
Sonnet 13: "Where's the way I must choose, and where is the path?"[5]

Part of the difficulty encountered in reading this text stems from the relentless tension between centifugal and centripetal forces. On the one hand, the poet is constantly asking himself questions concerning his identity, his self-consciousness, often contradicting himself; on the other, the classical sonnet forms and the obsession with the central image of the sun, the source of all human energy, maintain a sense of aesthetic control and unity.

Perhaps the most convenient way of reading this cycle is as a set of variations on the solar theme. The deliberate line-repetition format suggests the appropriateness of the musical comparison. The individual sonnets are bound together by repeat lines, i.e., each sonnet from the second on begins with the last line of the previous sonnet, and the last sonnet, the fifteenth, is composed of the first lines of each of the preceding fourteen sonnets. This repetition is more than a compositional tour de force. The variation that each sonnet presents on the solar theme is fused with the other variations by sharing with them lines that, while being identical, really impart different meanings because of their very situation in the respective sonnet. For instance, the last line of the first sonnet is identical with the first line of the second sonnet, but conveys a different meaning, perhaps even a different mood, than the previous line that it echoes, precisely because it is the closure of one artistic unit, but the opening of another. The subtle shifts of meanings and sounds visible even in the English translation animate the entire work. The following rendition of the flow of themes from sonnet to sonnet is an attempt to present the richness of the cycle and should be read in conjunction with the text itself.

The first seven sonnets are essentially autobiographical, establishing the poet's problematic relationship to the sun through a series of situations. The first two sonnets, for instance, establish the identity of the poet as one who, like the hyacinth and mallow, turned toward the pure nourishing sun. But despite this orientation, he finds himself living in the city, with its exotic unguents and spices, which he actually loves less than the raw sight of sap on the cypress or the scent of the pear tree. The pastoral gesture, the consciousness that the speaker is really a city dweller who yearns for, even worships, the natural world is used to establish the ideational mood of the poem as one of tension. The tension is intensified in the second sonnet, where, after a rush of lush similes comparing the poet to the golden ear of corn, he declares his ennui: "But my soul was ever thirsty." And after despairing of fulfillment of his dreams, he wonders if his father (the sun) has lied to him, has not kept his promise. What this promise was is not clear here, but it apparently has to do with some sense of personal fulfillment, a oneness with the forces of nature.

The promise hinted at in the second sonnet is elaborated in the third: the sun—his father—nourished him with such sensitivity and awareness of the wondrous details of the natural world—the mountains, the volcanos, the heavens, "For me to be the axis of the world that he fashioned, / Its essence, its utter center." This startling declaration of the poet's gift from the sun that made him who he is, is further elaborated in a dynamic description of the marvels of nature in the fourth sonnet, where we are overwhelmed by a catalog of colors and hues, in sea corals and fused rocks, in the veins of trees and the brilliant tints of dawn and sunset. All these are the expression of the one mysterious melody of nature, which can be interpreted not by the mathematician or the biologist, but by those of pure, innocent hearts—like this poet.

The preference of the simple-hearted lover of nature over the scientist is undermined by the language of the sonnet, which attests to both a modern awareness of scientific research of the phenomena and the precise nomenclature of these phenomena. Tchernichowsky, we should not forget, was a physician, certainly the first modern Hebrew poet with a thorough grounding in the natural sciences from his days at Heidelberg, one of the great centers of the exciting discoveries in physics at the beginning of the twentieth century, particularly in the area of high energy and light. The linguistic elegance here is not that of a Romantic reader, but of a poet whose wonder is aroused by the detailed study of nature as it was taught in the most advanced universities at the beginning of the twentieth century.[6]

Allied to this fascination with science is the poet's obsession with the precise knowledge of the Hebrew name for every flower, tree, and stone. In 1919, for instance, he published an article on the names of flowers in Hebrew; in 1933 he published his lengthy poem "Perek be'anatomiah" (A chapter on anatomy); and in the late 1930s he was engaged to complete Aaron Masie's medical dictionary in Hebrew.[7] This preoccupation with the precise names of natural objects is one of the features of the sonnets in this cycle. The naming of the object in Hebrew is tantamount to its appropriation, its incorporation in the Hebrew cultural web that each sonnet demonstrates and celebrates.

The erudition of the poet is paraded in the fifth sonnet, where the poet declares that he had learned of the universal awe of nature expressed in Egyptian hieroglyphs, in Druid runes, in shepherds' incantations, in magical invocations, in Chinese talismans, in all of which

... my curious gaze

Discovers but this prayer, the entreaty of flesh and blood:
   "You who dwell in being's recesses, pray keep for me the blood.
   Quench not your fire that you lit in me in your mercy,

Liquid fire, guarding fire, one spark from your flames!"— ...

This learned assessment of the universality of awe both returns us to the situation of culture and the city of sonnet 1 and conveys a sense of desperation, of fear that the fire of vitality and mystery might be extinguished. This spark is all the more precious, we learn in the last two lines, since "That's the great total sum, lodged in the bitter heart / The voice of the soul wrapped in light, voice of wanderer in foreign darkness."

This tension between light and darkness, between doubt and certainty, is his present psychological state (sonnet 6), like an unsettling dream. In this condition of uncertainty and ideological upheavals, he takes shelter in his dwindling innocence, in the memories of his childhood village, the smell of the soil, the chaff in the silo, the sound of the ploughshare and scythe. These memories have sustained him in battle, in his agonizing fears, as he stood between the living and the dying.

His extreme confusion and anxiety are dramatized in a vivid battlefront scene, a justly famous passage (sonnet 7) built on his experience as an army doctor in World War I and the civil wars following the Russian Revolution. We see him in a dark trench, scalpel in hand, tending to dying soldiers. The scene is etched in Expressionistic light: the flash of cannon, the light on the page on which he crossed out the name of a dying soldier, the last spark of life in the eye of a gasping man—all distant reflections of the glorious light of the sun, but terrifying enough to raise a fundamental question about his identity: Had be been born too early—or too late?

Once he raises this central question, he begins to reformulate his position in the second half of the cycle, sonnets 8 through 14: an enduring awe at the energy of life revealed in the details of both nature and history, all apparently manifested as reflections or embodiments of solar power. The cycle drives forward to the fourteenth sonnet, a paean to the wonders of atomic energy. But before he reaches this goal, he leads us through a series of hymns of adoration of his "gods" (he is careful to enclose them in quotation marks), the various "children of the sun." These include the entire arc of being from the stars, to the elephant tree and the peels of garlic, and finally to seething coal, metamorphosed light and heat. All existence becomes a prayerful voice adoring the energy of the sun: from the cry of mother jackals to the blast of battle trumpets. The poet joins this infinite song since in his heart still abides the dew falling "on Edom's field [steppes]."

The distance he has traveled from the naive exuberance of his student days to the current more balanced awe at the pervasive energy of the sun is clear in sonnet 9, in which he elaborates on the source of his vitalism. The source, "the field of Edom," differs radically even from his recollection of his childhood scenes of raw nature in sonnet 1. The reference to the "field of Edom" is biblical (Gen. 32:4) and strategically chosen: the term refers to the borderland of eastern ancient Israel through which Jacob traveled on his way home from Aram. The dew that still dwells in the poet's heart comes from there or the "sacred sands in the desert of God." It is not from Greece or Canaan, or the catalog of primitive cultures in sonnet 6. The scene of reverence he paints here in the second quartet is one of desert tribes worshiping at a nighttime ritual at the period of the new moon at the foot of "Mount Hor, abode of primeval God," an unmistakable allusion to the Sinai desert. The scene is primal, mysterious, but already within the traditional texts that any Jew would have learned as a child.

In his imagination, there appears (sonnet 10) on the peak of that mountain in clouds of light a "giant with law-fire"—Moses, to be sure—who eclipses with his radiance both the Chaldean Bel on the Euphrates and the Sphinx on the Nile. The biblical geography is precise: ancient Israel led by Moses rose between these two mighty nations and eclipsed them. Even more, Moses shatters all other gods: the pride of Zeus; Perun, the Slavic god of thunder; Lubian priests in Africa and Wotan's trees in Germany; Ethiopian idols; Persian divinities; the totems of Arabia. Yet this excited recourse to history is not enough since the new generation will create a new god that he, the poet, will worship. But this yearning for a god is still affected by his longing for Orion and the sun. The recourse to history in sonnets 9 and 10 seems to be an exploration of a possibility that is negated in the following sonnets.

The new god he seeks, we learn in sonnet 11, will not be one shared with other human beings; he cannot pour out his libation to a god shared by the masses. He cannot worship the god that seems to have the characteristics of the traditional God of Israel: devoid of imagery or glorified in a sacred literature. What, then, is his god? What does he have left after rejecting a wide range of possibilities? The first tercet states it explicitly: the holy inspiration and joyous trembling experienced during the creative act of writing is, in itself, an act of devotion to the god of creativity. Here, for the first time in the cycle, the poet implies that the ecstasy of poetic creation is analogous to the wondrous stirring of nature. Both are aspects of an intoxicating vitalism whose products are acceptable gifts to the god of life and energy. The Nietzschean traces are obvious.

This sense of vitality is mysterious and connects him with the history of both natural and human events. This sonnet (12) focuses on the permanence and constant revival of this kernel of energy manifested in vegetative life, in the ruins of civilizations, and in a wide variety of present manifestations, from "the brain of the greatest of geniuses" to "the flesh of the mosquito." These variegated, perennial, present manifestations of energy are gods of a vanished, destroyed world who seize him so firmly that he cannot escape them. One senses here the Nietzschean "eternal return." This effusive ecstasy, continued in the octet of sonnet 13, revolves around the idea, so central to the entire sonnet cycle, that he is bound by ineluctable feelings of identity with the sources of energy he has seen in his experiences, both immediate and mediated by his reading.

His biographical reference becomes more specific in the sestet of this sonnet, when he traces this inspiration to antiquity, to Canaan, to ancient Israel, and to Ur of the Chaldees. The reader acquainted with Tchernichowsky's poetry finds himself back in familiar ideational territory, in the poetry of his early student days. Yet the second tercet surprises by raising the question: "Where's the way I must choose, and where is the path?" Three possibilities of "gods" of energy are offered. The first two are conventional: the God of Israel or Zeus. But the third, not mentioned by name in this sonnet, but occupying the crucial fourteenth sonnet, is called here: "the last age's icon in the kingdom of the idol." This third possibility is presented here as a possibilty, marked with an implied question mark, but the entire following sonnet eliminates the force of the question mark and marks the statement (in the Hebrew) with an exclamation point, asserting a strong degree of certainty.

This new god of energy to whom "the song of strength's dream we'll establish forever" is none of the possibilities mentioned before, but the mystery of atomic energy, "matter's secret." The atom is to be found in everything: in inanimate objects, in the wide variety of vegetable life, and in animals. The final sestet details the qualities of this new god of energy, the ultimate goal of this entire sonnet cycle:

> And the secret of heat, electricity and light will be grasped,
>> The mystery of magnets, the riddle of barley's granule,
>> The vibration of the roused nerve, stretched without hiatus.

> And it will all become a single secret, the secret of all secrets—the living.
>> Then the song will be sung him: this sun of mine warmed me,
>> I was to my God like a hyacinth or mallow.

The sun that warmed him is now positively identified as the source of all energy, of all life: the atom. The repetition here of the first line of the entire cycle returns us to the initial scene of the childhood love of nature and thus signals the development from childhood naïveté, through a series of meandering questions, to the final answer, that the new object of admiration and source of vitality is the atom, or rather the poet's awareness of the awesome power of the atom.

The last sonnet in the cycle is composed, of course, of the first line of each of the fourteen previous sonnets. As such, it both recapitulates all the major themes of the cycle, and in binding them together, serves as an elaborate refrain, demonstrating the subtle flow of the poem from stage to stage through a variety of experiences, memories, and questions, finally arriving at the possibility, again marked by a question mark, that the new god of energy evoking awe may be the human understanding of the mysterious power of the atom.

While the entire cycle deals with aspects of the sun as the source of energy, the variety of perspectives and sudden turns generates a dynamic, coruscating flow of ideas and sentiments. The reader cannot escape a pervasive tension, even in scenes that seem to be pastoral, like the first sonnet. The corona, in fact, carries to epic proportions the verbal web of tensions found in each individual sonnet. While some critics regard the "classical form" of the sonnet as an escape from the turbulence of the world to the stability and security of form, Tchernichowsky's sonnets, particularly this cycle, is anything but this. As we have seen, the sonnet "El hasoneta ha'ivrit" espouses a sonnet poetics that animates this entire cycle.

Tchernichowsky was a poet, not an ideologue, but his poetry often reflected his interests in broad cultural questions and in events in the Jewish world. Even his early poems reflect his Zionist passions and his anger at the massacre of his fellow Jews—as did two of his poems written in 1919 and 1920, though published later in Berlin. The period of the gestation and writing of *To the Sun*, 1919 in Odessa, was, as we have stated above, one of the most trying in his life. For about a year after the Menshevik revolution, Russian Jewry enjoyed a brief period of release from tsarist repression and the attendant optimism about the future and its potential for cultural growth. This euphoria was short-lived. After the October Revolution in 1917, the Ukraine was a battlefield and its Jews often victims of bloody pogroms. The Bolshevik government dissolved the traditional Jewish institutions in

1918, and the Yevsektsiya had commenced its campaign against "bourgeois" Zionists and Hebrew, the traditional language of the Jews. The situation had become so intolerable by 1921 that many of the leading Hebrew writers, led by Bialik, left Odessa for Istanbul on 21 June 1921. Tchernichowsky, both a Zionist and a Hebraist, obviously knew he had no future in the Soviet Union. He left for Istanbul in early summer 1922.

To the Sun is strangely reticent about the events of those days. Tchernichowsky's second great cycle of sonnets, 'Al hadam (On the blood), written partly in Odessa, partly in Berlin, where it was published in 1923, is extremely explicit about his reactions to the events of the revolution and the pogroms, his scorn for the false prophets and world-improvers. To the Sun, however, is strangely contained, even narcissistic. I would suggest two possible explanations for this reluctance to engage the events of that period. First, the entire corona was conceived as an examination of the poet's personal identity and poetic persona in one of the most difficult periods of his life. After the months of optimism after the Menshevik revolution, by 1919 the closing of horizons for a Hebrew writer in the Soviet Union had become painfully obvious. The seemingly existential questions had assumed a real urgency. Since his existence as a Jew and as a creative writer was inextricably contingent upon his role as a Hebrew poet, the political currents in the Soviet Union left him no alternative but exile. The existential angst of To the Sun, is paradoxically balanced and reinforced by the pastoralism of the idyll—or mock idyll, "Ḥatunatah shel Elka" (Elka's wedding), written in Odessa in the fall of 1921.[8] Composed when it was clear that there was no future for Hebrew culture in the Soviet Union, it is a deliberate reconstruction of a traditional wedding held, as it were, in the late nineteenth century in Tavria, the locale of his childhood. Despite the idyllic setting, there lurks beneath the apparently tranquil surface of the steppes in the fourth canto of this poem violent volcanic forces that subvert and destroy the pastoralized portrayal of the traditional Jewish world. Second, the possibility of the open expression of anger or revulsion had become impossible. Poetic criticism of the regime in Hebrew could not be printed, and even To the Sun was not published in Odessa where it was written, but in Jerusalem. Both To the Sun and "Ḥatunatah shel Elka" may very justifiably be categorized as "esoteric" writing, as expounded by Leo Strauss.[9]

In addition to its justifiable fame as a major achievement in the history of modern Hebrew literature, To the Sun seen in its historical context, is a marker of a major shift in Jewish cultural history, for it may very well be one of the last major Hebrew creations written on Russian soil. Together with "Ḥatunatah shel Elka," it stands as a monument to the end of Hebrew culture in Russia.

Notes

1. For bibliographic references to Tchernichowsky's works, see *Sha'ul Tcherni-chowsky: Bibliografiah*, ed. Ziva Golan and Haviva Yanai (Tel Aviv: Machon Katz, 1981). Items with full annotation are numbered consecutively. "El hasoneta ha'ivrit" is no. 215, first published in *Hashilo'ah* 40, no. 1 (1921): 54–55.

2. *Bibliografiah* no. 207. *Hashilo'ah* 39, no. 1 (1921): 68–78.

3. *To the Sun: Masot 'al kelil-sonetot leSha'ul Tchernichowsky*, ed. Zvi Luz (Ramat Gan: Bar Ilan University Press, 1996).

4. Luz, 109.

5. All translations are by Robert Alter and can be found in this volume.

6. For correspondences between Hebrew poetry and science, see Ruth Kartun-Blum, *Alpayim* 3 (1990); *Halets vehatsel: Hagigat kayits* (Tel Aviv: Zemorah-Bitan, 1994), 165.

7. See *Bibliografiah* no. 194, no. 258, no. 493, no. 577 no. 603.

8. This long poem was written between the seventeenth and the twenty-sixth of the Hebrew month Heshvan, late 1921. See *Bibliografiah* no. 213.

9. Leo Strauss, *Persecution and the Art of Writing* (Glencoe, Ill.: Free Press, 1952). Some years ago my colleague Moshe Perlman, who was in Odessa in those years, told me the following story, which I have not found in any biography of Tcherni-chowsky. In 1921(?), as the Soviet regime continued in its efforts to suppress Hebrew culture, the young Zionists of Odessa arranged a protest assembly and invited the poet Saul Tchernichowsky to speak. Instead of a stirring harangue, he delivered—to the disappointment of his audience—a two-hour lecture on the names of flowers in Hebrew. It would seem that the poet knew that any open political statement would be dangerous and thus made his point by simply demonstrating the vitality of the Hebrew language, which had precise words for all flora and fauna.

Robert Alter

SAUL TCHERNICHOWSKY'S CORONA of sonnets *To the Sun* is, both formally and thematically, one of the most unlikely of the great modern poems. Its greatness, let me hasten to say, will scarcely be visible to the English reader because the intricacy of the Renaissance form adopted by Tchernichowsky stubbornly resists even distant approximation in translation. (The one available English version besides the literal version offered here is arrhythmic, ungainly in diction, and very frequently imprecise.) The corona (*kelil sonnetot*) consists of fifteen interlocked Petrarchan sonnets (Tchernichowsky strictly follows the rhyme scheme ABBA ABBA for the octaves, varying the sestets with CCD DEE, CCD EED, and other permutations of the three rhymes); the last line of each sonnet becomes the first line of the next one, with the fifteenth sonnet made up of all the first lines in sequence. *To the Sun* was composed in Odessa during the summer of 1919—while the Russian civil war was raging, less than two years after the Soviet Revolution, and less than a year after the end of World War I. The Russia in which Tchernichowsky had grown up was thus engulfed in cataclysm; the renascence of Hebrew culture within the old multilingual Russian empire to which for two decades he had made signal contributions was already threatened by the new political order. Beyond these pressing local circumstances, if one looks to the literary-historical horizon to the West, this cycle of poems was written just two years before the beginning of the *anni mirabiles*, as R. P. Blackmur called them, of 1921 to 1924, during which the most spectacular cluster of trailblazing modernist masterworks appeared in English, German, and French.

The most obvious question about *To the Sun* is why Tchernichowsky should have chosen so intricate a form at this moment of vast upheaval, both to address that very upheaval and to articulate his own poet's credo in the midst of it all. *To the Sun* is a poem suffused with a sense of history, ranging from the pyramids and the Canaanite cults and the Bible to the modern age of technology, and also embracing the sciences from geology and zoology to physics. The corona, to begin with, is for Tchernichowsky a vehicle of historical memory, at least for a limited span of history, anchored as it is in the humanism of the Renaissance that was one of his cultural ideals. He was particularly conscious of the use of Hebrew as a medium for this humanism: oddly, but also instructively, Hebrew was the first language after Italian in which sonnets were composed, beginning with the fourteenth-century poet Immanuel of Rome (to whom Tchernichowsky would devote a 1925 Hebrew monograph). By taking up this formally exacting elaboration of the sonnet at a dark crossroads of twentieth-century history, Tchernichowsky was affirming the continuing vitality of the European humanistic tradition he cherished and was also announcing through his sheer technical virtuosity his own role as its supremely accomplished heir.

Rhyme rules the poetic world of the sonnet, and in the corona rhyme is given a kind of symphonic orchestration through the interlacing of sound from poem to poem. Another consequence of such elaborately braided deployment of rhyme is an effect of incantatory magic (both orchestral music and incantation are, in fact, alluded to in the poem). Above all, rhyme is a means of creating connections, at times in defiance of conventional logic, between words disparate in meaning—and in this poem, often between disparate realms as well. The art of connection, let me propose, is the key to the achievement of *To the Sun*. This cycle is not merely a formidable technical challenge for the poet but a nearly comprehensive synthesis of the principal themes that had exercised his imagination since the beginning of his career (he was in his mid-forties at the time of writing), and as such, one of the most ambitious poems he would ever undertake. The Israeli critic Boaz Arpali has suggested that *To the Sun* reflects a fusion of two Romantic poetic genres—the ruminative philosophic poem and the poem that chronicles the growth of the poet.[1] The proposal is plausible, though the variety of topics brought together in the cycle goes beyond what any putative Romantic forerunners would have encompassed in a single poem. Tchernichowsky, as I have intimated, invokes the whole range of history, from the cultic practices of early man to his own recent memories of trench warfare on the Eastern front. The geocultural canvas is just as broad, stretching from Greece and the ancient Near East to China to Norseland to the Russian steppes. At the same time, the poem shuttles back and forth from history to science to art to religion and myth to the multifaceted beauty of the natural world, while repeatedly reflecting on the meaning of the poet's vocation in this vast interplay of forces and traditions. The ultimate impulsion of *To the Sun* may well be Tchernichowsky's need to work out the relation between poetry and violence: in a world of dizzying transition that appears to be tearing itself to pieces, what place could there be for this poet's devotion to intricate patterns of beauty and for this poet's seemingly anachronistic attachment to pantheistic vitalism?

I would like to try to bring all these questions into better focus by looking closely at the eighth sonnet in the cycle. The immediately preceding sonnet, the most explicitly autobiographical of the poem, conjures up an image of the poet-physician standing "between the living and one already dying" in the trenches, the scene illumined by the fierce glare of artillery fire. The sonnet that begins with the speaker's sense of impotence and awe as he watches a life he is helpless to save guttering beneath his surgeon's hand ends in a startling pivot. The light flickering out in the eye of the dying soldier bewilderingly recurs in "that fire-flash burning and shrieking," which then, with an echo of the "deep calling unto deep" of Psalm 42, becomes a cosmic vehicle of theophany: "In the fire calling to fire that bids disaster and destruction— / It was you who were in them, this your glory that stunned me [in the Hebrew, a great tympani roll of alliteration: *hoyiso atoh vom, zeh hodkho hamomoni*]; / Did I come too soon or was the Rock late who created me?"[2] The poet, altogether a more spontaneous, less consciously willed, modern pagan than D. H. Lawrence, wonders whether he has arrived too early for the pagan renewal of a future era or whether he, in fact, has missed his historical moment in an archaic age long past. This sense of anguished in-betweenness sets the stage for the great profession of faith of the eighth sonnet. Before considering this pivotal sonnet in detail, let me quote it in my literal English version.

> Did I come too soon or was the Rock late who created me?
>   'Gods' are around me and fill all existence.
>   Stars are my gods, I pray to them bewitched
> By their faces, light of day and pale moon.
>
> For beside you there is nothing, O sun that has warmed me!
>   Sun-children you are to me, the cocoons hanging high,
>   Sun-children—the elephant tree, the peel of each garlic,
> Avatars of light and heat, the combustible coal.
>
> And all existence becomes a voice of prayer, the prayer of all:
>   To you the mother jackals call as they litter their whelps,
>   To you the battle trumpet as light breaks in the camp,

The suns in the sphere above as the voice sweeps them up.
In the chorus of the infinite I'll sing out and not be still:
In my heart the dew yet lodges that descends on Edom's steppes.

The role of rhyme in the imaginative realization of the poet's credo is decisive. Let me describe the pattern of the rhymes, which, of course, is not visible in the English translation. The rhymemes of the octave are *oni* and *um* (the way the vowels involved sound in Hebrew would rhyme with the English *tawny* and *room*). Thus a *rime riche* alternates with an ordinary rhyme in the ABBA scheme; in the sestet, Tchernichowsky will go a step beyond *rime riche* by using homonymic rhymes (C and E in the CDD CEE pattern). The eighth sonnet offers a grand cosmic panorama in which the poet, teetering between two eras in the first line, affirmatively inserts himself as a chorister in the final tercet. It is a vast vision of interconnectedness in which the phonetic kinship of the rhyming units cinches the links of connection. The two words that end the first line are *tsur bro'oni*, "the Rock who created me." The verb, which is the second word in the text of the Hebrew Bible, has, of course, a strong monotheistic provenance, as does the sturdy designation of God as the Rock, which recurs frequently in the celebratory and thanksgiving Psalms. But this semantic unit is locked in by the *rime riche* with *sahar hivaryoni*, the pale moon that is redolent of pagan and erotic associations. Between the Rock of the first line and the moon of the fourth, Tchernichowsky introduces, in single quotation marks, 'gods,' shrewdly exploiting the dense ambiguity of the Hebrew *elohim*, which is God when construed as a singular, despite its plural ending, or gods, angels, divine beings, when treated as a plural, as it is here. This magical-divine presence of the natural world is reinforced by the inside rhyme of the ABBA pattern: *yekum* ("existence") and *qesum* ("bewitched," or "charmed"): the echoing sound suggests to us that the intrinsic character of existence is a kind of magic, that the world of lovely living presences enchants the imagination of the beholder.

To the Sun constantly returns to its mythically imagined central focus on fire, light, energy. In the first quatrain of the eighth sonnet, the radiance is banked down in the flickerings and glimmerings of the night sky, with just one passing reference to daylight. The last rhyming unit of the quatrain, *sahar hivaryoni*, pale moon, then flares up into full solar brightness in its rhyme mate at the end of the next line (the beginning of the second quatrain), *shemesh himemoni*, "sun that has warmed me." The semantic freight of these two word-pairs bracketed by rhyme is unpacked through the rest of the second quatrain. For Tchernichowsky, scientific observation and religious reverence are indissoluble: the whole universe is animated by solar combustion, from the distant stars and the reflected light of the moon to our own sun, which equally imbues with life energy the poet and the entire kingdom of animals and plants, down to the fossil fuels humankind uses to warm itself. The inside rhyme of the quatrain conjoins the top and the bottom of the great chain of being by pairing "high" or "height" (*rum*) with "garlic" (*shum*—in Hebrew idiom, "garlic peel" suggests something entirely devoid of worth, but according to Tchernichowsky's pantheistic theology, everything has its worth in the sun-suffused scheme of creation). The "sun that has warmed me," *shemesh ḥimemoni*, of the first line is matched by rhyme with *hapeḥom horashoni*, "the combustible coal") at the end of the quatrain, a warmth to bask in and burning heat seen as two ends of the same spectrum.

The structural split of the Petrarchan sonnet between octave and sestet has very often been exploited from the Renaissance onward to convey a sense of antiphonal play or actual opposition between the two main divisions of the poem. Antiphonal response is especially notable in the sestet of this sonnet. The octave had been devoted to a rapt scanning of the natural world, from starry sky to garlic skin. The sestet, moving from sight to sound, makes explicit the appropriate response of all living things to the presence of the "gods" that fill the universe: "All existence [*yekum*] becomes a voice of prayer, the prayer of all." The next two lines make clear that the prayer that pulsates through all being is inflected not by any Romantic version of pantheism but rather by Nietzsche and by the poet's exposure to collective violence in his own recent experience. The stipulated instances of the voice of universal prayer are not the song of the nightingale or the chirping of the cricket but she-jackals birthing their whelps and the trumpets of battle. (Both these instances owe something to the poem from the whirlwind at the end of Job—a vision of the violent beauty of Creation that is a vehement dissent from the biblical consensus.) A sense of violence in procreation itself is intimated by the rare poetic verb for "litter," *tefalaḥnoh*, which has the more usual sense of "to split apart" and also is made the rhyme-word here of *maḥaneh*, "camp." The singing of the battle trumpet in turn is coordinated—as part of a cosmic choreography, it would seem—with the dawning of the sun's light (*honets or*), a conjunction that recalls the unsettling notion at the end of the previous sonnet that the solar god of power manifests himself in the blast of the cannons as well as in the animation of the human eye.

The second tercet begins by introducing the first of the two homonymic rhymes, "voice," *qol*, picking up "all," *kol* (the two words are phonetically undistinguishable in the Ashkenazi pronunciation). In this instance, the rhyme confirms an easy semantic connection, given the poem's theological vision with its assumption of an indwelling harmony throughout the created world. By contrast, the homonymic rhyme that ends the sonnet operates like a *faux raccord* used as a bridge between two disparate scenes in a film, here conveying us from the universal choir of the sestet to the realm of history, conceived from the standpoint of the Hebrew poet, that is the setting of the next sonnet. The poet sings out in this grand choir—*eronoh*, the same verb used for the battle trumpet and, not accidentally, the same high-poetic term for singing used in the evocation of cosmogony in Job 39, "when all the morning stars sang together"—and affirms that he will not be still (*vel'o edom*). This profession of the poet's vocation and its bond with the song of all created things is immediately followed by his declaration that in his heart he still feels the fresh dew falling on the ancient fields of Edom (*sdeh edom*).

Through all this fine intertwining of sounds and words, Tchernichowsky beautifully implements the radical project that he had initiated with his first volume of poems two decades earlier—to use the language of the Hebrew Bible (the biblical stratum predominates in his poetic diction) not allusively, as did his predecessors and most of his contemporaries, but in innovative reconfiguration, in order to express an imaginative world that challenges the very ontological postulates of the Bible. The Hebrew Bible, as the narrative, poetic, and legal manifestation of a revolutionary monotheistic worldview, proceeds by making hard-and-fast distinctions, setting up hierarchies. Creation in the opening chapter of Genesis advances through orderly steps, the advent of the first two humans on the sixth day, who are enjoined to hold sway over all living things, clearly represented as the culmination of the process. The verb "to divide" figures crucially in this process and in the body of literature that follows: lines of demarcation are repeatedly drawn in story and law and poem—between land and sea, man and beast, Israel and the nations, the sacred and the profane, purity and impurity, what is enjoined and what is forbidden. All this Tchernichowsky wants not so much to attack as to displace. There is hidden harmony in the play of violent forces of his cosmos, but it is decidedly not hierarchi-

cal—the indwelling presence of the sun's divine energy is equally manifest
in the lowly garlic and in the lofty elephant tree, in the birth-pangs of the
jackal and in the pale moon. All biblical notions of commandment and
prohibition, pure and impure, are, of course, irrelevant to the world as it
is imagined here, and the idea that man is uniquely granted dominion over
Creation has no purchase in this poem.

In the embracing perspective of *To the Sun*, even Tchernichowsky's ideological nationalism is set in a framework that puts it at odds with the
national particularism of its ultimately biblical source. As an ardent pro-
ponent of Hebrew cultural identity, Tchernichowsky was also a militant
Zionist (indeed, sometimes stridently so, especially in some of his late
poems). His proud sense of imaginative connection with the ancient Near
East through the Hebrew language is manifested at several points in the
sonnet cycle, but the world of this poem does not really allow any hierarchical opposition between Israel and the nations. On the contrary, the Hebrew voice of the poet is just one strong voice in a polyglot chorus of
cultures. The speaker's repeated insistence that his imagination is nurtured
by tribal memories of daily intercourse with divine presences in the natural
world before the imposition of an exclusive overmastering God sets him at
the same level with the poets and priests and shamans who revered Zeus,
Perun, Wotan, and the gods of ancient Egypt and Iran. All things, high and
low, ecstatic and serene, creative and destructive, are interwoven in a cosmic
web of life, and the dense interweave of related sounds and images and
repeated lines in the cycle is the formal expression of that visionary sense
of universal connection.

This grand pagan affirmation is shot through with a paradox of conflicting cultural allegiances of which Tchernichowsky himself is acutely aware.
His own channel to a primordial rapport with the natural world is the
Hebrew language, which has the distinct advantage for the mythicizing
modern poet of having deep, living roots in the early Iron Age, a time easily
imagined, as it was, in fact, as a moment when there was immediate access
to the vital presences of a reality at once natural and divine. The poet can
readily identify himself with the archaic community of the Hebrew people
revering the potent 'gods,' *elohim*, in all things. The character of the Hebrew
people once it has been saddled with the heavy legacy of Sinai is quite
another matter. The implicitly democratic polytheism of *To the Sun* in principle should make the poet a kind of pantheistic populist, but in fact he
finds himself acting as spokesman for a vision of the cosmos that has been

anathema to his fellow Jews for two and a half millennia of monotheistic consensus. This disparity of belief drives him into a poet's elitism—a familiar Romantic posture—which, on consideration, is actually an elitism within an elitism, since the audience of readers addressed by the Hebrew literary revival in Europe was itself a tiny educated minority within the Jewish people. Tchernichowsky's awareness of cultural isolation as he celebrates the idea of cosmic connection is given its sharpest expression in the eleventh sonnet of the cycle. Let me offer my own alternate translation of the first quatrain in order to provide one brief English equivalent of the rhyme scheme of the original and at least a loose approximation of its meter.

> For my heart utters song to Orion and the sun—
> Will you judge me now harshly and doom me to dust,
> If to the God of the vulgar no libation I'll trust,
> If the dance of the vulgar to crown him I shun?

In the original, these lines conclude on the barbed point of a strategic pun. The rhyme-word at the end of the fourth line is *kelil*, "crown," paired with *kesil*, "Orion," at the end of the first Hebrew line. But *kelil* is also the corona or crown of sonnets, so the poet is declaring that the splendid crown of interwoven poems that he has fashioned is meant as tribute to the divine sun and the heavenly constellations, not to the God that his fellow Jews imagine and worship. The second quatrain is a frontal critique of that God of the ordinary people. This deity seeks to dazzle man with his own unsurpassed pedigree as master of the hierarchy of Creation, but the document in question—perhaps, one may infer, the Torah—is bogus because no deity can really have claim to undisputed dominance in the world as the poet conceives it. In this polemic impulse, as numerous critics have observed of Tchernichowsky's general enterprise, there is a certain continuity with the anticlerical, anti-obscurantist impetus of the Haskalah, or Hebrew Enlightenment. At the same time, Tchernichowsky, a connoisseur of varieties of worship and religious imagination in a way that no Haskalah writer would be, is capable of a momentary perception of the grandeur of the monotheistic idea as he evokes God "in his heavenly temple, stripped of all image and writ, / In the beauty-of-all-in-all." In any case, the octave ends with the word *evil*, "fool," pointedly rhymed with *gevil*, "writ" or "parchment," the emblematic material medium of desiccated monotheistic tradition.

The antithetical movement of the sestet is then signaled by its very first syllable, *akh*, "but." And the shift from the isolated first-person singular of the octave to the second-person singular of the sestet is a way of breaking out of the isolation and implicating the reader, at least hypothetically, in the poet's experience: any person may feel a surge of sacred ecstasy in the act of Creation. This surge Tchernichowsky closely associates, in a characteristic move, with sexual virility—*nedivos gever 'az*, "a virile man's noblesse."

The underlying connectedness of all things leads, as we have variously seen, to a constant interweaving of disparate terms and images through the formal structures of the poem. At the same time, as the poem progresses, this sense of connection also repeatedly generates dialectical turns in the argument of the cycle. Thus, at the end of this pivotal eleventh sonnet, the affirmation of ecstatic male energy—the word rendered as "pride" also means "surge" or "high tide"—leads to "acceptance," or "finding favor"— obviously, by the solar deity, not the God of Sinai, and this verb of pleasing the divine serves as a shifter from the realm of ecstatic potency to the placid realm of vitality of the vegetal world. Its pods and seeds, as the beginning of the next sonnet spells out, store up the warmth and energy of the sun that quickens all things, so the poet, now very far indeed from the ritual dance of the monotheistic populace, is participating in the larger dance of universal life even in imagining an affinity between himself and the green kingdom of growing things. From the garden, the poet moves back to history, envisioning both its eschatological horizon ("till time's ending") and its hazy beginnings when the dwellers of marshlands lived in houses perched on poles. He is now ready for the last lovely loop of his elaborately braided corona: his confession of bewitchment by the ancient world and its gods (the thirteenth sonnet), his dream of uniting science and mystic vitalistic vision (the fourteenth sonnet), and the grand recapitulation of the first lines and the themes of the whole cycle in the final sonnet.

To the Sun, in pulling all these different realms together in so intricate a poetic structure, represents a beautiful and precarious balancing act. When Tchernichowsky, after fleeing from Russia to Berlin, tried to repeat the performance three years later in a second corona of sonnets, *On the Blood*, he slipped from the complexity of great poetry into the simplicity of ideological rhetoric. The later cycle makes one appreciate all the more the rare achievement of *To the Sun*. It is a poem forged in the crucible of violent modern history that still conveys a sustaining vision of the continuities of culture and of the creative rapport of humankind with the natural world. Its technical virtuosity, moreover, is a dazzling demonstration of the capacity of the poetic imagination to confront chaos and encompass it in the beautiful order of art.

Notes

1. Boaz Arpali, "Innocence and Knowledge in the Corona of Sonnets *To the Sun* by Saul Tchernichowsky," in *Saul Tchernichowsky: Studies and Documents* [Hebrew] (Jerusalem: Mossad Bialik, 1994), 293–356.

2. All citations of the Hebrew text are from *The Complete Works of Saul Tchernichowsky*, vol. 1: *Poems and Ballads* [Hebrew] (Tel Aviv: Am Oved, 1990), 204–14.

[III]

THE SENSE OF SMELL

S. Y. Agnon

ARTHUR GREEN

1 THE EXCELLENCE OF THE HOLY TONGUE

THE HOLY TONGUE is a language like no other. All other tongues exist only by agreement, each nation having agreed upon its language. But the holy tongue is the one in which the Torah was given, the one through which the blessed Holy One created His world. Angels and seraphim and holy beings praise Him in the holy tongue. And when He comes to praise Israel, He also does so in the holy tongue, as it is written: "Behold thou art beautiful, my beloved, behold thou art beautiful." What language does Scripture speak? Surely the holy tongue. And when He longs to hear the prayers of Israel, what language is it that He longs to hear? The holy tongue, as He says: "Let me hear your voice for your voice is sweet." What voice is sweet to Him? The voice of Jacob, praying in the holy tongue. By the holy tongue He will one day rebuild Jerusalem and return the exiles to her midst. By the holy tongue He heals the mourners of Zion, their hearts broken by the destruction, and He binds up their wounds. Thus it is written: "The Lord builds Jerusalem, gathering the scattered of Israel; He heals the brokenhearted and binds up their wounds." For this reason all Israel should take care with their language, keeping it clear and precise, especially in these last generations so close to redemption, so that our righteous Messiah (may he be revealed speedily, in our own day!) will understand our language and we will understand his.

2 AGAINST THE SCHOLARS OF OUR GENERATION WHO WRITE IN EVERY LANGUAGE EXCEPT THE HOLY TONGUE

But someone might object and say: "Is it possible to speak a language that has not been spoken for more than a thousand years?" as some stupid folk

102

among the Jews have said. "Even most of the scholars in our generation cannot stand up to it, and they either make a mess of their language, even in the most simple things, or else they write in every other language except the holy tongue." Whoever says this hasn't paid attention to the most important fact. Even though speech passed from the lips, it never passed out of writing, and it is there for anyone who seeks it. How is this? A person reads Torah or studies Mishnah or learns Gemara and immediately all those treasures of the holy tongue that the blessed Holy One has stored up for His beloved are revealed to him. This is especially true on the Sabbath, when we are given an extra soul that understands the holy tongue just as well as do the angels.

Then why do certain scholars make such a mess of their language? Because they put worldly matters first and words of Torah second. If they would make Torah their basis, the Torah would come to their aid. As for those who write in every other language but not in the holy tongue, even a Gentile who writes in the holy tongue is more beloved than they, so long as he does not write words of folly. You can know this from the case of Balaam the Wicked. No man did such evil as the one who suggested that the daughters of Moab go whoring, by which one hundred fifty-eight thousand and six hundred of Israel were destroyed. But because he spoke in the holy tongue and in praise of Israel, he merited to have a section of the Torah called by his name, and to have all Israel open their prayers each morning with the verse "How goodly," which Balaam spoke in praise of Israel.

And if you should say, "But do we not find that some of our early sages composed a portion of their books in Arabic?" the early sages are different, because the people of their generations were made weary by exile and were far from Messiah's light. Therefore their sages wrote them letters of consolation in their own language, the same way you pacify a child in whatever language he understands. The language of Ishmael is also different, since the Land of Israel has been given over into their hands. Why was the Land of Israel entrusted to Ishmael? Because he had managed to wrest it from the hands of Edom. It remains entrusted to Ishmael until all the exiles are gathered and God returns it to their hands.

3 THE SECRET OF WRITING STORIES

For love of our language and affection for the holy, I darken my countenance with constant study of Torah and starve myself over the words of our sages. These I store up in my belly so that they together will be present to my lips. If the Temple were still standing, I would be up there on the platform among my singing brothers, reciting each day the song that the Levites sang in the Temple. But since the Temple remains destroyed and we have no priests at service or Levites at song, instead I study Torah, the Prophets and the Writings, Mishnah, laws and legends, supplementary treatises and fine points of Torah and the works of the scribes. When I look at their words and see that of all the delights we possessed in ancient times there remains only this memory, my heart fills up with grief. That grief makes my heart tremble, and it is out of that trembling that I write stories, like one exiled from his father's palace who makes himself a little hut and sits there telling of the glory of his father's house.

4 ALL THAT HAPPENED TO THE AUTHOR BECAUSE OF A CERTAIN GRAMMARIAN AND ALL THE SUFFERING AND WOE THAT CAME UPON THE AUTHOR

Since I just mentioned a hut, let me say something about one. It once happened that I had written a story about a sukkah, a festival hut. Using colloquial language, I wrote, "The sukkah smells." A certain grammarian rose up against me, stuck his pen into me, and wrote, "You cannot say: 'The sukkah smells.' Only a person smells the aroma of the sukkah." I was worried that perhaps I had strayed from proper usage and done harm to the beauty of the language. I went and looked in reference books but found no support for my usage. Most of the books either tell you what you already know or else tell you nothing at all. I went to the scholars of our time, and they did not know what to answer me. Scholars know everything except that particular thing you are looking for. Then I happened upon a certain Jerusalem scholar, and he brought support for my words from the book called Perfect Treatise by an early sage named Moses Taku, of blessed memory. I was somewhat consoled, but not completely. I still wanted further support. When I ran into people who were experts in the holy tongue, I would ask them, "Perhaps you have heard whether it is permitted to write: 'The sukkah smells.' " Some permitted while others forbade. Neither gave any reasons for their opinions, but just stated them, like a person who sticks his thumb out at someone and says, "Well that's my view," or someone who licks his lips and says, "That's my feeling." That being the case, I went to erase those two words against which the grammarian had raised a protest. But when I started to do so, the sukkah came and its aroma rose up before me until I really saw that it was smelling. I left the words as they were.

5   THE RIGHTEOUS FROM PARADISE COME TO THE AUTHOR'S AID

Once somebody came to ask me a favor. In the course of the conversation he revealed to me that he was a descendant of Rabbi Jacob of Lissa. I put aside all my other concerns and did him great honor. I took the trouble to offer him some honey cake and a glass of whiskey. I fulfilled his request gladly, out of respect for his learned ancestor whose Torah we study and out of whose prayer book we pray.

After I'd accompanied him on his way, I ran into a certain scholar who was carrying a book under his arm. I asked him, "What's that you've got there? Isn't that the prayer book of the Sage of Lissa?" He smiled and said to me, "Sometimes you get so clever that you forget a simple custom of prayer and you have to look it up in a prayer book." I said to him, "It shows a special quality of that true sage, one who had already written novellae and commentaries known for both sharp insight and breadth of learning, that he would take the trouble to briefly lay out the laws of prayer and other matters in such an accessible way. His is a book that anyone can use to find the law and its sources, written right there with the prayers themselves. Our holy rabbis have left us lots of prayer books, filled with directions and commentaries both hidden and revealed, with matters grammatical or sagacious, with permutations of letters, secrets, and allegories, all to arouse the hearts of worshipers as they enter the King's palace. But if not for my respect for our early teachers, I would say that the prayer book of the Sage of Lissa is better than them all. In many of those prayer books the light is so bright that most people can't use them, while this one appeals to any eye."

While I was talking, my own heart was aroused and I started to tell of some things that happened to that sage whose teachings had spread throughout the scattered communities of Jews, who in turn followed his rulings. I told of some of his good qualities, things I had heard from reliable sources and had found in books.

Finally we parted from one another, he with his prayer book and I with my thoughts. I went home and lay down on my bed to sleep a sweet sleep.

Since I had done a Jew a favor and had gone to bed after telling tales of the righteous, my sleep was a good one.

I heard someone trying to awaken me. I was feeling lazy and I didn't get up. On the second try I awoke, and I saw an old man standing before me. The prayer book *Way of Life* lay open in his hand; his eyes shone and his face bore a special radiance. Even though I had never seen a picture of Rabbi Jacob of Lissa, I recognized him right off. It wasn't that he looked like any of the members of his family. The great among Israel just don't look like their relatives, because their Torah gives their faces a special glow.

When a person darkens his face over study of Torah, the blessed Holy One gives him that radiant glow and makes his face shine.

While I was still staring, the prayer book closed, the old man disappeared, and I realized it had been a dream. But even though I knew that, I said: There must be something to this. I washed my hands, got out of bed, and walked over to the bookcase. I picked up the prayer book *Way of Life*. In it I noticed a slip of paper serving as some sort of marker. I opened up to that place and there I read: "One uses lots of flowers that smell sweet to make the holiday joyous." It seemed that I had once been reading that page and had put the slip of paper there as a marker.

I thought to myself: He wouldn't have used such language on his own, without some authority in Torah. In any case, I took the prayer book *Pillars of Heaven*, by his uncle the sage Javetz, of blessed memory, and there I found the same expression. I was glad that I hadn't failed in my words and had done no harm to our holy tongue. If these two great pillars of the universe wrote this way, it must indeed be proper. The grammarian who had shot off his mouth at me would one day have to pay his due.

6   RECITING PSALMS
HOW RASHI, OF BLESSED MEMORY, INTERPRETS FOR THE AUTHOR A VERSE FROM THE PSALMS AND LIGHTS UP HIS SPIRIT

It was hardly worth going back to bed, since most of the night had passed, but it wasn't yet time for morning prayers. I got up and took a Book of Psalms. Reciting psalms is good anytime, but especially early in the morning when the soul is still pure and the lips are not yet defiled by wicked chatter. I sat and read a few psalms; some I understood on my own, and the rest were explained to me by Rashi, of blessed memory, until I'd completed the first book of the Psalter. My soul still wanted to say more. I did its bidding and read psalm after psalm, until I got to the Psalm for the Chief Musician upon Lilies. This is a song in praise of the sages' disciples, those who are soft as lilies and pleasant as lilies, so that they come to love their learning.

That was a beautiful hour of psalm-saying. The lamp on the table was lit, crowning with light every word, every letter, every vowel point, every musical notation. Opposite it there was a window open, facing the south. Outside, the predawn breezes blew, but they didn't put out the lamp or even challenge its wick. The breezes danced about the trees and shrubs in the garden, and there wafted in a sweet fragrance of laurel and dew, smelling something like wild honey or perfume.

The light from the lamp had begun to pale. It seems that the night was over. It may be that God hangs up the sun in the sky at that hour for the sake of those simple folk who don't know the whole morning prayer by heart but who recite it out of the prayer book.

A sound was heard from the treetops, the voice of a bird reciting her song. Such a voice could interrupt a person's studies. But I didn't get up from my book to listen to the bird's voice, even though it was both sweet to the ear and attractive to the heart. I said: Here I am reciting the Psalms. Should I interrupt these to listen to the talk of birds?

Soon another voice was to be heard, even more attractive than the first. One bird had gotten jealous of another and had decided to outdo her in song. Or maybe she wasn't jealous and hadn't even noticed the other. She was aroused on her own to sing before her Creator, and her voice was just sweeter than the other bird's. In the end they made peace with one another, and each bird seemed to complement the other one's melodies. They sang new songs, the likes of which no ear had ever heard. Melodies and voices like these certainly could keep a man from studying, but I made as though I didn't hear. There is nothing especially wondrous or praiseworthy about this, because the psalm played itself like an instrument of many strings. A Song of Love, next to which all other songs are as nothing. I followed after its every word with melody.

"My heart overfloweth with a goodly matter. . . . My tongue is the pen of a ready scribe; . . . ride on in behalf of truth, humility, and righteousness; let thy right hand teach thee awesome things." I understood as much as I could, and the rest was explained to me by Rashi, of blessed memory. When I got to the verse "Myrrh and aloes and cassia are all thy garments," I did not know what it meant. I looked in Rashi's commentary and there

I read: "All thy garments smell like fragrant spices. And its meaning is that all your betrayals and foul deeds will be forgiven and will smell sweet before Me." My mind was eased, like a person smelling flowers that smell.

7   TO CONCLUDE WITH PRAISE AS WE OPENED WITH PRAISE

Come and see how great is this holy tongue! For the sake of a single word a holy man troubled himself to come out of the Academy on High in the Garden of Eden, bringing his book before me, causing me to rise up at night to recite the Psalms, so that I might find something I'd been seeking for many days.

Naomi Sokoloff

AN OLD JOKE ASKS, how do you keep a fish from smelling? The answer, of course, is: you cut off its nose. The joke pivots on the fact that the verb "to smell" can be either transitive or intransitive. In contemporary colloquial Hebrew, the verb *lehariah* has parallel possibilities, and so the joke transfers easily across languages. However, this verb was not always so flexible. Uncertainty over the usage of *lehariah* generates the central controversy of Agnon's "The Sense of Smell"—that is, whether it is proper to say *hasukah merihah*. In this story, the narrator has used this phrase to mean that a sukkah smells [nice], it gives off a fragrant aroma. However, a journalist who criticizes him insists that the verb must be transitive, taking both an agent and an object: "You cannot say: 'the sukkah smells.' Only a person smells the aroma of the sukkah" (104); *Ein lomar hasukah merihah, sheharei lo' hasukah merihah ela adam hu' hameriah re'ah hasukah*" (A19).[1] Insulted, the narrator embarks on a series of attempts to verify the correct form of the verb. Consulting a variety of scholars and texts, a sage who comes to him in a dream, and even the sukkah itself, he seeks authority to justify his own usage.

This may seem a trivial disputation about a minor point of grammar. The story, however, brings into play large issues of authority, tradition, and language change. The narrator's concerns are embedded in a plot that highlights the remarkable history of the Hebrew language, its role as sacred tongue over millennia, and its dramatic growth within the modern era as a secular spoken language. The text poses a special challenge for translation. At issue are not just grammatical subtleties or lack of semantic congruence between "the sukkah smells" and *hasukah merihah*. (In English, to say something "smells" is to impart a distinctly negative connotation.) Instead, at stake here are matters of theme and style central to the narrative. "The Sense of Smell" explicitly posits the uniqueness of Hebrew and extols it as a "language like no other" (102; A18). How does a text so focused on the inimitable qualities of Hebrew come across in another language?

It is a commonplace to emphasize the untranslatability of Agnon's art. Agnon is known as a particularly difficult author to grasp in translation because of his deliberate efforts to archaicize and because of the profound erudition that is part and parcel of his Hebrew prose.[2] Agnon devised a style that was distinctively his own and that changed very little over the years of his long career. It relied heavily on rabbinic vocabulary and locutions and made extensive use of citation, richly weaving into the fabric of the text references to sacred sources. Eschewing passing fashions and aiming to transcend the contemporary moment, this undisputed master of modern fiction in Hebrew held a grand vision for his art. He saw himself as part of a long tradition and not merely as a creature of his own time.[3]

In "The Sense of Smell," such issues are fundamental elements of plot as well as style. The narrator presents himself as a writer at the tail end of an immense tradition who expresses his respect for the Hebrew language through strict adherence to classical models and resistance to linguistic innovation. Congruences between narrator and author are more than coincidental. The primary episode of the story was based on an actual incident that took place in 1934. Agnon himself was criticized by a journalist for using the phrase *hasukah meriḥah* and he took great offense, since he prided himself on his knowledge of Hebrew. "The Sense of Smell," then, is a kind of revenge, and it confronts head-on some of the tensions Agnon felt between his own work and the modern Hebrew that was developing all around him. He saw himself as a champion of correct Hebrew, and his sometimes antagonistic relations with the Committee on Language were matched by the low regard he held for Eliezer Ben-Yehuda, the foremost ideologue and advocate of reviving Hebrew as a modern vernacular.[4] The narrator similarly insists that Hebrew can be used by Jews as their current language, but that it should derive its power from knowledge of the religious sources and not from contemporary wordsmiths. He remarks that "even though speech passed from the lips, it never passed out of writing and it is there for anyone who seeks it" in Torah, Mishnah, and Gemara.

Many aspects of the story transfer quite well to English. In Arthur Green's version, an archaic quality carries over quite successfully, thanks to the level of diction and to somewhat formal and anachronistic locutions, such as "priests at service"—a rendering of a phrase *kohanim be'avodatam* (104; A19), which might have been rendered more colloquially as "priests worshiping". In addition, many intertextual references are clear, since they are not hidden but manifest in the narrator's frequent and deliberate quoting of Scripture (particularly in the opening, which resembles homily). In the English, many phrases appear as direct citations, and the use of quotation marks signals the reader openly that there is a need to identify sources. However, surely one of the first things to change in English, no matter how skillful the translator, is the music of the text and the sounds of Hebrew that elicit reverence by evoking ancient tradition. Deep devotion to the holy tongue, expressed by Agnon's narrator, is likely to be appreciated by Hebrew readers, especially those well aware of Agnon's own profound erudition and commitment to Hebrew textual traditions. These matters may be less evident in English, which simply does not carry the same weight as the original. This is a key issue, since some readers have read the text reverentially and others have read it ironically.

An English-speaking audience, unschooled in Hebrew or Jewish texts and relying on translation, may well be inclined to read skeptically. It would be natural for them to view the narrator as a somewhat ludicrous figure whose concern with language is overwrought and who suffers an exaggerated preoccupation with textual authority. Such an understanding would then steer interpretation to questions about unreliable narration and about the ironic presentation of scholars in Agnon's fiction (topics that critics have discussed at length in connection with others of his texts).[5] Similarly, for readers unaware of the Jewish pious tradition in which nature is cast as a lure, a distraction from study, it may be self-evidently laughable that the narrator, toward the end of his tale, ignores the singing of birds in order to focus on psalms. These readers might well assume that his text-driven pursuits are tantamount to self-defeat and that he foolishly ignores the glory of God's Creation in order to praise God. The cultural lens that predisposes English-speaking audiences to underestimate the narrator's reverence for the holy tongue also provides sensitivity to ironic dimensions of the story.[6] Contributing to these are elements of plot (such as the narrator's obtuseness and xenophobia)[7] that appear particularly nakedly in the English because they are not offset or counterbalanced by the resonance and echoes of the Hebrew original.

More nuanced readings have concluded that Agnon's art is capacious enough to encompass both ironic and reverential readings of this story. As Anne Golomb Hoffman and Alan Mintz have emphasized, "The Sense of Smell" is a highly ambivalent piece. They note that in this text, Hebrew is presented as a language of plenitude and presence.[8] Agnon here approaches a mystical view of language that imagines Hebrew as existing prior to the creation of the world and capable of creating worlds. This belief in this power of the Hebrew language can be traced far back in Jewish tradition—for example, in Bereshit Rabba. Yet these critics also describe Agnon's story as "mock-heroic." They observe that the narrator presents himself as a figure on the margins of tradition, who, as a modern writer, performs a much diminished role in comparison with his predecessors, the priestly poets. His quest to ascertain the correctness of a single phrase both reveals his respect for tradition and exposes the triviality of his own concerns. Modern writing is, at the same time, admirable and diminishing; the character is both clownish and endowed with dignity because of the long chain of texts and traditions to which he attaches his work.

While some ironies emerge from plot elements, others emerge from multivalences in the Hebrew that are lost in translation. One such example is when the narrator makes reference to his writing as *ma'asiyot* (A19; translated simply as "stories," 104). He casts them as the mere writings of a modern author overshadowed by the sacred writing of yesteryear. At the same time, the Hebrew carries special connotations because it is associated with hasidic tales of Nahman of Bratslav.[9] The word *ma'asiyot* conveys a very distinguished pedigree and is invested with spiritual import. Consequently, Agnon's narrator may be making modest claims for himself or may be claiming a highly prestigious role. The dividing line between humble and great is elusive, and the use of language over time, as it brings layers of connotation, makes definitions unstable and opposites oddly interchangeable.

Similarly, other ironies accrue in the story, likewise emerging from and calling attention to the richness of Hebrew as it has evolved over time. To gauge this effect, it is fruitful to identify several points in the story that defy translation and to show how some key contradictions and ironies manifest themselves in these details. A salient example comes from the very opening of the story, where the narrator sets up an opposition between the holy tongue and all other languages.

> The holy tongue is a language like no other. All other tongues exist only by agreement, each nation having agreed upon its language. But the holy tongue is the one in which the Torah was given, the one through which the blessed Holy One created His world. Angels and seraphim and holy beings praise Him in the holy tongue. And when He comes to praise Israel, he also does so in the holy tongue. (102; A18)

The narrator praises the holy tongue and posits that it is unlike languages governed by human agreement and man-made conventions; it has a special God-given status prior to human history. Yet in the Hebrew, this passage complicates matters by placing the word *lekales* in a crucial position: *mekalsim oto belashon hakodesh* (the angels and other holy beings "praise Him in the holy tongue"). Embedded in the word *lekales*, to praise, is the opposite meaning: to denigrate or humiliate. The first sense is prevalent in rabbinic usage, while the second is more frequent in biblical Hebrew. While it would be preposterous to suggest that Agnon intends the negative meaning here, the choice of this word, in contrast to, say, *shevah* (a word meaning "praise," which does appear later in this story), calls attention to the fact that words change over time. The text thereby points to meaning and word usage as things that evolve. In another context, this word choice might not be significant. Here, though, it is enough to raise an interpretive eyebrow, since this story features a narrator so resistant to change, so intent on seeking a definitive truth about word usage in age-old sources. The use of *lekales*, then, is a kind of invitation to a deconstruction, implying the possibility of dismantling the rigid distinction between the holy tongue and other language—despite the bold pronouncements of the narrator at the opening of the story. The passage demonstrates the specialness of Hebrew, not as a language that is primordial, but as a language whose vast wealth of meanings and richness of possibilities allow even for opposite meanings at the same time. Hebrew is a language like no other, it could well be argued, because of its unique history, its remarkable longevity, and its spectacular growth in the twentieth century. As a modern vernacular, it is rightfully to be judged by the Language Academy here on earth, and not just the celestial Academy on High that Agnon's character prefers.

Another element of the text that hints at contrary meanings is the word *tam*. It appears in the title *Sefer ketav tamim* (A19), translated as "Perfect Treatise" (104). This polemical work is one source where the narrator finds justification for using the phrase *hasukah merihah*. It is, in fact, a historically authentic document written by a thirteenth-century tosafist, and so its primary function in the story is to add authenticity to the narrator's truth claims. However, the title also introjects ambivalence into those claims. The semantic range of *tam* includes variable meanings: perfect and complete, but also simple and foolish. Why should we attribute ambivalence to the word *tam* in this title? The answer depends on knowledge about the author of that treatise, Moshe Taku. Taku was known for taking a stance "fiercely opposed to any innovation in the realm of beliefs and theology."[10] He distinguished himself by rejecting the ideas of Saadia Gaon, Abraham ibn Ezra, the Ashkenazi Hasidim, and Maimonides, because he considered their doctrines a threat to orthodox belief. In other words, he was a man strongly resistant to change, whose endorsement of the phrase *hasukah meriḥah* carries certain weight. It is as if Agnon's narrator says, here's an opinion not to be taken lightly. It does not come from those who lack respect for time-honored tradition. At the same time, from the vantage point of the twentieth century, the fact that Taku was so very reactionary suggests that, in some sense, he missed the boat. To a certain extent, he got left behind by history. Maimonides and Saadia Gaon, after all, are towering figures whose names are much better known than his. And, curiously, his name may signify a tie, that is, a dispute in which there is no definitive answer.[11] Consequently, at one and the same time, this figure suggests positions that are both definite and yet not definitive. He has a firm stance, yet the text hints that—precisely because it is so firm—the reader should not be overly impressed. Perhaps Agnon is playfully telling us that to be too rigid is undesirable and that his own position in relation to tradition is not so one-sided. It seems that Agnon celebrates devotion to the holy tongue and to tradition, but distances himself from a narrator who overdoes the search for authority and who relies on an authority known, finally, for writing foolishness rather than a "perfect" treatise. The word *tam*, in its polyse-mousness and in conjunction with the felicitously equivocal possibilities of the name Taku, allows for a reading opposite to the explicit message of the narrator.

Another passage merits attention as it undercuts the narrator's rigidity. It appears at a particularly sensitive juncture in the story, the beginning of section 4, which first introduces reference to the sukkah and to that key phrase, *hasukah meriḥah*.

> It once happened that I had written a story about a sukkah, a festival hut. Using colloquial language, I wrote, "The sukkah smells." (104; A19)

This passage defies translation as it employs an idiom—rendered here as "using colloquial language"—that denotes making something easy to un-derstand. The words may be read as *lesaber et ha'ozen* or as *leshaber et ha'ozen*. According to the Even-Shoshan dictionary, the more prevalent *les-aber* is related to the verb *lehasbir* (to understand) and hence to the concept of making something understandable. However, the pronunciation *leshaber et ha'ozen*, which can be traced back to Rashi, has the sense of breaking, cracking open the ear so that someone will hear. An example of such usage, cited by Even-Shoshan, is, in fact, this very passage from Agnon's "The

Sense of Smell," so it is not far-fetched to read the phrase that way.[12] The verb *leshaber* indicates a rupture. Especially for anyone unfamiliar with the idiom, the expression might well convey or insinuate more of an assault on the ear or the hearing than something that eases. So the question that this choice of word raises at some level is, does the use of the phrase *hasukah merihah* make things easier? Is it a colloquialism that makes the language more accessible? Alternatively, does it grate on the ear? Is it a colloquialism that damages the beauty of the Hebrew language? The narrator himself frets over the suitableness of the phrase and finds scholars who support both the position that it is acceptable and the position that it is not. The instability of the phrase *leshaber / lesaber et ha'ozen* itself provides evidence that verbal meaning is not fixed and stable, but evolving and open to controversy. As such, this phrase may serve subtly as a flag to direct our attention to the instability also of the phrase *hasukah merihah*.

The English translation, while unable to capture such complexities of pronunciation, derivation, and accrued idiomatic meaning, has its own advantages. Substituting the word "colloquial" for *leshaber / lesaber et ha'ozen*, the narrator more explicitly refers to the revival of the Hebrew language as a historical phenomenon. More firmly placing this story in the context of that sociolinguistic process, he thereby more explicitly brings into view an opposition of innovation and tradition and helps the story highlight the antagonism Agnon felt toward linguistic invention. The English sharpens attention to those tensions because it acknowledges what is, in fact, basic information or common knowledge that the story in the original obscures: the phrase *hasukah merihah* is perfectly acceptable in contemporary spoken Hebrew, and it was even in 1937, the date of composition of this story. The narrator's entire enterprise of searching for justification is anachronistic, or at least indicative of an exceptional need to cling to the past. Pitting himself against his detractor, the narrator separates himself from the widespread, collective effort to turn Hebrew into the modern language of a contemporary people. The result is an odd kind of self-aggrandizement. The narrator casts himself as a hero singlehandedly fighting the forces of ignorance and defending the holy tongue, but this is not genuine heroism. It is the stance of a man who takes an aggrieved and isolated stance because he feels personally insulted.

As this example suggests, although there are things that cannot be conveyed in translation, it is important to keep in mind the advantages that translation may bring. In this text, which is so focused on a language like no other—where the narrator extols the holy tongue to the detriment of other languages and even excoriates Jews who write in other languages—it is interesting that there are times when the English shines. Adding felicitously to the text, for instance, is the title, "The Sense of Smell." The phrase may be read not only as referring to the sensory realm and to olfactory sensibility, but as a pun where "sense" refers also to definition or meaning. Used in this way, the title indicates that the story, to a large extent, is about definitions and thus highlights major issues in the text: Who has agency? Who has authority? Who defines words and who turns meaning from one thing to its opposite? As his narrator immerses himself in what at first seems like trivial disputation (leading the reader to ponder, what's the sense of all this?), Agnon lays out conundrums with far-reaching implications: What is the role of the modern writer at the tail end of a long tradition? Is it big or small, and from what does the writer derive his importance—from the humble position he occupies as a latecomer, or from starting anew, from constructing a new identity and exercising originality? Where and in what way does he insert himself into tradition and the startling process of revitalization that Hebrew has undergone in the past century and a half?

As contemporary readers, we can view these matters from our own privileged vantage point in time. Throughout the 1990s and until now, the Hebrew used in literary texts in Israel, particularly in fiction, has drawn increasingly closer to everyday spoken Hebrew. Agnon's distinctive register, his profound reliance on classical sources, and the dense tissue of allusion in his work contrast dramatically with much of today's writing. More and more, Agnon has become an author who is relegated to academic settings, studied in school but rarely read by the general public. However, other recent fiction has turned to a rich, deeply engaged use of traditional sources, even as religious themes, characters, and settings have come increasingly into view. The question of how literary language relates to colloquial language remains a timely one for Hebrew. As "The Sense of Smell" encourages us to sniff out that which is enduring and that which is not, it can remind Hebrew readers to examine their own relation to this extraordinary language. By the same token, it can alert English-speaking readers to some of the large issues of authority, tradition, and language change that come into play in the exceptional history of Hebrew writing and culture.

Notes

1. The English translation by Arthur Green, reprinted here, appears in *A Book That Was Lost*, ed. Alan Mintz and Anne Golomb Hoffman (New York: Schocken, 1995), 139–46. The Hebrew version comes from the volume *Elu ve'elu* in Agnon's collected works (Jerusalem: Schocken, 1974).

2. For insights into translating Agnon, see William Cutter, "Rendering Galicia for America: On Hillel Halkin's Translation of *Sippur Pashut*," *Prooftexts* 7 (1987): 73–87.

3. Robert Alter provides an overview of these issues in his essay on Agnon in *After the Tradition* (New York: Dutton, 1969). Gershon Shaked provides an excellent introduction to Agnon's use of allusion and pseudo-midrash in *Shmuel Yosef Agnon: A Revolutionary Traditionalist*, trans. Jeffrey Green (New York: New York University Press, 1989), 23–39.

4. Aharon Bar-Adon, *Shai 'Agnon utehiyat halashon ha'ivrit* (Jerusalem: Mossad Bialik, 1977), esp. pp. 165–95, and "Kenagen hamenagen, kemakor leheker lashon vehevrah bitkufat ha'aliyah hashniyah" in *Kovets 'Agnon*, ed. Emunah Yaron et al. (Jerusalem: Magnes, 1994). Agnon's skepticism about Ben-Yehuda is congruent with the outlook of sociolinguists and cultural historians, who since the late 1970s and the 1980s have set themselves the task of debunking the Ben-Yehuda myth. For the most prominent discussion of these matters in English, see Benjamin Harshav, *Language in Time of Revolution* (Berkeley: University of California Press, 1993).

5. For example, Esther Fuchs, "The Unreliable Narrator," *Prooftexts* 3, no. 3 (1983): 278–84, and *Omanut hahitamemut: 'Al ha'ironiyah shel Shai 'Agnon* (Tel Aviv, 1985); Naomi Sokoloff, "Passion Spins the Plot: Agnon's 'Forevermore,'" in *Tradition and Trauma: Studies in the Fiction of S. J. Agnon*, ed. David Patterson and Glenda Abramson (Boulder, Colo.: Westview Press, 1996), 9–26.

6. I base these remarks on my personal experience teaching "The Sense of Smell" in North America, both in university classes and in community settings with adult readers.

7. See discussion by Alan Mintz and David Roskies in this volume.

8. Mintz and Hoffman, *A Book That Was Lost*, 10, 81. Interpretation of this text is also to be found in Anne Golomb Hoffman, *Between Exile and Return: S. Y. Agnon and the Drama of Writing* (Albany: State University of New York Press, 1991), 115–22.

9. My thanks to William Cutter for this point. See also Arnold Band's comments on "The Sense of Smell," in *Nostalgia and Nightmare: A Study in the Fiction of S. Y. Agnon* (Berkeley: University of California Press, 1968).

10. *Encyclopaedia Judaica* (Jerusalem: Keter, 1971), 738.

11. According to the *Encyclopaedia Judaica*, the name Taku most probably derives from a place name, perhaps Dachau. However, in the context of "The Sense of Smell" it begs for other interpretation.

12. Avraham Even-Shoshan, *Hamilon hehadash* (Jerusalem: Kiryat Sefer, 1986), 4:1324.

David G. Roskies

DESPITE ITS BREVITY, Agnon's "The Sense of Smell" combines disparate elements that are not easily reconciled. The story's homiletic structure, storybook headings, archaic style, and anecdotal plot, and its coincidental encounters, dream sequence, and moment of mystical reverie bespeak a world of all-too-perfect harmony. Yet the narrative is riddled with riddles. Is the writer/protagonist a pious raconteur or a misanthrope? Does not the closed and self-referential world of Torah study, with its obsessive search for authority, clash with the solipsism of the artist, who lives in the subjective realm of the senses? The sukkah, furthermore, is both lowly and sublime; the "sense of smell" of the story's title implies a sensibility at once neotraditional and radically innovative. Having lavished so much attention upon the wording of a single phrase chosen, almost erased, and ultimately validated, what is Agnon trying to say about the relationship between writing as a craft and writing as a religious calling?

[1]

To begin with, the linguistic medium would seem to be the story's manifest message. Just as the homiletic style of chapters 1 through 3 avoids all signs of modernity, the message is resolutely antisecular. Hebrew cannot be confused with any other national language. It is *leshon hakodesh*, the language that predates Creation and that will usher in the messianic age. It is the vehicle of past, present, and future; of the Torah; the Holy One, blessed be He; the angels and seraphim; the people Israel; of Jacob, the exiles, the mourners of Zion, the Messiah. It is the language of prayer, the language that God most longs to hear; the language of Song of Songs, in which God sings the praises of His people, Israel; and the language of the Psalms, in which Jews seek solace through their long night of exile.

This is vintage Agnon, just the kind of densely allusive, sermonlike preamble that he made famous with "Agunot," his signature story of 1908. For the narrator is convinced that we live in an age of stammerers and skeptics. His opening homily is a preemptive strike, a polemic against all those who deride the revival of Hebrew as a spoken language; who fail to master even the rudiments of the holy tongue; who revert to writing in the languages of exile; who "put worldly matters first and words of Torah second." "If [scholars] would make Torah their basis," the narrator proclaims, "the Torah would come to their aid." *Sheʾilu ʿasu hatorah ʾikkar haytah hatorah mesayʿatam.* Indeed, this extravagant credo is borne out by story's end: the Torah will literally come to the author's aid. But not before he pulls out all the stops. So holy is the holy tongue, he polemicizes at the end of chapter 2, that it overrides even the wickedness of the worst Gentile. To wit, Balaam, whose most extreme act of betrayal was forgiven on account of his immortal Hebrew words in praise of Israel, *ma tovu ohalekha Yaʾakov.* For this one poem, he merited having a Torah portion named after him and having the morning prayers open with his words.

Never mind that the Balaam of folk memory flies in the face of this seemingly irrefutable proof; that, quite to the contrary, when you teach someone a lesson, *lernt men mit im Bolok,* you teach him "the Torah portion Balak". Never mind that the man who colluded in the downfall of 158,600 men of Israel should be forgiven and immortalized simply because he uttered his prophetic words in Hebrew. And never mind that, looking ahead to the Middle Ages, some of the great Jewish sages composed their works not in Hebrew but in Arabic. The narrator has this to say in rebuttal: These works (the *Kuzari*? the *Guide for the Perplexed*?) were but pabulum for babies! Besides, there is divine reason for the choice of Arabic. The Holy Land has been entrusted to Arab hands by God, until such time as God returns it to the Jewish exiles.

So what began as an exalted invocation of the cosmic merits of the holy tongue has ended with a rearguard, rednecked attack on:

1] Jewish scholars who refuse to master their ancient tongue;
2] the culture of the Gentiles;
3] the Golden Age of Spanish Jewry;
4] the attempt to liberate Palestine by political means; and
5] the whole secular enterprise.

Meanwhile, the lyrical tone of chapter 1, with its seductive and seamless rhetorical structure, has given way to the strident rhetoric of intellectual debate: *shema yomar . . . kol haʾomer ken . . . kol sheken . . . umipnei mah . . . mipnei she . . . tedaʿ lekha sheken . . . shema tomar . . . lefikhakh . . . veshoneh . . . velamah.* The narrator signals a further shift in tone in chapter 3, as he turns his attention inward, to his own state of exile. *Me'ahavat leshonenu umihibbat hakodesh ani mashhir panai 'al divre torah umar'iv 'atsmi 'al divrei hakhamim umeshamram bevitni kdei sheyakhonu yahdav 'al sfatai.* Not a Levite is he, officiating at the Temple among his singing brothers, but a lone Nazirite, on a self-imposed diet of Torah and the words of our sages. He lives in spatial and spiritual exile. Anne Hoffman calls this section Agnon's "imaginative geography," reading "sukkah" of the author's parable not as "lowly hut," but as "sanctuary," the word that houses.[1] This may be true in retrospect; but at this point in our reading, what we hear is a litany of loss: the solitary study of Torah replaces the communal singing of psalms; the living word is replaced by *zikhron devarim*; the resplendent house of God is replaced by a makeshift hut; and the ultimate expression of loss is the writing of *sippurei ma'asiyot*, mere *mayselekh* that tell obsessively of a world that is no more.

Thus, the first three chapters form a kind of triptych: praise, polemic, and lament. Since the diction and cadence remain so firmly rooted in traditional discourse, the shift to the first-person singular in chapter 3 is almost imperceptible. The craft of writing is here depicted as a tragic surrogate for the exalted Levitical calling, yet so long as the storyteller can on occasion construct a lowly sukkah, fiction still partakes of the same universe of faith and meaning that was once the preserve of the Temple brotherhood. As a Nazir, furthermore, dedicated solely to the preservation of the holy tongue and feeding exclusively off words of Torah, the narrator must honor and preserve each and every word.

How brutal, then, the fall from even this demoted status, when the narrator is forced from his solitary ministrations by a public accusation on the part of an unnamed grammarian. To make matters worse, the narrator is described in the chapter heading as a mere *mehabber*, or "author," no better than his opponent, who challenges him on the most hallowed ground, the aforementioned sukkah. Can one speak of a sukkah "smelling"? Not much to hook a story on, much less, a quest narrative. But a quest it becomes, "mock heroic" perhaps, but a quest nonetheless. And here we see the narrator at his most misanthropic. He is radically mistrustful of *sifrei shimush*, the tools of modern scholarship, as he is of the scholars themselves, who "know everything except that particular thing you are looking for." And he finds no answer even among his fellow Jerusalemites, native speakers of Hebrew, because each is motivated solely by ego and personal whim. Just as he is about to erase the offending word, however, the sukkah itself miraculously intervenes, its aromatic smells validating the narrator's linguistic usage.

What this last episode means is never explained, and is anyway superseded by an even greater miracle, announced in the heading of chapter 5: "The Righteous from Paradise Come to the Author's Aid." What has the narrator done to warrant such a miracle? He has gone out of his way to honor a descendant of Rabbi Jacob of Lissa. He has also engaged a scholar in dialogue, in the course of which he has praised the Sage of Lissa for the exceptionally useful prayer book that he had compiled. The narrator then falls into a sweet slumber and is visited by the sage himself, who holds the aforementioned siddur in his hands. Dream merges with reality when the narrator awakens, consults his own copy of the prayer book, and rediscovers in its pages the very words he has been seeking. Searching through another sacred tome, he finds additional linguistic proof. He ends the chapter with sweet thoughts of revenge.

Properly, the quest is over. All told, the author has found textual validation in three separate sources, and his credo, "If scholars would make Torah their basis, the Torah would come to their aid" has been borne out in fact. What's more, the quest has taken him out of his glorious isolation and allowed for meaningful interactions on a social and trans-temporal plane. Hoffman calls the dream sequence "something of a family romance," in which the narrator discovers kinship not in life, but in texts, the dream suggesting a community "where, ultimately, it is language that joins together sages of the past and the figure of the writer" (119–20). Again, paraphrasing Hoffman, the sage instructs his progeny that true innovation through the Torah means discovering what is already there, already written, already read, already copied.

The author makes much of the fact that he was able to identify the face of the sage in his dream; this, despite the absence of any known pictures and despite the well-known rule that "the great among Israel just don't look like their relatives, because their Torah gives their faces a special glow." What was so special about the Sage of Lissa's Torah? "Our holy rabbis have left us lots of prayer books," the narrator had said earlier, "filled with directions and commentaries both hidden and revealed, with matters grammatical or sagacious, with permutations of letters, secrets, and allegories, all to arouse the hearts of worshipers as they enter the King's palace." Yet none could match the prayer book of the Sage of Lissa for usefulness. None but he had made himself a true servant of the Torah, or had written "in such an accessible way." Does this not suggest an elective affinity between him and the dweller in a mere sukkah, a match for any man in scholarship, who nonetheless stooped to conquer in order to produce accessible stories of supreme usefulness?

If the true sage and he are revealed to be *mishpokhe*, members of a select brotherhood who "darken their faces over study of Torah," then why the reverie at daybreak, the pious recitation of psalms, and the discovery of a fourth and final proof, in Rashi's commentary? The Torah has already come to his aid. The anal grammarian has already been vanquished. Why the repetition? Why isn't the Sage of Lissa a good enough *yikhes*? Because Rashi's intervention comes against the backdrop of something new, the intrusion of real smells and real sounds emanating from a particular natural landscape. Whatever happened before, when a sukkah came and its aroma rose before him until he really saw that it was smelling, what happens now is acutely sensory and sensual.

Yet this most personal, overtly autobiographical, moment in the story is also the most intertextual. In a scene reminiscent of Bialik's "Hamatmid," the scholar is seated indoors pouring over a sacred tome while nature beckons outdoors. Recalling an episode in the *Tales* of Nahman of Bratslav, he hears birds singing exquisite melodies to one another. And in the language of the Song of Songs, the same passage, in fact, with which he began the story, the voice of the second bird "was just sweeter than the other bird's"; *vehayah kolah 'arev mikolah shel ḥavertah*, and together, the two birds "sang new songs, the likes of which no ear had ever heard." Pretending not to hear, the author sets their singing to the words of Psalm 45, the Psalm for the Chief Musician upon Lilies, and although he identified this psalm earlier as "a song of praise of the sages' disciples, those who are soft as lilies and pleasant as lilies," it is clear that he is reading the words as he has never read them before, nonmetaphorically, and in a way unsanctioned by tradition. That is when Rashi comes to the rescue, and glosses the words *kol bigdotekha* (45:9) in two different ways: contextually, as "all thy garments smell like fragrant spices," and midrashically, as "all your betrayals and foul deeds will be forgiven and will smell sweet before me." Whereupon the sukkah reappears in all its aromatic glory, and his mind is eased "like a person smelling flowers that smell."

On the manifest, homiletic, plane, one that is clearly privileged from beginning to end, the author is rescued by the Torah. On a psychological plane, he is rescued by his own sense of smell. Alongside the ideal portrait of the Torah scholar, modeled by Jacob of Lissa, who, for all his relative obscurity, had served his flock so much better than any other scholar, there is the real portrait of the contemporary Hebrew writer, living in a diminished world, at odds with his surroundings, reduced to writing *mayselekh* in an embattled language.

Why did Agnon write this story? Why did he write it in 1937? Why, sitting in Talpiot, Jerusalem, did he prefer the company of the sages long since dead? How credible is it that one sense of smell does not subvert, betray, the other?

[2]

Agnon is the master of what Bakhtin calls the "double-voiced utterance." Agnon appropriates the utterance of another as the utterance of another and uses it for his own purposes. His stylized tales are designed to be interpreted as the utterances of two speakers. The audience hears in a version of the original utterance the collective voice of the Jewish past and a second, contemporary, speaker's evaluation of that utterance. Left to their own devices, the two speakers would be in essential agreement, so that the success of the stylization would derive from the utterances of the second speaker corroborating the utterances of the first. The narrator functions here as a latter-day scribe, a *sofer stam*, as is the case in such late works as *'Ir umlo'ah*. Devoid of inner tension, these stories are eminently forgettable.

Not so "The Sense of Smell." Here, the first utterance, the collective voice of the past, is under attack. Its whole authority and semantic position are being questioned. This is why the writer must up the ante and preempt his attackers with a tour de force in praise of the holy tongue. Conscious throughout of an audience for whom Hebrew is neither holy nor viable, the speaker of the second utterance objectifies, personifies, hallows the first utterance in every way conceivable: through lyrical, polemical, tragic, and mock-heroic passages. The ultimate purpose of his discourse is not self-validation, not the quest, but the revival of the authority and vitality of the first utterance. If Rashi can speak to the present, then the present can speak through the past.

Hebrew, in Agnon's scheme, becomes the language of polyphony. The real enemy, therefore, is the grammarian, who insists upon using Hebrew monologically: one word, one meaning. God forbid that the revival of Hebrew as a living language be entrusted to people like him! If truth is dialogic, then Hebrew is the one true language. Note that Hebrew precedes Creation, precedes God, as it were, thus freeing the text of Torah for dialogue, commentary, agreement, and disagreement. Why, even the author, for all his erudition, doesn't understand everything he reads in Scripture! Agnon displays his genius by conjuring up a dialogue that works vertically instead of horizontally. On the horizontal plane of politics, society, and academic scholarship, language is debased and monologic. Only when one gives voice to the past, crediting each individual utterance and its author, recognizing that author's unique face, does Hebrew regain its open-endedness, its unfinalizability, its cosmic potential. Each recaptured utterance, moreover, rests upon an ethical event, upon the author / hero owning, or signing an act: praying, studying, helping a stranger, talking words of Torah with another scholar. In this way, *leshon hakodesh* becomes both the vehicle and tenor of true dialogue.

How does individual creativity enter into the system of sanctioned dialogue? Creativity begins when one feels at home in the world of the past. Creativity is predicated upon mobilizing the whole personality. Creativity comes when the recitation of the received words is accompanied by something unexpected, a birdsong unlike any that was ever sung. Creativity begins when nature comes to the rescue of culture, when the utterance beyond space enters into dialogue with the utterance beyond time.

[3]

Agnon's best stories are not stylizations at all. They are a species of "creative betrayal." As such, they belong in the mainstream of Jewish literary history, midway between Der Nister and I. B. Singer.[2] Agnon shares Der Nister's sense of election. The artist is a Nazir, who dedicates his life to the service of his craft. The measure of his self-discipline is the distance between mundane, profane speech and the carefully wrought language of his literary art. The plot is always the tale of a symbolic quest, undertaken by a lone hero who meets with many obstacles. Both writers swore allegiance to Reb Nahman. Both came of age in the heady atmosphere of Weimar Germany.

Even if there were no genetic link between them, both Der Nister and Agnon arrived at the art of creative betrayal via the same three-act drama of rebellion, loss, and negotiated return. In Agnon's case, each act played itself out in and through a different setting.

Act 1, the rebellion, as a member of the Second Aliyah.

Act 2, when he experienced the profound loss of Buczacz and all that it stood for.

Act 3, the negotiated return to the severed past, during Agnon's sojourn in Weimar Germany.

Creative betrayal was the art of triage, the art of rescuing what little could still be saved in an age of skepticism, fragmentation, and gross materialism: archaic language, storytelling, the figure of the sage. Creative betrayal was an artistic bulwark against national despair. What else could a Hebrew writer hold out to his audience in 1937, at the height of the Arab revolt, and against the rising specter of Hitler and Stalin? A little sukkah, and nothing more.

But the strength of creative betrayal lay in the very combination of its disparate strands: rebellion and retrieval, nature and culture, the sensual present and the spiritual past. When the Agnon narrator says, "There is nothing especially wondrous or praiseworthy about this," you know that something extraordinary has just happened. His coy modesty at story's end just about gives the game away, "because the psalm played itself like an instrument of many strings. A Song of Love, next to which all other songs are as nothing." This is a song that can be heard only by someone who has returned to the study house of Buczacz via the cultural revolution of Tel Aviv/Jaffo. This is a song rooted as much in the senses of the beholder as in the language of psalms.

And lest there be any doubt about this, Rashi himself comes out of the Academy on High in the Garden of Eden and explicates the key passage: *bigdotekha* from the root *bgd* means "thy garments," but it can also mean "your betrayals," from the word *begidah*. Like the art of creative betrayal, derived from the Hebrew *begidah yotseret*, the art of creative recloaking is preceded by the act of betrayal. Agnon, perhaps the greatest of the born-again storytellers, has written a fantasy about a writer, all of whose betrayals and foul deeds were forgiven, and who, in the midst of his anger, isolation, and despair, was granted a miracle: the early morning breezes, the sweet fragrances, and the birdsong emanating from his own garden suddenly endowed the language of Creation with new meaning and gave new promise to the language of redemption.

Notes

1. Anne Golomb Hoffman, *Between Exile and Return: S. Y. Agnon and the Drama of Writing* (Albany: SUNY Press, 1991), 117.

2. See David G. Roskies, *A Bridge of Longing: The Lost Art of Yiddish Storytelling* (Cambridge, Mass.: Harvard University Press, 1995).

Alan Mintz

"THE SENSE OF SMELL," a beguiling short narrative, provides a revealing glimpse into the contradictions of Agnon's self-conception as a modern religious artist, or, depending on one's point of view, as a religious modern artist. On the one hand, the story's narrator presents his vocation as a writer of stories as being continuous with the creativity of the sages and sacred poets of classical and premodern times; a Levite by birth, he views the prose fiction he writes as lineally descended—despite shifts and transformations imposed by history—from the Levitical songs sung in the Jerusalem Temple. The guarantor of this vertical continuity is the Hebrew language itself, whose sacred and revealed nature imposes a discipline of faithfulness upon its belated users. On the other hand, the modernist axis of the story is manifest in the self-conscious and even playful way the author creates the persona of the narrator and goes about manipulating the discursive forms of the story. The anachronistic style of the story and the grandiosity of the narrator's self-presentation open up a space of parody and irony that qualifies in subtle ways the sincerity of the narrator's religious vocation. Whether the story overcomes these contradictions or merely contains them is a difficult determination that likely depends on the stance of the interpreter in relation to the very issues of tradition and modernity raised by the work itself.

It should be noticed at the outset that the story breaks into two distinct pieces: chapters 1 through 3 and chapters 4 through 7. It is in the second, longer part that the actual story, such as it is, is told. This is the tale of criticism the narrator received for using a word in a particular grammatical construction and the eventual vindication that came his way by both natural and supernatural means. The first part, by contrast, has little directly to do with the tale and has no narrative of its own to offer. It serves rather as a kind of expository prologue that expatiates on three subjects: the glory and sanctity of the Hebrew language; the craven shortsightedness of scholars who write in languages other than Hebrew; and the factors that sanction the narrator's vocation as a writer of prose fiction. The purposeful heterogeneity of "The Sense of Smell" as a whole, as expressed in the disproportion between these two pieces, is part of the story's playful modernity even as it mimics the style of earlier forms of writing.

One of those antique styles is already in evidence in chapter 1, "The Excellence of the Holy Tongue." (There is, to begin with, a sense of mock seriousness conveyed in the very notion of dividing a short short story into formal chapters with at times long descriptive titles.) Although the style is not immediately recognizable as belonging to a particular text or period, the rhetorical ingredients suggest the discourse typical of a pious savant. The chapter begins with an ostensibly learned distinction between the languages of the world, whose meanings are based on the conventions of human usage, and the Hebrew language, whose meaning is guaranteed by the divine revelation of the Torah. But the pretense to scholarly observation is quickly swept aside by a kind of rapturous catechism in which the narrator poses a series of rhetorical questions, all of whose answers underscore the primacy of Hebrew. Rather than presenting historical evidence for his assertions, the narrator adduces quotations from the Song of Songs and from the liturgy in a manner that amounts to a midrashic exposition. (Because the passage is not, in fact, a real midrash—although it allows the reader to experience it as such—it belongs to a category special to Agnon that Gershon Shaked calls the "pseudo-midrash.")

After describing Hebrew as the language that embodies the intimate relations between God and Israel, the narrator brings his exposition to an eschatological apotheosis that is surprising in the practicality of its logic. When the Messiah reveals himself—which will be sooner rather than later, asserts the narrator, because we live in the later generations of history—he will of course speak Hebrew, and we shall not be able to understand him—nor he us—unless now, in the present moment, we exert vigilance over our use of the sacred tongue, guarding it from impurity and keeping it clear and precise. The linkage between proper language usage and the messianic age, while entirely taken for granted by the narrator, may not seem so manifestly self-evident to us.

In fact, the narrowly pious and messianic temper of these arguments is likely to make the contemporary reader more aware of what is excluded than included. Most of the arguments for the revival of Hebrew as modern written and spoken idiom were based on a nationalist premise: a nation needs a language of its own as well as a land of its own, Hebrew is the national language of the Jewish people, Hebrew bridges the gap between the ancient people and the people reborn, and so on. For the narrator of

"The Sense of Smell," however, there remains only the single divine, revelatory, and messianic axis.

After the loving encomium for the Hebrew language in chapter 1, the
polemical tone of the second chapter ("Against the Scholars of Our Generation . . .") comes as something of a surprise. The targets of the narrator's
ire are the majority of scholars who write Hebrew badly or who write in
another language altogether, in addition to those "stupid folk among the
Jews" who doubt whether a "dead" tongue like Hebrew can ever be revived
as a spoken language. Against these voices stands the narrator's conviction
of the utter self-sufficiency of Hebrew. In the chain of textual tradition
stretching from Scripture through rabbinic literature, he asserts, all the necessary linguistic resources are to be found in abundance.

The catch, however, is that it is only God's beloved to whom "all those
treasures of the holy tongue" are revealed; without immersion in these
sacred texts, this abundance is not vouchsafed. That the narrator sees himself as included in this circle of the divinely favored is made manifest in
chapter 3. In this chapter, his religious stance is disclosed by the method
of his argumentation. Although he discourses on the scholars of his time
and their failures, the way he uses evidence is very different from the practices of the academy. For example, to make his point that Gentiles who
write in Hebrew are to be preferred to Jews who write in other languages,
the narrator adduces evidence not from history but from Scripture. Even
though Balaam, the Moabite prophet who appears in the Book of Numbers,
is held accountable for the deaths of 158,600 Israelites in the desert, he
merits having a portion of the Torah known by his name and a quotation
from his prophecy placed at the beginning of the daily liturgy because of
the very fact that he uttered his oracles in the Hebrew tongue. The narrator's indifference to history is similarly evident when it comes to the
reasons he gives for why some of the great works of medieval Jewish
thought were composed in Arabic. While any literate reader might be expected to know something of the role of Arabic in the transmission of Greek
philosophy, the narrator offers an exclusively messianic explanation. Such
a reader will not find it easy to accept the presumption that such a work
as Maimonides' *Guide for the Perplexed* was written in Arabic solely because
the Jews of the time were exhausted by the exile and needed to be pacified
like children by being spoken to in "whatever language."

The distinctness of the narrator's voice, at times fervent and at times
querulous, has been wholly recognizable in the declarations and judgments

he has uttered so far. Yet those statements have been directed toward others, and it is not until chapter 3 that he speaks of himself; and when he does so, he takes off in a new direction rather than continuing to engage either of the subjects he has just taken up: the paean to Hebrew and the denigration of its betrayers. Instead, with no warning, he presents the reader with nothing less than a rationale for his vocation as a modern Hebrew writer. It is a moment of stunning self-revelation, although the elliptical concision with which the revelation is presented makes it fleeting and cryptic. The whole chapter is no more than fifteen lines in the Hebrew, and within that brief compass, the narrator presents a sequence of shifts and transformations whose import is heady but whose inner logic is elusive. We have to work hard to supply the connections.

The narrator begins by explaining that the reason he forgoes the pleasures of the world and devotes himself to studying the words of the sages is so that these words will be "present to his lips." There is a presumed comparison between the narrator and the so-called sages excoriated in the previous chapter, who complain about the poverty of Hebrew as a modern language. Unlike them, he experiences no such insufficiency because he immerses himself in the Hebrew texts of the tradition. But instead of a metaphor of immersion, we are given a metaphor of ingestion. The narrator stores up the words of the sages in his belly, and through an unexplained process of absorption and incorporation, the words—now his own Hebrew words?—present themselves on his lips.

Yet the ascetic life devoted to textual study, a high and virtuous calling, turns out to be distinctly second best. The narrator is a Levite—like Agnon himself, the biographically minded reader might recall—and if the Jerusalem Temple still stood, he opines, he would be singing in the Levitical choirs in the Temple precincts. In the present moment while the Temple is still destroyed (the emphasis on the "still" underscores his messianist outlook), he contents himself with study as a compensation for the stilled songs that accompanied the Temple worship. At this juncture, we are still at a distance from the enterprise of writing fiction, and the threefold sequence that leads to this end unfolds with telegraphic brevity.

First comes the sadness that arises from the realization that of the great tradition of learning there is nothing left but a memory (*zikhron devarim*). The sadness causes his heart to tremble, and it is finally this trembling that leads him to the writing of stories. The term the narrator uses for stories is *sippurei ma'asiyot*, and it would be a mistake to take it unquestioningly as a reference to modern fiction. If one is intent on reading "The Sense of Smell" as a story by Agnon about Agnon, thus conflating the author with the autobiographical narrator, then one arrives at that conclusion directly. Yet the term is, in fact, taken from the discourse of Hasidism and refers to allegorical narratives (as opposed to textual commentary and sermons) told by hasidic masters to convey esoteric religious meaning; it is closely associated with the tales told by Nahman of Bratslav. Consistent with his self-presentation so far, the narrator remains within the orbit of piety and does not identify himself with the enterprise of modern literature. Yet at the same time, he describes a trajectory of fallenness that passes from the sacred songs of the Levites through the textual erudition of the sages to the prosaics of telling tales.

As if to give us an illustration of this belated vocation, the narrator concludes with a parable; although the parable is familiar from the classical midrashim about the destruction of the Temple, it takes on new meaning in this context. In the midrash, the father's palace is the Temple itself; in exile, the Jews sit in synagogues and study houses, fallen substitutes for the Temple, and tell of the glory of the destroyed sanctuary. In the way in which the narrator is appropriating the midrash, it is the postbiblical writings of the sages (Mishnah, Talmud, etc.) that correspond to the father's house, and in the wake of the loss of that tradition the narrator sits in his hut (the impoverished house of fiction or stories, as it were) and tells (*mesapper*) of the glories that are no more.

It is the hut that serves as the thematic hinge between the story's discursive introduction and its narrative proper. The hut is, of course, nothing other than a sukkah, and in "The Sense of Smell" the notion of the sukkah is used in three senses: as a humble temporary dwelling, as a traditional epithet for the Jerusalem Temple, and as the booth that Jews erect and take their meals in during the week of the autumn Sukkot festival. Although it is in this last sense that the sukkah is understood in the remainder of the story, the echoes of the transcendent, lost sanctuary are never wholly absent. This is part of a larger fundamental duality in "The Sense of Smell" that is never overtly resolved. The narrator presents himself as embarked on a mission of high seriousness whose stakes involve nothing less than the purity and integrity of the divinely inspired Hebrew language. At the same time, techniques of parody deflate the high drama of the episode and present it as a tempest in a teapot that ultimately draws attention to the grandiosity of the narrator's self-conception.

The deflationary effect is chiefly conveyed through the story's stylistic register and outward organization. The division of this short text into full-blown chapters with cumbersome titles that importantly summarize the matter of each chapter—all this evokes the tracts and controvertialist literature of the eighteenth century in Western Europe, and later, the Haskalah in Hebrew literature. The deployment of grand rhetoric on behalf of a grammatical controversy about two words recalls such mock-epic works from an earlier period as *The Rape of the Lock* and *A Tale of the Tub*. The spat is given a mock-heroic elevation in which the conflict assumes the proportions of mortal combat. The carping grammarian lances the narrator with his pen, and the narrator swoons. "The Sense of Smell" could have been properly renamed "A Tale of Two Words." Even though the incident that gave rise to the story had taken place just before the time of the writing and within the arena of modern novels and their serialization in newspapers—a scene from Agnon's most secular novel *Sippur pashut* (A simple story) as excerpted in *Ha'aretz*—the language of the story is pointedly archaized. The figure of the narrator, moreover, resembles not the modern writer that Agnon was but a pious author from an earlier age. As Anne Golomb Hoffman has noticed, the narrator makes a point of referring to himself not as a *sofer*, a writer in the modern sense, but as a *meḥabber*, an older term for an author-compiler-redactor who has no pretensions to originality or artifice.

Chapter 4 summarizes the narrator's dilemma. He cannot dismiss the grammarian's attack because, in his eyes, the charge is far from trivial. For if he has, in fact, misused the verb in question by inventing a new grammatical construction, then he is indeed guilty of sinning against the divinely ordained properties of the Hebrew language as interpreted through the chain of tradition. The quest for vindication he now embarks upon, in fact, nearly ends in failure. The so-called experts he consults adduce opinions but no evidence, and the one obscure reference he is directed to does little to put his mind at rest. He is about to accept his guilt and recant, but at the last moment he is mysteriously rescued from the fateful act of erasure.

The first stage of the narrator's rescue revolves around the figure of Jacob of Lissa, a rabbinical scholar active in Poland at the end of the eighteenth century and the beginning of the nineteenth. While Jacob of Lissa is hardly an obscure figure, he is not one that would be immediately recognizable to the average Hebraically literate reader. The fact that his familiarity is limited to pious and scholarly circles is a further indicator of where the narrator

locates himself. The qualities the narrator admires in Jacob of Lissa also
tell us as much about the former as the latter. In conversation with the
scholar who was carrying the prayer book of the Sage of Lissa, the narrator
expatiates on Jacob's rare commitment to the ideal of utility. Even though
he was a master of sophisticated and erudite talmudic scholarship, the sage
took the time to compile a useful and usable compendium of laws and
customs related to prayer.

When later that night, the sage appears to the narrator in a dream,
holding his prayer book open in his hand, what is remarkable is not the
ghostly visitation itself but the narrator's confidence in recognizing the
identity of the sage, whose likeness he has never before seen. He makes the
identification on the basis of the radiance of the sage's face, which, he
explains, God bestows on scholars as a reward for the privation they endure
in their devotion to the study of Torah. The radiance is given to he who
"darkens his face over study of Torah," and this phrase, unsurprisingly, is
exactly the same one that the narrator uses at the beginning of chapter 3
to describe his own self-deprivation in the service of the study of Torah
and the purity of the Hebrew language. The linkage between the narrator
and the Sage of Lissa is further strengthened when, upon awakening, the
narrator goes to his bookcase, takes the sage's prayer book in hand, and
triumphantly discovers what he has been looking for: a passage in which
the verb "to smell" is used intransitively. Although the providential prompt-
ing to consult the prayer book surely comes through the dream, the exact
location of the exculpatory passage is marked by a slip of paper inserted
by none other than the narrator himself, who, at some time in the unre-
membered past, had marked—and apparently absorbed—the verb in this
unusual usage. The standing of the narrator is hardly diminished by this
fact. Not only do the "righteous from paradise come to the author's aid,"
as encapsulated in the chapter's title, but their intercession serves less as a
revelation of something unknown than as a catalyst for the narrator's recovered memory of his own scholarship.

The validation offered by the Sage of Lissa and his uncle Javetz (Jacob
Emden) is pleasing to the narrator, but there remains a final and more
exalted level of confirmation to be granted him. It is more exalted because
it issues not only from an earlier link in the chain of tradition but from
the greatest authority of that earlier age. The Sage of Lissa and his uncle
may be great lights of the latter authorities, the *aharonim*, but Rashi is the
greatest light of the earlier authorities, the *rishonim*. The story of how the

narrator is vouchsafed Rashi's approval of his intuitive use of the Hebrew language occupies the final movement of "The Sense of Smell." The earlier sections of the story concern the narrator's production of language as a writer and the responses it provokes from others. The final section concerns the consumption of the language rather than its production. We see the narrator in a private moment of communion with the text, and it is in that posture that he is given, as if by grace, the final consummation.

When the narrator awakes from his dream at the beginning of chapter 6, it is too late to go back to sleep and too early to recite the morning prayer. This time, between the states of sleeping and waking and night and day, is a limnal zone that is vulnerable to the unsettling vagaries of the imagination. The narrator takes the deliberate step of filling this interval with the recitation of psalms, a traditionally pious measure aimed at rescuing "dead" time from unwanted thoughts. The narrator frames his choice in terms of a substitution of one kind of language for another. Once the day comes with its social intercourse, one's lips will inevitably be "defiled by wicked chatter"; but now, while the "soul is still pure," he grasps the chance to infuse it with the discourse of the sacred. The posture of receptivity is the key here. Psalm saying is not "learning" in the traditional sense of an active engagement with the contradictions of a text in order to wrest new meanings from it. He is communing with the text and letting its words wash over him; he moves quickly and fluidly through dozens of psalms, pausing to consult Rashi's commentary only when he needs to.

The consummation of "The Sense of Smell" comes in the form of a textual reverie. The reverie is presented as a kind of contest between the realm of nature and the realm of the text. In the darkness before dawn, the two realms start out in sympathetic vibration; inside, the table lamp crowns every letter with light, while outside breezes and fragrances dance and waft without disturbing the quiet recitation of psalms indoors. At first light, the song of one bird is heard and then the song of a second bird; the two compete jealously at first and then join to sing in harmony "new songs, the likes of which no ear had ever heard." Although this music would ordinarily be irresistible, the narrator is at pains to point out that he had no trouble remaining absorbed in his recitation because the psalm he was reading "played itself like an instrument of many strings" and produced a "Song of Love, next to which all other songs are as nothing." The beauty of nature is thus ultimately absorbed and superseded by the greater beauty of sacred textuality in which the narrator has immersed himself. As he consults Rashi for a gloss on verse 9 of Psalm 45, he is given the ultimate gift of having his suspect deployment of a Hebrew verb vindicated by none other than the greatest of the medieval sages.

Why Psalm 45? Most modern students of the Bible read Psalm 45 as a hymn written by a court poet celebrating the marriage of a young king. In the rabbinic reading followed by Rashi—and followed in turn by the narrator—the subject of the psalm is Torah scholars as a class. The praise of the young king's military prowess is transformed by Rashi into admiration for the scholar's intense acuity in learned debates. The pen of verse 2 becomes the sword of verse 4, and vice versa. Rashi's appropriation of the trope of militancy brings us back to the polemical premise of "The Sense of Smell" as a story. (There are, in fact, an abundance of intertextual connections between the psalm and the story that a fuller analysis would profitably bring to light.) As a kind of scholar-knight militant, the narrator repulses an attack by his antagonist and is confirmed in the purity of his faithfulness to the Order of the Holy Tongue.

For the sake of a single word of this holy tongue, the ultra-short concluding chapter worshipfully tells us, a holy man bestirred himself from heaven and the narrator was guided to his psalmic revelation. Yet the attentive reader knows that this is far from the whole story. The pious naïveté of the narrator's persona is progressively undercut by the self-referential nature of the narrative; it is he and no other who is decisively there as the recipient of revelation. This becomes a principled and critical self-importance when the narrator locates his belated vocation of storytelling as the last link in the great chain of authority and learning. The narrator's self-regard, it should be kept in mind, is contained within the larger authority of Agnon the author. This is a saving distinction. For in his capacity for self-ironization, Agnon reveals himself as one of the great modernists of our literature.

[IV]

MAN'S HOUSE

U. Z. Greenberg

HAROLD SCHIMMEL

Only he who returns to the village toward evening: to his trees good-
  in-all-seasons,
To his portion of field which is a fruitful extension of his flesh
And to his well which cools for him his water with a gleam
Only he who returns at close of day to the village and not to the city,
Walks as one who returns to a goal and not as an exile's walk to his
  inn;   5
Walks on the trusted path, soft-to-the-step. For it's good:
From dew, from sun, from breath of skies, from a bird's steps on it..
With the rose-of-dusk in his ears, with heart beating as a bird at a
  window;
Approaches a fence of twigs, opens its door to a white cottage,
That one could almost hug . . . like an extension of his body.   10
Whose roof is of straw, and has much of the feminine and a bird's nest.
And blest darkness of night in a small window;
Comes and opens his mouth and says hello inside to woman and
  offspring
And sits down to eat the evening meal; and silence is there: as after
  strings
And flutes that were silent.   15
And sleeps there a night's rest, made good by many trees
And the nectar of fields is in it. And the forest is near and the river— —

Only he tastes of the precious taste of man's true homeland.
Which was every man's once upon a time in this universe,
Before he set his foot in a shoe and covered his shoulders to the ends
  of his body   20

135

And built a city and paved a road to-hide-from-eye the greening earth.
And became a body compounded of anger.

Only he who returns to the village toward evening, truly goes home:
Rolls from his back the exile-city, unravels the riddle of longing
And the worry-sadness thereby, that man bears within him   25
All the days of his being in this faultless, late world.
Homeland of the first man, uprooted from it, this the cause of the
    longing
And the sadness of detachment,
Secret of clipped-wings and they flutter still.
This is the secret anger of wandering— —   30

I returned to the village, as one returns to an ancient homeland:
To its smell, its resin, its sweetness, its security,
To first well water.

A return to the village is a return in which there is miracle.
The cut tree again joins up with its trunk.   35
Therefore always sorrow so catches all-in-me toward evening
When a train lingers near a village station
And one of the travelers gets down with his bundle there.
I see him walk the field path he knows,
I smell after him and it's as if I know it also   40
This path: soft from dew and bird and animal steps upon it
And from shadow of trees down its length— —

His goal is the cottage, with its roof of straw and this twig fence.
And what's inside—is everything.
Now he goes in and a gold heart is lit in the small window.   45
And I travel onward from this through the night, to the city,
That swallowed my ancient portion of field and a road covered it and
    great buildings.
And wherever I travel and wherever I come, that place is not my goal,
Because anger is there, strangeness.
A man in a village toward evening is just like a tree,   50
Which stands reflecting on thoughts of itself: now with dew and now
    with its pleasant tear.

The body is watered like a field and like the tree in it.
Man is master of his house, because his house in the village is no
   higher than his forehead
Whereas man in the city is not master of the wall, which is higher
   than his forehead.

Man walks in his city-dwelling like a household exile.   55

Lewis Glinert

ON FIRST LOOKING into Greenberg's "Man's House," a work of Hebrew's greatest Expressionist poet, some readers may feel cheated. Where are the imagistic and prosodic pyrotechnics, where is the sparking "I"? In place of the power and the glory, placid blandness.

But this is a work about the other side, the *sitra aḥra* of the modernist poet: the old world of simplicity and tradition, antedating the forces of alienation and anomie. This other side might then demand a different tone, another style and prosody. But then again, might one not expect "Man's House" to spare us nothing of the horror of the modern world, the world of the Gentiles, and of the conflict it creates? There is, however, very little here of conflict, of Greenbergian confrontation. This poem is a striking study in inwardness, in containment. And in place of the poetic extravagances one might have hoped to find, one finds a still, small subtlety of syntax, of sound symbolism, even orthographic symbolism, that powerfully states the theme of home and homecoming, and a holism that is the fundamental ethos of this poem.

At the same time, we have to grapple with a disturbing poetic ambivalence as to the nature of the human condition and its remedy. This ambivalence is embodied in the title. Does it denote "Man's home" or "Adam's home"? Or, as it occurs to you in absorbing the articulation and rhythm of the piece, might *beito* denote also "his [letter] *bet*"?

FIRST STANZA

The poem opens on a ringing note of (ostensible) certitude and security: *rak mi sheshav el hakfar*. And yet as verse follows verse, it becomes increasingly apparent that there is an underlying lack of stasis or repose: we opened with an implied negative *rak* and the beginning of an embedded clause *mi she*; it is normal for a Hebrew embedded clause to last one line, maybe two—but not until the eighteenth line and the second stanza do we come to a resolution: *rak zeh to'em miykar hata'am*. Here, then, is a paradox: the poet is painting a massive picture of calm, adding stroke upon stroke, but all the while turning up the tension. At the metalinguistic level, our gaze is being distracted toward the poet himself and his mood; and at the same time, we are being fed syntactic signals that there is a meaning to this whole picture—except that we are not allowed to know it. Meanwhile the stanza ends, and only then is this meaning vouchsafed to us: that the cottage home is an archetype and entrance to a profound primeval repose that once was man's and is now all but lost.

The mood is one of almost unsupportable longing, stress, anxiety: *kisuf, rogez, de'agah*. And the object of these emotions fills the picture. This is all about where one is going back to—and no mention of where one could be coming from. From one's work? From the city? From some existential fate? Again, the sheer eighteen-line scale of this exclusion strains the senses. The solitary allusion to "the other," allowing us just momentarily to orientate ourselves, is the mention of an alternative goal, *krakh* (*urbs*) in line 4, set in contrast with the *kfar* ("*rus*"). The result is a straining for total containment in this archetypal cottage-home.

The familiar forces of Greenberg the Expressionist have here been sublimated, by a formal tour de force, into a still deeper, more abstract set of tensions.

What is the nature of this *kfar*? All-ness and whole-ness are all around: from the trees that are *tovim-bekhol-'et*, "good at all seasons"—like the psalmist's fruit tree (itself a metaphor for the righteous, Psalm 1) whose leaves marvelously "shall not wither" and all of whose doings "shall prosper"—to the field that feels like a *hemshekh poreh livsaro*, "a fruitful extension to his flesh," yielding an organic bond between self and surroundings and thereby transcending the ubiquitous modern alienation of man from his means of production; and then to the cottage that is equally *kehemshekh guf*, "like a bodily extension," not by virtue of the tools of labor but by its intimacy and scale (*shekim'at efshar lehabkah*, "which one can almost hug"), unlike the massive townhouses (*batei midot*) of the sixth stanza, of which no one could say *eino gavoa mimitsho*, "it is no higher than his brow." The wholeness is captured, in a kabbalistic vein that runs through the work, as the nexus of the masculine and feminine principles at both a human and animal level in the embrace of the cottage: *veharbeh minashyut bah*, "with much femininity in it," *vekan tsiporim*, "and a bird's nest."

Holism is also evoked at the level of language and orthography: most obviously, orthographically, in the numerous ad-hoc hyphenated compounds such as *hatovim-bekhol-'et, hemshekh-poreh, harakh-litse'idah*. The first mentioned, in line 1, supplies by virtue of its meaning a structural code for them all: transcendence of the divisions and atomization of life seemingly built into Creation—the Creation characterized from the divine perspective of Genesis 1 as *ki tov*, "that it was good," but recast here by the poet with the telling addition of a mere *hu*, "it," as *ki hu tov*, "for it is good." (This "it" refers to "the trusted path," but, more significantly, seems here to fulfill man's privilege of naming and reifying his universe.) These hyphenated compounds will continue to appear and send their message with some frequency up until the central stanza of the poem. Thereafter they vanish, as if their job had been done; *kol-bi*, "all within me," in the sixth stanza evokes a quite different whole—nontranscendent, purely internal—while *krakh-meguro*, "the city of his residence," in the bleak one-line finale sets up a mocking urban echo of false, forced intimacy.

Linguistically, wholeness is embodied in the overarching structure: in the bracketing ("embedding"), already referred to, of the entire first stanza as a relative clause hanging on *mi sheshav*. And from linguistic greatest to linguistic least, a leap that is itself a metaphor of encompassment (could one get more metalinguistic than this?), the smallest of words, *bo* and *ba*, denoting "in" or "with," are marshaled to proclaim enclosure and wholeness: *mitse'idat tsiporim bo*, "of the walking of birds in it," *veharbeh min-ashyut bah*, "with much femininity in it," *ve'omer shalom bah*, "and says hello in it," *mitiv harbeh 'etsim vetsuf hasadot bah*, "has the quality of many trees and the honey of the fields in it." If our English gloss has something gauche about it, it is because the placement of *bo* and *bah* itself creates a gauche word order and rhythm; ordinarily tucked between subject, verb, and object as a weightless clitic, *bo* and *bah* are here methodically placed at the end, giving weight to in-ness and a thud of rustic simplicity. The effect is repeated later in the poem, with other significant consequences that we shall discuss presently.

The *kfar* comes rich with the tangibles of the real world, the trees, the plot, the well, and a whole catalog in line 7. At the same time, it harbors echoes of an ancient Eden. Well before the second stanza, one can hear them: *ki hu tov* (see above); a taste of patriarchal blessing in the phrasing of line 7: with no verb to govern the preposition *mi*, it is inviting to take *mital, mishemesh* not as "from dew, from sun" but as an echo of Deut. 33: 13f.: "of dew, of sun"; and a hint at the classic biblical statement of the pristine ideal of work-and-repose in Psalm 104 ("Man goeth forth to his work and to his labor until the evening").

SECOND STANZA

In the *kfar*, the poet finds a world that predates arts and sciences, shades of Rousseau's utopian *Discours sur les sciences et les arts* and with a strong flavor of a biblical Eden—or at least a world before the sin of Cain. The city, introduced laconically in the first stanza (lines 4–5) as locus of the traveler-exile (*velo kehelekh-goleh limlono*), is now branded, in the stark couplet *vayiven 'ir*, "and he built a city," as the habitat of the line of Cain. It was east of Eden that Cain, expelled from human habitation, built his alternative: the first city (*vayehi boneh 'ir*, "and he became a city builder," Gen. 4:17). A city for one man and his son, a city for the lonely. In the stark biblical account, the city served first and foremost to broadcast the name and the fame (*shem*) of his son, whose son in turn was named Irad ("urban"?) and whose line ended with the inventors of weapons of war.

Now the poem's title begins to assume new significance: "the house of Adam." As the contrast between *kfar* and *krakh/'ir* is fleshed out, so, too, is that between man and man. The alternative to the *guf*, "body," organically meshed with its world in the first stanza (line 10), is the *guf merubeh rogez*, "a much-stressed body." The syntax and sounds here set up shock waves. The open, paratactic structure, so archetypically biblical, of the line beginning *vayiven 'ir*—extended the length of the line into a set of four rhythmic couplets—hurtles ambitiously ahead and into the next line (*vayehi*, "and became"), only to grind to a halt in the dense, internally rhymed triplet *guf merubeh rogez*, an arresting use of Mishnaic phraseology. The contrast between biblical and postbiblical language has been much exploited since the Haskalah for a variety of metaphorical effects (selectively, since modern Hebrew draws largely on both); here, perhaps, the Mishnaism connotes the artifice of a "civilized" and urbanized world, as against the supposed pristinity of a rustic biblical age that knew no metropolis.

The second stanza has come to a defined end and a nadir. The preceding stanza, as we have noted, demonstratively did not come to a rest; nor will any of the other stanzas in this restless paean come to rest, except the fourth, central stanza—the zenith—and the epilogue.

THIRD STANZA

The poet seems to start all over again. But instead of the massive ingestive structure of stanza 1, we get right to the point and to the main verb. We are coming to the "mystery" of what we are fleeing from: angst and Welt-schmerz. (And is this not the true nature of angst, that we do not even recognize it for what it is?) Existence outside Eden. Thus, the city of exile is maybe just a trigger for a deeper existential condition, and rurality is its remedy.

The tone here is philosophical, the style in parts Zoharic (what else could it be? After having symbolically exhausted the biblical and the Mishnaic, one can only resort to the third great conventional "type" of Hebrew: the medieval-philosophic)—and nowhere more obviously than in the final line, *hi sod-rogez-hanedod*, "that is the mystery of the stress of wandering," structurally and phonetically evoking such Zoharic phrases as *raza deshabat ihi shabat de'itahadat*, "the mystery of the Sabbath, that is, the Sabbath that was grasped" (Friday evening prayers).

But the poet does not limit himself to kabbalistic tones; the spirit of the great anti-kabbalist, Maimonides, also haunts these lines: *moledet adam har-ishon . . . hi sibat hakisuf vetugat hatelishut*, "the home of the original Man . . . is the cause of yearning and the grief of rootlessness," is structurally an echo of the famous opening words of Maimonides' code of laws and beliefs: *yesod hayesodot va'amud hahokhmot leida sheyesh sham matsuy rishon*, "The foundation of foundations and pillar of wisdom is to know that there is a first entity." Truly, structure is at the heart of this poem. The binary con-struct (*semikhut*) structure of *sibat hakisuf* and *tugat hatelishut* is part of a buildup to a climactic set of three-part construct structures, *sod karet hak-nafayim* and *sod-rogez-hanedod*, whose density and ternary form echo and—in the tight hyphenation of *sod-rogez-hanedod*—actually eclipse the grim density of the *guf merubeh rogez* at the close of the preceding stanza. Struc-ture is theme.

But equally, these echoes of Maimonides have intrinsic thematic force. Maimonides sets out to establish the basis of knowledge and locates it in a higher knowledge of the Creator. Greenberg locates the basis of human meaningfulness in a deeper sense of a pristine world and in the very quest for it, the need to soar. Hence the image of the bird in the first stanza and of snapped wings and migration at the end of this one.

FOURTH STANZA

The fourth and middle of the seven stanzas is the eye of the storm and is the first to be set in the first person—a sharp shift (or perhaps a natural outcome?) from the philosophic abstractions that preceded it. Yearnings have translated into real return. This is also metaphoric of the discovery of a real "I," the "return" to authenticity. Or maybe to say: this is no theory, no Marxist dogma, no Expressionism, but, as the Talmud might have put it, *bedidi hava uvda*, "it really happened to me."

Here, again, open parataxis with an echo of biblical poetic iteration—*lereḥah, lisrafah, lemitkah, levit'ḥonah*—takes the place of the dense compound phrase *sod-rogez-hanedod* on which the foregoing stanza tensely ended. And, pointedly, the string of four nouns is not left in abstract detachment but "anchored" with possessive suffixes (note the simplicity of it, the eschewing of colorful images and epithets): "*her* smell, *her* resin" . . . , until all anchoring in turn gives way to the deepest belonging, *meimei ve'er rishonim*, the primal waters.

But a mystery remains, one that arises from the Hebrew medium but that might not have arisen in Greenberg's Yiddish or Polish—or in English: Does *shavti lakfar* mean "I (once) returned" or "I have returned"? In linguistic terms, is it imperfective or perfective? In practical terms, is the poet celebrating a success, a stasis, or a fleeting accomplishment for which he and every man have constantly to struggle?

FIFTH STANZA

After attainment of the goal, can the climax hold? Or must it needs fall away? The remaining three stanzas can only be read in this light. Training one's eye on the opening note of the fourth stanza, in place of the *rak* that tensely opened stanzas 1–3 comes a phrase, *beshivah lakfar*, "on returning to the village," which seemingly continues in the past-present mode of attainment—or might it be nothing but a regression into the aoristic philosophical tones of stanza 3? The nonfinite phrase is ambiguous, like all such nominalizations; time and person have been repressed. Equally, is *shav* in the next line in the present tense or the past, the perfective or imperfective? The language and context are both ambivalent.

For the moment, we do know that to return is as much a mystery as to yearn. *Shivah* is *nes*, just as *karet knafayim* was *sod*—the mystery at the heart of Greenbergian art and ideology.

But the suspicion soon forms that the poet is no longer in a state of return: Why should he now be seized with *tugah*, "grief"? Why should he now be watching another traveler alight at the village? And why the recurrence of the path *rakh mital umitse'idat tsipor uvehemah bo*, "soft with dew and the walking of bird and cattle on it"—recalling the perspective of the outsider looking in of the first stanza?

SIXTH STANZA

And now, with the "I" usurped by a nameless traveler who attains what the "I" had yearned and briefly known, the "I" enters the city and the city opens up to us.

The theme is now one of size and fit: The *batei midot*, "mansions" (literally, "buildings of measure"), which should "fit" him, dwarf him. He cannot be master of the walls designed to protect him, yet he fits snugly and perfectly into the little house in the country that only reaches his brow. The city seems to have swallowed his space whole. Here, body is organically detached from surroundings, and container has become contained.

We have referred to the metaphoric force of architecture, language, and orthography in this poem. Consonant with its philosophic and kabbalistic vein, the letters and sounds of Hebrew are graphically brought into play—above all, the contrast between labial and velar, the lip sounds and the back palate sounds, a classically abstract structuralist binarity but serving a powerful iconic purpose for both eye and ear.

We meet it first in the pointed contrast in stanza 1, line 4: *el hakfar velo el hakrakh*, "to the *village* and not to the *big city*"—*kfar* and *krakh* share the same letters but one, *f* versus *kh*, a contrast between labial and velar and also, in the shapes of the two letters, a minimal orthographical contrast. The significance of labiality is soon evident in the recurrent forms *bo, ba*, "in it," whose peculiar use we have already discussed. The letter *bet*, routinely used in Hebrew as a one-letter prefix to denote "in," has something of an iconic as well as a symbolic "in-ness," which the poet exploits to the full. It reaches its climax in stanza 5 in the form *bi*. As the poet loses his hold on the inner home, *tofeset tugah et kol bi*, "grief seizes the whole of in-me," his insides are themselves subject to seizure; and he has now rung the changes on the three major vowels, *i, a, u*, a kind of enigma variation on a theme of *bet*. *Bet*, of course, in turn *means* "house." And the very title of the poem seems now to refer to Hebrew lettering: *Beit* is associated, by paleolinguists and kabbalists alike, in its shape as well as its name with *bayit* and *be*, with containment and inwardness. *Beito shel Adam*: a man's *bet*, or Adam's *bet*. The primal poetic home.

Phonetically, too, the labials have associations with the first sounds and motherhood, mama, baby. The poet makes use of all three major Hebrew labials: *b*, *p/f* and *m*, as in alliterative *mital, mishemesh, minishmat shhakim, mitse'idat tsiporim bo* (stanza 1, line 7), *bevered dimdumim be'oznav, belev dofek katsipor.* (line 8) and climaxing at *meimei ve'er rishonim* (end of middle stanza).

Contrasting with this labiality is the velarity of the *k/kh*, which is the distinguishing letter of *krakh*. And the very same velarity stands out in the other leitmotifs that contrast with *bayit*: *guf merubeh rogez* (the nadir of the poem), *karet kenafayim*, and *goleh*. Maybe also *g*, *k*, and *z* (echoes of *rogez*?) marking the container in the first line of stanza 6: *gag la mikash vegeder zradim*, "it has a roof of straw and a wattle fence"—contrasted pointedly with the interior, which is the poet's "all."

SEVENTH STANZA

Thus, man in the big city finds himself in a space whose whole ostensible function would seem to be to provide housing and home; he is a *ben bayit*. But it is an illusion. The son (*ben*) in whose name the father Cain built (*vayiven!*) the city can be nothing but a wanderer. The true, biblical force of *gur* and *meguro* is not settlement, but temporary shelter. And the wholeness and rounded labiality of the *ben bayit* must give way to the grating velarity of the *goleh*.

Dan Laor

IN OCTOBER 1949, while acting as a member of the first Knesset (the Israeli parliament) on behalf of the Ḥerut party, and in the midst of a period characterized by the intensive publication of poetry related either to the Holocaust or to Israel's War of Independence, Uri Zvi Greenberg surprised his readers with a new cycle of poems, that had nothing to do with state matters or with anything in the public sphere. The new cycle, titled *Min haḥakhlil umin hakakhol: Mahalakh 'al erets raba* (From the reddish to the blue : A walk on the great land), appeared in *Lu'aḥ ha'aretz* for the year 1949/50, and soon after it was printed in a small booklet and distributed to a close circle of friends and colleagues.[1] An advertisement that announced the publication of the *Lu'aḥ* referred exactly to this point: "Uri Zvi Greenberg, the great national poet, will surprise the devotees of his poetry with the publication of a major poetic cycle written in a pure lyrical idiom and penetrated by a sad tone." An extensive statement on that matter was made by critic Yisrael Zemora, who happened to be the only person to review *Lu'aḥ Ha'aretz*: "Once again, Uri Zvi Greenberg has deviated from his daily poetic practice and made a feast for himself as he has rarely done in the past, writing something that may be defined as "chamber poetry": the theme is not—as it usually is—the eternity of the nation, and not its suffering ... but is ... the temporary nature of the individual, the suffering caused by his own physical self, his emotional and mental pain, as well as his personal, private way of thinking."[2] This cycle of poems was issued again a few years ago, in the framework of Greenberg's posthumous *Sefer ha'igul* (The book of the circle), a major collection of post–World War II lyrical poetry, originally planned for publication in the mid-fifties.[3]

Greenberg started working on these poems in 1940 and had concluded his work by 1949; these dates are mentioned in the original publication in *Lu'aḥ Ha'aretz* and again in the book itself, with additional information about where they were written: Jerusalem, 1940—Tel Aviv, 1949. More information about the dates in which some of these poems were written can be found in the handwritten as well as typed manuscripts of this cycle, which are housed in the Greenberg archives at the National and University Library in Jerusalem. The earliest poem to be dated is "Shir hanofim hayafim" (The song about the beautiful landscapes), which was written in Jerusalem, "the holy city," on 30 January 1940, and was copied over and corrected in Ramat Gan (Greenberg's place of residence near Tel Aviv) on 28 May 1949. The latest poems to be dated—"Hakelev veha'adam balailah" (Man and dog at night) and "Shir kol ha'adam (The song of everyman)— were written on 22 February 1949. This shows that Greenberg started to compose these poems during World War II, not long after his traumatic flight in September 1939 from German-occupied Warsaw, and completed his work in the aftermath of Israel's War of Independence, with both events being an inexhaustible source for his poetic genius.

Though no specific date of composition was offered for "Man's House," the poem that opens this cycle, the manuscript does provide us with alternative information as to where it was written: Ramat Hasharon, "on a Sabbath eve." During the forties—the decade in which this cycle was composed—Ramat Hasharon (established in Mandatory Palestine in 1923) was a small agricultural village, long before it became a midsize town and a lively suburb of Tel Aviv. The local population was small, little farms were located behind many houses, and most people made their living in various branches of agriculture—vegetables, orange groves, or raising cows and hens.[4] Greenberg was then living in a tiny apartment owned by the family of the Revisionist writer Y. H. Yeivin in the southern part of Tel Aviv; occasionally, he would go to Ramat Hasharon for retreat, as a guest of Haim and Sara Binyamini. Sara, like himself, was a radical Zionist, affiliated with the organization Lohamei Herut Israel (Lehi). Ramat Hasharon was the place to which Greenberg fled, together with the Yeivin family, as Italian military aircraft bombarded Tel Aviv (September 1940), and he went there at times during World War II and after. Greenberg, then a bachelor, was extremely welcome at the Binyaminis, who offered him room and board and made it possible for him to write in a tranquil environment.[5] It is therefore quite conceivable that Ramat Hasharon was the catalyst that generated "Man's House"—a modern pastoral that emphasizes the contrast between town and country to represent the complexities of human life against a background of simplicity.[6]

The village as represented in this poem brings immediately to mind a typical European, or rather, East European village, not an agricultural settlement in Mandatory Palestine, where this work was written. This impression is created by various images used by the writer, such as the forest, the river, the well, the small shed with a straw-covered roof, as well as that of a man, who by the end of the day makes his way from the village train station toward his home with a package on his back. The place that Greenberg probably has in mind is his own birthplace—a small village in eastern Galicia (now Ukraine), not far from the town of Zloczow. This village— Bialy Kamien—is mentioned by its proper name later in this cycle, in a poem entitled "Shir beit imi" (The song of my mother's house).[7] There the speaker mentions the location of his village on the bank of the river Bug (whose western part starts north of Zloczow) and describes in some detail the small house where both he and his mother were born—a typical village house painted white, with a low roof and small windows. Beside it is a well with a large pump reaching up to the treetops and inside one can see a large ornate clock on the wall. Images from Greenberg's native village are also scattered in some of his early works. For example, in a poem called "Hahekhrah" (Necessity), written shortly after the writer's immigration from Europe to Palestine, the speaker relates to the agony of immigration, using his native villlage—though not mentioned by name—as a metaphor for one's own land.[8] The village is represented by a catalog of images, such as the forest, the small river, the well, and the mill, as well as through more specific objects, such as "the white cottages with roofs of straw and red tiles" and "a fence of twigs," most of them echoed later in "Man's House." The earlier poem also speaks of the longing for "all flushed apples, for the blueness of the plums!"—signifying the blue and red colors in the title of the new cycle.[9]

According to the biographical data available to us, Greenberg was less than two years old when his family left Bialy Kamien and moved to the city of Lwow, the capital of eastern Galicia at that time.[10] Nonetheless, during his childhood and adolescence, the poet was a frequent visitor to his native village, as it remained the place of residence of his mother's family and that of his beloved grandmother, Yokheved Landman, who was still alive at the end of World War I. This may explain Greenberg's deep affinity for the countryside, as opposed to his early resentment to an urban environment: "And what happens in Lwov?" he wrote to his friend Haim Itzkovitz during a visit to Bialy Kamien in 1914. "Oh, I don't want to know about it. This huge city—how much blood it demands! And how many cries and moans are swallowed by it."[11] Future events took Greenberg far away from Bialy Kamien: first, World War I, in which he was a front soldier; his postwar years were spent first in Warsaw, and later in Berlin, which was the ultimate European urban center at the time; his immigration from

Europe to Palestine at the end of 1923; finally, the Russian-German conquest of his native Poland in the course of World War II and the annihilation of Polish Jewry. In this context, "Man's House" can be read as an elegy on the lost landscape that has been strongly associated with his childhood environment. In the original manuscript of the poem, though not in print, Greenberg even speaks directly about "the portion of the field *of my ancient village, with the best of my ancient childhood*," substantiating the identity between the rural environment and his own early life.[12]

However, the option for a personal, autobiographical reading of the poem cannot blur the poet's main strategy to transform the rural reminiscences of his early childhood into a general, rather philosophical statement about the human condition, focusing on what he perceives as the tragic shift of man from the harmonious mode of existence offered by the traditional, rural way of life to the anxiety and alienation created by the city— the emblem of modern times.[13] This position is established through an exhaustive treatment of the dichotomy between the country and the city: whereas the country is represented through natural, "soft" images and friendly constructions—the trees, the fields, the well, the "soft-to-the-step" path (line 6), the small white cottage with the straw roof and a birds' nest, located not far from the river and from the forest—the city is characterized by "hard," stony images and unfriendly constructions: "the paved road" (in contrast to the "soft-to-the-step" path), "the great buildings" (line 47) and "the wall, which is higher than his forehead" (line 54) (compared with the small, feminine cottage, "no higher than his forehead" [line 53]). It is therefore only in the village, and nowhere else, that—according to Greenberg—the individual becomes an integrated part of the world that surrounds him: the field is described as a "fruitful extension of his flesh" (line 2), the small cottage that houses the family is not only an object to be embraced, but is also "like an extension of his body" (line 10), and, elsewhere in this poem, "the body is watered like a field and like the tree in it" (line 52). Not so in the city, in which harmony and simplicity are replaced by anger, strangeness, and sorrow: the body, which previously enjoyed a sense of "extension," turns into "a body compounded of anger" (line 22), and the feeling of intimacy, rootedness, and domesticity is taken over by the individual's anxiety and restlessness. Indeed, whereas the country is synonymous with "homeland" (line 18), the key word for the city is "exile" (*golah*) (line 24): in the first stanza, man's return to the village is "not as an exile's walk to his inn" (line 5); in the third stanza, the word "city" is hyphenated with "exile" (*hakerakh-hagolah*—"exile-city" [line 24]), whereas the poet's final declaration in the sixth stanza is that "man walks in his city-dwelling like a household exile" (line 55). City life is thus associated with wandering ("secret anger of wandering" [line 30]), detachment ("sadness of detachment" [line 28]), strangeness ("anger . . . strangeness" [line 49]), and death: the image of the "clipped-wings" (line 29) in the third stanza includes the word *karet* (*karet-kenafayim*), which is the talmudic idiom for God's punishment manifested in premature death.

The shaping of the country-city opposition is substantiated in the course of the poem by several allusions to the early chapters of the Book of Genesis: Greenberg's Galician-Ukrainian village, described in the first stanza, is identified in the second and third stanzas with the mythical Garden of Eden ("man's true homeland / Which was every man's once upon a time in this universe" [lines 18–19] and even "homeland of the first man" [line 27]), a place where man could walk naked, "before he set his foot in a shoe and covered his shoulders to the ends of his body" (line 20). This allusion is intensified by the very use of the word *adam* (which means "man")— including in the title of the poem ("Beito shel adam" in Hebrew)—which is both a noun and the proper name of the first man. Though the ancient sin is not mentioned, Greenberg does refer to what may be considered one of its main products—the construction of the first city: "And [he] built a city and paved a road to-hide-from-eye the greening earth" (line 21). This reference is established through an indirect allusion to Gen. 4:17, where Cain, the notorious son of Adam and Eve, is recognized as the builder of a city: "And Cain knew his wife, and she conceived . . . and he built a city and called the name of the city after the name of his son, Enoch."[14] In this context, attention should be paid to the use of the conversive *vav* turning past into future, combined with the imperfect verbal form (*vayiven ir vayitsok kevish*), which is a typical biblical construction, and to the uncommon form of the adjective in "greening earth" (*adama madshi'ah*), which alludes directly to Gen. 1:1: *vayomer elohim tadshe ha'aretz deshe* ("And God said: let the earth bring forth grass"). Echoes from Genesis 1 can also be found in the first stanza: "Only he who returns to the village . . . / Walks on the trusted path, soft-to-the-step. For it's good" lines 1, 6 (the Hebrew *ki hu tov* stems from the biblical idiom *ki tov*). In his study of the pastoral, Peter V. Marinelli suggests that the movement from the garden to the city implicit in Judeo-Christian mythology "is a direct result of the Fall," and therefore the desire to escape from the town—so well reflected in this poem—is interpreted as "the desire to escape from the circumstances into which we were plunged by the fall and of which the city is, however glorious, really the result."[15]

No wonder, then, that the theme of return is of major significance in this poem, where the expulsion from Eden is a latent motif, and where the term "exile" is repeatedly associated with both man and space. This is exactly what Michael Seidel refers to as the "exilic state," which he considers the ultimate cause for "a lifelong scenario of estrangement."[16] According to Seidel, this state of affairs calls for a solution, which—at least in works of literature—is translated into an imaginary narrative of return to the much desired destination from which the individual has been disconnected for a long time. Thus, through what Seidel calls a "leap" from the concrete to the fantastic, the return to the past—repeatedly considered through the anaphora of the first and the third stanzas ("He who returns to the village . . ." (lines 1 and 23)—is suggested to be possible, at least in the realm of the imagination: "I returned to the village, as one returns to an ancient homeland: / To its smell, its resin, its sweetness, its security / To first well water" (lines 31–33). This imaginary act of return may even perform a "miracle" (line 34) by putting things, at least for a while, back into their previous position, as if "the cut tree again joins up with its trunk" (line 35). Yet the poem is written with a deep notion that paradise lost cannot be easily regained, and that man is doomed to accept this loss, for it is definite and irreversible. "And I travel onward from this through the night, to the city, / That swallowed my ancient portion of field and a road covered it and great buildings" (lines 46–47). (The Hebrew for "great buildings" is *beit midot*, with a clear reference to Jer. 22: 14, where it functions as a metonymy for social and moral injustice.) In the conclusion of this poem, the rather individual experience of the "I" versus the city is phrased like an epigram, making the one-line ending of this poetic work sound like the moral of the whole poem: "Man walks in his city-dwelling like a household exile" (line 55). Greenberg, as a writer of a true pastoral, knows well that moving away from an unsatisfactory time and place and returning to a time and place that are superior can be imagined but not implemented; thus, the sight of a traveler walking to the village train station, presented in a previous stanza, can be seen by the "I" only from a distance, because for him, as for Adam, the way back to Eden is blocked by the cherubim and by the flaming sword that turns every way.

In an afterword to the posthumous publication of *Sefer ha'igul*, Dan

Miron writes that as editor in chief of Greenberg's complete oeuvre, he decided to place *Min hahakhlil umin hakakhol* at the beginning of this volume, considering this cycle as the appropriate text to signal the poet's return to a personal and metaphysical poetry after abstaining from such writing for twenty years.[17] What Miron refers to are four major volumes of what he calls "lyrical metaphysical poetry," all of them published posthumously, which represent a poetic alternative to Greenberg's works that concentrate on political matters and deal with themes related to Jewish existence. This kind of writing differs radically from poems included in books such as *Rehovot hanahar* (Streets of the river) and *Sefer ha'amudim* (The book of pillars), produced in the forties and fifties, in which—according to Greenberg's own literary theory—poetry takes responsibility over the lot of a nation, not over that of the individual. Thus, it is occupied with the Holocaust, with the struggle for national revival, and with Israel's sovereign statehood. The main concern of Greenberg's "other" poetry is quite the opposite—man's place in the universe, nature, and that which is above nature, the relationship between man and woman, the child facing his parents and the parents facing their descendants, man and God, man facing death. This trend began with "Man's House," in which priority is given to the private over the public, to art over politics. In this sense, the poem under discussion serves as a prologue not only to the original cycle and to *Sefer ha'igul* at large, but for a whole new trend that has gained a tremendous momentum, unrecognized so far, in Greenberg's late poetry.

Notes

1. *Min Hahakhlil umin hakakhol: Mahalakh 'al erets raba, Lu'ah ha'aretz lishenat tav shin yud*, i–xxvii. *Lu'ah Ha'aretz* was an annual publication for literary and daily affairs issued by the *Ha'aretz* daily, for which Greenberg was a regular contributor.

2. Y. Zemora, "Lu'ah ha'aretz lishenat tav shin yud," *Ha'aretz*, 23 September 1949.

3. See Uri Zvi Greenberg, *Kol ketavav*, ed. Dan Miron, vol. 9, *Sefer ha'igul* (Jerusalem: Mossad Bialik, 1994), 11–35.

4. Ze'ev Aner and Dorit Yisrael, *Me'ir shalom lemoshavah: Sipura shel ramat hasharon* (1923–1993) (Ramat Hasharon: Moetzet Ramat Hasharon, 1993).

5. Based on a telephone conversation with Eliyahu Binyamini, May 1999.

6. I use the term "pastoral" or "modern pastoral" as it is defined in Peter V. Marinelli's *Pastoral* (London: Methuen & Co., 1971). See also Raymond Williams, *The Country and the City* (London: Oxford University Press, 1973), 289–306.

7. "Eima gedola veyareaḥ," in *Kol ketavav*, 9: 30–31.

8. Ibid. vol. 1 (1990), 66.

9. Visiting the Ukraine in 1992, I was rather amazed to find out how much the reading of Greenberg's poems—particularly "Hahekraḥ"—can serve as a useful guide for Bialy Kamien.

10. Dov Sadan, "ʿAl Uri Zvi Greenberg usevivav," *Nativ*, July 1993, 60–62; and a letter by Aliza Greenberg sent to me on 6 January 2000.

11. Quoted by Shalom Lindenbaum, *Shirat Uri Zvi Greenberg: Kavei mitʿar* (Tel Aviv: Hadar, 1984), 51.

12. See Greenberg's archives, Ms. 2:948.

13. In his 1925 volume *Eima gedolah veyareaḥ*, Greenberg connects the decay of the village with the rise of the modern city: "the village is doomed and nobody cares (and if one cares?!); all roads are running from the city and there is no more salvation." See *Kol ketavav*, 1:9.

14. See Baruch Kurzweil, "Heʾarot lemahut hanofim beshirei U. Z. Greenberg," in *Bein ḥazon levein haʾabsurdi* (Tel Aviv: Schocken, 1966), 65–67.

15. Marinelli, 10–11.

16. Michael Seidel, *Exile and the Narrative Imagination* (New Haven: Yale University Press, 1986) 1–19.

17. *Kol ketavav*, 9:219.

Hannan Hever

ON THE SURFACE, it seems that the poem "Man's House" presents a clear and sharp opposition between two modes of being and two opposing situations: between he who returns to the village toward evening and he who lives in the city; between he who is one with the organic, natural, unmediated existence and he whose existence is within the boundaries of the big city, with its paved roads that hide from the eye the greening earth.

This set of oppositions is crystallized, finally, into an opposition between "man's true homeland" (line 18), available to him who returns to the village, and the diaspora, or the exile-city, in which one lives as "a household exile" (line 55). The poem urges its readers to choose the option of returning to the village as the desirable, appropriate choice; this is, after all, the return to the homeland, which is the return to the object of national desire. The appropriate trajectory is from the diaspora to the homeland, and there is a clear hierarchy between the two: a hierarchy that privileges homeland over diaspora.

But a close reading of the poem reveals the inability to realize this recommendation. The homeland is a total, flawless essence: an organic mode of being, within which "he who returns to the village toward evening" (line 1) is, in effect, a material continuity of the object of his return, the village. He "approaches a fence of twigs, opens its door to a white cottage, / That one could almost hug . . . like an extension of his body" (lines 9–10). But it is this total being of the homeland that denies the ability of ever fully returning to it. Thus, Greenberg writes "that one could *almost* hug" it (line 10, emphasis added). Even the returning toward evening is a metaphor to a late return, one that is not whole, not total. It is a process of return, and "only he *tastes of the precious taste* of man's true homeland, / Which was every man's once upon a time in this universe" (lines 18–19, emphasis added)—tastes, but does not fully merge with. He who returns to the village toward evening and only tastes the precious taste of man's true homeland is so doing since it is a homeland that was every man's once upon a time, and therefore, because of its extreme totality, there is, of course, no way to perform a concrete, material, real return to it.

It thus follows that the object of desire that Greenberg constitutes in the poem is an impossible object. This object is so complete and total that it can never be achieved. Therefore, its very impossible existence becomes the reason for the constant absence. The desire for something that is unachievable becomes the sign of constant absence, which cannot be repaired and become present. An inversion of the hierarchy of homeland and diaspora thus happens. Not only is the homeland not about to annihilate the diaspora, as is implied in the recommended trajectory from diaspora to homeland, but the homeland is the very cause of diasporic existence. The very desired existence of the homeland is what maintains the diaspora, the absence. Greenberg himself phrases this point very clearly: "Homeland of the first man, uprooted from it, *this the cause of the longing* / And the sadness of detachment" (lines 27–28, emphasis added). Being uprooted is not the cause of the longing but the "Homeland of the first man, uprooted from it, this the cause of the longing / and the sadness of detachment," is. It is a metonymic move from cause to effect, which inverts their relationships. Instead of talking about being uprooted from the homeland as the cause of longing, of the desire to the homeland, it is the very existence of the homeland that is the cause of desire.

The homeland of the first man, which can never be obtained, is the source of sadness and will forever beget sadness. When Greenberg chooses to represent the dynamics of desire through the terminology of the expulsion from the Garden of Eden, he positions the Garden of Eden as the cause and the reason for exile and uprootedness. Therefore, the village is not only the desired object but also the source and the cause of detachment.

The return to the village toward evening, described as the liberation from the city/the diaspora, is presented not as a full return—emotionally and existentially whole—but as an answer to a riddle, the riddle of longing. It is not the longing that is repaired, or the desire that is fulfilled, but the intellectual riddle of desire that is solved.

The two central organic metaphors through which Greenberg represents the return or the connectedness contain within themselves their dismantling, or their lack of coherence. One is the metaphor of the bird, through which Greenberg describes the secret of return as the "secret of *clipped wings* and they flutter still . . . / This is the secret anger of wandering—" (lines 29–30). Similarly, the metaphor of the tree, which represents the return as "a return in which there is miracle. / The cut tree again joins up with its trunk" (lines 34–35), also contains its dismantling within itself. Later in the poem, as he develops the metaphor of the tree ("A man in a village toward

evening is just like a tree" line 50), Greenberg describes the organic connectedness as one that contains self-reflection that, in its turn, contains
sadness that threatens the inner and organic wholeness of the tree and
undermines it. The man "stands reflecting on thoughts of itself: now with
dew and now with its pleasant tear" (line 51). The damaging apparatus is
integral to the longing and desire.

In the second part of the poem (lines 31ff.), the person of the narrator
changes, and from a general discourse in the third person about he who
returned to the village toward evening, he becomes a first-person narrator,
saying, "I returned to the village, as one returns to an ancient homeland"
(line 31). But this mode of personal testimony is immediately revealed to
be an estranged representation, an external representation of the return of
someone else. My return is the return of the traveler who gets off the train
as it lingers near a village station. The return of the narrator to the village
is, then, a metaphoric return "as one returns to an ancient homeland" and
is described as "a return in which there is miracle." But the miracle happens
to someone else. My return to the village is the return of someone else
"when a train lingers near a village station" (line 37). My return, then, is a
mediated return, being materialized via the gaze focused on the return of
someone else: "I smell after him," and not as part of unmediated togeth-
erness but "it's *as if I know it also* / This path: soft from the dew and bird
and animal steps upon it / And from shadow of trees down its length"
(lines 40–42, emphasis added).

The return of the traveler who gets off the train and goes on to his
cottage in the village is analogous to the narrator's travel to the city. And
the narrator in the poem, who has presented himself as he who returned
to the village, now presents himself as he who cannot reach his goal at any
cost. And adopting an all-encompassing description referring to all places
at all times in any situation, he determines irrevocably: "And wherever I
travel and wherever I come, that place is not my goal, / Because anger is
there, strangeness" (lines 48–49).

The initial reading, that of the hierarchical recommended trajectory leading from the diaspora to the homeland, is the immediately available reading,
since it is commensurate with the national Zionist narrative and with
Greenberg's private world. But in effect, the poem turns out to be an exposure of the inner problematic of Greenberg's radical nationalism. From
this radical perspective, the notion of homeland appears to be an organic,
total concept. And because of that, this radical perspective finally under-

mines itself as it points to the diaspora as a necessary situation, stemming from Greenberg's totalizing concept of homeland. The binarism of homeland and diaspora, which implies a clear hierarchy according to which the homeland is positive and the diaspora negative, turns out to be one that necessitates the existence of the negative diaspora as a condition for the concept of the positive homeland. The hierarchy in which homeland is preferred over diaspora is inverted when the diaspora is revealed to be a constant condition to all longing for the homeland. When desire for the homeland is so total, organic, and atavistic, it negates the priority of the homeland. Greenberg's atavistic discourse, which developed as a continuation of Fascist thought and culture, is so radical that it contains its own destruction within itself.

This reading exposes the refusal of the poem to be included in a definitive manner in the national Zionist narrative. The ability to read in the poem traces of the struggle between a totalizing, radical understanding of "homeland" and the pragmatic Zionist desire stems from the attempt to read the poem outside the constraints and dictates of national reading, which submits all texts to the obligation of the Zionist metanarrative. In Greenberg's poetry, there is a duality: on the one hand, he portrays a political, pragmatic continuity from diaspora to homeland; on the other hand, the structure of desire that he constitutes in his poem is not easily compatible with this continuity. No doubt the manifest, explicit political message of the poem stands, and the poem emphasizes time and again the great effort invested in the desire for a homeland. But given the kind of total, organic homeland that the poem prefers, this desire cannot be materialized.

Not adhering to the authority of the reading that is submitted to the national metanarrative, which presents itself as the sole authority, means exercising a post-national reading of the poem. This is a reading that, rather than organizing the text in a smooth, coherent positioning of a clear, causal hierarchical relation of diaspora and homeland, tries to analyze the effort to submit the text to this hierarchy, to this national hierarchical narrative. Post-national reading is an attempt at understanding the limits of this effort of submission and the efforts to cover it up; and it enables the exposure of the inner duality that arises in Greenberg's text out of his profound and total commitment to the Zionist narrative.

[V]

BRIDAL VEIL

Amalia Kahana-Carmon

RAYA AND NIMROD JONES

GOD'S FIRE ON THE CHILDREN[1]

God's fire on the cities
God's fire on the houses, in the fields
God's fire, so beautiful, so divine.
Flames upon flames. Shofar blasts and angels' eyes.
Eyes of angels are much purer than children's eyes.
Angel seraphim singing praise.
Children are not angels, dirty children, evil children.
Screaming and demanding children, bad children, only sometimes sing.
Children are not angels and their voices do not halleluja.

Angels will come and kick the children, chase away dirty, ugly, mothers,
Stupid fathers with nothing of God's wisdom.
Stupid fathers sow evil, reap death, corpse fathers.
Dirt fathers, garbage fathers, stone fathers.
Child, where's your father, father's not in the clouds.
Who is flying in the clouds? Not stupid father, evil father, corpse father.
Come children, pray to God fire, to burnished angel seraphim
Say thank you, dirty child with dripping nose.
Clouds will give out rain, good rain upon the earth,
Angels will roll up robes of glory, give first aid to the world.
To you, too, dirty child, an excellent cookie.
Flowers will unfold, corpse father won't see the beauty.
Ugly mother will not look, she'll only curse, mother.
Angels will praise God, shofars will cry ah-ha.

Meir Wieseltier
(Translated by Gilead Morahg)

158

FATHER ACCOMPANIED HER and sat with her on the Egged inter-city bus. Until the journey began. It was the bus before last. Because Father had taken her to the pictures. Now he was impatient. Irritable for some reason.

A group of UN soldiers were getting on the bus. One got on and Father said: "Looks like Anthony Perkins, that one." Another one got on. Looks even more like Anthony Perkins, reflected Shoshana but did not say.

For many hours she had waited for Father. An evening in another town. The park. Empty playground. Through branches and leaves, lights: dwell-ings. Residences, windows. Strangers' homes.

Since the early afternoon she had waited there. The gardeners were still having a rest in the shrubs' shade. Two long-haired vagabond tourists, one with hair like the sun in a poster, equal and matching tongues of flames in a blazing circle, with intense concentration measured and cut in two a single cigarette with a razor blade. Little boys and girls began arriving. Some of the little boys had their hair held to one side by a hair clip. Some of the girls had tiny toy handbags. Some little white woollies folded over the arm. Chilly in the evening in the mountain town.

Later on, deaf-mute children were brought to the park. With them two teachers. Or minders. Very young, dressed like sluts.

The minders went and sat on a bench. The mute children invaded the playground, swarming over every seat. Or, blank-eyed, violently spinning roundabouts, making swings and their sitters fly. The nice children scat-tered, scurried for mothers' or child-minders' laps. The mute children, like pirates, snatched at the vacated seats. Signaling to each other pleasure and delight; voicelessly, with gestures and grotesque faces only. Among them fully grown girls riding the infants' seats of the seesaws, on their faces the expression of mental retardation. One lanky boy, somber, most obstinate, his shirt torn at the shoulder, kept on disturbing them. Trying to grab their rubber flipflops, rising and falling, while they draw back their feet and kick out at him lazily. Under his chin, in his stomach, his ribs, wherever the seesaw takes them. And whenever he, with his eyes shut, gapes in soundless pain, one can see, his teeth are false.

The park emptied. Soon it will be completely dark. And now it is. The recorded voice of a woman trails past. Clear and vivid as though a singing siren were sitting on the hood of the passing car. Silence again. Then the trail of the familiar voice of an announcer, reading the evening news. From a first-floor balcony, across the trunks of the pine trees, once or twice, questions are asked aloud. Of members of a family, settling for the night. Then the vertical slats of the blinds were turned slightly, their backs inward, their insides outward, just enough to seal off.

Shoshana took out and started eating the food her mother had given her for the journey. Brown bread. A little smoked mackerel. One or two apricots. A little halva.

A man—an Ashkenazi, bald and pot-bellied in too-wide khaki shorts, once everyone sported clothes like that, with a shabby briefcase, like a middle-aged clerk—went in and out, in and out of the park. Earlier, when he had passed by her, she could still make out the grooved buckle, held in the last hole of his belt. Beads of sweat on his forehead and the front of his bald head. Also his eye, fixed on her sideways, like a rooster's. Fixed on her all the time. Later on, one could hardly make out the features of his haggard face. The darkness deepened more and more. Shoshana made up her mind and went to wait on the pavement, under the street lamp. She was worrying that Father might not find her, as he had told her to wait in the park, in the playground, like all the children. And what if Father should come in through the other gate? What if he went away. But that's how it is. In another town. A strange town.

She stood on the street corner, peering furtively at the section of the main street, there beyond the alley. People were passing there. True, fewer people. But people were passing there. And cars. All along there had been some mistake, it was revealed to her now. She hadn't thought about it, but must have assumed that life outside came to an end when one went to bed, after supper. Except on special occasions. And here's something new, secret: there's the ordinary life of day. And there's the ordinary life of night. Life carries on at night. Differently though. At night everything is different. Houses, people, thoughts.

The bus lingered. Father started to grumble.

Since when do UN soldiers travel by bus, Shoshana reflected. Two were sitting in front. A third one stood over them, chatting.

Ice-blue eyes they had. And though they certainly had broad shoulders, something about them was seemingly narrow. They were as though made of drier stuff. As though we ourselves, our end is to shrink, leaking a spreading puddle. And later on, when all but shrunk to thin skin, to get all wrinkled, to evaporate and be no more. But they, their end is to crumble, turn into dust, and be no more. They were all similar, but each in his own way. Like guavas. They all taste good, but each tastes also slightly different, giving its own interpretation of the taste of the guava.

A man carrying a high cardboard box entered. On it, in big red scrawl, like a finger smear, it read: Parts—Incubators. He blocked the exit with it.

Again Shoshana was reminded of the story called "Excerpt" in the *Paths Reader* Part Four. A chick hatches out of its egg in the incubator. To whom will the chick turn its inborn human need for attachment? Will it turn to the electric incubator, it was written there, will it turn to the poulterer who breeds it in order to have it transferred to the electric poultry abattoir, to whom? The inborn human need, it was written. The human need of he who is not human.

From one of the seats could be heard the voice of a young man, of Oriental Sephardi stock, excited, even though whispering. "Give it to me. Let me be the secretary of the committee. No, not because you like me. Because I've got the hang of it. And you'll see if, within four years, I don't turn this place into a political springboard. First-rate. If each one of them wouldn't need me, look for me, come to me for favors. Here's Ben-Dov. Who's Ben-Dov. All right, he's head and shoulders above. Today. Fifteen, twenty years ago, what was he. A seaman. And today, you can see for yourself. And I, I'll get you the whole of the construction lot going. Think of it: power. True, true. But Anaby got demolished politically because he doesn't have the makings of a public figure. Just not a strong man. True, he was seen all over the place. Ran around. But he doesn't have the makings. It's a question of having an influence over people. You have to know how to get them going. How? Work at the source. Besides, you know that with me you'll get the works. Balance sheets, reports, deals, the lot."

The bus lingered on. Father got up, parted abruptly, and left.

As soon as Father got off the bus, the UN soldier who had been standing up came over and sat down beside her. Perched on his seat, craning his neck forward, he picked up his chatting with his friends.

Freckled, young, good-looking. But the light went out and he stopped talking. Shoshana wondered about his sitting next to her. Moreover, she had noticed that before he sat down he had considered her, then the empty seat across the aisle, and making a quick decision chose to sit by her. As soon as he sat down, it was as if a prize had fallen her way.

Even in the dark it was possible to see, his lips were finely drawn. The fleshy hand, grasping the rail of the seat before them, firm. And he's one of the boys. Very much one of the boys.

The bus started moving off. Outside, a tall woman passed, crossed its path walking very upright, and the driver cried out furiously: "Greta Garbo." Shoshana peeped at the UN soldier, saw him smiling in surprise.

Unaware, she too smiled inwardly. But now the strap of the flight bag—
the blue El Al bag, with Father's laundry, that Father had placed on the
shelf above—slipped down, swung about and almost touched the beret of
the soldier sitting in front of her. Meaning to put it back, Shoshana struggled to get up, tried to stand on the curve of the wheel at her feet. Trouble:
the UN soldier was sitting on the edge of her skirt, Mother's wide skirt
given for the trip. As the bus swerved to leave its bay by the platform side,
Shoshana slipped, found herself in the dark waist up across a hard and
alien knee.

"Sorry," she cried out in Hebrew, reaching out with both hands, as if
for a raft, to the rail of the seat in front, while the embarrassed UN soldier
was saying in English: "I'm sorry. I'm sorry. It's all right."

Trying to stand up again, the UN soldier still sitting on the edge of her
skirt, the bus swerving the other way, she flew to his knees once more.
This time he hastened to help, to raise her like a package in order to put
her back in her place. But with the bus jolting and straightening itself, he
put his hand in the wrong place. "Sorry," he let go at once, alarmed.
Straining to rise, Shoshana said: "It's all right," echoing his English,
"sorry." And she tried a word from her schooldays: "Dress." "Dress? Oh,
dress. I'm sorry," his alarm increased and he rose. "It's all right," she
mouthed in shame. The shadow of a smile was wiped off her face now.
With it, her self-assurance.

Once, when Father still worked in Tiberias, a waitress, with a wink to
her friend, volunteered to display her skills in making small talk. She announced, she'd ask a soldier if he was married. She couldn't find the word.
Then she did: "You, papa?" "Perhaps I am and I don't know it," the soldier
laughed, very much taken by surprise. All the waitresses shrieked. What
did he mean? Married or single. He invited the waitress to go out with
him. "Where to?" she asked. "Dancing cheek-to-cheek," translated Father,
for all to hear the soldier's reply. What did the soldier mean. "UN soldiers,
they are like sailors of a ship." Father had explained to her at the time.
Father had a song in French, and once on a weekend, he translated it for
us like this, with feeling: "I see the harbor lights / Only they told me we
were parting / The same old harbor lights / That once brought you to me
/ I watch the harbor lights / How could I help if tears were starting /
Goodbye to tender nights / Beside the silvery sea." And throatily: "I long
to hold you near / And kiss you just once more / But you are on that ship
/ And I am on the shore." And again, as before: "Now I know lonely nights

/ For all the while my heart is whispering / Some other harbor lights / Will steal your love from me."

Along the nocturnal road were trees, nodding heads like people. The light of the speeding bus falls on them, withdraws from them. And the vapor-veiled moon crescent is getting blurred. But why is her throat so dry? Shoshana gazed through the window for a long time.

Once, while she was traveling home with Father's laundry, a nice young man, maybe a student at the Polytechnic, sat next to her reading a paperback. Entitled *It Was Murder by Moonlight*. When it got dark, the young man put the book in his pocket and turned to touch her nape so artfully that until they reached the junction she couldn't make out whether he had, or she had imagined it. Then as now, at the first moment, the same panic. A blind panic. Like a wild animal's. Only this time there was no room for error. The UN soldier beside her is, he is, pressing his elbow on to her arm. This time she did not rise to leave her place and did not move to another seat. She sat on like a statue. Doing nothing. Gazing through the window.

Now, with his other hand he is seeking hers. And just as it's not for exercising their throat muscles that people utter sounds. But for saying things with words, the things matter. So it is here. He is seeking to say something, only in another way. What is he asking. Yes, I know. But it's not clear what he is asking right now about it. And what does he expect from her. Hard to know, let alone when one is confused.

She stole a look at him. And learned that he was already sitting very close, much closer than she had realized. Deadpan-faced, as though he had nothing to do with her. Passing his arm behind to surround her. UN soldiers in front of us, UN soldiers behind us. How does he have the nerve?

At the junction the lights came on. The UN soldier hurried, moved away abruptly.

Cheerful girl-soldiers boarded the bus. "Smadar, Smadar," they cried out to another who was still outside, buying something from a young vendor. Good-looking, grown-up, laughing. Here goes, reflected Shoshana, this will put an end to me. Besides, there's no escape: I know what he must think of me now—she didn't dare look his way. As he sat staring straight ahead, so did she. As he folds his arms, so she folds hers.

The girl-soldiers spread out boisterously over the vacant seats. The ticket inspector got on. And the UN soldier beside her smiled to himself, privately, tilting his chin a little, as a UN soldier seated distantly threw a side-comment in a loud voice, probably a joke. Shoshana took out the two tickets from the pocket of her plaid blouse. The return ticket and the late-night surcharge one, holding them both in her hand.

And she saw: the UN soldier who was sitting still grinned at her. As if asking permission. Before she could know what he wanted, he took her tickets from her hand. Holding them with his ticket, entirely together, he handed them to the inspector.

As ever and always she, the eldest daughter, has had to manage on her own—what is it that passed through her now, piercing through the bark, penetrating the sapwood, making it ooze. She felt herself shattered, knowing nothing.

Returning her tickets, he attempted to strike up a conversation with her: "Israel?" he pointed at her.

Shoshana nodded.

He pointed at himself:

"Riff-raff."

Where is Riffraffia? she tried to remember.

"Canada," he smiled as if in confirmation, raising a shoulder to push his ticket into his pocket.

All she knew about Canada, she reflected, was what Father had once told them. A Canadian walked into the hotel kitchen. He sat down and said, to Father and the rest of the assistant chefs, that where he came from, normally, they entertained in the parlor. But a specially welcome guest was always received in the kitchen. This was what the man had said, and dropped off. Totally drunk. Only later they found out he'd fallen asleep on the spice mill, which they had been looking for all that time.

The UN soldier pointed backward with his thumb. To know whether she is a resident of the city they had left. Shoshana pointed ahead. The city they were heading for. He got it and laughed, as if by this she had proved herself sharp-witted. He pointed back again, shaking his other hand, as if inquiring. Shoshana pointed at Father's bag. "Papa," she said. The UN soldier's face became respectful, and Shoshana felt pleased. Very.

Then she remembered. Tried her hand at making small talk:

"You. Papa?"

He didn't understand. But pointed at himself, and smiled: "No papa. No mama. No brother. No sister. No wife. No children. Nobody," he said. And he took off his beret. Put it on her bag. On her bag he put it. Now, with his red hair, he was better-looking sevenfold. And as soon as the light went out he returned to her. Once the bus danced. And he, using the inside of his arm which was on her back, pressed it on her hard then, deliberately. As if to protect her, to spare her the bumps.

In the vicinity of the city boundaries, but a good way from the station yet, the road was blocked with buses and cars. "A traffic jam?" people said. "An accident?"

For a long time they waited there. More cars drove up, stopped. People began to get off the bus. Got tired and boarded it again. A man wearing the bus company hat appeared. A real veteran. There had been a road accident, he explained. They would have to proceed on foot. Passengers going farther would be provided with transport. Saying this, he left. The driver translated it into English, and picking up his satchel indifferently, left too.

The UN soldier got Shoshana's bag down from the shelf, but people were shoving between them. Especially one woman, her fleshy bulk quivering, who continued her conversation while alighting, as if incapable of stopping: "Twenty years later I saw her, the one he left me for," it was unbelievable that she was saying. "Quite my look-alike. And he did the same thing to her too. The bastard, the worthless bastard," she said. "How do I know? He did it with me," she spoke ordinarily. The ordinary life of night.

Almost the last one to get off, down there waiting for her was the UN soldier.

"Goodbye," Shoshana was glad to have found the word. She took her bag from him, while here too was a novelty: the language not her own language in her mouth. A man-made, contrived automaton. Look, as if at the press of a button it suddenly works, alive, performing: another secret new thing is revealed. Suddenly the world is full of questions and surprises. Meanwhile, she was overhearing a passing Israeli youth, who, casting a glance at the UN soldier, was saying about him in Hebrew: "Some body." And it was as if it were she who had been paid a compliment.

The UN soldier did not go. He was standing, hands in the belt of his narrow trousers, and waiting. Shoshana pointed at his friends, the UN soldiers who were walking away, after they had set themselves apart and crossed to the other side of the road. He shook his head signaling no, and took her bag from her. Smiling and saying, "Little girl," he pointed at his watch. Meaning, it's late and it won't do for little girls to be on their own.

They were the last ones there now. And as she turned to follow the crowd, which was making its way along the stalled vehicles, he stopped her. Catching her lightly by the edge of her sleeve. Tacitly, as if conspiring. Now that she had stopped with him, Shoshana felt that he had her consigned to his charge entirely. Under his patronage. Now she was his. All she had to do was to rely on him. For his part, his contribution or guarantees were in evidence by the quality of the skin of his arms, for instance. Fine, sand-colored, strewn with freckles and as if brave, very appropriate. Or his watch, his square wrist-watch, this too was sort of appropriate, and by that an attested proof. Also his vest, like a white gym shirt, peeping out of his open collar. And so forth.

When there were no more passengers, the UN soldier pulled her to him, moved her to his other side, and led her with him down a path—many paths were here—leading toward the city. All went over there, whereas they go on a way that is theirs only. That too was right. She joined him unquestioningly.

From time to time he stopped her, hugged and fondled her. Once, kneading and kneading her, he said into her hair, slowly, so she would understand, "You'll see. I'll be good," and kissed her on her hair.

The words astounded her. Another secret new thing is revealed: this is what the grown-up girls are privileged to. Canadian girls. Blissful girls. Mysterious, haughty, and deserving. Is it they who got them instructed, trained them. On evenings of paths through boughs in leaf, and lanterns hanging from branches amid twigs, foliage and tendrils. His chest in uniform, to which he held her when he spoke, belonged there too. His surprising chest, close, straight, all vacant and free; and how is this, a safe haven. But what had he said. As though she had been asked, in astonishment: "All these years, and you didn't know? Did you really not know that there is, there is a Mediterranean Sea in the east as well?" Of course. A sea, and a beach. And why the scary relief. "I didn't know," I answer, and already am not sure: did or didn't I. But what did he say? Did he propose to her? A little girl. Does it mean he intends to wait until she grows up? To take her with him, in the fullness of time, to Riffraffia? Run along, days, run. The only thing unclear yet is how, without ever knowing me, he recognized immediately that I am Shoshana more than any Shoshana, and that is why I should be singled out.

In the floral skirt too large for her, made to fit her waist with a safety pin. In the plaid blouse too short for her, the sleeve not quite hiding the slipping bra strap. The same Shoshana. And another Shoshana. Mysterious, deserving. Beautiful girls, beautiful women, like beautiful fans. Always, whenever she perceives the beautiful, it's a pleasure. As if she partakes of their beauty, from a distance. And now, there she is, a proper partner herself, deserving. And at a threshold.

Like then, in the dream? I stand in a large public square. Daylight fades. A very beautiful African lady, an ambassador's wife, stands spellbound before one of the flower beds in the square. A corner of tall, giant funnel-like arum lilies. Gaudy. Striped, streaked and spotted, in supernatural hues. "Harare-Horse," she says in a low voice, "Harare-Horse." I too fall under the spell. "Harare-Horse?" I ask. "Harare-Horse: the piles of sweets in our marketplaces." And someone comes to call her. To the airliner. To the night sky. Already studded with stars like jasmine flowers. Run along, days, run.

Holding her hand in his all the time, at the end of the path they came to a very tall wire-mesh fence. Looking new. They turned back. Over and over, at the end of every path, was the same fence. Impossible to walk along it. Tall thorns, impassably tangled. No choice, the fence has to be climbed.

He threw her bundle over to the other side. Helped her climb the fence. Then joined her. He swung his legs over to the other side and jumped down. But she, she couldn't get down! Putting up his arms to catch her, she let herself go, fell into his arms.

Having received her, why didn't he allow her to go, steadily enfolding all of her, tightly against him? And why has he changed so? Why don't they keep on walking? And why is she suddenly again in the panic of a wild animal—she tried to free herself. But how very strong men are, it dawned on her. And he breathes as if he has a fit of shivers. Why did he abruptly fling her to the ground. And isn't it wrong to force down a person's head backward into the dust. Wriggling to set herself free, half of her trapped between his legs, and he keeps her legs clasped together, her top half locked in one of his arms, he only sprawled on her, hard, in his clothes and shoes, that's all, with his other hand, forcing her face toward his, seeking her mouth, as if looking for closeness and consent. Himself, giving, offering, donating his only pair of lips, the ones that matter to him, it must be, of lips that seem so well cared for. Yet, at the same time, he cruelly prevents her from freeing herself, as if forbidding her to make a move, what sort of a plan is all this, and he is sighing and is so worked up. Suddenly he lets go. Everything isn't clear, isn't good. Haven't we been friends? And I, for his sake, I am no longer of Israel. I am of the UN.

Sitting beside her he asked, slowly, so she could make it out:
    "How old are you?"
    Shoshana showed with her fingers: thirteen.
    He laughed. Buried his face in her shoulder.
    "God," he said, laughing, "forgive me." Now he tapped the top of his head, meaning: he had thought. To explain, he stuck out his fist three times, opening and closing it, and added fingers, meaning: eighteen. He twisted his left hand, meaning: maybe. He stuck out his fist again and added with his right hand fingers, meaning: seventeen. Stuck out again and with one finger: sixteen. Thought it over, and only stuck out: fifteen. Shoshana was watching it all earnestly, patiently, trying to comprehend the sign language. But now he laughed, tapped her nose with his finger. Shoshana raised her head towards him, and he hugged her with one arm, drawing her to him. The private fair skin of his arms is nevertheless very appropriate. His chest in uniform, a safe haven.
    "Mosquitoes," he said. Of course, mosquitoes. He patted his back pocket, as if to check, brought out a crushed packet of foreign cigarettes. And matches, their heads a lighter color than their bodies, attached in rows to a small book. He lit a cigarette. He pointed to the cigarette smoke and clarified: "The mosquitoes," making with his palm as if he is dispersing them. Smoke drives mosquitoes away, she learned. He's a learned man.
    He kept on smoking. Looking ahead. Turned and offered her the cigarette. Shoshana took the cigarette. He laughed and corrected her hold of the cigarette, encouraging her to smoke. But Shoshana gave him the cigarette back. And so, making a move to lean on her forearm, she gave out a small cry: she had laid the inside of her wrist on a piece of glass, and cut herself. She searched, picked up the piece of glass, clear glass of a bottle neck. He took it from her hand, hurled it away. "Let me," he asked to see the cut.
    Shoshana hesitated. Put her hand behind her back, smiling at him shamefully. He resumed smoking, looking ahead. Shoshana brought out her hurt hand gingerly, sucked it covertly. He saw, laughed. Turning to her, he took the whole arm in his free hand. Could see nothing in the dark. Pressed her arm as if promising, and returned it to her. Having finished his cigarette, he stuck the butt in the ground. Rose up, almost without

using his hands, she noticed. Went to fetch her bag, slinging it effortlessly over his shoulder.

He came over and pulled her up. "Little girl," he said tapping his watch smiling.

Shoshana rose up, yielding. He said something, speaking slowly, so she could make it out. And she couldn't. He repeated it, again and again, and she couldn't make it out. "Never mind," he laughed lightly.

Now houses could be picked out clearly. Everything seemingly colorless. And the street lamps' lights over there going out all by themselves. Is it so that, in an ordered way, day after day, the sky is rinsed white by the steadily increasing pure light, without hindrance, simply and in silence day slips out of night? A neat, uncomplicated solution. So very right. All the earth is full of heaven's glory. No need for witnesses. But the eyes see. Raising his hand, the UN soldier wiped off dust from each of her eyebrows with his thumb. In her heart it was as if he had sworn her in.

They were walking between the road and the line of trees along it. To the northeast, among the trees and across the flat roofs of the houses, she saw a reddening mark overlaying a suggestion of blue. And the clouds of reverence. The dwarfed cylinders of the solar tanks and their sloping panels, the ladders and spindly matchsticks of the television aerials, all blacker than black, against the background of incandescent sea, gradually igniting. It is of the revelations made visible, an inheritance in the possession of the sworn in, the initiated ones, to whom the mysteries of the world are every-day affairs.

Earlier, when they were looking for the way, they heard a gang of boys passing far away. Probably trainees at the vocational school. One was strumming the guitar, others singing indistinctly. She remembered that it had been the last day of school. The UN soldier even did a "Bang-bang" in the direction of the sounds, as if holding a rifle in his hands. Now, in the light of daybreak, the boys were seen coming back. A reminiscence of colors: tight trousers, reminiscent of light blue; a belt, reminiscent of stripes of black and red; a shirt, reminiscent of yellow. Still singing, stopping to sniff each other's mouths, they were crossing the road, marching down towards the houses: the time is four o'clock in the morning, they'll wake up the whole street. "I have no idea what I wrote in the exam. But what I wrote was the right thing."

The UN soldier turned quickly, fixed her nimbly to one of the eucalyptus trees. Leaning against the tree with his arms held above her, he stood hiding her. She was astonished. By herself, it would never have occurred to her. She attempted to say something, but he put his hand promptly over her mouth, and she was breathing the fresh pungent tobacco smell on his fingers. Then he lowered his gaze to her, smiling amiably. UN-Soldier!—her heart clung to him. UN-Soldier!—thus she stood watching him all the time, her head tilted up to him, her eyes staring wide-open at him, his hand on her mouth. Until, when the boys were not there anymore, and bending his knees, he held her by the shoulders, jokingly attached his cheek to hers. Remembering, he rubbed his hand against his cheek to show the reddish stubble which had started growing, grimaced to make her laugh, and released her. "Little girl, good girl," he said.

UN-Soldier!—Shoshana plucked up courage, put out her hands, took hold of his waist, did not wish to walk on. Then joined him, continuing to walk.

Free of any dependence known to me. Unknown dependences have lent here character and grit, without which you are not a person—he strides as though without moving his head. Regards everything before him as though all, and this means all, is equal and the same. And speech is not a must for him, with or without it will do. This, you can tell, is his natural state. There's a kind of admirable quality here, like a sort of luxury. Serenity arising from a reservoir of strength—Shoshana tried to match her footsteps to his. And all the while his face, arms, uniform—all of his familiar self, is both old and new in the new light.

A truck, still nocturnal, its lights still on, passed them with a great clatter. Full of Arab laborers, stooping. On the other side of the road, the football pitch. The two goals, and the hard ground cleared of scrub, surrounded by a stand consisting of two rows of stadium benches, one above the other, like scaffolding. And a bus stop. The billboard. From here, whoever is not in the know couldn't have guessed that the dark rectangle on the billboard is the big illustrated poster of the Indian film. The girl has a red pea in her forehead, above her nose, and an amber necklace; the beads thick and squarish. While the man has an inclination towards a double chin.

The UN soldier scanned the highway, looking lost, passing his palm over his ruddy neck. Inspecting her as if he's uncertain of her ability to lead the way. Perhaps he thought she kept looking at him all the time with great interest, waiting for his resourcefulness. But she keeps looking on at him as she walks only because she cannot take her eyes off him: I could not imagine him with a mustache, for instance, or with sideburns, or a beard. Now, that he is need of a shave, I can. Or, here. Despite the peeling nose owing to this country's sun, here are the azure shards of ice-mountains. Shards from the faraway country where his home is, the keepsake embedded in his face instead of eyes. His face, permanently wearing the sudden foreignness that a woman of ours has on her face, for a fleeting moment, when she first puts on her earrings. Like a foreign perfume. A foreignness that has a touch of class. Like fastidious sinisterness. Sinisterness that is the product of your own imagination, the product of your own effacement. Or his colors, for example. The colors of another earth, different—as far as the eye can see, other fields, different. With different electricity pylons, vanishing into them. With different tractors and combine harvesters, looking minute when they pass through them. The men who drive them wear different overalls. Perhaps dungarees? Are their hats straw hats frayed at the edges? In the heat of the day in the field they all drink whisky out of jerry-cans.

Shoshana stopped. To shake a bit of gravel out of her shoe. She tried to indicate that she was stopping.

He halted, smiled comprehension.

Shoshana resumed walking. The shards of faraway, they come complete with an arrangement of golden lashes. The colors, all the colors of a different, freckled earth, in the land across the ice-mountains: if you break with your axe a little ice in the valley, you'd be able to draw out with a hook a fish that is about man-size. And look, lo and behold, they have arrived, fallen right here. Striding right here. With our very own football pitch behind us, and in front, our neighborhood. All the birds in the boughs of the eucalyptus trees welcome the future sunrise in concert, but I know: it is also in our honor, also in our honor. Is there anyone like you in the world, that like you is just right.

And here's the neighborhood.

A cat could be seen passing from a house roof to a shed roof. All the houses are deep in slumber. The end of the wooden cart is showing, laden high with watermelons. Of the first ones this season. But it seems, none of the Ezra brothers is asleep on the mattress over there. Even the hanging hurricane lamp is out of sight. In a slow death, devoid of any noble fortitude, the two abandoned houses crumble away. Cracks on the wall, the yards are thorn bushes. They say, among their foundations' low cement stilts there are snakes.

At the back fence of the house she stopped. Pointed at the house. But the UN soldier bent back his thumb and stuck it pointedly between his teeth, as he tilted his head backward, demonstrating to Shoshana, with eyes surveying around, that he wished to drink. She understood. Pointed at the tap beside the dustbin.

He rode the fence, then was over. The shoulder-line straight as a coat hanger, the big shirt hanging down his back like a scarecrow's, he turned on the tap. Leaned forward above it, legs apart, and drank. A cat, probably lurking there the whole time, suddenly made up its mind, leaped out of the trash bin and fled to the neighbors' yard, hid behind the old icebox that lies there, its side on the ground. The UN soldier wiped his mouth with his wrist.

He came. Stood before her. Lifted the bag, hung it over her shoulder laughing, saying something in his language. Shoshana did not leave. He looked at her. Shoshana did not leave. With his finger he moved his beret from the back of his head too far forward. From his forehead too far back. As if mimicking someone, good-naturedly. Shoshana did not leave.

He started rummaging in his pockets. Took out the Egged bus ticket. Examined the Egged bus ticket. Folded it correctly, and folded it up again. Put the ticket in her palm and closed her fingers over it, grouping them together into a brown fist enclosing the ticket. "Souvenir," he smiled. Shoshana did not leave. He stroked her cheek lightly, and left. Turned once, waved to her with his hand, and left.

When he could no longer be seen, Shoshana looked at the ticket. I don't know his name, it occurred to her now. He doesn't know mine, she looked at the ticket. Buried her face in the ticket. Then steadied the burden on her shoulder.

She entered home on tiptoe. Skirting the baby pram at the inside of the front door, she passed her sleeping brothers. Solemn, to the point of fear-inspiring, as if they are crucified. She changed in silence. And cautiously got into bed, together with her little sister, who was snuggled all curled up, and with her arms as if sheltering her head and face.

Her mother, her hair disheveled, the eternal red dressing-gown now thrown hastily over her nightgown, came in from the other room. Pushing aside the yellow striped curtain, she stood in the entrance: Shoshana looked her mother in the eye. Her mother looked Shoshana in the eye. Didn't say anything. Left. And Shoshana could hear how her mother was suppressing her sobs, over there, in her creaking bed in the other room. Then how the baby woke up. And fell asleep again.

She wiped one last dust-grain, or two, off her thin eyebrows, off the base of her neck. From behind her earlobe. Rosita is my name, I would have told him. A name to conjure with in the world. My birthright name, until it was changed into a Hebrew one by Teacher Hephzibah's decree. Little-Girl my name will now remain. I've indeed shrunk to a small-finger size, yet have grown simultaneously by an arm's length: surrounded by the familiar, that at the same time is different. As with the girl Alice, in the show they sent us. For the adoption ceremony, when they adopted us on "Love Thy Brother as Thyself Day." There were all those misfortunes. The loudspeakers went dead on us. Then the truck broke down. And the guests fated to wait were irate: they were given tea, said thank you, but hardly touched it. Teacher Hephzibah even organized us, the "Clowns" choir, to start a sing-song, for them to join in. None of them did. Zvi performed for them his "Dancing with the Lady Zvia" dance. In a lady's hat, a borrowed dress, a handbag and unshaven cheeks, he danced in ballroom style, embracing and stroking his imaginary partner. But some nervous ones whispered among themselves all the time: truck—tow vehicle—a disgrace. Who's interested in these ones? Go on Mama, go on washing the laundry. Maybe in two weeks time, maybe in three: over there, where all of them are good-looking, all are kind-hearted, all loving, in their dashing greenish fatigues, in the barracks yard, in front of the gray pillared arches, taking pleasure and in no hurry, all of them will be watering with buckets, scrubbing or combing, each his own pet horse. One by one they'll stand still, their work at a halt. They'll be restored into motion again as I'll go on, passing along the fence, set on searching. "Hail to my cousin / All ruddy and fair / Is he doing well / Our King David?": the last in the row he'll be. Doing his work. Lovingly. Unaware. There I shall stand. Shall wait. Until he sees me. Recognizes me. He will put down his brush. Will come out to me. Bring me in. And everyone will laugh, but be glad, the Regiment's Sweetheart. In two weeks' time perhaps, perhaps in three, on an Egged intercity bus. With a blue El Al bag. To my destiny.

"But my name is Little-Girl / The Regiment's Sweetheart / And UN-Soldier is thy name / I see the harbor lights ..." And maybe, even in another twenty years. And even if I see those for whom they'd give me up.

Those will be quite my look-alike. And they will be cheated on too. How will I know? for they will cheat on them with me!—she buried her face in the bus ticket. With a sinking heart. Sensing herself as one who is brought to court, and at the end the clerks hand him a formidable paper to sign. And he signs. Among other things, also with a touch of satisfaction. A satisfaction which is not unlike a destruction wish, at once alluring and frightening. But the chick hatching out of its egg in the incubator, the one with problems, what about the chick—she was beginning to doze off. Prevented herself from falling asleep: as if without any restraints, how is it, suddenly a person is compelled to draw close. Extends attention, tokens of good-will, of affection, pampers without reservations. Unafraid. Giving, getting exposed in front of a stranger. He ought to be fond of that stranger. Must be. Surely he needn't have anything to do with all this otherwise. Moreover, to do it willingly. Out of himself. He's fond, yes fond. And sinking into sleep, like one striving laboriously, who toward the end of his journey is shedding any superfluous load, this is what she was left with: a person wants. Wants to receive, to give. A person extends, attention, care, is fond, makes one take part, as if they are not strangers. And then he leaves. Does not come back. She fell asleep.

She heard her mother getting up, passing into the kitchen. Mixing the feed for the chickens. In the heat that already filled the world, like laundry air, was all the humdrum of the drudgery of the newborn day. Born without a mask: no blessing, no chance, no reconciliation, no change, no novelty. No stir in the leaves of the creeper; this calabash-like, gourd-like plant, it decks out only the yards of the poor, as she had observed long ago. Twining over there, raising its yellow flowers, clinging to the posts of the pergola in the yard, its end can be seen from her corner in the bed. She heard her mother attaching the hose to the kitchen tap, to fill the two large galvanized laundry tubs and the pail for the baby diapers outside, under the kitchen window. The way she had told us once. Told us of a story that had taken place in their homeland. A story about a brother who strangled his adulterous sister and threw her body into a well. "Blessed are the hands," his mother had blessed him—she told us full of sacred awe.

But me, I am never more of this place. Ever more of the UN.

And the backlash swept her over. Like a forgotten melody. The burst of freshness of a power that draws one back, and anguish, akin to regrets, over that which is massacred here at your feet each time anew and gets trampled, you know not what it is. They recapture that which is extinct and by now is nothing but tenderness, all the tenderness. Yet in it are preserved all its lost flavor, fully retained, and its true colors—with a punch that is like a fist-blow to the jaw. In the great wide world only this time, only for me, only in my case—won't I, please—some day find you again.

Note

1. This poem appears as an epigraph in the original Hebrew edition of "Bridal Veil," including the one reprinted in the appendix to this volume (see A25). It is omitted in the Jones translation but is restored here for the reader's reference.

Nancy E. Berg

AMALIA KAHANA-CARMON'S TRIPTYCH *Magnetic Fields* opens with her powerful story "Bridal Veil." On the surface, it is a portrait of a naive and innocent young girl, a lyrical coming-of-age story, a tale of seduction. The plot follows Shoshana, a thirteen-year-old girl traveling home in a bus with her father's laundry. The UN soldier who sits next to her takes advantage of her innocence. When the passengers are forced to disembark at the entrance to the city, the soldier takes charge of Shoshana, tries to force himself on her in an abandoned field, and eventually parts from her at the entrance of her home at daybreak. The shallow plot belies a deeper structure of connections and disconnections. The real story exists beneath the surface, in the subtleties of language. The narrative itself is fractured yet cohesive, from the sentential level, where many phrases stand as sentence fragments in an almost telegraphic style, to the szujet as a whole. Any more linear narrative would be a lie. It is only by examining the language of the story—repeated words, metaphors, recurring patterns, and echoes of other works—that the richness of the story is revealed.

The fractured nature of the narrative reflects the ruptures within the protagonist herself. The greatest disjuncture is perhaps the break between now and then, but other fissures include that of foreignness (us/them, issues of belonging and identity, and alienation from her parents).

On the other hand, the connectedness of the story exists from the level of single lexical items up through patterns and images. Parts of the story that seem unrelated illuminate other parts through the repetition of a specific word, phrase, or image imbuing the story with echoes and shadows.

The protagonist's character is revealed in the texture of the language itself. Her central trait—as with other characters created by the same author—is her passivity, her self-effacement. The language of the narrative contributes to her characterization in the way that pointillism paints a scene. Her most assertive moment comes when she is at her most passive. Simply by analyzing parts of speech, her personality is revealed.

There are fewer verbs than nouns in Amalia Kahana-Carmon's style, and many of the verbs associated with Shoshana reinforce the reader's sense of her passivity. We see this from the very beginning, when her father remarks that one of the UN soldiers looks like Anthony Perkins, and Shoshana thinks—but does not say—that another one looks more so. Shoshana's verbs and verbal phrases are of inaction ("waited," "went out to wait," "sat like a statue,"), inwardly directed ("thought," "wondered," "found herself," "recalled," "smiled inside"); and rendered inactive by negation ("didn't say," "didn't think," "didn't know," "didn't get up and didn't move to another seat," "didn't do anything," "didn't dare look his way"). Some verbs are diminished by adverbs, actual and implied ("peeped," "looked furtively," "peeped at him secretly," "sucked in secret," "entered her house on tiptoes"), and some are minimized by multiple verb chains ("went out to wait," "started to try to stand," "wanted to try to say something," "tried to remember").

Additionally, many of the verbs of the UN soldier's agency include Shoshana as a direct object—without the accusative marker *et*—as if his verbs have absorbed her ("stopped her," "caught her," "pulled her," "passed her to his other side," "led her," "fondled her," "kissed her"). In this, as elsewhere, the soldier appears to take the father's place. For example, earlier in the narrative Shoshana worried that her father might not find her.

The verbs, scant as they are, serve as keys to the story. The verb *'oleh* (to go up) makes an interesting link between the deaf-mute children in the park and the UN soldiers boarding the bus, thus comparing the soldiers to the deaf-mute children—plundering, sinister, and taking someone else's rightful place. ("The mute children invaded the playground, swarming over every seat . . . like pirates, [they] snatched at the vacated seats.") These children echo the dirty snub-nosed children of the poem proem.[1] So, too, the deaf-mute children are alien to the children from the "good families," who are properly chaperoned by their nannies. They use a different language, a language of grunts and gestures, not unlike the language Shoshana and her soldier use, because "words do not suffice."

The recurrence of the verb *'over* (pass by or cross over) adds to the sense that life is passing Shoshana by, especially life at night. In the park, the Ashkenazi man with the shabby briefcase passes by her, music from a moving car passes by her, and while she is waiting outside the park, other people and sounds pass by her. So, too, the tall woman crosses in front of the bus, the UN soldier crosses over and sits next to her, and—in *hiphiel* (the transitive form)—the UN soldier moves his arm to encompass her, and passes her to his other side. In contrast, Shoshana does not cross to another seat after the soldier makes a pass at her. The uses of this verb suggest passivity, change, and abandonment.

Even more so, the repetition of verbs of leaving (*yarad, halakh, nifrad*) reinforces this last sense. The father, impatient and irritable, leaves abruptly. The harbor lights of the father's song tell the woman in the song that her lover has left. When the bus is stopped at the site of the accident, a veteran bus-company employee alights, states the situation, and leaves (165, A30). The bus driver "translates [the announcement] into English. He also left." (165, A30). They abandon Shoshana to her fate, to the "protection" of the UN soldier. The soldier himself does not leave until later. At the back fence of her house, "he stroked her cheek lightly, and left [*vehalakh*]. Turned once, waved to her with his hand, and left [*vehalakh*]" (172, A35). Again this contrasts with Shoshana's actions. In the paragraph preceding the soldier's departure, it is stated three times: "Shoshana didn't leave" (172, A35).

In a story climaxing in a situation that is clearly "inappropriate," it is telling that the word *nakhon* (translated by Raya and Nimrod Jones as "appropriate") is used so repeatedly. In a conversation overheard on the bus in which a young Mizrachi argues for a more significant political role, his words draw the connection between strength or power and correctness: "more important than this, power. Correct. Correct." Later in the story, as Shoshana gets to know her soldier, she describes parts of him as "correct": his fair skin, his watch, his uniformed chest (*ken bitaḥon*, "a safe haven," 168, A31) before and after her discovery of his strength. On one level, the connection is made between strength or power and correctness or appropriateness; on another, the equation is clearly ironic. Within the cultural milieu described by the story, the UN soldier's behavior is terribly "inappropriate"; so, too, is Shoshana's reaction.

Even more revealing is the repetition of the word *ʿatah* (now), occasionally juxtaposed with *paʿam* or *kodem* (then). The fracture is between now and then, divided by night and Shoshana's discovery of life at night, and the attempted rape. The division fractures her identity and belonging, shifting her affection from her home to the UN.

Different kinds of connections are also made by the striking metaphors that make connections between disparate entities. The tropes of personification, beastification, and even vegefication create something organic. There is a process of transfer or projection from one life form to another. The UN soldiers are compared to guavas:

They were all similar, but each in his own way. Like guavas. They all taste good, but each tastes also slightly different, giving its own interpretation of the taste of the guava (161, A27).

Shoshana's UN solder strides without moving his head, contrasting with the trees along the road "nodding like people." Houses are in slumber. The soldier lifts Shoshana "like a parcel." Conversely, the chicks from her school reader—with their "need to imprint,"—are humanlike. The personification implies a reverse beastification: Shoshana is chicklike, needing to imprint on the young man. When she feels trapped—first on the bus when she discovers him sitting closer to her than she realized, and then when he catches her over the fence and doesn't let her go—she feels the "blind panic of a wild animal" and she wriggles to get away from him. While she is the one likened to the wild animal, he is the panting beast.

Metaphors usually find the similar in the dissimilar. Specific metaphors here focus on the dissimilar, on the quality of foreignness. The UN soldiers as a group are different, as if "made of drier material." Shoshana's soldier, in particular, is different, and much of his difference is described in colors. His eyes are described as bluish shards of icy mountains from his homeland, his coloring is foreign, and Shoshana imagines even the earth of his foreign land is a different color, worked with different tractors driven by farmers in different-looking overalls. His pale skin and red hair contrast with Shoshana's brown hand curling around the ticket-stub souvenir.

Shoshana, however, has her own foreignness. Her outsider status extends beyond the family, but it starts there. Like the picture painted by Wieseltier's poem,[2] she is virtually estranged from her parents. Her father lives in another city, leaves her to wait in a dark park for hours, and "abandons" her to the UN soldier. Indeed, the UN soldier at the center of this story takes over Shoshana's father's place as soon as he leaves the bus. (When the girl trips—an inadvertent action—she falls over the soldier's knee in a grotesque tableau of a father-daughter interaction. Tellingly, she trips when the father "reasserts himself" metonymically through the strap of the bag holding his dirty laundry.) Her mother looks at her without words. There seems to be a great undercurrent of animosity or competition between the mother and daughter for the father—the traveler. Shoshana looks at the image of what she will become (in the eternal dressing gown, hair disheveled, tired, burdened) and hates what she sees (just as her mother sees herself reflected in her daughter and is fearful of this similarity).

Shoshana is estranged from the outside as well. The lights at the beginning of the story are from other people's homes, "strangers' homes" in another strange city. "And the parallel slats of the venetian blinds were turned slightly inward, their backs inside and their faces toward the outside, enough to close off." She is left on the outside.

The memory of "adoption day" also points to her outsider status—her foreign name that needs changing, the attitude of the people there to "adopt" her and the other immigrants, the truck that breaks down (in contrast to the functioning truck filled with Arab workers that drives by). "Surrounded by the familiar, that at the same time is different." Her neighborhood contains elements of foreignness—the new fence, the imported Arab workers, the Indian movie poster, the presence of the UN soldier himself. A marvelous cascade of metaphors describes him:

> His face, permanently wearing the sudden foreignness that a woman of ours wears on her face, for a moment, the first moment she puts on her earrings. Like a foreign perfume. A foreignness that has a touch of class. Like fastidious sinisterness. Sinisterness that is the product of your own imagination, the product of your own effacement.

Shoshana's imagination is fertile ground for the wonderful metaphors—and the source for her picture of her future reunion with the UN soldier. (This, despite the clear pattern of men leaving their women: from the sailor in the French song, to her father who lives in another city, the husband of the woman on the bus, the bus-company employees, and the UN soldier who places his cheek next to hers, echoing the proposition of the soldier in Tiberias.) Her effacement is what allows this story to happen. Her effacement is her story.

Allowing herself to feel the soldier's "protection" shatters her, bewilders her, pleases her. She gives herself up completely to him; the physical "surrender" seems much less significant than her inner surrender. "And I, for his sake, am no longer of Israel. I am of the UN," she declares, later accepting his appellation of her as her name: "Little-Girl will be my name now."

The sinister lies under the surface. Even the attempted rape—if that is what it is—is brief and not traumatic, and yet that makes it somehow more threatening. Similarly, there is something vaguely sordid about the men in this story: the predatory UN soldier, the shifty man lurking in the children's playground, the father represented by his dirty linens. The real divide between now and then—between Shoshana's state of innocence and her state of knowing—seems to be her discovery of the night. The significance of the night is reinforced by the play between light and dark in the narrative.

The first lights we encounter are those mentioned above of the apartment houses in the strange city where Shoshana meets her father—"strangers' homes"—emphasizing her lack of belonging. They also contrast with her own home, which is dark when she returns from her adventure.

As she waits for her father in the park, night falls and she stands under a street lamp. Street lamps are turned off at the end of her night. The story is bracketed by the fading daylight right before her discovery of "the ordinariness of night" and the breaking dawn ("a reddening mark overlaying a suggestion of blue") right after her other, more sinister, discovery.

On the bus, the UN soldier stops talking when the lights go out and moves closer to Shoshana. He moves away from her when the lights are turned back on, foreshadowing his leaving her when day comes. Similarly, the harbor lights of the song signal abandonment (the same song into which she daringly inserts herself before falling asleep). Lights mean foreignness, alienation, and abandonment.

Only in the dark do Shoshana and her soldier come close to communicating—though mostly through gestures, and still riddled with incomplete interactions: he didn't understand," "she didn't understand," "never mind," "she wanted to try to say." Shoshana is left without clear comprehension. The rape scene is even less understood, narrated from Shoshana's perspective through a series of questions.

> Having received her, why didn't he allow her to go, steadily enfolding all of her, tightly against him? And why has he changed so? Why don't they keep on walking? And why is she suddenly again in the panic of a wild animal— she tried to free herself. But how very strong men are, it dawned on her. And he breathes as if he has a fit of shivers. Why did he abruptly fling her to the ground. And isn't it wrong to force a person's head backward into the dust.[3]

The soldier leaves her with his ticket stub as a souvenir. It is little more than trash, something used up and no longer of value, and it duplicates what she already has. A symbol of parting or of travel, the ticket stub has also brought them together, if only for a moment.

This is not a story of sexual initiation or education. It fits uneasily with the plot of seduction. Shoshana's legs stay clenched tightly together; the soldier remains fully clothed. But the idea of sexual initiation is threaded throughout the story. The woman on the bus who tells of her ex-husband's infidelities, and even more so, the man with the rooster eye, foreshadow a sexual encounter. The man could easily be interpreted as a sexual predator, he "went in and out of the park, in and out"; his belt buckle—grooved—is more prominent than his face; and his eye, like a rooster's, is fixed on the young girl. So, too, after the puzzling incident in the field, when the soldier and young girl are intertwined on the ground, wriggling and panting, he lights a cigarette, shorthand for postcoital repose. Shoshana, for her part, cuts her hand on a piece of glass in the grass. Although her bleeding is out of sync—everything in this interaction is just a bit off kilter—it resonates with the idea of rape or at least loss of virginity. The symbolic moment of breaking the hymen is gestured at but does not happen, like the rape itself. Also her change of identity and affiliation implies that he has taken possession of her, made her his own. The incident neither destroys her nor leaves her wholly the same. Ultimately, she does not understand what has happened or why, so it is hardly a story of sexual awakening and initiation. Shoshana remains naive. The story begins with her waiting at the *gan ye-ladim* (children's playground) and ends with her, dream-singing "My name is Little-Girl" and dreaming of finding her UN soldier, as if part of the cinematic world that hovers in the background.

This work echoes with Hebrew literary intertextuality. Shoshana cutting her hand calls to mind the scene in Amos Oz's "Navadim vetsef˓a" (Nomads and viper)[4]—and thus the story as a whole—in which the protagonist Geula cuts herself on broken glass. Geula is a repressed single woman on a kibbutz who is both attracted to and repulsed by a young Bedouin man. The young Arab represents a freedom to Geula no less enticing than the freedom and escape that the UN soldier seems to offer Shoshana. (In both stories, the men are type characters; neither is named.) In an ambiguous ending, Geula seems to substitute a rape fantasy for the reality of a snake-bite. Although much older, she seems as naive, inexperienced, and intrigued as Shoshana. Sex pulsates throughout the narrative but is never realized. The motif of cutting oneself on glass both calls up and distances from sexual initiation, thus playing with the interface of knowledge and innocence.

Some of the details in writing also reflect an almost Agnonesque sensibility. Snatches of overheard conversations and glimpses of other people seen as shadow images work both to establish the realia of life and to foreshadow later events or parallel other characters. So, too, the narrative seemingly emphasizes the trivial and downplays the principal, as if looking through the wrong end of a telescope. Characters appear to mirror or complete each other. Scenes in which not much "happens" are played out fully. These elements are most prominent in Agnon's stories about male-female relationships and the difficulty of communication between men and women, such as in "Panim aherot" (Another face).[5]

In Dahlia Ravikovitch's short story "Ihur katan" (A slight delay),[6] a young woman in the army turns down an officer's advances despite her inexperience and her interest. Her naïveté and strength are similar to Shoshana's. The character is less passive than Shoshana but not necessarily more sympathetic.

Amalia Kahana-Carmon's own story "Ne'ima Sasson kotevet shirim" (Ne'ima Sasson writes poetry)[7] parallels the story under discussion. In both, the protagonist is a young woman on the threshold of maturity. The eponymous Ne'ima Sasson engages in a delicate dance with her teacher (from an Orthodox girls' school) negotiating an impossible relationship that ends without consummation. As in the story under discussion, "nothing" really happens, and the real story is in the language.

In none of these stories do the parents play a central role. The girl is on her own. Only in "Bridal Veil" are the parents present at all, the father at the very beginning of the narrative, the mother at the end. Neither gains the reader's sympathy. The father is impatient and irritable, the mother disheveled and despairing.

"Bridal Veil" is firmly a part of the modern Hebrew literary fabric. The figure of a young woman and her sexual exploration is served well with delicate treatment and is a subject of interest, even—especially—in a literature once thought of as a literature of fathers and sons. This is a story about dumbness and noncommunication, reflected by the fragmented narrative style. The fact that Shoshana and her UN soldier cannot communicate is paradoxically at the heart of what is said in this story.

The story defies and denies expectations of genre. It does not belong to the traditional narratives of seduction, assertion, or self-discovery. Shoshana remains curiously detached and unaware, manipulated by those around her, and living in a fantasy. The sexual initiation that is promised does not actually happen; the young girl who did not understand the soldier's joke in her father's story (" 'You, papa?' 'Perhaps I am and I don't know it.' ") still does not understand. She has learned only about the ordinariness of night. A forsaken snub-nosed child.

Notes

I am grateful to Rebecca Copeland, Dick Davis, Robert Hegel, and the participants of "Reading Israel in America" for their comments.

1. "God's Fire on Children," Meir Wieseltier. In this volume, see pp. 158–59 and A25.

2. Compare to Philip Larkin's oft-cited "This Be the Verse."

3. The implication is that the soldier reaches his climax without even undressing and therefore does not need to continue. Even without penetration, he is still forcing the young girl to cater to his sexual needs.

4. Amos Oz, *Artsot hatan* (Lands of the jackals) (Tel Aviv: Masada, 1965).

5. S. Y. Agnon, "Panim aherot" (Another face), *Davar*, 12 December 1933.

6. Dahlia Ravikovitch, *Mavet bamishpahah* (Death in the family) (Tel Aviv: Am Oved, 1976).

7. Amalia Kahana-Carmon, *Bekfifah ahat* (Under one roof) (Tel Aviv: Hakibutz Hameuchad, 1996).

Gilead Morahg

THE MEANING OF Amalia Kahana-Carmon's elegantly crafted story "Bridal Veil" does not emanate so much from the events of which it tells as from the manner in which it is told. It emerges from the way in which the narrative voice selects and arranges the tapestry of sights, voices, memories, and thoughts that constitute the story. A key element in this design is the inner voice in which Shoshana, the story's thirteen-year-old protagonist, reacts to events she encounters, seeks to explain them to herself, and struggles to relate them to her life. Equally important is the narrator's practice of placing semantic markers at key junctures of the design in order to signal its thematic directions.

The story opens on an Egged bus. Shoshana and her father, who accompanied her to the station but will not join her on the trip back home, are sitting in the bus waiting for it to depart. Earlier that day, Shoshana spent long hours waiting for her father in the children's section of the public park. From the bright noon hours into the encroaching night she had waited, observing sights, experiencing emotions, and thinking thoughts that would lead her to the first of that night's discoveries:

> All along, it was revealed to her, there had been a mistake. She hadn't really thought about it, but she must have assumed that life outside the house came to an end when you went to sleep, after supper. Except on special occasions. But here's something new, hidden: there's the ordinary life of day. And there's the ordinary life of night. And it's different. At night everything is different: houses, people, thoughts.[1]

As her journey progresses, Shoshana will discover much more that is new and hidden in the ordinary life of the night. But in the meantime, the bus isn't moving. Shoshana's father grumbles, impatient to send his daughter on her way so that he can get back to his.

Additional passengers get on the bus. First, a group of UN soldiers, one of whom will play an important part in Shoshana's experiences of the night. Then a man, who—like all the other figures who accompany her on this nocturnal journey, except the soldier—will have no contact with Shoshana or any awareness of her existence. Yet, like several others, this man creates an experience, stirs a memory, and evokes a thought that is integral to the story and becomes part of the pattern that creates its meaning: "A man came in, carrying a tall cardboard box. On one side, in smeared red letters: 'Parts—Poultry Incubators.' He blocked the exit door with it" (161; A27). This sight, like many of the story's other sights and sounds, elicits a revelatory response. Observing the man with the cardboard box,

> Shoshana was reminded of the story "Excerpt" that she read in her schoolbook, *Paths* (part 4). A chick hatches from its egg in an incubator. To whom will it direct the natural human desire for attachment? Will it turn to the electric incubator, the book said, or perhaps to the poultry farmer who is raising it in order to send it to the slaughterer, to whom? The natural human desire for attachment, it said there. The human desire of that which is not human. (161; A27)

Since lexical repetition is a common means of literary signification, attention should be paid to the context in which the motif of the chick hatching in the incubator recurs toward the story's end. When Shoshana finally gets back home and curls up in bed, exhilarated, agitated, confused, and fatigued from her experiences that night, the predicament of the baby chick resurfaces again.[2] As she is about to fall asleep, Shoshana suddenly thinks: "But that chick hatching from its egg in the incubator, the one with the problem. What about that chick—she began to doze off" (174; A36). But she fights sleep off, and her ensuing thoughts constitute an answer that relates Shoshana's character to the image of the chick hatching from its egg in the incubator and connects the entire story to "the natural human desire for attachment":

> What about that chick—she began to doze off. She prevented herself from falling asleep: as if without inhibitions, how is it, suddenly a person is impelled to get close. Gives attention, signs of fondness and goodwill, becomes tender. Unafraid. Gives. Opens himself to a stranger. He must be fond of that stranger. Otherwise why bother with all that? After all, of his own free will. Of himself. From him. Fond, yes, fond. And sinking onto sleep like a long-striving person who, toward journey's end, casts off all unnecessary baggage, this is what is left: A person wants. Wants to receive, to give. A person bestows, adores, shares, not like strangers. Then leaves. Does not return. She fell asleep. (174; A36)

This insight into the nature of the need to share the self with another is the essence of the lesson that was learned from the experiences of the night in which Shoshana hatched like a chick from the shell of her childhood and took a crucial step toward her emotional world as an adult.

One of the critical questions posed by this story concerns the degree of irony with which it presents Shoshana's inner world. The story is not designed to create ironic distance between the narrating voice and the young protagonist.[3] On the contrary, it is designed to put this voice in the service of creating a close empathic proximity to the rhythms of Shoshana's changing life. I read this story as a literary examination and an ideological exploration of the awakening of the natural human desire for attachment to another, and of the first steps toward integrating this emergent emotion into a personality that is just beginning to recognize its own self and to forge its own way.

"Bridal Veil" constitutes a highly nuanced contemplation of the sources from which a young girl constructs the story of her identity and of the manner in which reality and fantasy, frustration and aspiration, innocence and intelligence, converge in the dynamic through which a personality begins to define itself and to form an independent view of the world and of her place within it. In many ways, it is a story about the ability of people, even at an early age, to employ fortuitous events as a means of understanding themselves and their relations to others. The saliency of this ability is emphasized by the fact that Shoshana must construct the story of her identity entirely on her own. It is not by chance that the image that defines her is of a chick hatching from its egg in an incubator. The physical orphanhood of the baby chick that is born into an anonymous and arbitrary world suggests the spiritual orphanhood of Shoshana, who cannot learn a thing about the natural human desire for attachment from her parents.

The harsh indifference of Shoshana's father and mother to the inner world and outward needs of their daughter relates this story to the poem by Meir Wieseltier that serves as its epigraph. It suggests a concern with a more universal sense of orphanhood—the internal bereavement of children deprived of love by their parents and forced to rely on their own meager resources in their quest for a good way to satisfy this natural human need that is so inhumanly denied them by those who were supposed to provide for it. Shoshana's father and mother appear to be among those parents whom Wieseltier's poem describes as "dirty, ugly, mothers, / Stupid fathers with nothing of God's wisdom. / . . . corpse fathers. / Dirt fathers, garbage fathers, stone fathers." There is no redemption in such parents and no capacity for guidance. This is why Wieseltier concludes his poem with an appeal to every miserable dirty child with dripping nose to turn to other sources that he calls "God the fire" and "angels lovely seraphim":

> Angels will roll up robes of glory, give first aid to the world.
> To you, too, dirty child, an excellent cookie.
> Flowers will unfold, corpse father won't see the beauty.
> Ugly mother will not look, she'll only curse, mother.
> Angels will praise God, shofars will cry ah-ha.

Shoshana's father shows little regard for his daughter. He is very late in coming to pick her up, making her wait for hours in the children's section of a darkening public park. After he finally arrives and takes her to the movies, he is anxious to send her off again. There is no conversation or any other evidence of a connection between them. Her mother is a miserable, bitter woman whose attitude toward her daughter's awakening emotional world is summed up, according to Shoshana, in a story the mother once told her children: "A story that took place in the country from which they came. A story about a brother who strangled a fornicating sister and threw her body into a well. 'Blessed are the hands,' his mother praised him—she told us in awe" (203; A36).

Thus, when Shoshana hatches from her childhood shell, leaves the children's section on her own accord, and takes her first uncertain steps into the unfamiliar night world of adulthood, she is truly a defenseless innocent, eager to attach herself to the first person who offers a measure of recognition and warmth—much like that baby chick that is ready to direct the natural human desire for attachment to the poultry farmer who is raising it for the slaughter. For Shoshana, this person is the UN soldier who takes the seat beside her, finds a way to put his arm around her, and takes advantage of the circumstances that force them to leave the bus in order to initiate more intimate physical contact. Today, such a narrative paradigm almost inevitably elicits the culturally conditioned expectation that this will be yet another story of sexual aggression and physical violation. One of the satisfying surprises offered by "Bridal Veil" is that this is not the case.

Despite the anxious moments experienced by the girl, and by the reader, this is not a story about callousness, domination, and defilement. It is, rather, about a very human dynamic of fumbling exploration and dawning realization that leads to the discovery of surprising new resources of the self and to useful insights into how that self might best proceed in life.

There are many textual indications that Shoshana's encounter with the soldier is the metaphoric "excellent cookie" offered to a miserable child in one of those rare moments of grace in which, according to Wieseltier, "Angels will roll up robes of glory, give first aid to the world." At such a moment, he writes, "Flowers will unfold, . . . Angels will praise God, shofars will cry ah-ha." This is the moment in which Shoshana experiences an understanding of the place of the natural human desire for attachment within her own emerging sense of self.

The experience of a strong emotional connection of the self to another informs "Bridal Veil" with little regard for the identity and personality of this other. This is not a story of love between two people. It is, rather, a story of the emergence of the emotion of love and of the initial measure of its value within a single individual. It is also about the causal connection between the emotion of love experienced by the individual self and the recognition of the uniqueness and value of this self by another. Ultimately, it is about the importance of reaching for an understanding of the value and the province of the natural desire for attachment to another in the life of the individual. The story captures the moment in which this need takes specific emotional shape within Shoshana, sparked not by the gradual increase in physical contact between her and the soldier, but by the act with which he surprises Shoshana—who, "from the very beginning, being the eldest daughter, always had to fend for herself completely by herself": he takes her bus tickets from her hand and presents them, together with his own, to the conductor (164; A29).

It is at the precise point of this modest gesture that the narrating voice places one of the semantic markers that provide thematic guidance. Here is the entire passage, with the marker toward its end:

> She saw: the UN soldier smiled at her. As if asking permission. And before she could understand what he wanted, he took her tickets from her hand. Putting them together with his own, completely together, he presented them to the conductor.
>
> She, who from the very beginning, being the eldest daughter, always had to fend for herself completely by herself—*what is this that, piercing, now passed in her through the phloem, penetrated the parenchyma, making oleoresin flow.* She felt shattered, knowing nothing. (164; A29. Italics added)

The italicized sentence is equally obscure in the Hebrew original: *mahu asher poleah, ʿavar bah ʿatah et hashifa, ḥadar lakakai, veshotet haktaf.* The deliberately abstruse terms constitute a directive for the reader to pause, to ponder, and to seek out the precise meaning of this moment. For me, the only way to do this was to consult the dictionary, where I found that phloem (*shifa*) is the fibrous tissue that protects the inside of a plant's stem; parenchyma (*kakai*) is the soft marrow of cells that is the fundamental tissue of a plant's stem; and oleoresin (*ktaf*), also known as balsam, is a fragrant resin exuded from certain trees, especially trees of the genus *Commiphora*, used in antiquity for medicinal purposes and for incense.[4]

There is something audacious, and perhaps presumptuous, in a move that assumes that the reader will bother to consult a dictionary at this, or any other, narrative juncture. But the reward for such effort is a clear understanding that what is occurring here is the emergence of an unfamiliar emotion that pierces to the core of the organism and generates joy, healing, and a numinous fragrance. Given this understanding, I read "Bridal Veil" as an exploration of the place, nature, and significance of this emotion in the future life of a girl on the verge of adulthood; as an attempt to answer the question, "What is this that, piercing, now passed in her through the phloem, penetrated the parenchyma, making oleoresin flow." The scope of this discussion does not allow for a detailed examination of the process of Shoshana's vacillation between escapist juvenile fantasies and flashes of emotional and existential insight through which the answer to this question is pursued. But a consideration of a few key narrative junctures may serve to define the direction of this quest and to indicate its outcome.

One of these junctures is the difficult moment in which the soldier grabs Shoshana and imposes himself upon her. Here, in the midst of the frantic jumble of painfully innocent questions that flood her mind, a profoundly different question emerges and begins to transform her innocence into a more useful understanding of her experience. Why, why, why, she asks, after jumping off a fence and into the soldier's helpfully extended hands:

> Why didn't he let her go, clasping all of her to him like this. And why has he changed all of a sudden. And why aren't we continuing on our way. And why suddenly like a terrified animal again—she tried to free herself. But men are so strong, she discovered. . . . Why did he throw her so rudely on the ground. Isn't it wrong to push a person's head back like this, into the dirt. (167; A31)

And then, as he lies heavily upon her, forcing her face to his, seeking her lips, she begins to find some answers and arrives at the most important question of all:

Struggling to free herself, half of her trapped between his legs that were pressing her legs tightly together, her upper half locked in one of his arms. He just lay on her, hard, in his clothes and his shoes, that is all, and with his other hand he twisted her face toward his, seeking her mouth, as if seeking closeness and compassion. Himself, giving, offering, bestowing his own and only pair of lips, *does he care, he must*. (167–68; A32. Italics added)[5]

It is on this question, "Does he care?" and on the answer that she immediately provides, "He must," that the narrative turns. This internal exchange is not presented as a pitiful attempt at self-delusion but as a pivotal perception of human truth. Shoshana is right. This soldier does care. Until this moment, she had done nothing to discourage his cautious advances, although she was not unaware of their implications. On a previous bus trip, when Shoshana suspected that the nice young man seated beside her was deliberately touching the back of her neck, she hastened to move to another seat, her heart beating in terror. "But now, unlike then, there could be no question about it. The UN soldier sitting beside her was definitely, definitely, pressing his elbow against her arm. This time she did not get up and did not move to another seat. She sat still as a statue. And did not do a thing. Staring out the window" (163; A28). Shoshana is clearly prepared to let this experience develop.

When the soldier tries to take her hand, she seems to understand more than she is willing to admit to herself, thinking, "What does he want. Yes, I know what. But it's not clear what he's asking now, right now, in this matter. And what he expects from me. It's hard to know. Especially when you're so confused" (163; A29). And when he puts his arm around her for the first time, she can only wonder, "Where does he get the courage?" (163; A29). But the soldier's courage is limited. When the bus stops at a station and the lights come up again, he quickly pulls away and Shoshana thinks, "I'm done for. . . . There's no way back: I know what he'll think about me now" (164; A29). But when the lights go down and he puts his arm around her again, she lets him. (164; A30). Thus, the narrative makes it very clear that the young soldier had every reason to believe that this girl "in the floral skirt . . . clinched to her waist with a safety pin, and the checkered blouse that was too short for her, the sleeve barely covering the slipping bra strap," (167; A31) was older than she really was and was knowingly responding to his advances. But now, sensing his mistake, he draws back, verifies her age, laughs in embarrassment, and apologizes. And when he hugs her again, drawing her close to him, Shoshana recognizes that this is not a prelude to sexual violence but a gesture of comfort and protection:

"The private skin of his pale arms was right after all, and his uniformed chest—a safe haven" (168; A32).

The narrative precludes the possibility of reading Shoshana's reactions as wishful delusions of a perilously innocent girl, through the semantics of the ideational context in which it places another gesture by the soldier. As the night draws toward morning and the two of them approach Shoshana's neighborhood, the narrative voice deploys the image of light emerging from darkness in order to point toward a possible solution to all the confusion. This is a solution that expunges Shoshana's initial perception of a radical distinction between the daytime world and the nighttime world, and replaces it with a more harmonious vision of a world in which the light flows naturally out of the night:

> Now the houses could already be seen clearly. Everything as if without color. And the streetlights turning off on their own. And thus, as always, day after day, the skies are washed clean with brightening light, simply and quietly the day slips forth from the night. A correct and uncomplicated solution, a solution that embraces the world. It has no need for witnesses. But the eyes do see. Raising his hand, the UN soldier wiped dirt off her eyebrows with his thumb. To her, in her heart, this was as if he had sworn her in. (169; A33)

Some of the mystical overtones here are still not completely clear to me. But it seems that the key to the universal solution mentioned here is to be found in the gentle gesture with which the soldier brushes the dirt from Shoshana's face. To amplify the sense of initiation that is generated by this simple act, the narrative voice deploys a cluster of images that ascend from the narrow streets of the neighborhood to the very verge of mystery: "They were walking between the road and the trees alongside it. And in the northeast, through the trees and beyond the flat roofs, she saw a trace of red. Above a trace of blue. And the clouds of glory." Against this backdrop, the black skyline of the shabby neighborhood is etched "as if on the background of an illuminated sea, increasingly incandescent. Of the revelations known only to the initiates, who have been brought into the secret circle. For them the mysteries of the world are commonplace events" (169; A33).

The connection between Shoshana's sense that the soldier had sworn her in and "the revelations known only to the initiates, who have been brought into the secret circle," and for whom "the mysteries of the world are commonplace events," is a critical key to understanding this story. By means of this connection, the narrative casts the moment in which the soldier wipes the dirt from Shoshana's face as a moment of epiphany in which a vital hidden truth is revealed to her; as a moment in which the soul cries, Ah-ha. The fact that this epiphany is sparked by the soldier's gentle gesture points to the substance of the secret that was revealed to Shoshana: that the natural desire for attachment need not be arbitrary, that its correct fulfillment is to be found in mutual recognition of the humanity, vulnerability, uniqueness, and dignity of the other.

This reading is reinforced by the episode in which the soldier covers Shoshana with his body a second time. Now, however, not in order to seek contact with her body, but in order to protect her honor: "He turned, pinning her quickly against one of the eucalyptus trees. And, leaning on the tree with his arms encircling her, he stood over her to conceal her" (170; A33). He does this to hide Shoshana from a group of young men from the neighborhood who are passing by, so that they won't see her coming home at dawn with a foreign soldier. And when he looks down and smiles cheerfully at Shoshana, who would have never thought of protecting herself this way, the natural human desire for attachment erupts in full force. Shoshana's inner voice merges with the narrating voice, crying: "UN soldier! Her heart clung to him. UN soldier!" (170; A33). The remainder of the story enhances the sense that the experience of this emotion and the insight into its possibilities enable Shoshana to integrate the desire for attachment into the evolving story of her identity. The ecstatic ending of "Bridal Veil" extends the possibility that Shoshana will be able to do this in a manner that will enable her to free herself from the stifling emotional world of her childhood home and to have greater freedom and more hope in entering her emotional world as an adult.

Notes

1. Parenthetical page references in the article will be to the translation appearing in this volume. For purposes of greater accuracy, I often found it necessary to provide my own translations. Consequently, the quotations given in this article will often differ from the text of the English translation.

2. For a discussion of the significance of the image of the motherless baby chick in the stories of Amalia Kahana-Carmon, see Lily Rattok, *Amalia Kahana-Carmon* [Hebrew] (Tel Aviv: Sifriat Poalim, 1986), 14. My reading of the specific use of this image in "Bridal Veil" differs considerably from Rattok's general observation.

3. On this, I am in disagreement with Gershon Shaked, who, in his perceptive discussion of "Bridal Veil," claims that "the story is based on the ironic opposition

between the illusion that persists in [Shoshana's] mind and the reality that is revealed in the cruel plot." Gershon Shaked, *Hebrew Narrative Fiction 1880–1980* (Tel Aviv: Hakibbutz Hameuchad, 1998), 5:323.

4. Here, it seems to me, the translators missed the authorial intent by using their translation as a ready-made explication: "What is it that passed through her now, piercing through the bark, penetrating the sapwood, making it ooze," p. 164.

5. At this critical juncture, the translators misread the Hebrew of the last sentence.

Hannah Naveh

CONTEXT AND AUTHORIAL INTENT

"BRIDAL VEIL," a short story by Amalia Kahana-Carmon, after having been originally published separately (1968; see appendix for publication details), was subsequently incorporated into the volume *Magnetic Fields: A Triptychon* (1977), where it was positioned as the first of three stories. Its first discrete publication relatively close to Kahana-Carmon's short-story collection *Under One Roof* (1966) certainly may have encouraged its acceptance as a continuation of the poetic principles established in that collection. Yet its repositioning in the triptych required both a reexamination of the individual story and, not surprisingly, a new evaluation of the author's total thematic range. This last was not in the least due to Kahana-Carmon's own claims regarding the significance of the triptych as an "integral work," i.e., not merely a "collection." The author's claim for the integrality of the triptych calls special attention to the new closure that the single story was given, by undoing its finality and subjecting its plot (and theme) to further development. It was as if in its first publication, the story's "final word" had not been said (or understood) and the unfinished business found its better position and closure with the new arrangement. What was significant in this case was the subtitle *Triptychon*, which ordered the reading of the story in both its position as an opening to an evolving narrative, as well as in its position as a mirror image of its two counterparts—both concepts equally suggested by the title *Magnetic Fields*. And then Kahana-Carmon took a third turn in controlling the context of "Bridal Veil" by positioning it as the first chapter of her composite novella, also titled *Bridal Veil*, in *Here We'll Live: Five Short Novels* (1996). Here it was again the first of three stories, only this time it was joined by two works, each of which had been previously published (in two different preceding volumes), disregarding the order and context of their original publication. At this point, I suggest that Kahana-Carmon "wrote" "Bridal Veil" three times, without actually changing one word of the story, and that the main aim of the rewriting was to change the story's most significant, most telling, feature, i.e., its closure. She retains for it its place as "first" (the opening chapter,

so to speak) in the two composite works following its initial discrete publication, thus emphasizing its primary, proactive, and generative quality. It
is always the onset. Yet in its repositioning, she offers different options for
its closure. The concept of narrative closure regards the end of a narrative
as its most heavily laden segment in terms of establishing, stabilizing, and
finalizing its meaning. Therefore, by giving "Bridal Veil" three different
closures, each one canceling out its predecessor, Kahana-Carmon performed corrective artistic surgery to control the story's meaning and theme
and to finally create, from her point of view, its true, or most desired,
contextual position.

Kahana-Carmon, more than most contemporary Israeli authors, participates actively in current literary critical discourse by giving interviews and
public presentations as well as by writing literary reviews and essays. More
often than not, her subject focuses on her own writing, whether by direct
reference or by indirect inference. She often presents her views on writing
in general (the literary tradition) and on the responsibility that a writer has
to represent an internal vision and subjective understanding by finding the
precise externalizing principles and practice that govern the transitional
process from the inside out. Her philosophical turn is also evident, as many
discerning and concerned readers have commented (most critical have been
Tzurit and Rattok), in her works themselves, in her controlling comments
and reflexive thematic moments.

She also often puts her protagonists in the position of mouthing poetic
principles, whether overtly or metaphorically, which are easily detected as
her own credo. I, for one, shall seriously and respectfully assign utmost
importance to Kahana-Carmon's "letters of intent," i.e., to her comments
(internal) and commentary (external) about her work, although I shall also
aim to point out the discrepancies between her two modes of confession:
self-representation and self-analysis.

This essay will follow the career that "Bridal Veil" took over the years
by considering the significance of the authorial control that Kahana-
Carmon exerted over it in revisiting it and rewriting its place or role within
the project of her master narrative. She obviously had not intended the
story's independence and relative autonomy (first visit: 1968)—or at least
she felt the story had not fully subsumed her vision. Nor was she satisfied
with its place or role in the subsequent triptych (second visit: 1977), perhaps
because of critical response but perhaps also because of a changing sensibility. In fact, I shall propose that Kahana-Carmon herself came over the

years to recognize better her own story—and, in fact, her total master narrative—and found that instead of rewriting it, she could simply change its closure to assist in revealing its true narrative role and ideological import (third visit: 1996).

In this project, two driving forces are at war: on the one hand, Kahana-Carmon revels in every new revelation that she has of the drama of love and writes it from a fresh start every time; this is a search for difference and innovation. She has stressed many times that her writing reflects new understandings and changing sensibilities, and she has insisted many times on the developmental aspect of her works. On the other hand, there is a basic uniformity, an unchanging perpetuity, to her account of the love drama, which leads to a continuous rewriting of its theme; this is a search for sameness and repetition. It may be that the apprehension of the second of these two forces, which has dominated the reading and appreciation of Kahana-Carmon's work as a whole, is responsible for her critical classification as a "writer with one story." Instead, I propose, she is the hedgehog, who knows "one big thing" (I. Berlin); so is Dostoevsky, so is Monet. Not bad company. She concedes to this place: here we'll live. In the telling of the "one big thing," she exposes both sameness and difference, and so she may magnetize and demagnetize her stories, constantly destabilizing and contextualizing them, diverging and converging alternately, and setting before us the deconstructed result of the sameness-difference rivalry.

THE QUEST FOR TRUE LOVE: FIRST VISIT

The two previous essays in this volume, by Berg and Morahg, have illuminated the possibilities of reading "Bridal Veil" as a separate and entirely autonomous work. It is certainly tempting to read "Bridal Veil" in the context of Kahana-Carmon's previous short stories and indeed as part of the one setting of *Under One Roof*. Berg and Morahg have demonstrated the nature of the heroine (Shoshana) and her plight in light of a narrative already posited by previous girls and young women in Kahana-Carmon's works. This narrative consists mainly of the drama of love—the quest, the encounter, the enchantment, and ultimately, the disenchantment, and finally the ecstatic coda. Although most critics agree to this schema, with its variations in tone and degree, they use the term "love" reluctantly to describe the central experience of the heroine (usually a woman); moreover, Kahana-Carmon herself, who continuously offers insightful ideas and commentary to her work, hardly ever uses the term. Instead, the reference is to "enchantment," "charm," "magic," "visionary," "revelation," "epiphany," and so on. Yet a serial inquiry and anatomy of love are nevertheless what Kahana-Carmon's work is about, and her entire oeuvre is a personal and original discourse of love. She has invented a thrilling account of love as a possible project in terms of inventing the self (the project of individuality) and as the penultimate intersubjective experience. This essay aims to underscore the unique role that "Bridal Veil" plays in the unfolding of the drama of love and to claim that Kahana-Carmon sharpened and honed this role by rewriting the story's closure. The three visits of "Bridal Veil" constitute a metamorphosis of Kahana-Carmon's discourse of love.

Shoshana is Kahana-Carmon's youngest girl-heroine. Although she has (in Ne'ima Sasson before her) and will have (in Clara after her) colleagues in her role as ingenue, she is still the only complete girl-child, not even close to making the crucial step of crossing the divide that separates women from girls. Her story is fraught with misunderstandings and blundering mistakes, which stem from her unexpected confrontation with a discourse (and its practice) to which she has not yet been initiated. Moreover, even after having experienced what could have been an initiating rite to feminine maturity, having met a man who is no longer a boy and who mistook her for a woman, she retains her naïveté completely. Her experience has left her exhilarated in a way that is incompatible with the idea of maturity, and she is astonishingly untarnished by the disengagement (which is by no means a disenchantment). More significantly, her story lacks the final subdued and distancing coda, which is so typical of other Kahana-Carmon dramas of love. When the story takes leave of her, she is totally engulfed in the romantic vision of her life as a mission of reunion with the UN soldier: "It is you that I shall—shan't I, oh please—one day find again!" This is a promise she makes, to shape her life as a mission of love-finding, fastening her fate to love.

In this, Kahana-Carmon leaves her heroine just short of recognition, which would normally entail a retreat from absolutes and totalities. Shoshana's affirmation of true love has circumvented the site of compromises and grim reality (which is where *Magnetic Fields* will eventually take her), and there is no disenchantment and no concluding comment or philosophical reflexive coda to her story that might suggest mature retrospection. Instead, her experience lands her directly in the mythical landscape of true love as if it were an attainable reality, as if it had a tangible geography, as

if it were a country to which one may travel—Canada, in this case. She is
not familiar with the topos of the ever elusive Promised Land or of Paradise
Lost; she is a great believer in the physicality and materiality of metaphors:
Somewhere Over the Rainbow would be an appropriate example of a real
accessible location to her. Whereas Ne'ima Sasson, Shoshana's more mature
counterpart, who knows that she, too, "will find again" an object of true
love, resorts to artistic creation as the locus of refinding and recapturing
her initial experience of love, Shoshana will probably buy a travel ticket
and obtain a visa to get there.

This the narrative makes evident: Shoshana is poised on a brink. She
will be making a transition by the end of the long day, and it will not
merely be that of arriving home; she has been traveling home from various
locations for a long time, going back and forth between her parents on a
misunderstood mission (she believes that it is her business to deliver her
father's soiled laundry to her mother's wash barrel). She seems to know her
route well enough, and her parents seem to deem her capable of traveling
it alone. But this exceptional journey leads to a disruption of safe regularity:
she is about to discard her original license of leave and assume a new and
completely different quest. This discovery comes at a junction in her life:
it occurs on the last day of school (the very same time and place in which
Ne'ima Sasson makes her discovery). She is no longer comfortably en-
sconced in being a child: she fears the intentions of a man lurking in the
quickly darkening spot her father had chosen to meet her, yet she retreats
with unease to the children's playground, since the playing children, too,
are frightening and demonic. She suddenly and unexpectedly, and also certainly unpreparedly, inhabits a bewildering "contact zone." The school shirt
she is wearing is embarrassingly too tight but her mother's skirt, which she
borrowed for the trip, is too large and needs fastening at the waist with a
pin. In this, like a mermaid, she is not yet "sexed." She struggles for individuality and recognition and feels lost, threatened, and abandoned. She
overhears a young man on the bus, begging to be hired for a job, claiming
with passion that the future employer will not regret choosing him. Her
whole fragile being totters toward him, repeating and recapturing his cry:
"Choose me!"—this is the profound unvoiced plea of this young, unwanted, unchosen girl. Symbolically, she has no room of her own.

This feeling is enhanced by her general disorientation and feeling of
ineptitude: no one had told her that life goes on after dark in a manner as
regular and unceremonious as during the day. This is what she discovers

now, waiting for her overdue father, just as she would soon learn that there are countries west of the Mediterranean Sea; she is quite dismayed to learn that for some people, "the sea" (the Mediterranean) is to their east. Thrice she reiterates: a new and secret thing had been introduced into her life. Her borders had suddenly been stretched, her world expanded, and the possibilities find her unprepared and unguided. Having completed school and formal instruction, she is now coming out as an autodidact, taking charge of interpreting the events, whereas previously she relied on others to inform and shape her concepts. And so we are about to behold an intuitive, spontaneous, and uncontaminated reaction—a reaction that figures for Kahana-Carmon as the ultimate, primordial participation in the drama of love and that constitutes the protagonist as a subject in love.

The discourse of love for Kahana-Carmon in this story (and ultimately, as I shall suggest) focuses on the instance of an imprinting recognition, when one subject recognizes another as a bestower of significance. The crucial concept here is that of subjectively and independently choosing the bestower. To be in love is thus to choose self-constitution by the experience of believing to be chosen by the eye of the beholder, who thereby becomes the loved one. The knowledge or certainty of having been chosen is what produces, in Shoshana's case, the total self-generated and self-willed deliverance of the self to the grace of the other, in complete confidence. The future that may lie waiting for her is evident in other Kahana-Carmon stories, which lead the drama of love to its conclusion: she may fall into captivity and experience humiliation and subjected submission; she may be sold to pay off a gambling debt; she may marry a cold and indifferent man; she may have a baby for which she cannot profess caring intimacy; she may become impoverished of her material and mental assets; she may live in the sheltering fantasy of another life, secretly coveting and creating an alternative to her own failure; she may become paralyzed and be rejected—all these options attest to the fact that Kahana-Carmon regards the location of love as a temporary and fragile sanctuary (a bell jar) from real life. It was this imaginary context that controlled the reading of "Bridal Veil" 's first visit. Shoshana was regarded as a "beginner" who will soon meet her fate—exemplified in stories of other girls and women. And although none of the grim results of the love drama has the power to destroy the heroines' basic, underlying, indefatigable, undefeated, experience-defying and totally transcendental and transphysical belief in love, they still come to distance themselves from it for their self-preservation.

Yet this is not the case for Shoshana. Shoshana represents the untampered, uncontaminated quality of pure love, before the devastating onset of real life. Her ecstatic concluding vow therefore is not a negation of her experience, and it does not strike (or irritate) the reader as the idiosyncratic Kahana-Carmon signature. On the contrary, it is sound both narratologically and psychologically. For Shoshana, real love is the total response that one experiences when confronting one's imprinting agent. This encounter enables the self to become its authentic best self. It is the most desired self-constitution experience. This response disregards rational social contracts and exerts a totally head-on reaction to the encounter. The encounter is understood as a demonstration of fate, and no evidence can alter the belief in its inevitability and design. Finding herself in this most significant encounter, Shoshana is prepared to be totally reckless and completely spontaneous. She has never before actually visited the scene of love, although she now understands it to be the focal point of all her accumulated, scattered, and chance memories and mementos. They all acquire a shape and design when reviewed as a prolonged and protracted preparation for this moment of meeting with love. She has found a room of her own, which, in this discourse, always means that it is occupied by the two lovers. A solitary room of one's own, in terms of this discourse, is a place of loneliness and dereliction—this she has learned well from both her parents. Loneliness, in terms of this discourse, is what leads to philosophical resignation and to the deliverance of the self to a higher divine authority.

The dominant element of love as Shoshana performs it is in the complete resignation of the self to the compassion, mercy, and protection of the other. Shoshana, who has known only limited and circumstantial statutory protection by her father and mother (both are clearly unfit and precarious protectors), recognizes true love by its precisely fitting her (so-called childish) imagination of what love consists of, i.e., that it is a protectorate. Living in a protectorate is compared in other stories to having "a room of one's own," to being in a "glass [bell] jar," to finding "the heart of summer, the heart of light." The protectorate of love is not inhabited by inferior or lesser persons who seek the benign and beneficiary protection of a powerful, higher authority (although it may easily be mistaken for just that, bearing in mind the initial captor-captive relationship of Peter and Clara in *Up in Montifer*). It is rather a place of its inhabitants' complete security in being totally accepted, of being precisely fitting and adequate, and therefore it offers them a sense of enhanced and authentic individuality and of having been chosen and anointed. It is a place of coming into one's own and of becoming one's self. It is a place of ultimate self-discovery and identity constitution. It is life-giving. That is Shoshana's understanding of true love, and that is Kahana-Carmon's suggestion for autonomous selfhood.

Is this a child's notion? Is this a notion to be discarded and exchanged for a more valid one eventually, once subsequent chapters to the story have been imposed on its closure? And more interesting (for this reader): Is this idea at all compatible with any form of feminist ethics, or is it a pre-feminist concept, to be corrected by future experience? Kahana-Carmon endeavors to control our answers to these questions by visiting "Bridal Veil" again, in her subsequent triptych *Magnetic Fields*. She thus poses it more clearly as a beginning begging a denouement. It retains its powerful quality to represent the germination of the idea of true love at its first encounter. Thus she invests the story with the narratological and psychological force of a primal scene—that which is forever imprinted in the mind as an ideal and which is the object of constant yearning. She also thus addresses herself to the question of "a woman [not a girl] in love," and so supplies to the story her understanding of Shoshana's future.

IS THIS THE ROOM?: SECOND VISIT

Kahana-Carmon is famous for her accounts of her own writing and her rather illuminating, although sometimes limiting, interpretation of her own works. *Magnetic Fields* was not received extremely well—indeed, it quite baffled its readers, even the most deft and qualified ones, who tried to explain the threefold narrative of the volume as a whole, and, as a rule, failed to do so. Kahana-Carmon found that she had to come to the rescue of her work and endeavors to explain its compositional principle. She refers in interviews to the two stories succeeding "Bridal Veil" as continuations and conclusions to Shoshana's initial position. She concedes to a necessary "fall" and withdrawal from the dignity and ecstasy of "Bridal Veil" 's closure; and she discloses the nature of the comfort to be found after the disenchantment: it is always conceptualized in terms of a so-called religious experience. Yet although the two sequel-stories in *Magnetic Fields* fit her schema, and, moreover, they are resonant with the tone and mood of *Under One Roof*, they do not seem to be at peace with "Bridal Veil."

Obviously, Kahana-Carmon's main concern is the compositional problem that the volume presents. She has already well established herself as an

acclaimed and prizewinning short-story artist; yet she has also already suffered rebuttal and criticism for her attempt at a novel (*And the Moon over
Ayalon Valley*, 1971). Now, what was *Magnetic Fields*? Here was a hybrid
work that readers could easily deal with on the individual story basis, but
that was seriously questioned for its integrity as a novel, albeit segmented.
Kahana-Carmon's explanation of her project goes to the need to establish
linear development and narrative sequentiality as the guiding principles of
the volume. I find no problem with her intention or with its execution,
taking account of Kahana-Carmon's preference for the "divergent" mode
of textual representation of time and spatiality ("hoping the illusion of
action will form in the imagination of the reader," in "Primary Principles").
It is nevertheless obvious that she herself felt the stories retained a strong
and vital separateness, which enabled her to modulate, correct, and adjust
their meaning (magnetize) by a shift of context (such as in the third visit).
Indeed, so strong was her sense of the incompatibility of "Bridal Veil" with
its two succeeding stories in the triptych that after publishing *High-Risk
Gambling* (1980), she claims that its two stories are an alternative closure
for "Bridal Veil"! She thus corrects the "mistake" of *Magnetic Fields* by
providing a new closure for Shoshana's plot. In her own words, she says
that the two stories of *High-Risk Gambling* take their departure from "Bridal
Veil" and lead it to a new closure. This virtual sequence could be considered
still another rewriting of "Bridal Veil," bringing the total number of its
productions to four.

What was it exactly that failed in the composition of *Magnetic Fields*? I
believe that the leap from the initial discourse of love in "Bridal Veil,"
including the subject position that it assigned to Shoshana, to the final
conclusion of the project in the two following chapters or stories, was felt
to be overextended, and inasmuch was discredited. Moreover, that the initial position was destroyed by them, in that they took the project to total
disillusionment, and consequently to a resigned philosophical contemplation. This was not only incompatible with Shoshana's subject-position but—
much more significant—was incompatible with what Kahana-Carmon
could bear to be conveying. I believe that Kahana-Carmon could not finally
resign Shoshana to the fate that her mature and grown counterparts in
Magnetic Fields came to suffer. Whether the fate of the lonely, unhappy
Zevulun of "The News Room Is There" or that of the glum, dispirited
Tamar, the heroine of "The Ship Negba Glided Majestically"—although
both were living "abroad," which is crucial for Shoshana's discourse of

love—neither could represent Shoshana faithfully. Even Wendy of "The News Room Is There"—who easily fits the notion of finding a room of one's own—represents the coldness and loneliness of the autonomous self-sustained woman. Indeed, a grim vision for the famous room.

The full scope of this triptych's narrative implies not the price that one pays for far-fetched ideals and fantasies but rather their complete inadequacy and the devastating loneliness and desolation that ensue with their collapse. The closure of the triptych casts Shoshana as a victim of her initial intuitions and, much worse, as slightly pathetic. It emphasizes her immaturity and reduces her vision of love to childish fantasy, as if to say: grown women know better.

The total isolation and dejection that is the fate of the two heroes in the triptych's second and third stories belie and slightly ridicule Shoshana's devotion, and are indeed a grim conclusion to her project. Although it was part of Kahana-Carmon's intention, it seems that the passing of the metaphorical torch from one protagonist to the next was unsuccessful. Having pledged to "find again" her true love, Shoshana (in her counterparts) travels far and wide to discover that love is not to be found (although several "rooms" are optional) and that one must eventually find comfort in metaphysical notions. The metaphorical torch is thus dropped and lost, and love is thus relegated to the realm of intra-subjectivity, where it is a futile soul-searching and self-battering procedure, rationalized and explained away philosophically. Whereas "Bridal Veil" promises further future possibilities for encountering true love, the unfolding of *Magnetic Fields* is quite adamant in its refusal to allow and to envisage this future. It claims rather that ideals must be abandoned in face of reality, and dreams must find their place in contemplation.

RESUMING THE QUEST: THIRD VISIT

And so finally, Kahana-Carmon reshapes Shoshana's future in *Here We'll Live*. Again, "Bridal Veil" takes its place as a beginning, as an initial position, thus reaffirming the importance of primal scenes and of primary imprinting experiences. It also lends its title to the whole novella (novella 4 of the volume), which is of utmost significance for a narrative of development and evolution. Naming the whole project by its first segment poises that segment as the total governing idea of the whole narrative and binds all future development to the initial concept. It is as if there is no real moving away from the original position—the child's pure vision of love, which is controlled by the bridal veil (*Bridal Veil*). Thus, Shoshana's quest-pledge is not rejected but is rather reaffirmed in older and more mature contexts. In the third visit, the room of her own is not impoverished but rather magnified to its extremes. The "news room" (*ḥadar haḥadashot*) of *Magnetic Fields*, the direction to which the hero had lost, is found in new circumstances.

It now becomes clear that by presenting the readers again with "Bridal Veil" in yet a new context (not being "new" in the full sense only emphasizes the point), what Kahana-Carmon wishes to correct is not her writing of the story, but rather our reading of it. She is giving us a better indication of the nature of her discourse of love, which we (and she) may have misinterpreted. Transferring the story to a new "home" allows Kahana-Carmon to identify from among her previous works those that provide a better closure for it, a closure that is compatible with her (new? changed?) discourse of love instead of one that violates and misrepresents it. The stories chosen this time are famous for their heroines' resolution to carry the torch of love even in the face of the most adverse circumstances. Although the circumstances of love seem to have changed in the process of the protagonist's progress in life and experience, she herself retains, in almost heroic proportions, the basic subject position to which Shoshana swore eternal loyalty. Indeed, it seems that no degree of betrayal or abandonment, whether by actual persons or by circumstances, could shatter Sarah-Jane's (*High-Risk Gambling*) or Tirtzah's confidence in her position ("Scenes from the House with the Pale Blue Steps"). They wish to remain the true bearers of the proverbial torch, come what may, and they both insist on the loved one being a part and parcel of their "room."

The protagonist of the drama of love is one who defines her sense of individuality and autonomous selfhood in terms of being in love. Although it would seem that her understanding and enactment of being in love defy notions of autonomy—and, in fact, almost seem opposed to it—I believe it is we who need to examine our limited and restricted definition of autonomy. Kahana-Carmon has offered in her two sets of closures for "Bridal Veil" these two possibilities: either a departure or retirement from love, a withdrawal of energy and libido from the love exchange (*Magnetic Fields*); or self-abandonment and self-absorption in the love exchange, self-dedication to it in a vision of symbiotic fusion.

The first of these is generally considered the main narrative course of

206 | BRIDAL VEIL

Kahana-Carmon's work, and it is conceptualized as the option of auton-omy: it is the terminology of autonomy that infuses the discussion and presentation of the disenchantment segment in the drama of love for many critics. Kahana-Carmon, too, in her essay "Partial Truths" (1977), defines the culmination of "the charm" in terms of ecstatic revelation and epiphany, which alleviates and dulls the sharp pain, fury, and humiliation that the heroine undergoes with the termination of love. She says: "Wherever you turn, the world is governed [activated] by intelligence [thought, design, wisdom, reason]—call it divine design. And nothing is unintentional or born of chance; it is all a consequence of causality and authorship; it is all part of a grand master plan." This certainty compensates for the impossi-bility of finding a more realistic relief or comfort for the suffering of dis-enchantment and disengagement (*post coitum omne animal triste est*), and it enables the heroine to retreat with a certain sense of worth, self-preservation, and a feeling of having retained autonomy. It relegates the drama of love to an incidental and functional role in the project of self-invention, something to have visited and have emerged from, perhaps scathed—but bearing a prize. Rattok says that the finalizing ecstatic com-ment aids the heroine to overcome the failure of her relationship. Berman calls this procedure "a passion for the Binding [*'akedah*]," emphasizing the psychological urge to make sense of personal experience by referring it to a universal sacrificial fusion with a higher order. But I would suggest that it is exactly this procedure that is responsible for the destruction of indi-viduality, since it bonds the self to a high-order "cause" ("a grand master plan") external to it. No intersubjectivity is possible between the two orders, because of their difference; it is this unbridgeable gap that enables and demands the epiphany in the first place. The heroine is thus entrapped in surrendering her individuality in the name of autonomy (a constructed fictional and misleading concept, I suggest) and successful emergence from the drama of love.

On the other hand, what the composite novella "Bridal Veil" (in *Here We'll Live*) offers is the second optional closure, that of fusion with the beloved and celebrating the individuality that is constituted in the negoti-ation of self with another self. Much has been said about the relevance of the Buberian concept of the I-Thou relationship for understanding the par-ticular type of intersubjectivity that Kahana-Carmon endorses (mostly in Balaban), and I support this intertextual inference. To put it *in extremis* is to assert that not only is it morally virtuous to engage in an I-Thou relationship, but it is even more rewarding psychologically to perceive of self-hood and individuality in this context. The individual thus perceives itself not as diminished because of dependence (which I believe to be the result of the ecstatic mode of closure), but rather as enhanced by the enchantment of having encountered its *basherte* (the chosen, intended one). For Ortega Gasset in his *Essays about Love*, this loosening of ego borders is typical to true love as we know it; for Barthes in his "Discourse of Love," it is this self-abandoning attachment of selfhood to another that figures as a central symptom of love. I propose, therefore, that for Kahana-Carmon in her final (so far) account of love, we must not be misled by the seemingly grim endings of the two stories succeeding "Bridal Veil" (in *Here We'll Live*). This avenue was consummated in *Magnetic Fields*, and any reader can easily feel that in the new configuration a different tonal mode is employed. The insanity, victimization, and masochism, which seem to permeate the novella throughout, are merely extreme situations in which the heroine's dedication and addiction to love are tested and she emerges triumphant.

It is this concept of individual selfhood and independent subjectivity that is preferred: advocating loneliness and desolation under the name of autonomy and independence merely exposes the artificiality and prejudice, which are inherent to these basically masculine concepts. On the other hand, glorifying the individuality that one experiences in a room of one's own, having defined it as the room of enchantment in which the enchanter is a necessary component, is another way of perceiving autonomy. The self is thus produced most significantly in the "glass jar" with a partner.

It is evident that Kahana-Carmon sees the project of "the production of the self" and the ritual of self-constitution as a venture for two. True, this stretches our notion of independence to its limits, but it is worthwhile.

Appendix: Publications of "Bridal Veil"

FIRST VISIT

1968: in *Sh'demot* 34: 14–24; a short story in a literary journal (after: 1966: *Under One Roof*, a volume of short stories)

SECOND VISIT

1977: in *Magnetic Fields: A Triptychon*; the first of three stories; for the other two, it was a first publication: "The Ship Negba Glided Majestically" and "The News Room Is There" (after: 1971: *And the Moon over Ayalon Valley*, a novel)

THIRD VISIT

1996: in *Here We'll Live* the first story of three in a composite novella also titled *Bridal Veil*; the other two: "After the Annual Ball" (previously published in *High-Risk Gambling*) and "Scenes from the House with the Pale Blue Steps" (previously published in *Under One Roof*); the novella *Bridal Veil* is the fourth of five composite novellas in the volume (after: 1980: *High-Risk Gambling*, two stories; and after: 1984: *Up in Montifer*, a collection including *High-Risk Gambling* and "Scenes from the Green Duck Bridge")

SOURCES CITED AND EXCERPTED:

Balaban, Avraham. *A Different Wave in Israeli Fiction: Postmodernist Israeli Fiction*. Jerusalem: Keter Publishing House, 1995 [Hebrew].

———. *The Saint and the Dragon: Studies in the Fiction of Amalia Kahana-Carmon*. Tel Aviv: Hakibbutz Hameuchad, 1979. [Hebrew]

———. "Zevulun Leipzig Writes Plays," *Siman Keriah* 7, pp. 436–55 [Hebrew].

Barthes, Roland. *A Lovers Discourse: Fragments*. Noonday Press, 1979.

Berlin, Isaiah. *The Hedgehog and the Fox*. Chicago: Ivan R. Dee Publisher, 1993.

Berman, Emmanuel. "The Longing for the Binding." *Siman Keriah* 7, 1977, pp. 431–36 [Hebrew].

Brooks, Peter. *Reading for the Plot*. Cambridge, Mass.: Harvard University Press, 1984.

Buber, Martin. *I and Thou*. Walter Kaufmann, trans. New York: Simon & Schuster, 1970, 1974.

Naveh, Hannah. *Twin Stories: A Genre of Fiction*. Dissertation, Tel Aviv University, 1978 [Hebrew].

Ortega Y Gasset, Jose. *Estudios Sobre El Amor*. Yoram Brunowski, trans. Jerusalem: Keter Publishing House, 1981 [Hebrew].

Pratt, Mary Louise. *Imperial Eyes: Travel Writing and Transculturation*. London & New York: Routledge, 1992.

Rattok, Lily. *Amalia Kahana-Carmon: Monograph*. Tel Aviv: Sifriyat Poalim, 1986 [Hebrew].

Roemer, Michael. *Telling Stories: Postmodernism and the Invalidation of Traditional Narrative*. Lanham, Md.: Rowman & Littlefield Publishers Inc., 1995.

Shaked, Gershon. *Hebrew Narrative Fiction 1880–1980, vol. 5*. Jerusalem: Keter Publishing House, 1998 [Hebrew].

———. *Literature Then, Here and Now: Literature, Poetry and Society*. Tel Aviv: Zmora-Bitan Publishers, 1993 [Hebrew].

———. *A New Wave in Hebrew Fiction*. Merkhavia & Tel Aviv: Sifriyat Poalim, 1971 [Hebrew].

Shirav, Pnina. *Non-Innocent Writing: Discourse Position and Female Representation in Works by Y. Hendel, Kahana-Carmon & R. Almog*. Tel Aviv: Hakibbutz Hameuchad, 1998 [Hebrew].

Tzurit, Ida. "Heretic Thoughts," *Haaretz*, March 25, 1977 [Hebrew].

FOR A LIST OF AMALIA KAHANA-CARMON PUBLICATIONS AND INTERVIEWS [HEBREW] SEE:

Rattok, Lily. *Amalia Kahana-Carmon: Monograph*. Tel Aviv: Sifriyat Poalim, 1986, pp. 202–3 [Hebrew].

SELECTION OF ADDITIONAL AMALIA KAHANA-CARMON PUBLICATIONS [HEBREW] AFTER 1984:

Kahana-Carmon. "To Waste on the Marginal," *Yediot Aḥronot* 19.9.1985, p. 23.

Kahana-Carmon. "Brenner's Wife Rides Again," *Moznayyim*, May 1985, pp. 10–15.

Kahana-Carmon. "She Writes Quite Nicely, But About the Marginal." *Yediot Aḥronot* 5.2.1988.

Kahana-Carmon. "The Song of the Bats in Flight," *Moznayyim*, vol. 64 no 3–4, 1989, pp. 3–7.

Kahana-Carmon. "Why a Flood of Women Writers?", *Haaretz*, 8.3.1996, p. 53–54.

Kahana-Carmon. "A Portrait of the Book 'Here We'll Live,'" *Davar Rishon*, 3.5.1996.

[VI]

HOVERING AT A LOW ALTITUDE

Dahlia Ravikovitch

CHANA BLOCH AND ARIEL BLOCH

I am not here.
I am on those craggy eastern hills
streaked with ice,
where grass doesn't grow
and a wide shadow lies over the slope.   5
A shepherd girl appears
from an invisible tent,
leading a herd of black goats to pasture.
She won't live out the day,
that girl.   10

I am not here.
From the deep mountain gorge
a red globe floats up,
not yet a sun.
A patch of frost, reddish, inflamed,   15
flickers inside the gorge.

The girls gets up early to go to the pasture.
She doesn't walk with neck outstretched
and wanton glances.
She doesn't ask, Whence cometh my help.   20

I am not here.
I've been in the mountains many days now.

The light will not burn me, the frost
won't touch me.
Why be astonished now?   25
I've seen worse things in my life.

I gather my skirt and hover
very close to the ground.
What is she thinking, that girl?
Wild to look at, unwashed.   30
For a moment she crouches down,
her cheeks flushed,
frostbite on the back of her hands.
She seems distracted, but no,
she's alert.   35

She still has a few hours left.
But that's not what I'm thinking about.
My thoughts cushion me gently, comfortably.
I've found a very simple method,
not with my feet on the ground, and not flying—   40
hovering
at a low altitude.

Then at noon,
many hours after sunrise,
that man goes up the mountain.   45
He looks innocent enough.
The girl is right there,
no one else around.
And if she runs for cover, or cries out—
there's no place to hide in the mountains.   50

I am not here.
I'm above those jagged mountain ranges
in the farthest reaches of the east.
No need to elaborate.
With one strong push I can hover and whirl around   55
with the speed of the wind.

I can get away and say to myself:
I haven't seen a thing.
And the girl, her palate is dry as a potsherd,
her eyes bulge,   60
when that hand closes over her hair, grasping it
without a shred of pity.

Barbara Mann

THE PROBLEM OF WITNESSING is at the heart of Dahlia Ravikovitch's "Hovering at a Low Altitude," a poem that addresses a universal
situation within a particularly Israeli frame of reference. In its vacillating
placement of the speaker, who is both omniscient and detached, the poem
critiques the position of "hovering" above reality in order to escape the
brutality of everyday life. It is also a phenomenological exploration of one
woman's struggle to engage the world through the zone of poetry. The
poem should be read against the background of the relation between artistic
creation and ethical responsibility as well as the role of literature in the life
of the nation. The notion of a more private, individualized self was ubiquitous in Israeli poetry in the 1960s and 1970s and was the hallmark of the
work of Ravikovitch's contemporaries, the poets Yehuda Amichai and Natan
Zach. Their poems have been understood as one response to the over-
whelmingly collective nature of the first-person voice in Hebrew literature
from the turn of the century, and to the enormous ideological and national
expectations placed upon the writer. Ravikovitch's early volumes were crit-
ically well received and were particularly noted for their crafted language.
These books were followed by a relatively long period of poetic silence,
which was broken in 1982 with the publication of "Hovering at a Low
Altitude." On the one hand, then, the poem marks an important turning
point in Ravikovitch's work: it may be read as a self-incriminating reflection
upon a poetic self that she was partly responsible for creating. On the other
hand, the poem asks us to reconsider this distinction between a collective
and an individual voice, compelling us to question our own practice as
readers.

The poem's opening terrain is a dramatically ominous wasteland. We
follow the turnings of the last day in the life of an anonymous shepherd
girl, who is both doomed and slightly damaged from the start. The poem's
speaker seems comfortably, enigmatically, aloft. Four times the speaker repeats: "I am not here."[1] This declaration is a performative contradiction:
like the Liar's Paradox, its content contradicts the premises of its performance. The poem's speaker must be "here," in order to say that she is not.
(The gender of the poem's speaker is revealed later in the poem.) Likewise,

she must be watching in order to describe what it is that she has not seen. This type of contradiction, and the accompanying impulse to create a reliable narrator, is the driving force of much imaginative expression. This impulse becomes particularly problematic, however, in situations such as that depicted in "Hovering at a Low Altitude," where the power of the gaze is first denied, then asserted, again and again. In keeping with the self-conscious impossibility of its refrain, the poem's language is vivid and slightly stylized, as if to foreground the surreal situation it depicts.

The speaker's declaration of absence is not only a description of physical location; it is a state of mind that persists and deepens throughout the poem, alongside the tragic approach of violence in a desolate and foreboding landscape. At first, the speaker is "not here" but "in the crevices of the eastern mountains," "not here" but observing a monstrous, devouring sunrise; by mid-poem, she is still "not here" but has "already been in the mountains many days." Apparently untouched by the extremes of climate or the knowledge of impending violence, she has "seen worse than this in [her] life." Finally, toward the poem's brutal conclusion, she is "not here" but "above the wild threatening mountain range," on the edges of the East, akin to the exotic climes of Ravikovitch's earlier work.[2] The phrase "I am not here" is a means of coping with the world's horrors. In the poet's own words: "I am a witness to things that I haven't the ability to change, and I hope that this doesn't dull my revulsion."[3] However, all the while that she is "not here," the speaker offers a premonition of future events, which are themselves described as having already occurred: the girl and her herd of goats move toward the pasture at sunrise, while at noon a stranger climbs the mountain, his movements witnessed by the floating speaker, who seems powerless to act. Something about the uneasy cooperation of verb tenses both underscores the inevitability of the violence and enables the speaker's cagey yet persistent distance from it. The changing relation between the speaker and the girl—and the distance between the speaker and the scene that she "does not see"—allegorizes the position of the writer in the world; the poem questions the ethical possibility of writing that "cushions" itself from a brutal reality. Beyond this metapoetic critique, however, the poem contains a wider, implicit judgment of the society in which the poem was produced, as the reader shares in its privileged and seemingly all-knowing viewpoint. The poem's power derives from both its self-indictment and this implication of its readers: it insists on the ethical untenability of remaining aloof, a position that fails to act against violence and injustice and leads to

BARBARA MANN | 215

a moral erosion of the self. This meditation on the connection between writing and power and between moral outrage and action is complicated by details of the local Israeli context and by Ravikovitch's position as a woman poet.

"Hovering at a Low Altitude" was first published in the fall of 1982 and has been read in the context of the Lebanese War, a period of great social and political turmoil in Israel. The war itself, and the years immediately surrounding it, provoked an enormous amount of political poetry, as well as literary reflection on the place of politics in belles-lettres. Ravikovitch, like many Israeli writers, participated in public demonstrations against the government and against the Israeli invasion of Lebanon. Throughout her career, she has commented, in often contradictory fashion, on the relation between poetry and politics. For example, in 1959, on the occasion of her first volume's publication, she claimed that as a poet she was not preoccupied by the "problems of the generation: the establishment of Israel, the ingathering of the exiles, making the desert bloom, even the atom bomb."[4] At the time of the publication of *True Love* in 1987, the volume in which "Hovering at a Low Altitude" was eventually collected, she viewed the politics of her Lebanon poems as nothing new; the invasion itself she saw as a continuation of abuses that predated the war.[5] More recently, when asked whether she accepts the definition of political poet, she replied, "I am political to the same degree that I have always been, and I don't see *Mother with Child* [published in 1992] as particularly political."[6] However, "Hovering at a Low Altitude" was written and submitted for publication in the literary journal *Siman Kri'ah* before the war began.[7] Furthermore, in *True Love*, the poem is not grouped with the volume's other poems explicitly connected to the war: "They're Freezing in the North," "You Can't Kill a Baby Twice," and "Get Out of Beirut." Instead, we find it in a section called *The Window*, alongside a poem of that name that describes the self's withdrawal from external events: "What have I done already? I haven't done anything for years."[8] As readers, we thus come to "Hovering at a Low Altitude" in the wake of a critique of the position of viewing a scene from the relative safety of a window. This situation provides one way of understanding the poem within the context of the war, which was in large part witnessed by the Israeli public through the firsthand accounts of soldiers and secondhand media accounts.

The poem itself, regardless of these specific circumstances, raises the question of the worth of poetry during any period of extended public trauma. Hebrew poetry has often served as a realm in which to record and debate the relation between public trauma and private experience. In this regard, Ravikovitch's poem participates in a rich tradition in Jewish culture.[9] For the poet, one special locus within Hebrew literature may have been a short essay by Leah Goldberg. Hebrew women poets have characteristically relied on this kind of web of intertextual relations. Goldberg—poet, translator, critic, teacher—was a major literary figure from her arrival in Tel Aviv in the 1930s until her death in 1970. Ravikovitch paid homage to her as "hidden yellow rose" in a pool of "toads," who "only because of her wonderful courage/ . . . doesn't look for another pool."[10] In September 1939, Goldberg published an article in response to the friends and colleagues who repeatedly asked, "When will you start writing war poems?"[11] Goldberg objected to poetry that glorified heroism and warfare, contending that the poet's task must always be to celebrate life. Her response to the war in Europe was to write nature poetry: "I have taken upon myself a disreputable role, the role of a fool rushing in, in order to say that I . . . in September 1939, see myself as obligated . . . to appear before literature with the opening phrase, for instance, in these words: 'On a September morning / the sea in our land is clear and cool.' "[12] Goldberg's essay was part of a larger debate among modernist Hebrew poets regarding the writing of explicitly political poetry and the role of writers and their work in the establishment of the state. Her declaration is a bit disingenuous; nature poetry in modern Hebrew has historically been connected to the national program of renewal in "Eretz Israel"—the Land of Israel. This is not to claim that modern Hebrew nature poetry is always necessarily polemical; it is simply that landscape description is often mediated by a wider social and political discourse. Goldberg was not unaware of these connections, and we can find more explicit references to the politics of landscape description in other of her nature poems.[13] The poet's defense of nature poetry and her critique of the heroic mode are meant to problematize the strict distinction between the political import of the two genres. This distinction points to the seeming divide between two more fundamental categories—the individual or private versus the collective or public voice. The collective voice necessarily includes traces of those voices that it represses or masks in its efforts to appear universal. At the same time, the private self must speak in the generalized terms of the collective in order to be understood and effective as a poem. Even Goldberg's seemingly innocuous couplet cited above speaks in the compact, possessive first-person plural—*artsenu* (our land)—and refers to the month of Elul, associated with a particularly sacred time of the Jewish calendar year—the New Year and the Days of Awe.

This blurring of the personal and the collective may also be found in "Hovering at a Low Altitude," where the poet embeds biblical allusions concerning the relation between God and the people of Israel in descriptions of the anonymous shepherd girl.[14] Thus, a poem that ostensibly depicts an individual's flight from involvement in the world—"I am not here"—reverberates with the words of the prophets, who, one might say, invented the problem of personal responsibility toward the nation. In its depiction of the violent death of an unsuspecting child on a mountaintop, the poem also skirts a centrally defining motif in Jewish culture and in much modern Hebrew poetry—the binding of Isaac.

Nevertheless, some seed of the sensibility behind Goldberg's "nature-poetry-during-wartime"—its rejection of certain poetic modes in the national arena—became the hallmark of Ravikovitch's literary generation, what she calls "the history of the private individual."[15] Their poetry spoke in the first-person singular, detailing the individual, often esoteric experience of the poet without any ostensible connection to the political or social world within which it was produced. Yet just as Goldberg's nature poetry pushed subtly against conceived notions of collective and individual voice, these poets, Ravikovitch among them, sharply critiqued the social and political structures in which they lived and wrote. Perhaps because of the strong generational identification in Hebrew literature and in Israeli culture generally, implicit and explicit dialogue with other Hebrew poets was one characteristic mode of their work.

In *True Love*, "Hovering at a Low Attitude" is bracketed by two poems that constitute a kind of testimony to another woman poet, Yona Wolloch, the most influential Israeli poet of the last twenty years, and a controversial figure in her own right. Both poems—"Finally I'm Talking" and "True Love Is Not What It Seems"—meditate upon the connection between Wolloch and her work, her death in 1985, and something called "true love." In these poems, literary inheritance, even a misappropriation, is also a form of love, albeit one that is often confused with, or marred by, self-love. Of the many "heirs" Wolloch left behind, Ravikovitch says: "You gave them permission / but you didn't give them responsibility." Her own poems about Wolloch are hyper-engaged and brutally honest, forcefully addressing the poet in what Ravikovitch calls Wolloch's "new situation"—"you are a dead woman."[16] They also question the degree to which people (including the poet) "truly loved Yona," asking, "Do we truly love our friends? . . . Do we truly love our children?"[17] What is the relation between this "true love" and "Hovering at a Low Altitude," which describes a violent encounter from a detached, "love-less" position, at the window? The poem's almost anthropological, detached "hovering" records with patience and fidelity the details of even the most brutal scene. What is the proper relation between a poet and her subjects, especially when these subjects are victims, actual or imagined? What kind of ethical complications derive from a voice that repeatedly claims, "I am not here"? What special fabric of relations exists among women poets and their relation to these ideas?

The answers to these questions depend on, to quote Raymond Carver, "what we talk about when we talk about love." Women poets in many traditions have characteristically exploited the expectations of women's poetry to be "merely" personal, while fine-tuning a sharp critique of dominant literary genres and societal expectations regarding women, especially women artists. In her essay on nature poetry during wartime, Goldberg also mentions love poetry, arguing that "not only is the poet allowed to write love poems during wartime; he *is obligated*, because during wartime the value of love is still greater than the value of murder."[18] She cites both the *Iliad* and David's biblical eulogy of Jonathan as examples of great love poems that have been mistakenly read as war poetry. Just as "true love is not what it seems," and nature poetry may be deeply political, true love poetry is also not what it seems. In Ravikovitch's work, love is about suffering, and suffering is always political. In framing "Hovering at a Low Altitude" with these questions about love and literary relations, the poet asks us to consider what kind of love hovers absently in a poem that repeatedly declares "I am not here." On the one hand, love is dependent upon genuine sympathy and identification: the shepherd girl is referred to as "the little one," and the speaker tries to imagine "what the girl was thinking." On the other hand, this empathy is complicated by the seeming necessity of aesthetic distance necessary to artistic creation, a distance that often precludes sympathy or involvement and implies a form of power. Unlike some of her poems that are more explicitly connected to the war, "Hovering at a Low Altitude" has been admired as a great philosophical achievement because it simultaneously embraces both the distance of aesthetics and the passion of engagement.[19] Therefore, within the context of the volume as a whole, "Hovering at a Low Altitude" occupies an interesting position: it serves as a kind of intermediary link between the engaged talk of love in the Yona poems and the volume's more overtly political poems, almost as if the poem's detached drama serves as a conduit through which the passion of the Yona poems infuses the war poetry. The narrator in "Hovering at a Low Altitude" seems to be powerless to prevent the violence before her, yet her position may also be construed as voluntary, even necessary as a survival strategy. The poem is an attempt to deal with this self-erasure, to describe it, in effect—to turn it into something else. Pronouncements of victimization or powerlessness are a staple of Ravikovitch's poetry; from the start, it is the orange's adoration of its devourers that is the central focus of her work.[20] Love, even at its most self-destructive, is a form of agency, of power. However, her poems recognize that the space between describing a powerless position and truly occupying one is vast.

Nonetheless, "Hovering at a Low Altitude" hinges on the degree to which the poem's speaker identifies with the girl. Despite her repeated proclamations of detachment, the speaker follows the girl's actions with rapt attention. Their connection is most strongly suggested nearly halfway through the poem, in line 27, as the speaker gathers up her skirt, and her gender is decisively revealed in the feminine singular verb form: *osefet*. This banal, almost domestic gesture leads to the fantastic movement of hovering at ground level, like a spirit. There is also, however, in this particular description of flying close to the ground, something vaguely threatening, like the movement of a surveillance or attack helicopter. Despite her surreal position above the earth, the speaker is privy to brutally real and intimate details concerning the girl's body—her cheeks, the frostbite on her hands, and her hair in the poem's closing lines. While the hovering enables the speaker to question and wonder at a comfortable distance—her feet don't touch the ground, she feels neither the cold nor the light—the gathering of her skirt connects her physically to the girl's sexuality. The leisurely gentility of the speaker's gesture—the luxury of gathering her skirt so that not even its hem sweeps the ground below—symbolizes a final attempt to shield herself. She is far away but must watch until the end. Ironically, it is the girl who is alert, though unsuspecting, while the speaker lets her thoughts pad her protectively with cotton quilting. Her aloof position is, however, further eroded as the poem draws to its violent conclusion, a deterioration suggested in the tentative language of the final stanza: one *may* move at "the speed of the wind," and "I *can* get away and say to myself: / I haven't seen a thing." Does this disavowal in fact describe her position at the end of the poem? Though the speaker claims that she has seen worse, she seems to be trying to convince herself. As the poem ends, the location of the speaker is multiple and shifting: on the edges of the East, she is also close enough to view the ostensibly innocent approach of the man as he climbs the mountain. The poem ends as the attack begins; the speaker's intimate knowledge of the girl's body—her palate, her eyes, her scalp—places her, and the reader, in a position of heightened, purely omniscient, sympathy. The space in which the poet is "not here" is also the space in which the reader must acknowledge her own silence, and perhaps her own complicity, in the violence unfolding before her.

Notes

1. This repeated "non-witnessing" is a variation on the psychological trauma recorded by Ravikovitch's nightly witnessing of her father's death when she was a girl, "Standing by the Road," in *The Complete Poems So Far* (Tel Aviv: Hakibbutz Hameuchad, 1995).

2. For example, "Tirza and the Wide World," "War in Zanzibar," "Australia," and "Chad and Cameroon," in *The Complete Poems So Far.*

3. "Interview with Dahlia Ravikovitch," *Maʾariv* (8 February 1991).

4. *Davar hashavua* (23 December 1959): 17.

5. "After the Silence," *Haʾaretz* (24 October 1986).

6. "Interview with Dahlia Ravikovitch," *Maʾariv* (22 January 1993).

7. The poem first appears in *Ḥadarim* 3 (fall 1982) and is collected in *True Love* (Tel Aviv: Hakibbutz Hameuchad, 1987). See Nissim Calderon, *The Feeling of Place* (Tel Aviv: Hakibbutz Hameuchad, 1988), for original publication details.

8. *The Window,* in *True Love,* 27.

9. See Alan Mintz, *Ḥurban: Responses to Catastrophe in Hebrew Literature* (Syracuse: Syracuse University Press, 1996).

10. "The Toads," in *The Complete Poems.*

11. Originally published in the literary weekly *Literary Pages.* Reprinted in A. B. Yoffe, *Leah Goldberg: A Memoir* (Tel Aviv: Tchirkover, 1984).

12. Ibid.

13. Leah Goldberg, "From Songs of Zion," in *Writings* (Tel Aviv: Sifriyat Poalim, 1986).

14. See Chana Kronfeld's essay in this volume.

15. The poem lists series of dates and events, concluding "In all these, I was alone." "History of the Individual," in *The Complete Poems So Far.*

16. "Finally I'm Talking," in *True Love,* 30.

17. "True Love Is Not What It Seems," in *True Love,* 53–54.

18. "Poetry in Wartime," in *Leah Goldberg.*

19. See for example Yochai Oppenheimer, "Keshirut politit: ʿAl halirikah vapolitikah bashirat Dahlia Ravikovitch," *Siman Kriʾah* 22 (July 1991): 417–30.

20. For example, "Love of an Orange," in *The Complete Poems,* 15.

Nili R. Scharf Gold

READING DAHLIA RAVIKOVITCH'S "Hovering at a Low Altitude"[1] as a political poem[2] has become nearly its only reading. So accepted is its understanding as a semi-confessional, Israeli guilt-ridden text, that even careful poetry readers such as Shimon Zandbank refer to its political implications without questioning them.[3] Critics also discuss the poem's self-referential character, but again, in the context of a debate about the artist's role vis-à-vis the reality of oppression and war.[4] Even the selection of Ravikovitch's poems translated into English implicitly shares this reading. In it, "Hovering at a Low Altitude" immediately follows the explicit "On the Attitude toward Children in Wartime."[5]

True, in 1983, the poet included "Hovering at a Low Altitude" in a joint collection of political poetry protesting the war in Lebanon.[6] She has also made her views publicly known by writing militant antiwar articles and poems.[7] However, these facts do not justify the almost exclusively political interpretation of the text. The reader ought not to ignore other qualifying factors. It is known that the poem was submitted to the magazine *Hadarim* before the battles in Lebanon broke out; hence, it was not written in direct response to the war.[8] Moreover, when "Hovering at a Low Altitude" finally appeared in the book *Ahavah amitit* (True love) in 1987, Ravikovitch nestled it among other lyrical poems, under the inside title *The Window*, and not at the end of the book, under the marked political inside title *Questions in Contemporary Judaism*. This placement, I believe, is not a coincidence, nor is it an oversight or an attempt to camouflage the poem's true meaning. It is an interpretative signal from the author, that "Hovering at a Low Altitude" is first and foremost a personal, lyrical poem.

The spectacular imaginary landscape that opens the poem is arid, a space forsaken by God and man (lines 1–5). Although the mountains' wide shadow (*tsel*) is described idiomatically by the verb "lie," or "spread" (*natush*), it is hard to ignore the echo of that verb's primary meaning. *Natush* means "abandoned," "forsaken," "deserted," according to the dictionary (line 5). Nature, then, is not only the locus of events; it also forebodes, even mirrors, them. Abandonment and its terrifying consequences may be at the core of this poem, the emotional wound that motivates this text. The oxymoron-like declaration at the head of the poem, "I am not here" (line 1), throws the speaker to an existence there, elsewhere, on bald carnivorous mountain gorges. Although the poem's title informs of a disconnected state (i.e. hovering), the speaker, at least at the outset, is on, not above, this ominous landscape (line 2). The mountains' icy streaks resemble an animal of prey; they are spotted, *menumarim*, like *namer*, a tiger (line 3). The speaker's "I," whose feminine gender is not certain at this point in the poem, in attempting not to be "here," finds herself in a desolate place of danger. There is no protection "where grass does not grow" (line 4), let alone a shady tree. The absence of a hiding place in the mountains is intimated only through the landscape in the first stanza; yet in the assault that ensues at the end of the poem, it is almost a culprit.

The "I" who utters the poem's first five words lets the terrain dominate the four lines that follow. When another human being, "a little shepherd girl" (*ro'ah ketanah*), comes into sight with her flock, she is almost merged with the scenery (line 6). The shepherd burst forth from a tent in a birth-like, or animal-like, emergence (as indicated by the verb *hegiḥah*, line 8). She may resemble the black goats in her care, so much a part of the land-scape, almost invisible and just as vulnerable. Goats, *'izim*, recall for the Hebrew reader kid or goat, *gedi-'izim* or *se'ir-'izim*, the quintessential sac-rifice or victim (Gen. 37:31; Lev. 3:12; 5:6).[9]

It is important to note that at this point, the speaker and the "little shepherd girl" are both invisible, and they are both there, on the mountains. It is not unreasonable to ask whether vulnerability is a common trait for them both as well. However, the two differ in the level of their awareness. While the speaker sees, the girl does not. The latter part of the poem ret-roactively suggests the presence of a third, knowing and threatening figure on the mountains, one who the speaker most probably recognizes.

The existence of evil is apparent in the opening stanza. First, in the haunting, horror-movie-like vista, and then in the irreversible verdict dis-closed by the omniscient speaker ("She won't live out the day / that girl," line 10). The detachment-refrain, "I am not here," is repeated immediately after the "verdict." The knowledge of what is about to happen may drive the urgent need to escape. Yet the "I am not here" means that the speaker is still there, "on the mountains," where the shepherd girl is unknowingly awaiting her fate. The foretelling of catastrophe is rendered in a language of certainty, not premonition. The "I," then, is either divine or is recol-lecting an experience. If the latter is true, the text may be read as a quasi-cinematic flashback. While the chain of events unfolds in the present in front of the eyes of the dumbfounded reader, for the narrating voice, it is but a remembrance of things past.

The second stanza repeats the structure of the first: four lines of eerie mountain-scape follow the "I am not here" refrain. A sickly-looking sunrise is exposed. A flying red ball (*kadur*) with a whitish spot is turning over in the mountain's inflamed throat before becoming a hot sun (*hamah*). The cruel, tiger-like gorges of the first stanza open a devouring, repulsive maw (*lo'a*) in the second stanza (lines 13–14). In Ravikovitch's poetry, a red, sore throat or a suffocating "ball" or lump in the throat is often connected to a sense of despair and helplessness.[10] The self-declared "detached" speaker, it seems, almost physically feels the danger of this ailing, hostile landscape.

Then the mountains' prey reappears. As in the opening stanza, she emerges immediately after the picture of her "carnivore." The cracks in the speaker's attempt to disconnect herself from the event seem to widen even further. The vocabulary of the third stanza's opening line betrays the empathy: "And the little one hurried so to rise for pasture" (*vehaketanah hishkimah ko lakum el hamir'eh*, line 17). "The little shepherd girl" of the first stanza is now tenderly called "the little one." The verb *hishkimah* ("rose early") recalls Abraham's fateful early rising with his son who was about to be sacrificed (Gen. 22: 3), and the adverb "so" (*ko*) illustrates the girl's earnest attempt to do her work, thus disclosing the narrator's compassion.

The lines most densely packed with biblical allusions in the poem are found here. The polarity between the shepherd girl, the essence of innocence, and the cruel world surrounding her is too grave, so to speak, for one poet's words. Ravikovitch turns, then, to the ultimate text, representative of divine justice. Only by negating the Psalmist's assurances of the reign of justice, only by deconstructing the prophets' notion of right and wrong, will the fate of this pure creature gain its appropriate dimensions. Biblical vanity is juxtaposed with the girl's humility and absolutely pure intentions. She does not "walk with an outstretched neck and wanton eyes" (lines 18–19) like the "daughters of Zion" (Isa. 3: 16), nor does she "enlarge her eyes with paint" (line 19) like Zion, the sinner (Jer. 4: 30). Yet no god helps her. Following the deconstruction of the prophets' negative female portrait is the negation of the Psalmist's deliverance. While the Psalmist lifts his "eyes to the mountain," asking, "Whence cometh my help?" (Ps. 121: 1), the little shepherd girl, unaware of the approaching threat, does not. While the Psalmist's mountains contain God, her slopes are without mercy.

The inverted allusions to the Scriptures intensify the sense of God's abandonment and injustice, which now dominate the scene.

"She doesn't ask, Whence cometh my help" (line 20). The quintessential call to God "Whence cometh my help?" (*me'ayin yavo 'ezri?*) carries here, through the line's punctuation; an added possibility for interpretation. If indeed, the desired reading of this line is that the little, unaware, shepherd girl is not asking about her own source of help, the punctuation would read: She doesn't ask: "Whence cometh my help."

Instead, the quotation marks are missing, as if to imply that she, the girl, is not "not asking" for her own help, but rather, she is "not asking" about "my," meaning the narrator's, salvation. In other words, the line suggests that the girl is not wondering from where the speaker's (the "I") help would come. Although this meaning is only implied here, one may argue that the ambiguity, created by the punctuation, deliberately blurs the boundaries between the girl and the poem's "I." For that fleeting moment in the poem, the adult who is recounting the story and the helpless girl become one and the same. As the poem progresses, the narrator identifies increasingly with the little girl, and the text intimates that it is a reworked reconstruction by an adult of her own childhood experience. As the adult looks back, she may ask questions about the event, but the child undergoing the trauma does not. This reading explains why the girl did not ask about the continued survival of the woman she was to become; it makes sense of the girl's obliviousness of the adult's need for help; and it adds another layer to the almost obsessive refrain and its insistence on distance and detachment.

The passage from the third to the fourth stanza mirrors the leap from the first to the second ("She won't live out the day, / that girl. / I am not here," lines 10–12). The greater the proximity of the "I" to the girl's fate, the more urgent is the need to escape. That need is echoed in the refrain and magnified, in the fourth stanza, by a declaration of immunity to suffering ("the light will not scorch me. The frost will not touch me," line 23). The "I" admits that past trials and tribulations are responsible for her apathy: "I've seen worse things in my life" (line 25). The reader ought not to ignore the possibility that the story told here is actually the speaker's own, one of the "things" she has seen, or rather, lived through.

The fifth and central stanza is choreographed to be the most revealing and longest in this seven-stanza, sixty-one-line poem.[11] Themes from the first and third stanzas are replayed here with greater intensity. The girl's quasi-feral, primitive character and her pure, unpretending nature are now observed from a closer vantage point and are graphically delineated. Unaware of being watched, she crouches, unwashed, wild, almost animal-like, a victim in a few hours (lines 29–30). Furthermore, this stanza's first line, "I gather my dress and hover" (line 22), finally reveals the gender of the hovering entity (*osefet*, "gather," is in the feminine form of the verb). The greatest physical proximity between the woman who narrates and the little girl occurs at this point in the text. For the first time, she is "very near to the ground" (line 27). So close is the "I" that she can read the seemingly absentminded expression on the girl's face and is able to see the cold sores on the back of her hand. She can almost touch "her cheeks, as soft as silk" (lines 31–33).

This intimate portrait of the girl recalls another. Although I am aware of the pitfalls of such connections, I suggest that the girl's features bear resemblance to Ravikovitch's persona. Hers is the concentrated / distracted look; the porcelain and silky skin; the hand rashes and the sensitivity to the cold.[12]

The eighth and ninth lines of this stanza blur the reader's perception of the girl's countenance. Depending on how one reads the punctuation and line division, she is either attentive or dreaming. "Absentminded, seemingly/attentive, as a matter of fact" (lines 33–34) is the literal translation that follows the original punctuation and line division. If read according to the punctuation, the girl is absentminded; she only seems attentive. However, the same lines, read according to Ravikovitch's line-division, lead to the opposite conclusion: she is truly attentive, she only seems absentminded. Earlier in the poem, the suggestive punctuation binds the woman and the girl with the call, "Whence cometh my help." Here, too, the punctuation plays a similar role, pointing to the adult's and the girl's duality and unity at once. The girl is oblivious, while the recollecting adult is watchful as she counts the hours until the assault. "And there still remain just a few hours" (line 35).

The counting of the remaining hours is followed by a variation on the refrain: "I, I was not thinking about that matter" (*ani lo ba'inyan hazeh hagiti*, line 36). This "substitute refrain" agrees with the pattern, already established in the poem, where excessive closeness to trauma is followed by an intensive attempt to detach or deny. However, at this pivotal point, a mere "I am not here" does not suffice. An added cotton-wool padding is required to insulate the speaker from the horrific vision in store. The text refers to itself, interpreting, and finally repeating the title. Hovering, it claims, is a simple solution to existential problems. "Neither feet touching the ground nor flying" (line 39). Hovering at a low altitude allows the speaker to survive despite the heart-wrenching sight. The poem could have neatly ended with the reiteration of the title. Instead, a slow-motion play-back follows.

"That man," seemingly innocent, climbs the mountain. The man, who, on the surface, appears in the sixth stanza for the first time, is called *ha'ish hahu* ("that man," line 44). By referring to him in this way, the narrator discloses, perhaps, a previous encounter with him. The preposition *ke*, "as if," intimates a knowledge of the man's intentions and of the story's end. Even the hovering ceases now. "That man went up the mountain / as if he were innocently climbing" (lines 44–45). When he reaches her, there is "no one else around" (line 47). One must wonder to where the "I" had disap-peared. If the entire "plot" were to occur in the poem's here-and-now, the "I" would be present, at least through the "I am not here" refrain. But in this sixth, laconic, stanza, even the speaker's declaration of "non presence" is missing. While up to this point, she reported every step in great detail, including the girl's tent and goats, skin, posture, and facial expression, now there is a void. The sixth stanza closes with "And if she tried to hide or screamed / there is no hiding place in the mountains" (lines 48–49). Why did the hovering speaker not hear the scream? Not see the desperate search for refuge?

It seems to me that the only way to understand the "if" in "if she tried" is to believe it. The narrator is truly uncertain of what had happened at that climactic moment. It is blocked out from her memory. Even now, years later, when the story is reconstructed, that moment is too painful to revisit. The careful account is that of "screen memories," details that surround the main incident, but are not the actual event.[13] What is described in the poem as "Hovering at a Low Altitude," then, is a psychological defense mecha-nism that enables a survivor of trauma (or a victim in the midst of an assault) to distance herself from the pain. In the case of this poem, it is as if the speaker leaves her body and is able to look down on it from above, at one of the worst moments in her life.

The price of this "hovering" is revealed only at the end of the poem. The mountains are more dreadful then ever. Only through a violent hurl, *taltelah 'azah*, through swift circling in the wind and self-imploring is the

"I" capable of removing herself from the scene of the crime (lines 54–57). The actual execution of the very deed committed by "that man" is absent in the poem. "The little one's" bulging eyes and dry mouth and the man's merciless hand grabbing her are the only evidence (lines 58–61). The oxymoron reaches its height at the end of the poem. The narrator claims, "I haven't seen a thing" (line 57), yet she sees (or perhaps feels) the girl's eyes popping out of their sockets and her palate "as dry as a potsherd." Although the separation between the "I" and the "girl" is maintained with great effort throughout the poem, there remained slips—traces, if you will—for the careful reader to unveil and fill in the gaps.

The two options available to Ravikovitch's personae in earlier works were either flying high in "the sky's amazing blue" ("In the Right Wind," line 29), or touching fire, being in the place of danger. Taking off to the heavens often ends with a catastrophic fall. So is the fate of a man who "falls from an airplane in the middle of the night" ("The End of the Fall," line 1), or of Saint-Exupéry, who disappeared over the Mediterranean, or of others who "fly in the right wind / and die suddenly" ("In the Right Wind," lines 36–37). Reaching to the depth of experience, touching, and living passion and pain to their fullest are equally as hazardous as flying. Ravikovitch's female personae: the daughter who must return to the place where her father was killed; the young woman who reaches for her "Dress of Fire"; the lover so consumed by desire that she is either swallowed or drowned[14]— all are destroyed physically or emotionally.[15]

The horrific feeling of abandonment by a parent who dies or by a remaining not-good-enough parent, as well as the continued vulnerability of the child, may be replayed in "Hovering at a Low Altitude." The words *bemakom she*, meaning "in the place where," which curiously appear in the opening stanza (in the place "where grass does not grow," line 4), recall the very early line "In the place where he stands, there is fear of danger" from the autobiographical poem "On the Road at Night" (line 9). That early poem is Ravikovitch's only direct retelling in verse of how she became orphaned. Its speaker is an "eldest daughter" (line 4) who is obsessively compelled to return "to the place where" her father was run over by a car. As mentioned above, flying is merely an alternate danger route to encounter the dead father.

In "Hovering at a Low Altitude," however, a new strategy is being tested, a method for survival: Hovering. It is preferable to physically touching danger or to flying high above. Hovering is "a very simple method, / neither feet touching the ground nor flying" (lines 38–39). Yet the trauma, either of loss or of its consequences, still haunts the "I," who repeatedly insists "I am not here."

"Hovering at a Low Altitude" may represent a poetic stand or even a political one. But it ought to be read first as a text that touches hidden corners of the soul, a struggle to confront a memory, this time without being consumed or destroyed by it and not by escaping or repressing it.

Notes

1. The quotations from "Hovering at a Low Altitude" in this essay do not always follow Chana Bloch and Ariel Bloch's translation reprinted in this volume. For the purpose of analysis, I often use my own, more literal, translation, which also follows the original's line and stanza division. The line numbers provided throughout the essay correspond with the Hebrew original and its complete, literal translation given as an appendix to this essay. All references made to poems in Hebrew refer to *Kol hashirim ʿad ko* (Tel Aviv: Hakibbutz Hameuchad, 1995).

2. "The political poem is, simultaneously, a political tool that employs poetic means, as well as a literary text that evokes and promotes political action." Hannan Hever, *Paytanim uviryonim: Hashirah hapolitit beʾerets Yisraʾel* (Jerusalem: Bialik Institute, 1994), 14. (My translation N.G.)

3. "Ahavah amitit," printed excerpts from a radio broadcast, Ilana Zuckerman, host, Shimon Zandbank, Dahlia Ravikovitch, and Yosi Sharon, participants, *Proza* 108 (1987): 38–41.

4. Nissim Calderon, "Meḥaʾah," May 1986. Ariel Hirschfeld, "Ravikovitch aḥare ʿasor," *Yediʿot ʿaharonot*, 1 August 1987.

5. See 102 n. 1.

6. *Veʾen tikhlah lakeravot velahereg: Shirah politit bemilḥemet levanon*, ed. Hannan Hever and Moshe Ron, (Tel Aviv: Hakibbutz Hameuchad, 1983).

7. For example, "On the Attitude toward Children in Wartime," in *Kol hashirim ʿad ko*, 255, *The Window*, 102; and "Latset mi-Berut," in *Kol hashirim ʿad ko*, 251. "You Can't Kill a Baby Twice," in *Kol hashirim ʿad ko*, 249, *The Window*, 100.

8. Calderon, "Meḥaʾah."

9. For "The Kid" as sacrifice, see Nili Scharf Gold, *Prooftexts* 4 (1984): 141–152.

10. "Cinderella in the Kitchen," in *Kol hashirim ʿad ko*, 226, *The Window*, 90.

11. The fifth stanza is divided into two in the English translation.

12. See "The Marionette," in *Kol hashirim ʿad ko*, 162, *The Window*, 50. Hand sores play a central role in Ravikovitch's autobiographical account of abuse. See "Hatribunal shel haḥofesh hagadol," in *Kevutsat hakaduregel shel Winnie Mandela* (Tel Aviv: Hakibbutz Hameuchad, 1997), 87–117.

13. Freud, "Screen Memories" (1899[SE3], 301).

14. For "survival strategies" and the treatment of traumatic memories in Ravikovitch's work, see Nili Rachel Scharf Gold, "Staying in the Place of Danger: The Disobedient, Poetic 'I' of Dahlia Ravikovitch," in *To Speak or to Be Silent*, ed. Lena B. Ross (Wilmette, Ill.: Chiron, 1993), 97–108.

15. Line numbers for poems that recall the options for Ravikovitch's lyrical personae (other than those in "Hovering at a Low Altitude") refer to the English translations as they appear in *The Window*. For flying, see "The End of the Fall," in *Kol hashirim 'ad ko*, 128, *The Window*, 65; "To the Memory of Antoine de Saint-Exupéry," in *Kol hashirim 'ad ko*, 146; "In the Right Wind," in *Kol hashirim 'ad ko*, 130, *The Window*, 63. For touching danger see "No Fear of God in That Place," in *Kol hashirim 'ad ko*, 311; "On the Road at Night," in *Kol hashirim 'ad ko*, 24, *The Window*, 3; "A Dress of Fire," in *Kol hashirim 'ad ko*, 122, *The Window*, 57. "Love of an Orange," in *Kol hashirim 'ad ko*, 15, and many others.

HOVERING AT A LOW ALTITUDE

I am not here.
I am on eastern mountains' crevices
striped with bands of ice
where grass does not grow
and a wide shadow is spread on the slope.   5
A little shepherd girl with a flock of goats
black
burst forth there
from an invisible tent.
She will not live her day that girl   10
in pasture.

I am not here.
In a mountain's maw a red ball sprang up,
not yet a sun.
A frost patch reddish and sickly   15
is turning over in the maw.

And the little one hurried so to rise for pasture
her throat not outstretched
her eyes not enlarged with paint, not winking
she is not asking, whence cometh my help.   20

I am not here.
I am already in the mountains many days
the light will not scorch me. The frost will not touch me.
I am not stricken with astonishment anymore.
I've seen worse things in my life.   25

I gather my dress and hover
very near to the ground.
What did she think to herself that girl?
Wild-looking, unwashed
for a moment bending down crouching.   30
Her cheeks as soft as silk
cold sores on the back of her hand.
Absent minded, seemingly
attentive, as a matter of fact.
And there still remain for her just a few hours.   35
I, I was not thinking about that matter.

My thoughts padded for me a cotton-wool padding
I found myself a very simple method,
neither feet touching the ground nor flying.
Hovering at a low altitude.   40

But as noon was approaching
many hours
after sunrise
that man went up in the mountain
as if he were innocently climbing.   45
And the girl very close to him
and there is no one besides them.
And if she tried to hide or screamed
there is no hiding place in the mountains.

I am not here.   50
I am above wild and dreadful mountain ranges
in the far edges of East.
This is a matter upon which there is no need to dwell.
It is possible with a violent hurl and with hovering
to circle at the speed of the wind.   55
It is possible to leave and convince myself:
I have not seen a thing.
And the little one, her eyes only popping out of their sockets
her palate as dry as potsherd,
when a hard hand clasped her hair and seized her   60
without a shred of pity.

                          (literal translation, N.G.)

Chana Kronfeld

Perhaps it is precisely the ripeness of the lyrical "I," so sensitive it may appear excessive at times, which makes it possible for quite a few Hebrew poets to respond in their work to the human suffering that cries out to us from across our northern border and from behind the Green Line. This individualist sensibility can serve as a substitute for the sense of a national collective that shattered before our very eyes in such a brutal fashion. Gradually an alternative national consensus is emerging. . . . A superior example of the way such a distanced "I" gets confronted with the immeasurable cruelty brought on by the Lebanon War is offered by Dahlia Ravikovitch's poem "Hovering at a Low Altitude." This poem illustrates with sharp concreteness the terrible pressures exerted upon the lyrical consciousness and the literary patterns suitable for it when they find themselves defenseless amid the horrors of war.

Hannan Hever and Moshe Ron

A LEBANON WAR POEM?

MORE THAN ANY OTHER POEM by Dahlia Ravikovitch, with the possible exception of "You Can't Kill a Baby Twice," "Hovering at a Low Altitude" has come to represent Israeli poetry's return to an ideologically engaged poetry of protest.[1] It is often singled out—for praise or condemnation, depending on the reader's point of view—as the paradigm example of the antiwar poetry written in the wake of the 1982 invasion of Lebanon. Yet, as Nissim Calderon has pointed out in *A Sense of Place* (Tel Aviv: Hakibbutz Hameuchad, 1988:12 [Hebrew]), the poem can't be taken to actually refer to wartime events because Ravikovitch first submitted it for publication (in the literary journal *Ḥadarim*) before the war started.

The poem's somewhat confusing history of publication is only superficially a matter of dates. Nor is it merely a mark, as several critics have suggested, of some deep-seated ambivalence about writing political poetry.[2] By the late seventies and early eighties, the political was once again established as a legitimate mode of literary discourse. It engaged, interestingly enough, not just the new generation of writers but even the same Statehood Generation poets who some twenty-five years earlier had struggled to make room—in the collectivist spirit of the times—for a personal, modernist "skeptical and ironic poetics," almost to the point of valorizing any distance from direct "social engagement as a form of cultural heroism."[3]

By the early eighties, Dahlia Ravikovitch was in a unique position to lend literary and moral legitimacy to the return of the political. She was the youngest of the Statehood Generation poets and therefore more likely to be identified with a literary change of guard. And she was the only female poet of the group to have achieved a central place in the canon and to have become an influential model for younger female and male writers alike. Moreover, having recently become a mother for the first time, she had just attained what was still in Israeli society the culturally sanctioned condition for a woman's ethical right to speak out. Indeed, Hever and Ron's antiwar anthology, where "Hovering" appears roughly one year after the war, ends with a photograph, taken during the invasion of Lebanon, of Dahlia Ravikovitch holding a "Begin, Resign!" plaque and standing next to the gray-haired veteran poet Amir Gilboa at a writers' demonstration in front of the Ministry of Defense in Tel Aviv.

The different frames within which Ravikovitch herself positions this poem suggest that it is a somewhat more complex example of the turn in her work, a turn marked thematically by a triangulation of concerns with war, woman, and child. The female subject in Ravikovitch's later poetry can be described as hyphenating the titles of her 1986 book, *True Love* (*Ahavah amitit*) and of her 1992 collection, *Mother with Child* (*Ima 'im yeled*). That the true love of these later poems is now the love between mother and child need not be reduced to the accidents of personal history, although the temptation to read women's poetry as mere biography is as great in Israeli critical circles as it is elsewhere.

Politically explicit, yet far from being merely a political statement or a one-dimensional *J'accuse*, "Hovering at a Low Altitude" has come to occupy an emblematic position in contemporary Hebrew poetry. The poet's self-critical account of her own—and her generation's—"disengaged" aestheticism resonates with the urgency of ethical condemnation and extends to the culture of political detachment and escapism. For many Israelis who have grown up on Ravikovitch's work, this poem reads at times as an unflinching self-criticism, even self-parody, of the signature poetic scenario of her early work: a young woman fleeing from an oppressive reality to exotic regions of the globe and to the far reaches of the poetic imagination (*mehozot hadimyon*). But this is not all there is to this new turn in Dahlia Ravikovitch's poetry. The meshing of the poetic and the political in her later work is also informed by a heightened sense of the genders of grammar and the grammars of gender. It is a mistake, I would argue, to account for it in purely political or biographical terms.

THE DILEMMA OF WITNESSING

Thematically, "Hovering at a Low Altitude" dramatizes the dilemma of witnessing: how can the speaker—as woman, as Jew, as ethical subject—observe in harrowing detail the rape and murder of a young Arab shepherd girl in the mountains of Lebanon and not share in the responsibility for the crime? And beyond that, how can the poet aestheticize such violence through the very process of making it the subject of the poem, without being implicated herself? As always in Dahlia Ravikovitch's poetry, it is through resistance to the realistic mode that she makes the reality of the violence unavoidable; it is through insistence on the first-person singular that she implicates the collective; and it is through a series of negations, or a poetics of *litotes*, that she affirms the innocence of the victim and the guilt of both perpetrator and witness. Common to all these strategies is the subtle but relentless work of Ravikovitch's craft, of her extraordinary command of Hebrew as a language of poetry. In a series of radical uses of ambiguity and metaphor, and equally radical reversals of the topos of the nation-as-woman, Ravikovitch rejects any possibility to mitigate or ignore the rape-murder, or the larger analogy between sexual and national violence. In the process, the Arab girl is constituted as a subject, even while the speaker—and her implied audience—risk losing their own subject position.

The title, "Hovering at a Low Altitude" (*Rehifah begovah namukh*), uses media or army Hebrew in the style of the all-too-familiar news bulletins of the late 1970s and early 1980s. These would typically refer to low-flying helicopters in hovering formations, perhaps patrolling over southern Lebanon. Only in the beginning of the fifth stanza does it become unambiguously clear that what does the hovering in this poem is not the military chopper but, quite surrealistically, the female speaker floating in midair as in a Chagall painting: "I gather my skirt and hover very close to the ground."[4] The title, which appears just once in the body of the poem, at the end of this crucial fifth stanza (lines 41–42 in the English; 40 in the Hebrew) establishes the fantastic "dramatic situation" within which the speaker observes and narrates (in the present tense and the first-person singular) the events of the last day in the life of the little Arab shepherd girl. The speaker cuts short her eyewitness account right at the point where the violent attack begins. The poem reverses the popular conventions of narrative suspense by telling us from the start in no uncertain terms that the little girl will die before the day is out, but also by alternating between the girl, the landscape, and the female speaker, and focusing away from the "plot." In leaving off exactly where a horror movie would be reaching its climax, Ravikovitch resists the obscene exploitation of violence against women in the imagery of mass culture. This resistance is crucial if the poem is to collapse the distance between eyewitness and victim, and turn the reading process itself into part of the inescapable witnessing.

Temporally, the poem spans the hours between the early-morning prediction of the girl's death (stanza 1), and the afternoon when "that man" first appears on the mountain, and the girl is unable to hide or find refuge from him (stanza 6 in the Hebrew; 7 in the English). Although a close reading suggests that the girl is raped before she is murdered, both actions occur outside the boundaries of the poem's narrative. And whereas we are told by the speaker in the first stanza (lines 10–11 in the Hebrew; 9–10 in the English) that the girl will die, it is only by engagement with larger issues of social and textual history that we may infer that the girl was raped as well. Ravikovitch asks quite a lot of the reader here: first, to reject the biblical metaphor of the nation as promiscuous woman; and second, to extrapolate from this rejection an invalidation also of the tendency to accuse rape victims of having brought it upon themselves (see discussion of stanza 3 below). But no such close interpretive work is required in the poem in order to identify with the girl's experience of extreme physical terror. It is from the girl's internal, embodied perspective that Ravikovitch conveys this terror, even to the point of focusing on her palate feeling "dry as a potsherd." The man is reduced to a disembodied metonymy of "the hard hand," which may be all the little girl could see at eye level, as that hand "closes over her hair, grasping *her*" (lines 60–61 in the Hebrew; 59–60 in the English).[5] The Hebrew makes it clear that it is her body that the hard hand grasps, not just her hair, "without a shred of pity": *kesheyad kashah laftah et se'arah ve'aḥazah bah lelo kurtov ḥemlah*; since *se'ar* (hair) is masculine, the third-person feminine singular pronominal preposition *bah* must refer anaphorically back to *haketanah* ("the little one," line 58 in the Hebrew; "the girl," line 57 in the English).

Structurally, the poem starts with a joint focus on the speaker and the girl (stanza 1), a focus that is then split, in the following three stanzas, between the landscape (stanza 2), the girl (stanza 3), and the speaker, all three characterized primarily by what they are not (a variation on the classical *litotes*). This insistence on separation and negation is, I think, not accidental. It supports Ravikovitch's attempt to destabilize the powerful cultural topos of the land as woman, and with it the sexual or erotic figuration of both. This is related to, though not identical with, Ravikovitch's critique of the cognate biblical topos of the nation as woman, an equally powerful foundational metaphor that also has its roots in biblical poetry. Note, for example, that stanza 2 depicts the moments before sunrise as a "not yet sun[fem.]," *'adayin lo ḥamah*, an unusual enough way to describe dawn, which, when taken literally, means "it / she is not yet a [fem.] hot one." This is a subtle analogy to the argument in stanza 3 that the girl was just that—a girl, and not a seductive woman who brought the attack on herself. Note that Ravikovitch could have used here the ordinary word for "sun," which is masculine (*shemesh*), but chose instead the feminine (and less common) noun *ḥamah*, which is identical to the feminine singular form of the adjective "hot." Furthermore, sunrise on the mountaintop is not presented as a moment for aesthetic contemplation but as an ambivalent site connoting childhood, danger, and disease, metaphorical implications that are evident primarily in the Hebrew. The red ball of the not-yet-sun makes the mountaintop look like the mouth of a volcano; the reddening frost— like the cheeks of a tuberculosis patient. (See the analogous depiction of the girl in stanza 5. The English translation underscores this analogy "her cheeks flushed / frostbite on the back of her hands," lines 32–33 in the Bloch translation, perhaps to avoid what would be a sentimental cliché in English: "Her cheeks are soft as silk," in a more literal translation; lines 31–32 in the Hebrew.)

The fifth stanza, which in the Hebrew is also the longest in the poem, brings the speaker and the girl together in the same poetic space, inscribing in the poem's structure the speaker's growing identification with her perspective, just before "that man" appears. But even as the speaker starts to panic in empathic terror because she knows what is about to happen, she begins to mouth the clichés of her culturally sanctioned prejudice (against women and against Arabs), in a futile attempt to make herself feel less complicit in the girl's horrible murder. A clear example is line 28 in the Hebrew (29 in the English), whose sustained ambiguity supports—indeed, calls for—two contradictory readings. The first could be paraphrased roughly as "What was it she was thinking about, that girl?" namely, a genuine attempt on the part of the speaker to look at the girl closely and empathically (her silky soft cheeks, her frostbitten hands), to understand her state of mind and to see things from her subject position (this is reinforced by lines 33–34; or 34–35 in the English: "She seems distracted, but no / she's alert"). The second reading construes the question as rhetorical, and is something quite different: "What [the hell] was she thinking, that girl"—the Hebrew uses the past tense and the dative of reference (*la*) after the verb—which together can reflect a dismissive or defensively angry tone. The implied accusation is a familiar one: if something terrible happens, it will only be her own fault. What is she doing out there on the mountain all alone, a young girl like that, and so forth. Some of the speaker's other stock reactions of this sort are also articulated here for the first time. She focuses on the girl being "unwashed," and "wild to look at" (the Hebrew is literally "half-wild," suggesting the racist notion "semi-savage").

By the time the title recurs in the closing line of this crucial stanza, hovering can be understood, in a brilliant Ravikovitch double-take, as a typically Israeli version of a detached "cool," a state of mind actually referred to in the slang of the period (particularly in Tel Aviv "with it" speech) as "hovering," *lerahef*. This disengaged mode of existence marks the attempt to dissociate oneself from the political "situation" (*hamatsav*), its pressures and moral implications. It invokes a personal and collective defense mechanism that is perceived as necessary in order for life to go on as usual. Ravikovitch selects the feminine term for hovering (*rehifah*) rather than the more common masculine noun from the same root, *rihuf*, because of the military connotations. This allows her to grammatically signal ever so slightly how inevitable is the identification of perspectives between the speaker and the girl, an identification that the poem's structure evinces as well. The grammar sets off a rich orchestration of nouns, adjectives, possessive pronouns, and third-person singular verbs—all with the feminine ending *-ah*, or endings that sound as if they were; and the pattern runs through the poem like a persistent wail that reaches its apex in the attack scene (line 60): *rehifah begovah* (title), *ro'ah ketanah* (6), *hegihah* (8), *yomah, hayaldah* (10), *belo'a* (13), *hamah* (14), *semukah* (15), *balo'a* (16), *vehaktanah hishkimah* (17), *gronah* (18), *einehah* (19), *einah* (20), *yigah* (23), *mah, tadhemah* (24), *hakarka* (27), *mah, ḥashvah lah hayaldah* (28), *reḥutsah* (29), *bikhriʿah* (30), *leḥayehah* (31), *yadah* (32), *kashuvah* (34), *lah* (35), *bir-fidah* (37), *shitah pshutah* (38), *reḥifah begovah* (40), *hazriḥah* (43), *alah* (44), *vehayaldah krovah* (46) *nistah, tsaʿakah* (48), *betaltelah azah uvireḥifah* (54), *vehaktanah eynehah* (58), *ḥikah* (59), *kashah laftah, seʿarah veʾaḥazah bah* (60), *ḥemlah* (61).

Witnessing the violence is articulated from a physically impossible, literally surreal vantage point, hovering above the scene, which, paradoxically, makes it visually inescapable. The reiteration of the title at the end of stanza 5 (6 in the English) thus also describes the poet's self-conscious self-criticism about aestheticizing the horrors from the "comfortable, gentle" distance of poetic imagination. The Hebrew here (line 37; corresponds to line 38 in the English) uses overtly excessive and inappropriate poetic diction, a pastiche of the luxurious erotic imagery used in the Song of Songs (2:5 and 3:10), and nowhere else in the Bible. But here it appears not in the context of love but to describe the speaker's anxious attempts "to think pleasant thoughts," to add extra padding (literally, "a down lining") to her insulation from the brutality she knows she is about to witness.

Ravikovitch ironically adds the realistic touch of the speaker tucking her skirt tight around her legs (line 26 in the Hebrew; 27 in the English) just as the speaker tries to rationalize her surreal solution to the dilemma of witnessing as collaboration. A woman's automatic defensive gesture of modesty resonates here with psychological nuance. It suggests, for example, that the speaker has been identifying with the Arab girl, who, at this moment, is still unaware of the imminent danger she is in. And that she realizes that as a woman, she, too, could be vulnerable to the same murderous male gaze if it were to be turned upon her. From her panoramic, omniscient point of view, the speaker / narrator cannot but see and feel, nor can we: she is not only all-knowing but also all-telling. As Ravikovitch has her "unconsciously" project the consequences of the male gaze onto her own body, the reader is included in her cycle of knowledge and terror. The irony of her foreknowledge—and ours—is already established at the end of the first stanza, as the speaker asserts: "She won't live out the day / that girl." In this manner, Ravikovitch undermines from the poem's very beginning the sincerity of her persona's—and projected audience's—predictable excuses that they didn't know and didn't see what was happening. By the time the speaker explicitly invokes this familiar line, in the final stanza of the poem, she is clearly understood as infelicitous: "I can get away and say to myself: / I haven't seen a thing."[6]

The poem's recurring mantra and refrain, "I am not here," *ani lo kan*, marks two contradictory forms of dissociation, both of which, strictly speaking, are impossible, since the semantics of the deictic pronoun "here" (*kan*) by definition precludes the absence of the speaker. Typical of Ravikovitch's ideological uses of grammar, it is the ambiguous reference of "not here" that makes this impossible assertion meaningful. The speaker is either "not here" in her normal Western Israeli context, but is instead hovering (in the surreal or fantastic sense of flying low) over "craggy eastern hills"; or she is "not here" with respect to the violence on the craggy eastern hills, "hovering" psychologically and emotionally (in the slangy, escapist sense, somewhat similar to the English "floating"), not allowing what she is witnessing to affect her.

These attempts at being not here, wherever the "here" happens to be, are exposed as ethically and poetically insupportable in the last three lines of stanza 5 (stanza 6 in the English), one brief poetic moment before the violence begins to unfold. Ravikovitch ironizes the speaker's attempts to justify her hovering as a "compromise solution" between involvement and dissociation:

> I've found a very simple method,
> not with my feet on the ground, and not flying—
> hovering
> at a low altitude.
>
> (Bloch and Bloch translation, 211)

This ironic bit of self-characterization generates some of the poem's most potent social critique of the "Tel Aviv state of mind." Enlisting several arrays of idiomatic meaning and biblical allusion, Ravikovitch depicts and subverts with mock precision the impossible "physics" of her persona's solution. "Hovering at a low altitude" is not a feasible compromise between excessive attachment to political reality and a complete flight from it, not only because of the laws of gravity but also because of biblical law. "Not with my feet on the ground" translates here a Hebrew idiom that is more or less analogous to "having no foothold in" (*lo midrakh kaf regel*). This idiom appears only once in the Bible (Deut. 2:5), in a context whose contemporary political implications for an Israeli readership are an unmistakable condemnation of the Occupation. Speaking through Moses, God commands the

Israelites not to attack the lands of "your brethren the children of Esau": "Meddle not with them [*al titgaru bam*]; for I will not give you of their land, no, not so much as a foot breadth [*'ad midrakh kaf regel*]." Similar echoes saturate the linguistic texture of the entire poem, much as they did in Ravikovitch's earlier poetry, which is often construed, quite erroneously, as apolitical.[7] I will only be able to focus on a few brief examples, all combining to predict and subvert a stereotypic reaction to the Arab girl and the "hard hand" [*yad kashah*] that murders her.

The poem never names the victim or the victimizer, nor are they identified ethnically in any explicit ways. The place is also only indirectly referred to, but the history of the poem's publication and the geography of the region, where only in the north and northeast are there any ice-capped mountains, encourage the reader toward a rather specific identification of the locale as Lebanon (though "eastern mountains" doesn't quite fit and could actually be typological rather than geographic—*mizrahiyim* in the sense of "of the Levant"; see line 2). Yet, Israeli readers, even those who are upset by the poem's ideology—and perhaps especially those—would undoubtedly agree that the victim is Arab. Moreover, I would venture to suggest that many Israeli readers would see her attacker, while literally just "that man," as representing metonymically armed forces of one type or another. Ravikovitch depends on the readers' cultural and political knowledge—indeed, on their stereotypes—to perform this identification. It is important, however, that in refraining from labeling the girl, the man, or, for that matter, the speaker, Ravikovitch also resists reducing her poem to simplistic "identity politics." Similarly, as I suggested above, it is significant that she leaves the narrative of the rape-murder incomplete, "off stage," and the rape, in fact, only as an inference. Yet it is equally important to note that her use of implication and nuance does not result in any moral equivocation, nor does it make the power relations represented by the figures of the girl and the man any less unequal.

The girl first appears in the poem in the middle of the first stanza. A more literal translation of these lines (6–11 in the Hebrew, 6–10 in the Bloch translation) will underscore the cultural materials the poet invokes only in order to subvert them. Ravikovitch undermines our expected responses, and interpolates instead a reader's identification with the Arab girl.

> A little shepherdess with a herd of goats
> black ones
> emerged there

from an invisible [unseen] tent.
Won't live out the day this [young] girl
in the pasture.

But even this literal rendition cannot convey to the English reader the force of stereotype reversal in the Hebrew, beyond some added emphasis on the shepherd's youth and ethnicity. The Hebrew describes her first as "the little shepherdess" and again as "that girl." The term used here for girl, *yaldah*, makes it clear that she is indeed quite young, not even an adolescent. Unlike "girl" in English, *yaldah* cannot be used colloquially to refer to a woman. More saliently, however, "the little shepherdess" invokes a beloved folksong and dance, a classic of the popular Israeli nostalgic return to the music of early statehood. The girl's youth and the positive cultural echoes of her depiction make it harder for the Israeli reader not to feel some affection for her. Hebrew word order, where the adjective follows the noun, enables the enjambed one-word line (7 in the Hebrew), first deferring and then disclosing through coded language the shepherdess's ethnicity by emphasizing the black color of her goats. Black goats as metonymies for the Palestinians have been part of the "national narrative" since the early stages of the *Yishuv*, the pre-statehood Zionist settlement in Palestine. They have become the almost mythic "bad guys" of popular history, blamed for the deforestation of the land and contrasted with the pioneer goats that are prototypically portrayed, of course, as white. This is a technique practiced throughout the poem: Ravikovitch has the girl constituted as Arab and as "other" by the cultural stereotypes only after the reader has found it difficult to ignore her humanity—in other words, can no longer emotionally accept her as other. It is therefore the fact that she is just a little girl—rather than an Arab, or a shepherd, or a tent dweller, for that matter—that the female persona emphasizes ("this girl") as she exercises her omniscience, telling the reader what will happen before the day is out. As the poem progresses, the shepherd girl is referred to twice as "the little one" [*haktanah*], a term of endearment used to talk about a young family member (in line 17, and again, just before the murder, in line 58).

SHE DIDN'T ASK FOR IT: THE NATION IS NOT A WOMAN

Ravikovitch performs her most nuanced work in the radical use of biblical allusions to undo stock interpretations produced by the culture. This work is most pronounced in giving the lie to the "she asked for it" reaction to a woman's rape, while at the same time implicitly establishing the rape as part of the narrative. The crucial point is that in order to upend the modern misogynist reaction of blaming the rape victim, Ravikovitch chooses a rather large target: she challenges the validity of the foundational biblical metaphor of the nation-as-woman. In this metaphorical system, which has become a central topos for Hebrew literature throughout the ages, the nation is figured as woman or wife; God, speaking through the (male) prophet-poet, is figured as the husband, and the nation's ethical and religious conduct determines whether it will be figured as a beloved, faithful, and obedient wife or as a loose woman whose behavior must be punished. The most familiar extension of this metaphor in the prophets maps a woman's deviations from traditional sexual norms such as modesty and fidelity onto the nation's deviation from the norms of biblical monotheism. Even as Ravikovitch invokes this topos, however, in the first three lines of stanza 3, she introduces a sustained allusion to Isa. 3:16–17, an allusion that inverts not only the language but also the metaphorical basis of the biblical text.[8]

In Isaiah the sins of Israel are metonymically projected onto "the Daughters of Zion," who parade their seductive bodies in public. The (literal) rape and murder that the poem describes alerts us to the disturbing rhetoric of sexual violation that recurs in the prophets' condemnation of Zion. But in Isaiah the figurative women of the nation are accused not of unfaithfulness but of "haughty" (today, we'd say "assertive") behavior. In the process, the poet draws attention to the harrowing sexual brutality of divine retribution, represented in the less familiar conclusion of this famous verse:

> Moreover the Lord saith, because the daughters of Zion are haughty, and walk with stretched-forth necks [*netuyot garon*] and wanton eyes [*mesakrot 'eynayim*], and making a tinkling with their feet. Therefore the Lord will smite with a scab the crown of the head of the Daughters of Zion, and the Lord will discover their secret parts [*pot'hen y'areh*, which could also mean "their vaginas he will empty or destroy"].

On one level, the point of the allusion is to affirm via negation the innocence of the shepherd girl, leaving no room to accuse the victim: She "doesn't walk with neck outstretched and wanton glances," as in Isaiah, nor does she "rent [her] face with painting," as in Jeremiah (line 19 in the Hebrew; allusion not included in the English translation). On another level, however, given the power and dominance of this cultural topos and its profound effect on the discourse of the nation, a reversal of the biblical metaphor is bound to be rife with implications: the Arab girl is not a metaphor. As an Arab, she is not a metonymy for the Jewish nation. Literally, she is not even a woman, never mind a whore. She is simply a hardworking young shepherd who gets up *so* early in the morning (the Hebrew uses the emphatic *koh*, subtly establishing the speaker's sympathy for her), to take the goats out to the pasture (line 17). All aspects of the stock metaphor are negated one by one.

The last line of stanza 3 brings the rejection of the normative stance of the national/religious subject, helplessly seeking—and receiving—God's help. In the Psalms verse "I will lift up mine eyes unto the hills [*el heharim*], from whence cometh my help," the hills (in Hebrew, "mountains") are a metonymy for God. In a sardonic twist, it is "that man," not God, who appears on the mountain, and the girl can find no refuge from him "in these mountains." The supplicant's question in the psalm is not only negated but reduced here to a rhetorical question, reflecting common Hebrew usage, where *me'ayin yavo 'ezri* ("whence cometh my help") can be used simply to express helplessness, forgetting that in the Bible the question has a real answer in the next verse: "I will lift mine eyes unto the hills, from whence cometh my help. My help cometh from the Lord, which made heaven and earth" (121:1–2). Grafting the allusion to Psalms onto the allusion to Isaiah (and Jeremiah) allows Ravikovitch to go beyond the argument for the girl's innocence to a critique of both the discourse of the nation and of patriarchy, exposing the tacit links between the two in the textual archive of the culture. The Arab girl does not fit the sexual seduction model, she doesn't represent other stereotypes of normative "feminine" behavior, and she doesn't express dependence on a higher authority.

Finally, the juxtaposition of the girl's rape-murder with the biblical metaphor of sexual punishment itself has far-reaching implications because the allusive process works both ways:[9] If Isaiah is reread through the intertextual lens of the rape-murder of the shepherd girl in this poem, then the implicit analogy between the sexual brutality against women by God and by "that man" becomes inescapable. As usual in Ravikovitch and other Statehood Generation poets, the most crucial segment of the intertextual dialogue is absent and must be supplied by the reader, down to the parallels between the details of the female anatomy that both God and "that man" attack.

Read in its intertextual context, "Hovering at a Low Altitude" is not just a political protest poem where the rape and murder of the Arab girl represent metonymically the larger ethical implications of the Occupation. It is also, even in the strictly ideological realm, a poem that rejects the view of the national subject (as Jew and male) on the metaphorical model of female sexuality, and suggests instead the flesh-and-blood shepherd girl (as Arab and female) as a (literal) national subject, a subject who can no longer be dehumanized by an ethics and aesthetics of "hovering."

Notes

1. Both "Hovering at a Low Altitude" and "You Can't Kill a Baby Twice," were published in Ravikovitch's book of poems *True Love* [*Ahavah amitit*] (Tel Aviv: Hakibbutz Hameuchad, 1986), 31–33, 63–64, and subsequently in her *The Complete Poems So Far* [*Kol hashirim ad ko*] (Tel Aviv: Hakibbutz Hameuchad, 1995), 219–221, 249–50. English translation by Chana Bloch and Ariel Bloch, *The Window: Poems by Dahlia Ravikovitch* (Riverdale-on-Hudson, N.Y.: Sheep Meadow Press, 1989), 100–101, 103–4. In the first stanza of "You Can't Kill a Baby Twice," Ravikovitch employs a chilling parody of Psalms 137, the exemplary lament of exile and destruction, to invoke the massacre in the Palestinian refugee camps Sabra and Shatila during the 1982 invasion of Lebanon:

> By the sewage puddles of Sabra and Shatila,
> there you transported human beings
> in impressive quantities
> from the world of the living to the world
> of eternal light.

2. The issue of *Hadarim* where "Hovering" was first published appeared only after the war and contained many protest poems, among them by Rami Ditzani, a wounded soldier who published his first poems during the war. The editor, Hillit Yeshurun, featured "Hovering at a Low Altitude" prominently as the opening poem of the journal, followed immediately by a selection of Ditzani's work. See *Hadarim* 3 (1982/83): 4–6. The poem was also included, with the poet's consent, in *There's No End to the Battles and Slaughter: Political Poetry of the Lebanon War*, ed. Hannan Hever and Moshe Ron (Tel Aviv: Hakibbutz Hameuchad, 1983), 90–92 [Hebrew]. But when Ravikovitch subsequently published it in her own 1987 and 1995 collections of poems, she placed "Hovering" in the section *The Window* [*hachalon*] among poems concerned with a woman's voice and a woman's life and death, and not in the section of national-political poems ironically named *Issues in Contemporary Judaism* [*sugiyot beyahadut bat zmanenu*]. For the poet's purported ambivalence about writing political poetry, see, for example, Yochai Oppenheimer's "Political Competence: On the Lyrical and the Political in the Poetry of Dahlia Ravikovitch," *Siman*

Kri'ah 22 (1991) 422–24 [Hebrew]. New information that enhances the argument of this essay came to light as this volume was going to press and could not, therefore, be included here.

3. "Afterword," in Hever and Ron, 1983: 134.

4. The fifth stanza is divided into two in the English translation, where this line therefore occurs in the sixth stanza.

5. Simply "that hand" in the English translation. The Hebrew plays off the images of dryness and hardness in re-creating the attack scene with curt palpable detail. But idiomatically, the language replicates the analogy between sexual violence against women and political violence against Palestinians, echoing perhaps the phrase used to describe the government "policy of the hard hand" (*mediniyut hayad hakashah*) against Palestinian resistance.

6. Note that the Hebrew alternates between the impersonal (*efshar lehistalek*, lit., "it's possible to escape") and the first-person singular used in the rest of the sentence, again suggesting that feigning ignorance is more of a collective escapist response. "Say to myself" translates here the biblical form of the idiom (*ledaber 'al lev atsmi*, lit., "talk upon the heart of myself"), meaning both to cajole and to comfort. See, for example, Isa. 40:2 in reference to Jerusalem. The ironic implication is that the speaker would have to exercise extraordinary measures of self-persuasion to be able to claim that she hasn't seen a thing.

7. An alternative to the common view that the early poetry is apolitical is offered by Tamar Hess and Hamutal Tsamir in two articles with a joint introduction, "Two Readings of Dahlia Ravikovitch's Early Poetry"; T. Hess, "The Poetics of a Fig Tree: Feminist Aspects in the Early Poetry of Dahlia Ravikovitch"; and Hamutal Tsamir, "The Living and the Dead, the Believers and the Uprooted: A Reading of the Poem 'The Arrival of the Messiah,' " *Mikan: Journal for Hebrew Literary Studies* 1 (May 2000): 25–63 [Hebrew].

8. Within the primary allusion to Isaiah, Ravikovitch embeds a secondary allusion to Jer. 4:30, "And when thou art spoiled [=ravaged], what wilt thou do? Though thou clothest thyself with crimson, though thou deckest thee with ornaments of gold, though thou rentest thy face with painting [*ki tikre'i bapukh eynayikh*], in vain shalt thou make thyself fair; thy lovers [lit., those who were after your sexual favors; *'ogvim*] will despise thee, they will seek thy life."

9. I have proposed in *On the Margins of Modernism* (Berkeley: University of California Press, 1996), 114–40, that bilateral allusions are especially typical of the radical modernism of biblical intertextuality in the poetry of the Statehood Generation.

Contributors

Robert Alter is Class of 1937 Professor of Hebrew and Comparative Literature at the University of California at Berkeley. His two most recent books are *The David Story* (1999) and *Canon and Creativity* (2000).

Arnold J. Band, Braun Professor of Modern Hebrew Literature at Brandeis University for 2001–2003, long served as a professor of Hebrew and comparative literature at UCLA. His interest in the intersection of literary form and historical contexts has led him to the investigation of a variety of modern Jewish writers, primarily those writing in Hebrew. His best-known works are *Nostalgia and Nightmare: The Fiction of S. Y. Agnon* and *The Tales of Nahman of Bratzlav.* He is preparing a volume of his essays for the Jewish Publication Society Distinguished Senior Scholars Series.

Nancy E. Berg is an associate professor of Hebrew and comparative literature at Washington University in St. Louis. Author of *Exile from Exile: Israeli Writers from Iraq* (1996), she is currently working on a book about the politics of literary reception.

William Cutter is a professor of education and Hebrew literature at Hebrew Union College–Jewish Institute of Religion, and director of the Kalsman Institute on Judaism and Health. He is currently preparing annotated translations of the essays of Micha Josef Berdyczewski and has just concluded a study of aspects of Berdyczewski's correspondence.

Aminadav A. Dykman coedited *Homer in English* (1996) with George Steiner and has published several volumes of poetry translations in Israel, including a selection of Ovid's poems of exile (2001), poems by W. H. Auden and Joseph Brodsky, and an anthology of French Renaissance poetry. He has published articles on Mandelshtam, Tsvetaeva, and other Russian poets, and on Tchernichowsky's translations. He is also a literary critic and the director of the newly created Program for Translation Studies at the Hebrew University of Jerusalem. His book *The Psalms in Russian Poetry: A History* was published in 2001.

Lewis Glinert was professor of Hebrew and director of the Center for Jewish Studies at London University before assuming his present position as professor of Hebrew studies at Dartmouth College. He has published widely on Hebrew linguistics and the sociology of Hebrew and Yiddish, including *The Grammar of Modern Hebrew* (1989), *Hebrew in Ashkenaz* (1993), *Mamme Dear* (1997), and, based on his BBC documentary, *Golem: The Making of a Modern Myth* (2001).

Nill Rachel Scharf Gold teaches modern Hebrew literature at the University of Pennsylvania. Her monograph in Hebrew on the poetry of Yehuda Amichai won the Israeli Minister of Science and Culture Award. Her numerous articles in Hebrew and English on modern and postmodern Israeli writers are informed by semiotic and psychoanalytical theories. Her book *Inside the Apple* is forthcoming from the University of Wisconsin Press.

Hannan Hever is a professor in the Department of Hebrew Literature at the Hebrew University, where he teaches theory and criticism of culture, nationalism, postcolonial theories, and Hebrew literature. His most recent books are: *Captive of Utopia: An Essay on Messianism and Politics in Hebrew Poetry in Eretz Israel between the Two World Wars* (1995); *Literature Written from Here: A Short History of Israeli Literature* (1999); *Suddenly the Sight of War: Nationality and Violence in Hebrew Poetry of the 1940s* (2001); and *Producing the Modern Hebrew Canon, Nation Building and Minority Discourse* (2002).

Anne Golomb Hoffman is a professor of English and comparative literature at Fordham University. With a particular focus on psychoanalytic and feminist theory and gender studies, she writes about modern Hebrew literature and is the author of *Between Exile and Return: S. Y. Agnon and the Drama of Writing* (1991). Together with Alan Mintz, she edited *A Book That Was Lost and Other Stories by S. Y. Agnon* (1995).

Avner Holtzman is a professor of Hebrew literature and head of the Katz Research Institute for Hebrew Literary Research at Tel Aviv University. He is director of the M. J. Berdyczewski Archive in Holon. His recent books include: *Toward the Rent in the Heart: M. J. Berdyczewski—The Formative Years* (1995); *Literature and the Visual Arts* (1997); *Aesthetics and National Revival: Hebrew Literature against the Visual Arts* (1999).

Chana Kronfeld is a professor of Hebrew and comparative literature at the University of California, Berkeley, where she also teaches Yiddish literature and Jewish studies. She is the author of *On the Margins of Modernism: Decentering Literary Dynamics*, and co-translator (with Chana Bloch) of Yehuda Amichai's last book, *Open Closed Open*.

Dan Laor is a professor of modern Hebrew literature and dean of the Lester and Sally Entin Faculty of Humanities at Tel Aviv University. His 1998 biography of S. Y. Agnon won the Yitzhak Ben-Zvi Prize for the Study of the History of Eretz Israel; an English edition is forthcoming.

Barbara Mann is an assistant professor of Hebrew literature at Princeton University, where she also teaches Jewish studies and comparative literature. She is currently writing a book on Tel Aviv, which focuses on the relation between place, identity, and memory. Her articles on Tel Aviv's urban space have recently appeared in *Representations*, *Jewish Social Studies*, and the *Leo Baeck Jüdischer Almanach*.

Alan Mintz taught at Brandeis University for ten years before joining the faculty of the Jewish Theological Seminary as the Chana Kekst Professor of Hebrew Literature. Two of his recent works are *Popular Culture and the Shaping of Holocaust Memory in America* and *Translating Israel: Contemporary Hebrew Literature and Its Reception in America*. He has been coeditor (with David Roskies) of *Prooftexts: A Journal of Jewish Literary History* since its founding in 1980.

Gilead Morahg is a professor of Hebrew literature at the University of Wisconsin–Madison. He has served as president of the National Association of Professors of Hebrew and of the National Council of Less Commonly Taught Languages. He is a recipient of the Chancellor's Award for Excellence in Teaching. His publications include: "Outraged Humanism: The Fiction of A. B. Yehoshua" "New Images of Arabs in Israeli Literature"; "Breaking Silence: Israel's Fantastic Fiction of the Holocaust"; and "Israel's New Fiction of the Holocaust: The Case of David Grossman."

Hannah Naveh is a professor of Hebrew literature at Tel Aviv University and was head of the General and Interdisciplinary Studies Program in the Humanities. She currently chairs the NCJW Women and Gender Studies

Program. She is the author of *The Confession: A Study of Genre* (1987); *Captives of Mourning* (1993); *Men and Women Travelers* (2002); and coauthor of *Sex, Gender, Politics* (1999).

David G. Roskies is the Sol and Evelyn Henkind Professor in Yiddish Literature at the Jewish Theological Seminary. He is the author, most recently, of *The Jewish Search for a Usable Past* (1999) and *A Bridge of Longing: The Lost Art of Yiddish Storytelling* (1995). Roskies is cofounder and editor of *Prooftexts* and editor in chief of the New Yiddish Library.

Naomi Sokoloff teaches Hebrew literature at the University of Washington (Seattle). Her research covers a range of modern Jewish writing, with special attention to Israeli and American Jewish authors. Her publications include *Imagining the Child in Modern Jewish Fiction* and several coedited volumes, including *Gender and Text in Modern Hebrew and Yiddish Literature, Infant Tongues: The Voice of the Child in Literature,* and *Books on Israel: Volume 6.*

Bibliographical Note

ONE OF THE PROBLEMS that this volume was intended to make less severe is the scarcity of critical writing in English about Hebrew literature. With the exception of several critical studies of S. Y. Agnon, it is difficult to give the English-speaking reader many productive points of referral for the specific writers whose work is interpreted in these studies. It is therefore useful first to cite a number of works that deal with modern Hebrew literature as a whole or with major themes within it.

There are, to begin with, three journals in which articles about Hebrew literature can frequently be found: *Prooftexts: A Journal of Jewish Literary History* (Indiana University Press); *Hebrew Studies* (National Association of Professors of Hebrew–University of Wisconsin-Madison); and *Hebrew Literature* (Institute for the Translation of Hebrew Literature, Tel Aviv). An excellent introduction to modern Hebrew poetry in general and to the three poets discussed in this volume in particular is *The Modern Hebrew Poem Itself*, edited by Stanley Burnshaw, T. Carmi, and Ezra Spicehandler (Cambridge: Harvard University Press, 1989). See Chana Kronfeld, *On the Margins of Modernism: Decentering Literary Dynamics* (Berkeley: University of California Press, 1996), for a discussion of modernism with many examples from Hebrew poetry. David C. Jacobson, *Does David Still Play Before You?: Israeli Poetry and the Bible* (Detroit: Wayne State University Press, 1997), deals with the persistence of biblical motifs in Hebrew poetry.

An overview of the development of Hebrew prose can be found in Gershon Shaked, *Modern Hebrew Literature* (Bloomington: Indiana University Press, 2000). For a volume emphasizing more recent prose, see Alan Mintz, ed., *The Boom in Contemporary Israeli Fiction* (Hanover, N.H.: University Press of New England, 1997). The emergence of Hebrew as a modern literary language is examined in Robert Alter, *The Invention of Hebrew Prose: Modern Fiction and the Language of Realism* (Seattle: University of Washington Press, 1988). The spiritual crisis described in Hebrew prose at the turn of the twentieth century is explored in Alan Mintz, *Banished from Their Father's Table: Loss of Faith and Hebrew Autobiography* (Bloomington: Indiana University Press, 1989). On the reception of Hebrew literature in America, see Alan Mintz, *Translating Israel: Contemporary Hebrew Lit-*

erature and Its Reception in America (Syracuse: Syracuse University Press, 2001).

The classic study of Agnon's work with a full bibliographic apparatus is Arnold J. Band, *Nostalgia and Nightmare: The Fiction of S. Y. Agnon* (Berkeley: University of California Press, 1968). A thematic and generic overview can be found in Gershon Shaked, *Shmuel Yosef Agnon: A Revolutionary Traditionalist* (New York: New York University Press, 1989). See also Anne Golomb Hoffman, *Between Exile and Return: S. Y. Agnon and the Drama of Writing* (Albany: State University of New York Press, 1991). For a recent anthology with notes and introductions, see Alan Mintz and Anne Golomb Hoffman, eds., *A Book That Was Lost and Other Stories by S. Y. Agnon* (New York: Schocken Books, 1995).

Alan Mintz's *Banished from Their Father's Table: Loss of Faith and Hebrew Autobiography* contains a chapter on Berdyczewski's fiction. Another aspect of Berdyczewski's work can be glimpsed in his *Mimekor Yisrael: Classical Jewish Folktales* (trans. I. M. Lask; prepared and annotated by Dan Ben-Amos; Bloomington: Indiana University Press, 1990). For a study of Uri Zvi Greenberg's Holocaust poetry together with an introduction to his poetics, see Alan Mintz, *Ḥurban: Responses to Catastrophe in Hebrew Literature* (Syracuse N.Y.: Syracuse University Press, 1996). For a discussion of the fiction of Amalia Kahana-Carmon, see Yael Feldman, *No Room of Their Own: Gender and Nation in Israeli Women's Fiction* (New York: Columbia University Press, 1999). For a selection in English of Dahlia Ravikovitch's poetry, see *The Window: New and Selected Poems*, translated and edited by Chana Bloch and Ariel Bloch (Riverdale-on-Hudson, N.Y.: Sheep Meadow Press, 1989).

נספח: טקסטים בעברית

מיכה יוסף ברדיצ'בסקי I

פָּרָה אֲדֻמָּה

מעשה בפרה אדומה, והמעשה קרה לפני ימים לא רבים בעיר קטנה סמוכה
לחורן, מקום מושב רבי רבים אחד; ואמנם, אני, המספר, לא הייתי שם ולא ראיתי את
הדברים בעיני, אבל שמעתים מפי אנשים נאמנים. לא אכחד, המעשה מרגיז מעט.
רגע אמרתי: אכסה על זה, וכרגע אמרתי: יִכָּתֵב זה לעינינו.
הנה אנו בני הדור הולכים למות, וקם אחרינו דור אשר לא ידע אבותיו ומהלך
חייו בגולה, – והיה אם יקרא בספר ויבקש לדעת מהחיים האלה על־ידי קרי וכתיב,
נֵדע מה היו חיינו אז, נֵדע גם האור וגם את הצללים. נֵדע כי היינו יהודים, אבל גם
בני בשר ודם, ועם כל מה שמשמע בזה...

בעיר דַשְׁיה הקטנה היה שו"ב אחד, שהיתה לו „קבלה" על שחיטות, וכבר היה
קרוב להשיג משרה של שו"ב שני בעיר אחת; והנה נמצא בו פסול ולא יכול עוד
להיות שו"ב בישראל. ותחת לתפוש אחר־כך אומנות המלמדוּת, או להיות קורא
ובעל־תפילה, או להיות בכלל פועל־בטל, בלי מלאכה קבועה בחיים, וחי מן „הרוח"
או מחנות קטנה, בחר לו האיש הזה אומנות, שאמנם קרובה מאד בטבעה למלאכת
השחיטה, אבל במעמד החברתי והדתי של עיירות בני־ישראל היא רחוקה הימנה
מהלך רב... נאמר את הדבר מפורש: מי שהיה מוכן להיות שו"ב, והרי יש באומנות זו
מעין יראת־שמים וכל הדברים השייכים לדת היהודים, היה לקצב פשוט ברחוב
היהודים, ויפתח לו חנות של בשר. הוא עזב את הלימודים, את ה„לבושי שׂרד"
והלכות שחיטה וטריפות ויהי לקצב סתם, כשאר הקצבים, ולאדם מגושם העומד כל
היום בחנות, תולה את הפרים והכבשים השחוטים על יתדות, פושט את העורות,
מנקר ומוכר את הבשר ליטרה ליטרה...

ולא די בזה, הוא היה ל„קל" במעשיו ולבלתי נזהר במצוות, כשאר הקצבים בישראל,
שאינם מהדרים מן המהדרים; ואם רק לא תתגלה מילתא הם שוכחים לפעמים
ומוכרים בשר־טריפה בתור בשר כשר, מפני הדבר הפשוט, שבשר־טריפה בעיירות
כאלה, שרובן בני־ישראל ומיעוטן איכרים האוכלים בשר־החזיר, הוא כמעט ב„חצי־
חנם", ובשר כשר, על ידי ה„טַקסה" והמכס ועוד דברים כאלה, הוא דוקא לא בחינם
ומחיריו ארבעים או ארבעים וחמש פרוטות כל ליטרה. ואם ייסרו אותם שם בגיהינום
לעתיד בגלל המעשים האלה, הלא מרויחים הם פה בעודם על פני האדמה, והרוַח

3

הוא דבר נחוץ לכל בן־ישראל בעל אשה ובנים. וזאת למודעי: הקצבים אוהבים לאכול ולשתות ולפרנס את בני־ביתם בארוחת הבוקר, הצהרים והערב ממש, ולא בקטניות וברוחניות, כאשר יעשו התורנים ויראי־שמים "לשמה".

ובעצם, יש במעשה הקצבות ובהכאת הגרזן בגוף של בהמה, ואם גם שחוטה, כדי לגדע יד ורגל או לשסע אותה לשנים, מעין אכזריות. עוד אתמול היתה העז רועה באחו, הכבש רץ מן העדר לבית מלונו, והיום כבר הוציאו מהם דם ונפחה נפשם, והם תלויים על גבי מוט ופניהם למטה. הדם הוא החיים, והוא עתה נדבק בידי הקצבים ובאצבעותיהם: והם, הקצבים, הם העוזרים הראשיים לעקוד פר לשחיטה או שור בעת השחזת הסכין של השוחט. הוא, השו"ב, ישאר ירא־שמים, כי הדת ומצוות הדת שומרות עליו ומגינות על נפשו. והאכזריות שבדבר תבוא בקצבים והיא ירושתם. בכלל הקצבים אינם חלושי־הכוח, וכשריב מתפרץ בעיר ובא הדבר לידי הכאות ממש, הקצבים הם המכים הראשיים. כל העם הרוחני ירא את הקצבים הגופניים, כי המה עזי־פנים; ואם יכעיס אותם אדם לא ידעו חמלה.

צריך לומר גם את הצד הטוב שבדבר. עם בני־ישראל היה ימים רבים עם חלש וירא מקול עלה נידף; וכשהיו פרעות ביהודים היו נסים מפני מאה איכר שיכור אחד, ויקבלו עליהם את שבירת החלונות וקריעת הכרים והכסתות ואין מוחה. תחת זה הקצבים למדו למחות, להזדיין במקלות ובגרזנים ולהיות למגן בעת צרה. דבר כזה קרה בדשיה פעם אחת בחג הפסחא שלהם בין מלכא למלכא, דור שלם לפני זה, בטרם למדו בני־ישראל לעשות כמעשיהם בכל מקום ולהיקהל ולעמוד על נפשם. היפלא כי להם הרשות לעטר את שמם בתור ראשונים לגיבורי ישראל!

החמירה התורה בגנב יותר מבגזלן, שזה האחרון חשוה כבוד עבד לכבוד רבו, והראשון אינו משוה כבוד עבד לכבוד רבו, ואם דייקנים אנו בכלל הזה באים אנו בחיי הקצבים לשני הפכים בנושא אחד. גיבורי ישראל אלה, שאינם מוגי־לב כלל ולא יראו מפני כל, בטבעם כש"לוקחים" לפעמים שור או פר מאחרים בלי תשלומים חם עושים זה בצנעה, ודוקא שלא מדעת בעלים, ודוקא על ידי אחרים. ואולי אין זה כבר "לקיחה" כלל או מין גניבה, כי אם ענין הפרנסה. – ענין הקצבות מחייב שפר או שור שנשחט, שור או פר שקנו אותו ממש ושילמו כל מחירו עולה פי חמישה על שור שנשחט, שלא שילמו בעדו לבעליו ממש. הוא, השור, היה תועה בדרך ולקחו אותו אנשים והביאו אותו להם, לקצבים, או היו כחמישים פרים בעדר, ועתה שם רק ארבעים ותשעה, מספר המספיק עוד לבעלים; וצאו וחשבו כמה היזקות שכיחים בשחיטת פר: לפעמים יטריף אותו השו"ב בשעת השחיטה, ולפעמים יטרף בטריפת הריאה או בדבר אחר מי"ח טריפות... העיר דשיה בכלל עניה ויהודים אינם לוקחים הרבה בשר בכסף: בשר ששהה שלושה ימים בלא מים גם כן יטרף ובימות הקיץ יתקלקל. – איך יכול הקצב, שואלים, להתקיים בלי "מציאות" מן הצד?

תאמרו, הלא זה אסור, לא נכון לכל בר־ישראל כך. אבל האם לא גם שאר מסחרים וחנויות וכל גניבת דעת הבריות או רמאות, מאותם שיש בכגון אלה, אינם גם כן

אסורים? – בעיקר אין הבדל בין אלה לאלה, רק זה, שהללו, הסוחרים והחנונים מבעלי־הבתים, הפסלנות שבהם אינו דבר ביטוי בשפתים וקרוי בשם, ולא יעצור את עושיהם כלל מללבוש מעין איצטלה של אנשים כשרים, המתפללים במקומות הראשיים בבית־התפילה; והללו, כלומר, הקבצים וכל כיוצא בהם, בקהל היראים בל יחָשבו ומתפללים הם לא בבית־התפילה המרכזי שבעיר, כי אם ב„שומרים לבוקר". הללו, בעלי־בתים, שותים „תיקון" אחרי התפילה ויש להם איזה כינוי יראי לכל מה שעושים לצורך גופם – והללו, הקבצים, שותים יי"ש ממש, בלי אמתלאות, גם בלי מות אב ואם ושאר יומא דפגרא... הקבצים בודאי אינם צדיקים ואיני רוצה לחפות עליהם, אבל לולא אותו מעשה, כי אז לא היו בעיני כרשעים. רשעים! מי יבטא מלה זו בכל מרירותה? בני־אדם רוצים לחיות ויש להם יצר־הרע בתוך מעיהם, וגם הוא אינו מחותל במשי ודרכו קשה אף קשה. –

וכך היה הדבר:
בעיר דשיה היה בעל־בית אחד ושמו ראובן, אדם בינוני, שלא הצטיין מימיו במאומה; ומי יודע אם גם היה נודע שמו בין יושבי העיר, לולא היו פרותיו נודעות.
לרוב אנשי דשיה, שידם משגת, יש פרות נותנות את החלב לביתם ואינם צריכים לקנותו בחוץ. אבל לראובן היתה תמיד הפרה היותר טובה שבעיר; הוא היה מוצלח לזה והיה גם מבין בזה; הוא ידע לכלכל את פרותיו היטב ולשכלל את גופן ולעשות אותן בריאות וטובות־מראה. ראובן לא התבייש כלל, בבוא פרתו מהעדר, להכין לה מעצמו מזונות הבית והביא לה מים לשתות. הרפת שלו בחצרו היתה תמיד נקיה ועיניו צופיות תמיד, שלא יאונה לפרתו כל רע. השגחתו ועידון פרתו – זה היה תוכן חייו האחד כל ימיו, ובזה קנה לו גם שם בעיר ההיא.
אמנם אנשי דשיה הם עירונים ממש, ואין להם שייכות הרבה אל הטבע, אבל הפרה הנותנת חלב לבעלי־הבתים, והעזים הנחלבות אצל דלת העם, עוד נותנות שארית למגע עם הטבע. – מכירים בכל פינות העיר פרות הרחוב ההוא ועזיו; ובשוב הבהמות הגדולות והדקות מן העדר יעמדו השכנים והתבוננו אל כל פרה ואל כל עז, להגיד דעתם על ערכן ועבי גופן וסכום חלבן שנותנות לבעליהן. איזו חיבה לכל בית לבהמות־הבית שלה, ומתהלך אדם עם פרה ועז יחד כְרֵעַ. ומדוע לא יעשה כהן? גם הבהמות הנן בעלות־חיים ויש להן שעת שובע ורעב, רגשי צער וחדוה ואהבת אם לבנה וגעגועים. אם לא תדעו את זה קחו לכם לביתכם פרה או עז או כבש, ותראו את נשמת החי.
ובימים ההם היתה לראובן פרה אדומה הולנדית, שכמוה לא ראו עוד אנשי דשיה ליופי ולבריאות ולעיגול הגוף. כמלכה היתה צועדת קוממיות בראש, בבוא העדר מן המרעה; ורעותיה, הפרות בעצמן, היו חולקות לה כבוד, והיא באמת היתה מגזע נעלה, ומבנה גופה, עטיניה, עורה הנעים הראו מוצאה. כמאה וחמישים רו"כ ביקשו לתת לראובן פעם במחירה; ומחיר יתר הפרות של בני העיר, גם אותן של הנגידים,

עולה לכל היותר לשבעים או לשמונים רובל. איך בא ראובן לפרה כזאת, והוא לא
היה עשיר – לא נודע, אבל יושבי העיר לא התפלאו על זה כלל, אחרי שמזלו של
ראובן בפרותיו כבר ידוע היה. פרתו של זה צריכה להיות הפרה היותר טובה בדשיה
ובסביבותיה; כך כתוב בספר המזל וכן היה תמיד.

ומאושר היה ראובן בימים ההם, בהיות לו פרה אדומה זו, כאיש אשר השיג עילוי
בלתי־מצוי בתור חתן לבתו; והיה נהנה במלוא רוחו כאשר שמע מספרים בשבח
המתו ומפארים ומרוממים אותה. גוזמאות ונפלאות סיפרו על פרתו של ראובן
בדשיה, כמו שמספרים, להבדיל, מרבי. אמרו שפרה זו נותנת ארבעה הין חלב בפעם
אחת. אמרו כי מחמאה בלבד, שעושים מחלב הנותר מצרכי היום, ולראובן היה
בסך הכל י״ג בנים, והרי חמישה־עשר פיות ערב ובוקר וצהרים, מרוויח ראובן שלושה
רובל לשבוע. בקצרה, פרתו האדומה של ראובן, אשר ילדה שנה שנה בבוא האביב –
ובמחיר בן־הבקר בלבד לקח חמישה־עשר כסף – היתה נותנת חומר רב לשיחות
יושבי בית־התפילה.

דשיה שמחה כי עלתה בחלקה פרה מצוינת, שיכולה להיות לצבי ולתפארת גם
בעיר גדולה לאלהים. ולנשים השכנות, בעלות "עין הרע", שקינאו בה ורצו לסגור
חלבה בקרבה על ידי לחש, לא עלה מאומה ברחשי־ליל שלהן. אם ה' יברא בריאה
טובה לו ויעמידה על רגליה לשמחה ולראוה לכל רואיה, אז אין שליטה גם לשטן
ולבני־השטן.

ושערו בנפשכם: כל זה לא הועיל ביום עברה! הגיעה השעה ונחתם גזר־דינה של
פרה זו, שהיתה באמת מקור חיים למשפחה שלמה ולדבר נעלה ממשכיות העיר. לו
פקודת כל החי באה עליה ומתה הפרה בימיה המלאים; דבר כי יהלוך בארץ, או
מגפה או מיתה סתם הכריתה אותה מארצות החיים, גם אז נעצב רוחנו, אבל החרשנו.
גם על בני־אדם חיים יעלה הכורת. בית יפה, שהרבה עמלו בו בוניו, יהיה ללהב;
מדינה כי תינגף כולה לפני אויב, או כי יקשה עליה עול מושל ומרד ומרד רב יעמיד
אותה על עברי פי פחת, מי יעצור בידי גלגל ההשגחה? מי יטיח כלפי שמיא? ולו רוח
שטות נכנסה בראובן, או עמדה הפרה מלדת שנה ושנתים ונמכרה לשחיטה, והשו״ב
בירך על השחיטה כהוגן, ובדקו את הפרה ונמצאה כשרה, ופשטו את עורה וניקרו
אותה כדין, ומכרו את הבשר השמן לבני־ישראל ליום השבת, ונעם לחכם כשהוא
מטוגן ומבושל, והיה להם לעונג שבת, כי אז נדו בראש לגורל פרה חולבת כזו –
לשחיטה, אבל זהו דרך העולם, ומקרים כאלה יקרו בחיים. אבל בפרתו זו של ראובן
נעשה רצח, רצח נורא מאד, כאשר יארבו לאדם ביער להכותו נפש; והדבר היה שלא
בדרך הטבע ולא פילל אדם כי כזה יקרה בישראל!

היתה שנת בצורת, נתיקר הבשר. הפרנסות בדשיה היו דחוקות מאד, וגם לקצבים,
שמעמדם תמיד אינו נרע, נעשה קשה בימים ההם. קרו גם איזה דברי ריבות ומשטמות
בעיר ונפלגו "לצדדים שונים", כנהוג, וראובן, איש־שלום מנעוריו, לקח הפעם חלק
ב"מחלוקת", והקצבים היו מצד השני, שכנגדו. אמנם אין די סיבות לבאר את אשר

קרה אחרי־כן, ובכל זאת אני מרצה אותן לפני הקורא אחת לאחת. איני שופט פה,
רק מספר; אבל אחרים יבואו לשפוט ולצרף ולבאר את מהלך הדבר.

הגורל יצא על פרתו של ראובן מאת חלק אחוז של קצבי עיר דשיה ל"הילקח"
מבעליה – עינים עינים הביטו אחריה בשובה מן המרעה, והיא לא ידעה את גורלה.
נתאספה השיירה חרש בבית הקצב השו"ב הפסול, נתאספו שנית אצל שואל, הקצב
הראשי, בעל הכתפים היותר רחבות בדשיה, ויתיעצו על הצפונות, ויקבעו את היום
ואת השעה ואת המקום, וכולם מוכנים היו לזה כאיש אחד.

היה הדבר במוצאי־השבת, בשלהי דקייטא. עוד ישבו בבין־הערבים ראובן וביתו
ויררוו נחת מהפרה. הקטנים החליקו את עורה, הגדולים אמרו שבחה בפניה. הבת
הגדולה קמה ונתנה לה את הסובים הרטובים, ותציג לפניה גם שוקת המים; ולפתע
הוציאה הפרה אנחה שוברת את הגוף; ולא ידעו האנשים מה אירע ויתחלחלו. כי
יבוא החורף יתחילו העננים לכסות גם את לב בני־ישראל, בזכרם אחד אחד כי אין
עצים להסקה, כי אין בגדים חמים ובני־אדם צריכים לכסות מערומיהם. הרעו את
מעשיהם וקילקלו את פרנסתם!

השעה היתה שתים־עשרה בחצות הליל. כבר ישנו אנשי דשיה על משכבם, ובכל
בתי ישראל גם זיק אור אחד לא יאיר מן החלונות. חולמים הם האנשים קשה באופל
הליל, וממחרת היום יחלו ימי החול הקשים ללחם... והנה בן קצב אחד חוצה את
החושך וצועד לאט אל רפת ראובן, אשר שם הפרה עומדת. אין מנעול לדלת, רק
חבל עב יעבת רגל הפרה אל עץ אחד. ויחתוך אותו המתגנב בסכינו הַחַד, ויקח את
הפרה בקרניה ויוביל אותה במשעול צר, והפרה הולכת בתמהון רב.

והנה הס, האדם והחי, עומדים לפני פתח המרתף הגדול של שואל הקצב, ששם
נועדו יתר החברים; ויצאו שני אנשים לקראתם ויחליקו בידיהם את הפרה וימשמשו
בה, והיא קישקשה בזנבה באין חפץ. לפתע התחילו למשכה בכוח אל תוך המרתף
ולנהלה על המעלות והמורדות, בעל כרחה צעדה ותמאן ללכת, וידחפו אותה בחזקה,
ותנהם ותחרד מבוא המרתף.

הנה הפרה עומדת מטה בזעף. כשבעה אנשים קמו מהמרתף לקבל פניה, והם
לבושים אדרת־שער וחגורים כאיכרים ופניהם פני להבים. כבר שתו איש איש איזו
כוסות ל"חיזוק", והנרות הקטנים הדולקים באופל המרתף נתנו לו צורת שאול.
התחילו העומדים לסבב את הפרה ולמשש אותה.

ולפתע קם קצב גיבור כארי ויאמר להפיל את הפרה ארצה, אך רגליה חזקות
כברזל. באו חבריו ויעזרו לו בשארית כוח ויאבקו עמה קשה, והיא נעצה רגליה
בקרקע, ובעיניה שצף קצף. והנה קמה הפרה ותאמר לנגח איש, ותך בראשה בקיר
האבן, ויתנודד כל המרתף. קצב אחד גדול וחזק זחל מבלי משים אל תחת גחונה
ויהדק את רגליה האחרונות בחבל עב. ושני לו עשה כזאת ברגליה שלצד הפנים;
ויקומו האנשים כולם ויחגרו כוח, ויעמיסו את עצמם על גבי הפרה ויהדפו אותה
בחזקה. ותפול לארץ ותנהם בחזקה, ותאמר לנתק את החבלים. והקמים עליה החזיקו

בה באיזו נקמת־איבה, אשר לא ידעו תמול־שלשום. בחוץ החל הגשם לרדת ולהכות בגג המרתף והרוח השמיע קולו, וממצחי הקצבים נוטפים נטפי זיעה כגודל קטניות מרוב עמל; ויביטו איש אל רעהו כזרים ויסירו את בגדם מעליהם, קיפלו עד השחי את בתי־היד אשר לכותנתם ויהיו מוכנים, כמו לשעת־קרב גדולה. מה היה להם? איזה רוח עצור בהם ביקש לו מפלט. –

ואחד הקצבים, מי שהיה שו"ב, עמד במנוחה בצד וישחז את החלף הישן, שהוציא אותו מתערו ועבר על חדודו בצפרנו. ועוד הפעם כרעו הקצבים על גב הפרה, הללו אחזו אותה ברגליה העבות מלמטה והללו מלמעלה, ושנים מהם, אמיצי־כוח מאד, הטו את ראשה, כוחם התגדל לבלי שיעור. היה הדבר כמו קטב ממלא כל האויר, כמו גזר־דין נורא נחרץ זה עתה – והנה הרים הקצב־השו"ב את החלף ויעביר על הצואר החלק בהולכה והובאה. ותגאה הפרה בקול מחריד, הבוקע את האדמה, ויזנק קלח דם, ויהי כמו נפתח מעין דם גדול וישטוף כקשת רחבה, והיא מאירה באמצע לאור העששית, התלויה ממעל על גבי תקרה. והדם הולך ושוטף ויז על התקרה ועל הכתלים ועל הקרקע ועל מכנסי האנשים ובפניהם ובידיהם, ותילחם הפרה בשארית כוחותיה ותפרפר, ויהי כל הקרקע אשר מסביבה לנהר דם. קמו הרוצחים ויסיעו אותה ממקומה הצדה ותעבור שעה והפיחה נפשה האדומה ותמת. ניצח בן־אדם את החי!

ויקח קצב אחד סכין חד ויתחב בבטן הפרה הגוועת ותצא הפרשדונה החוצה ויחלו האחרים חבריו לפשוט את עורה, ויקרעו אותו כמעט מעל הפרה, והכל עשו במין כוח עצור ובמין רגש מוצק, שכמוהו לא ידעו עד עתה.

נפשטה הבהמה, החלו האנשים לחלק אותה לחלקים, לחתוך את ראשה, את רגליה. קצב אחד לא יכול לעצור ברוחו, ויקח את הכבד השמן וישטחהו על גבי גחלים בוערות, ששמו אחרים בפינה. ובבוא הדם באש אכלו אותו כולם בלי מליחה ובתאוה עזה נמרצה וילוקו את אצבעותיהם בחמדה. ובקבוק גדול של יי"ש היה עומד מוכן על הקרקע וישתו ויאכלו מלוא תאותם. ככוהני־הבעל בשעתם היו האנשים האלה בשעה ההיא, בחיתולק הקרבן לפני המזבח. והדבר לא היה בבית־אל או בדן, כי אם בעיר היהודיה דשיה, לא לפני גלות עשרת השבטים נעשה הדבר, בממלכת ישראל הצפונית, כי אם בשנת חמשת אלפים שש מאות ארבעים וחמש ליצירה...

עברה האשמורה השניה, הגשם ירד בחזקה והרוח סוער. חילקו האנשים את הפרה לעשרה חלקים, וישימו איש איש חלקו בשקו. ויעמיסו אותו כל אחד על שכמם, ונפוצו איש איש אל חנותו בחשכת הליל, לשימו שם ולהסתירו שם. העיר דשיה ישנה והוזה, כלבים נובחים, השמים מעולפים בערפלי הגשם. מי יודע מה שנעשה עתה בחלל העיר? –

שכחו הקצבים בחפזם לסגור את המרתף של שואל, ויבואו כלבים ללקק את הדם. בבוקר ראו כי פרתו של ראובן נעלמה מן הרפת ויאמרו כי נגנבה, ויחפשו

אותה; והנה מצאו בעוד שעה את עורה האדום, שהיה עוד מונח כמעט בלחגתו. ויחרדו האנשים למשמע הדבר הנורא הזה, וַתצלנה אזני כל שומעיו. ובבית ראובן האומלל תאניה ואניה ואֵבל כבד!

מיום אשר נוסדה דשיה לא היה לה יום כבד כזה. הלכו אנשים בחוצות וברחובות, נשים נשים באו ומלחשות ומדברות. היה כמו באו בעיר ליקוי-חמה וליקוי-לבנה כאחד, וכל אחד הביט בפני חברו ואשה בפני רעותה, כאילו נהפך העולם לעמק רפאים. אמנם נורא המעשה אשר עשו להרוג בהמה בשלַת ימיה, נורא מאד!

ואשר קרה לקצבים, שהשתתפו במעשי רצח הבהמה, דברי ריבות ומשפטים שונים בערכאות, ועּנשם של הקצבים האלה, גם בידי אדם גם בידי שמים – אם אספר כל אלה לפרטיהם יכילו הרבה. בקצרה, כל אחד שלקח חלקו בהכחדת הפרה האדומה, ראה אחר-כך דברים רעים בביתו וכמו רבצה בו אָלה להפילו למדחפות, אותו ואת ביתו, לבלתי השאיר לו שריד. הדברים ההם הלא כתובים בספר דברי הימים של דשיה ובפנקס העיר.

יקחם נא הקורא משם.

שאול טשרניחובסקי II

לַשֶּׁמֶשׁ
כליל סוניטות

אבותינו שהיו במקום הזה,
אחוריהם אל היכל ה' ופניהם קדמה,
והמה משתחוים קדמה לשמש

(סוכה פ"ה, מ"ד)

א

הָיִיתִי לֵאלֹהַי כְּיָקִינְטוֹן וְכַאֲדָנִי,
שֶׁאֵין בְּעוֹלָמוֹ לוֹ אַךְ שִׁמְשׁוּ זֶה הַצַּח,
וּמַלְאָךְ בָּא דּוֹפְקוֹ: "קוּם גְּדַל, בֶּן־צִיץ, וּפְצַח
רְנָתְךָ, רְנַת־חָג, בְּחָרוּל הַנַּשְׁכָּנִי!"

וְאֵינֶנִּק רְטֹב־נִיר. כַּיַּיִן עֲבָרַנִי
זֶה רֵיחַ אַדְמַת־בּוּל עַל רִגְבָּה, רֶגֶב רָךְ.
הֲמִבְּלִי אֵין לוֹ אָב וְכֹהֵן בְּמִקְדָּשׁ־כְּרָךְ,
כִּי הֱבִיאַנִי לְכָאן וּלְנָבִיא לוֹ שָׂמָנִי?

הַיֵּקֶל בְּעֵינַי שָׂרָף עַל גַּבֵּי כֶסֶף־בְּרוֹשׁ
מִשַּׁמְנֵךְ הַטּוֹב, הַמַּזְהִיב עַל הָרֹאשׁ,
וְרֵיחוֹת הָאַגָּס וְהַשָּׂדֶה שֶׁנָּטָרְתִּי

מֵאַבְקוֹת רוֹכְלֵי־שְׁבָא, מִנֶּרְדִּי וּמִקְטָרְתִּי?
וָאֶקֹּד־לָךְ בַּלָּט. אֶשְׁתַּחֲוֶה בִיקָר,
וּכְאַחַת שִׁבֳּלֵי־פָז בַּקָּמָה כְּבֻדַּת־בָּר.

ב

וּכְאַחַת שִׁבֳּלֵי־פָז בַּקָּמָה כְּבֻדַּת־בָּר,
שֶׁעָלְתָה בְּרָב־נוֹי וַתִּשְׁגַּשְׂג בְּכָל מְאֹדָהּ,
כְּשִׁבֹּלֶת אַחַת זוֹ צוֹפֶנֶת בְּחֵיקָהּ סוֹדָהּ,
עֲרֻבַּת חַיֵּי־עַד וּפְלֵיטַת־מַה מְּכֻבָּר;

כְּשִׁבֹּלֶת גְּנוּבַת־נִיר, הַיּוֹנְקָה שַׁד־הַכְּפָר
וְרֻטְּבָה עֲסִיס חַי, חוֹלֶמֶת חֲלוֹם־הוֹדָהּ,
צָמַחְתִּי גַּם אָנִי! אַךְ נַפְשִׁי צְמֵאָה עוֹדָהּ.
אֲהָהּ, יוֹם יִרְדֹּף יוֹם! הַאֶגְבַּהּ אֶת הַשְּׁטָר?

10

חֲלוֹמִי טֶרֶם בָּא! מֵעֵינַי נִצְפַּן שְׁבִילִי.
כִּי אֶפֶן כֹּה וָכֹה – אָפוּנָה: מַה־לִּי, מִי לִי...
הֲבָאתִי עַד הַגְּבוּל? אוֹ אִם עֲבַרְתִּיו כְּבָר?

הֲשֶׁקֶר אָבִי לִי, לֹא יִשְׁמֹר מוֹצָא פִיהוּ?
אֲנִי צִיץ־בָּר אֲנִי, וְאָבִי שִׁמְשִׁי לִי הוּא,
וַיְמַן לִי גִּשְׁמֵי־חֹם, וַיְצַו עַרְפְלֵי־הַר.

ג

וַיְמַן לִי גִּשְׁמֵי־חֹם, וַיְצַו עַרְפְלֵי־הַר,
דְּמְדּוּמֵי עִמְקֵי־יָם, מְעוֹן דּוּמִיָּה רַבָּה,
עֲתַר עֲנַן אֵשׁ קֹדְחָה עַל אֶשְׁנַבָּה,
וּבְטֶרֶם תִּפְרֹץ עָל, לָהּ קֶרֶב־אֶרֶץ צָר;

וְלוּחַ־שְׁמָשׁוֹת צַר מֵהָכִיל אֶת הַסֵּפֶר,
הַחַמָּה בַהֲמוֹן אוֹקְיָנוֹס־אֵשׁ עַל גַּבָּהּ,
וּנְצָרוֹת מִנִּי־עַד, שֶׁקִּבֵּל אָב מֵאַבָּא,
שְׁגִיוֹנוֹת חוֹלֵי־כָרֶךְ וּמִסְרוֹת תְּמִימֵי־כְפָר,

לִהְיוֹת אֲנִי הַצִּיר לְעוֹלְמוֹ אֲשֶׁר יָצַר,
תַּמְצִיתוֹ, מֶרְכַּז כָּל מֶרְכָּזָיו, הַרְבֵּה אָצַר
לַהֹוֶה וְלַבָּא, לְעָבֵר אֲשֶׁר גָּז.

וּלְמַרְבֵּה כָל־הַחֵן בִּצְבָעִים לֹא בִישָׁנִי.
וַיְעַשְּׁרֵנִי רָב – וּכְכֹחוֹ, אֲשֶׁר עָז –
סִמְפוֹנִיּוֹת אוֹר וָצֵל, וּכְחָל, וּסְרָק, וְשָׁנִי.

ד

סִמְפוֹנִיּוֹת אוֹר וָצֵל, וּכְחָל, וּסְרָק, וְשָׁנִי,
חֲנוּטֵי גָבִישׁ קַר וְיִשְׁנֵי כְרוּם־הַיָּם,
הַחַיִּים חַיֵּי־דַק שֶׁל נִיצוֹץ נִתַּז חָם
תּוֹךְ בַּהַט כְּבֶד־גָּוֶן וְשִׁפוּנֵי נַחְשׁוֹל אֲנִי;

וְרִקְמוֹת גִּידֵי־עֵץ עַל נֵסֶר מַהֲגוֹנִי,
אִילָנוֹת סְפוּגֵי־דָם מְקַלְחִים בָּעֵים,
וּגְנָנִים טֶרֶם־יוֹם וְשֶׁל עֶרֶב רוֹחֵץ בְּדָם,
הַמַּשִּׁיל אוֹצְרוֹת פָּז וּלְעוֹלָם לֹא יֵעָנִי, –

מַנְגִּינָה אַחַת הֵם, שִׁיר אֶחָד נִפְלָא, רָם.
הַמְצָרֵף סְפָרוֹת הוּא הוּא יִמְצָא אֶת הַחִידָה?
אוֹ, חוֹקֵר תּוֹרַת חַי, הַאַתָּה לִי תַגִּידָהּ?

לֵב־תְּמִימִים פָּתְרָה כְּבָר; וּמִן הַלֵּב הַתָּם
קִבַּלְתִּי גַם אֲנִי, כִּי לִבִּי לֹא רִמָּנִי!
בִּינוֹתִי צַעַר־דּוֹר, שִׁיר גּוֹי וָגוֹי קְסָמָנִי.

ה

בִּינוֹתִי צַעַר־דּוֹר, שִׁיר גּוֹי וָגוֹי קְסָמָנִי:
חֲלוֹם חַרְטֻמֵּי־אוֹן, הַמְתֹאָר עַל פִּי קִיר,
וּכְתָב דְּרוּאִידִים זֶה, טָבוּעַ בְּאַבְנֵי גִיר,
קָמֵעַ עַל־פְּנֵי קְלָף, שִׁיר קוֹסֵם – גִּמְגּוּם עָנִי.

וּבְשִׁרְטוּט נוֹתֵן צוּ לְדוֹר וּלְאֹם קַדְמֹנִי,
בְּהַשְׁבָּעוֹת רוֹעֵה־צֹאן, הַלּוֹחֵשׁ עַל סַף דִּיר,
בִּפְלֵיטַת שִׁגָּיוֹן־מָג, כִּי אֲחָזַהוּ צִיר,
וּבְטַלִיסְמָאוֹת־סִין מִבְּטֵי הַסַּקְרָנִי

יָגֵל אַךְ תִּפְלָה זֶה, אֲרֶשֶׁת בְּשַׂר־יָדָם:
"הַהֹוֶה בְּסֵתֶר־יֵשׁ, נָא שְׁמָר־לִי אֶת הַדָּם.
אַל תְּכַבֶּה אִשְׁךָ, בִּי הַצַּתָּ בְּרַחֲמֶיךָ,

אֵשׁ נוֹזְלִים, נוֹטְרָה אֵשׁ, זִיק אֶחָד מִלְּהָבֶיךָ!" –
זֶה סַד־הַכֹּל הָרָב, הַלָּן בַּלֵּב הַמָּר,
קוֹל נֶפֶשׁ עוֹטָה אוֹר, קוֹל תּוֹעָה בְּמַחְשָׁךְ זָר.

ו

קוֹל נֶפֶשׁ עוֹטָה אוֹר, קוֹל תּוֹעָה בְּמַחְשָׁךְ זָר
מִתְרוֹצְצִים תּוֹכִי, כִּי לֹא הִתְקַדַּשְׁתִּי לְמַדַּי
תְּחוּם אֵינוֹ אֶלָּא סָפֵק־סָפֵק, סָפֵק־וַדַּאי,
סְבָבַנִי כַּחֲלוֹם בְּשִׁגְיוֹנוֹת מְשֻׁזָּר.

וּבְהַהְפְּכוּת חַי מִתְרַפֵּק עַל כָּל גְּזַר־
דִּין נוֹקֵב דִּין, בַּחְתֹּר חֲתִירוֹת תַּחַת שַׁדַּי,
סוֹחֶרֶת אֵמוּן־תֹּם לָבַשְׁתִּי מֵעַל לְמַדַּי
וּבְחֵלוֹ שֶׁל יוֹם־יוֹם לִי נִשְׁאַר מְעַט מִזְעָר.

וְאִלְמָלֵא רֵיחוֹת גּוּשׁ אֲדָמָה שְׁמֵנָה, פְּרוּרָה,
חֹם מַחֲנִיק נוֹדֵף עִם הַמֹּץ מִן הַמַּמְגּוּרָה,
צְלִיל אֶת פּוֹלֵחַ נִיר וּמַגָּל רַן בַּבָּר,

סְפַגְתִּים בִּי בַּכְּפָר, בַּדְּרוֹר, עוֹדֶנִּי בְּאַבִּי –
מִי עָמַד לִי בַּצַּר, בַּקְּרָב, בְּהִתְכַּוֵּץ לִבִּי,
בְּעָמְדִי בֵּין הַחַי וּבֵין הַגּוֹסֵס כְּבָר?

ז

בְּעָמְדִי בֵּין הַחַי וּבֵין הַגּוֹסֵס כְּבָר
(אָמָּנוּת מַה־נּוֹרָאָה!) וְאִזְמֵל חַד בְּכַפִּי,
יֵשׁ בּוֹכֶה מִתּוֹךְ גִּיל וְיֵשׁ מְקַלֵּל בְּאַפִּי,
סָפַגְתִּי אַחֲרוֹן אוֹר תּוֹךְ אִישׁוֹן גּוֹסֵס זָר.

אֶל רַעַם תּוֹתְחֵי־אוֹן מִתְגַּלְגְּלִים בַּכָּר,
לְאֵשׁ נוֹצְצָה בְּאִשּׁוֹן מְנַהֲרִתִּי לִי בְּגַפִּי
הִתְוֵיתִי אַחֲרוֹן־קָו, מָחַקְתִּי חַי מִדַּפִּי,
מִסַּף מְשֹׁהָם כָּךְ תֵּעָקֵר אֶבֶן־יְקָר.

וְאוּלָם בְּאוֹתוֹ זִיק בָּעַיִן הָעוֹמֶמֶת,
בָּאוֹר הַסּוֹפֵג אוֹר וּבְטֶרֶם קָם לְעַד;
וְאוּלָם בְּאוֹתוֹ בְּרַק אֵשׁ קוֹדְחָה וְצוֹרֶמֶת,

בָּאֵשׁ הַקּוֹרְאָה לְאֵשׁ, הַמְצֻוָּה אֵיד וּשְׁמָד, –
הָיִיתָ אַתָּה בָם; זֶה הוֹדְךָ הַמֻּמְנִי; –
הַאִם קַדְמָתִי בָּא אוֹ אַחֵר צוּר בְּרָאָנִי?

ח

הַאִם קַדְמָתִי בָּא אוֹ אַחֵר צוּר בְּרָאָנִי?
'אֱלֹהִים' סָבִיב לִי וּמְלֵאִים כָּל הַיְקוּם.
כּוֹכָבִים אֱלֹהַי, אֶתְפַּלֵּל לָמוֹ, קְסוֹם־
פְּנֵיכֶם, מְאוֹר־יוֹם וְסַהַר חִוְּרָנִי.

כִּי בִלְתָּךְ אֵין כְּלוּם, הוֹי שֶׁמֶשׁ חַמָּנִי!
בְּנֵי־שֶׁמֶשׁ אַתֶּם לִי, הַגְּלָמִים תְּלוּיִים רוּם,
בְּנֵי־שֶׁמֶשׁ – עֵץ הַפִּיל וּקְלִפּוֹת כָּל הַשּׁוּם,
גִּלְגּוּלֵי אוֹר וָחֹם – הַפֶּחָם הָרַתְחָנִי.

וְהָיָה כָל הַיְקוּם קוֹל תְּפִלָּה, תְּפִלַּת־כֹּל:
לְךָ קוֹרְאוֹת אֲמוֹת־תַּנִּים, גּוּרֵיהֶן כִּי תְפַלַּחְנָה,
לְךָ יָרֹן שׁוֹפַר־קְרָב עִם הָנֵץ אוֹר בַּמַּחֲנֶה,

הַשְּׁמָשׁוֹת בְּגַלְגַּל־עָל, כִּי יִגְרְפֵם הַקּוֹל.
בְּמַקְהֵלַת אֵין־הַסּוֹף אֶרְנֶה וְלֹא אָדָם:
עוֹד בִּלְבִּי לָן הַטַּל, הַיּוֹרֵד עַל שְׂדֵה־אָדֹם.

ט

עוֹד בִּלְבִּי לָן הַטַּל, הַיּוֹרֵד עַל שָׂדֶה־אָדֹם.
וּמַרְטִיב אֶת הַחוֹל הַקָּדוֹשׁ בְּמִדְבַּר־אֵל;
וּבְאָזְנֵי חַי הַשִּׁיר, הַבָּא עִם בֹּא הַצֵּל
וְנִצְנֵץ כּוֹכָב רַךְ לִנְגִינוֹת מִנִּי קֶדֶם,

וְהֶאֱפִיל עַל הַיְקוּם בִּכְנָפָיו לֵיל־הַקֶּדֶם,
וְהָיָה אֶחָד סוֹד הַמִּדְבָּר וְהַלֵּיל,
וּמֵאַהֲלָיו יֵט קְהַל־עַמִּים עַל כָּל תֵּל,
וְהִשְׁתַּחֲווּ לוֹ בְחִיל בֶּחָג לָמוֹ וּבְאֵידָם.

וּבְהַמִּיר עַל הַגּוֹי שְׁמֵי־שָׁמָיו, שְׁמֵי־הַכְּחֹל,
כִּי יוּעַם עָלָיו פְּנֵי כוֹכָבָיו, וְאִם בְּעַל
רְקִיעַ־נָכְרִי לוֹ גַּם יִסֹּב אָחוֹר וָקֶדֶם, –

לְחֹדֶשׁ אַחַת יֵשׁ שֶׁיֵּצֵא בְּלֵיל־הָרָז
לְקַדֵּשׁ לְבָנָה זוֹ, וּכְשֵׁם שֶׁקִּדְּשָׁהּ אָז
עַל פִּסְגַּת הַר־הָהָר, מְעוֹנָה אֱלֹהֵי־קֶדֶם.

י

עַל פִּסְגַּת הַר־הָהָר, מְעוֹנָה אֱלֹהֵי־קֶדֶם,
מוֹפִיעַ בַּעֲנַנֵי־אוֹר עֲנָק וְלוֹ אֵשׁ־דָּת!
מִנֶּגַה נֶגְדּוֹ שָׁח בֵּל־כַּשְׂדִּים עַל נְהַר־פְּרָת,
וְחָוַר מַרְאֵה סְפִינְקְס בַּשִּׁיחוֹר, בְּאָפִיק יָאֹדָם.

וּבְיָדוֹ מַטֶּה, בּוֹ יְקַרְקֵר אֵל – וְנָדַם
גְּאוֹן זֶבֶס מְחַיֵּה שֵׁשׁ, וְשָׁמַע דְּבָרוֹ וְנָס
הַיַּעֲרָה פֶּרוּן, וּפָגַשׁ עָשׁ אֶת סָס
עַל חֹשֶׁן כֹּהֵן־לוּב, וְאִילָנֵי־ווֹטַן צֵידָם.

וּזְמַן כִּי יָמִיר זְמַן וְהֵאִיר מִזְרָח שׁוּב –
וְחָפְרוּ צַלְמֵי־כּוּשׁ, וּבוֹשׁ הוּרְמִיז וּכְרוּב
וֶאֱלִילֵי בְּנֵי עֶרֶב מֵאוֹר חֲצִי הַלְּבָנָה.

וְעוֹד חָזוֹן... וְיָצַר דּוֹר, כַּצּוֹרֵף בַּעֲלִיל,
אֶת אֱלֹהָיו הַבָּא – וְנַעַבְדוּ בְרִנָּנָה –
כִּי לִבִּי דוֹבֵב שִׁיר לַחַמָּה וְלַכְּסִיל.

יא

כִּי לִבִּי דוֹבֵב שִׁיר לַחַמָּה וְלַכְּסִיל –
הִתְמַתַּח עָלַי דִין וְלֶעָפָר תִּשְׁפְּתֵנִי,
כִּי לְאֵל הֲמוֹן־הָעָם אֲנִי לֹא אֶסֹּךְ יֵינִי,
בִּמְחוֹלוֹת קְבַל־עָם לֹא אֶתֵּן בְּרֹאשׁוֹ כְּלִיל?

וּבְמִקְדָּשׁ־שָׁמָיו לוֹ, חָסֵר כָּל דְּמוּת וּגְוִיל,
בִּיפִי־הַכֹּל בַּכֹּל בְּכָרוּב לֹא יַעֲנֵנִי,
וּבְסֵפֶר־יַחֲשׂ לוֹ לֹא בָא לְסַמֵּא עֵינִי,
וּבוֹ חֲתִימַת־יָד כֹּחַק לְשַׁטֵּר־אֱוִיל.

אַךְ אִם עֲבָרֵךְ גַּל הִתְלַהֲבוּת קְדוֹשָׁה־רַבָּה
וְרֶטֶט־גִיל בִּשְׁעַת הַיְצִירָה הַמִּתְנַבְּאָה,
בַּעֲטֶרֶת חַיֵּי לֵב מִשְׁתַּתֵּף לְכָל רָז;

בְּגָאוֹן־אַהֲבָה כֵּן בִּנְדִיבוּת גֶּבֶר־עָז –
נִרְצֵיתָ לוֹ כְּשֵׁם שֶׁנִּרְצֶה גַּן־מַתָּנוֹת
מִשֶּׁיִּתְרְמַל פּוֹל וְגָמַל פְּרִי־אִילָנוֹת.

יב

מִשֶּׁיִּתְרְמַל פּוֹל וְגָמַל פְּרִי־אִילָנוֹת,
עֲשָׂבִים שׁוֹטִים, כָּל מַסִּיגֵי גְבוּל וּסְיָג,
מִשֶּׁיָּבְשִׁילוּ הֵם חַרְצַנָּם בְּחֵיק הַזָּג
וְנִצְפְּנוּ קַרְנֵי־אוֹר וְנִגְנְזוּ מִסְּעָנוֹת;

מֵהֶם עַד יָקִיץ קֵץ לַזְּמָנִים, וּבְהִשְׁתַּנּוֹת
אַקְלִימֵי אֶרֶץ זוֹ וְרֵיחַ־יַעֲרָה פָג,
עִם שִׁיר בִּנְיָנִים עַל כְּלוֹנְסָאוֹת, פְּלִיטֵי־מָק,
וּבְקִבְרוֹת רוֹזְנֵי־עָם, בְּאַמְפּוֹרוֹת וּבְצִנְצָנוֹת.

וּלְאַחַר אַלְפֵי־דוֹר וּבָא מִמְּכֵרָה צָר,
יוֹפִיעַ עַל מְרוֹם מִגְדָּלִים בֶּחָצֵר
כָּל מִנְזַר עוֹבְדֵי־אֵשׁ, בְּמַדּוּרוֹת הֶעֱלוּ בָנוֹת;

וּבָעַר בְּמֹחַ גְּאוֹן־הַגְּאוֹנִים, וּבְבְשַׂר
הַיַּתּוּשׁ, אֲשֶׁר רָן, וּבְדוֹר רֵיק וַחֲסַר־
אֱלִילֵי עוֹלָם גַּז – תְּפָסוּנִי וְאֵין לִי מָנוֹס.

יג

אֱלִילֵי עוֹלָם גָּז – תְּפָסוּנִי וְאֵין לִי מָנוֹס!
אֱלִילֵי גּוֹי זֶה, יַיִן כָּל הַנּוֹגֵעַ בּוֹ,
נוֹי הָיָה לְחָכְמָה לוֹ, וְחָכְמָתוֹ הָיְתָה נוֹי,
וַיַּז מִיָּפְיוֹ לוֹ עַל שְׁאוֹל וְעַל אוֹקְיָנוֹס.

קָסְמוּנִי רוּחוֹת צָפוֹן־הַיָּם מִבֵּין אִילָנוֹת,
מִסְפָּרוֹת מִן הַכְּפוֹר הָעוֹטֶה תַּשְׁבֵּץ־שֵׁבוֹ;
וּבֵין חַמָּנֵי־אוֹן, וּבְמִקְדָּשׁ תַּרְתִּי בוֹ,
דְּמִיתִי נִיצוֹץ זֶה, הָאוֹמֵר בִּי הַשָּׁנוֹת, –

אַךְ זִיק מִמִּזְרָח הוּא, מִכְנַעַן אֲנַצְּרֶנּוּ;
תְּבָעוּנִי פְּסִילֵי־דָן, אֲשֶׁלִים מְלֵאִים חַיִל,
אֲשֵׁרוֹת, גָּלְמֵי צוֹר, בְּאוּר־כַּשְׂדִּים אֲעָבְדֶנּוּ.

אֵי דֶרֶךְ אֶבְחַר בָּהּ וְאֵיפֹה הוּא הַשְּׁבִיל?
הַאֶמְשַׂח שַׁמְנִי לְיָהּ אוֹ זֵאוּס אֲבָחֲרֶנּוּ,
אוֹ פֶסֶל אַחֲרוֹן־דּוֹר בְּמַמְלֶכֶת־הָאֱלִיל?

יד

אוֹ פֶסֶל אַחֲרוֹן־דּוֹר בְּמַמְלֶכֶת־הָאֱלִיל,
אוֹ שִׁיר חֲלוֹם־אַיָּל נָקִימָה לְעוֹלָמִים.
וּבְחֶנָּה עֵין־אִישׁ וְגִלְּתָה סוֹד־הַגֹּלָמִים,
צְרוּפֵי אָטוֹם דַּק בַּזָּהָב וּבַבְּדִיל.

וּמִן הַדּוֹמֵם יֵט וּמָתַח קַו וּשְׁבִיל
לְמַמְלְכוֹת הָעֵץ וְהַצֹּמְחִים הַנַּעֲלָמִים.
וְשַׁלְשֶׁלֶת אַחַת לוֹ: פִּטְרִיָּה שֶׁבַּכְּתָמִים,
יְרוֹקַת הָאֲגַם, הַלּוּז וּשְׁגַר־הַפִּיל.

וְנִקְלַט סוֹד הַחֹם, הַחַשְׁמַל וְהָאוֹרָה,
מִסְתּוֹרֵי הַמַּגְנִיט, רָז פְּרִיחַת עִנְבַת־שְׁעוּרָה,
זַעֲזוּעֵי עֶצֶב עֵר, הַנִּמְתָּח וְאֵין לוֹ פָנַי,

וְהָיָה לְאֶחָד סוֹד, סוֹד כָּל הַסּוֹדוֹת – חָי.
אָז יוּשַׁר לוֹ הַשִּׁיר: זֶה שִׁמְשִׁי חִמְּמַנִי,
הָיִיתִי לֵאלֹהַי כְּיָקִינְטוֹן וְכַאֲדָנִי!

טו

הָיִיתִי לֵאלֹהַי כְּיָקִינְטוֹן וְכַאֲדָנִי
וּכְאַחַת שֶׁבְּלֵי־פָז בַּקָּמָה כְּבָדַת־בָּר;
וַיָּמָן לִי גִּשְׁמֵי־חֹם, וַיָּצֻו עַרְפְּלֵי־הָר,
סִמְפוֹנִיּוֹת אוֹר וָצֵל, וּכְחָל, וּסָרֹק, וְשָׁנִי.

בִּינוֹתִי צַעַר־דּוֹר, שִׁיר גּוֹי וְגוֹי קְסָמָנִי,
קוֹל נֶפֶשׁ עוֹטָה אוֹר, קוֹל תּוֹעָה בְּמַחְשָׁךְ זָר,
בְּעָמְדִי בֵּין הַחַי וּבֵין הַגּוֹסֵס כְּבָר;
הַאִם קַדְמָתִי בָּא אוֹ אַחַר צוּר בְּרָאָנִי?

עוֹד בְּלִבִּי לָן הַטַּל, הַיּוֹרֵד עַל שְׂדֵה־אֱדֹם,
עַל פִּסְגַּת הַר־הָהָר, מְעוֹנָה אֱלֹהֵי־קֶדֶם,
כִּי לִבִּי דוֹבֵב שִׁיר לַחַמָּה וְלַכְּסִיל.

מִשֶּׁיִּתְרַמֵּל פּוֹל וְגָמַל פְּרִי־אִילָנוֹת
אֱלִילֵי עוֹלָם גַּז תְּפָסוּנִי וְאֵין לִי מָנוֹס –
אוֹ פֶסֶל אַחֲרוֹן־דּוֹר בְּמַמְלֶכֶת הָאֱלִיל?

אודיסה, אב–אלול תרע״ט, 1919

ש"י עגנון   III

חוש הריח

פרק ראשון / מעלת לשון הקודש

לא כשאר כל הלשונות לשון הקודש, ששאר כל הלשונות אינן אלא הסכמיות, שהסכימו
עליהן אומה אומה על לשונה, אבל לשון הקודש ניתנה בה תורה ובה ברא חקדוש
ברוך הוא את עולמו, ושרפים ואופנים וחיות הקודש מקלסים אותו בלשון הקודש,
ואף הוא כשבא לקלס את ישראל בלשון הקודש הוא מקלסן, כמו שכתוב הנך יפה
רעייתי הנך יפה. באיזו לשון הכתוב מדבר, הוי בלשון הקודש. וכשהוא מתאווה
לתפילתן של ישראל, לאיזו לשון הוא מתאווה, ללשון הקודש, שכן הוא אומר השמיעיני
את קולך, כי קולך ערב. איזו קול ערב עליו, זה קולו של יעקב שמתפלל בלשון
הקודש. ובלשון הקודש הוא עתיד לבנות את ירושלים ולהחזיר הגליות לתוכה.
ובלשון הקודש הוא מרפא לאבילי ציון שלבם שבור מן החורבן ומחבש את נגיעהם,
כמו שנאמר בונה ירושלים ה' נדחי ישראל יכנס הרופא לשבורי לב ומחבש לעצבותם.
לפיכך חייבים כל ישראל להקפיד על לשונם שתהא ברורה ומדוייקת, כל שכן בדורות
האחרונים, קרובי גאולה, כדי שמשיח צדקנו שיתגלה במהרה בימינו ישמע את
לשוננו ואנו נשמע את לשונו.

פרק שני / כנגד חכמי הדור שכותבים בכל לשון
ואין כותבים בלשון הקודש

שמא יאמר אדם וכי אפשר לדבר בלשון שנעקרה מן הפה זה אלף וכמה מאות שנה,
כדרך שאומרים קצת טפשי ישראל. ואפילו רוב חכמי הדור אין בהם כח לעמוד בה,
או שמשתבשים בלשונם אפילו בדברים הפשוטים או שכותבים דבריהם בכל לשון
ולא בלשון הקודש. כל האומר כן לא שם עיקר הדברים על לבו, שאף על פי שפסק
הדיבור מן הפה לא פסקה הלשון משנה ולומד גמרא מיד מגלין לו כל גנזי לשון
הקודש שגנזי הקדוש ברוך הוא לאוהביו, כל שכן בשבת שניתנה בו נשמה יתירה
שמכירה בלשון הקודש כמלאכי השרת.
ומפני מה מקצת חכמים משתבשים בלשונם, מפני שעושים דברי חול עיקר ודברי
תורה טפל, שאילו עשו התורה עיקר היתה התורה מסייעתם. ואותם שכותבים
דבריהם בכל לשון ואין כותבים בלשון הקודש, אפילו גוי וכותב בלשון הקודש חביב
מהם, ובלבד שאינו כותב דברי תיפלות. תדע לך שכן, שהרי בלעם הרשע שלא
הרשיע אדם כמותו, שנתן עצה לזנות אל בנות מואב ואבדו על ידיו חמש עשרה
רבוא ושמונת אלפים ושש מאות מישראל, בשכר שדיבר בלשון הקודש ודיבר בשבחן

18

של ישראל זכה שנקבעה על שמו פרשה בתורה וזכה שכל ישראל פותחין תפילתם בבוקר בפסוק מה טובו שבו שיבח בלעם את ישראל.

שמא תאמר הלוא מצינו בחכמים הקדמונים שכתבו מקצת ספריהם ערבית. שונים הם חכמים הקדמונים שבני דורם היו עייפים מן הגלות ורחוקים מאורו של משיח, לפיכך כתבו להם חכמיהם איגרות תנחומים בלשונם כדרך שמפייסים את התינוק בלשון שהוא שומע. ושונה לשון ישמעאל שארץ ישראל נתמשכנה בידיהם. ולמה נתמשכנה ארץ ישראל לישמעאל, מפני שזכה להוציאה מידיו של אדום. ועדיין היא ממושכנת בידיו עד שיתקבצו כל הגליות ויחזירנה לידיהם.

פרק שלישי / סוד כתיבת סיפורי מעשיות

מאהבת לשוננו ומחיבת הקודש אני משחיר פני על דברי תורה ומרעיב עצמי על דברי חכמים ומשמרם בבטני כדי שיכונו יחדיו על שפתי. אילו היה בית המקדש קיים הייתי עומד על הדוכן עם אחי המשוררים ואומר בכל יום השיר שהלויים היו אומרים בבית המקדש. עכשיו שבית המקדש עדיין בחורבנו ואין לנו לא כהנים בעבודתם ולא לויים בשירם ובזמרם אני עוסק בתורה ובנביאים ובכתובים במשנה בהלכות ובהגדות בתוספתות דקדוקי תורה ודקדוקי סופרים. כשאני מסתכל בדבריהם ורואה שמכל מחמדינו שהיו לנו בימי קדם לא נשתייר לנו אלא זכרון דברים בלבד אני מתמלא צער. ואותו צער מרעיד את לבי, ומאותה רעדה אני כותב סיפורי מעשיות, כאדם שגלה מפלטרין של אביו ועושה לו סוכה קטנה ויושב שם ומספר תפארת בית אבותיו.

פרק רביעי / כל מה שאירע למחבר על ידי דקדקן אחד וכל הצער והיסורים והטורח שבאו לו למחבר

והואיל והזכרתי ענין סוכה אומר בה בדבר. מעשה, פעם אחת כתבתי סיפור סוכת החג, וכדי לשבר את האוזן כתבתי הסוכה מריחה. בא עלי דקדקן אחד, נעץ בי קולמוסו וכתב אין לומר הסוכה מריחה, שהרי לא הסוכה מריחה אלא אדם הוא המריח ריח הסוכה. חלשה דעתי עלי שמא שניתי ממטבע הלשון ופגמתי ביופייה. עמדתי ופשפשתי בספרי שימוש ולא מצאתי סמך לדברי. שרוב ספרי שימוש או שמודיעים לך את שאתה יודע או שאין מודיעים לך כלום. הלכתי אצל חכמי הזמן ולא ידעו להשיב לי. יודעים הם החכמים הכל חוץ מאותו דבר שאתה מבקש. עד שנזדמן לפני חכם ירושלמי והביא ראיה לדברי מספר מסר כתב תמים לחכם קדמון ר' משה תיקו ז"ל. נחה דעתי קצת, ולא נחה כל צרכה. ועדיין הייתי מבקש תוספת חיזוק. וכשהייתי מזדמן עם אנשי לשון הקודש שאלתי אותם אפשר ששמעתם אם מותר לכתוב הסוכה מריחה. אלו התירו ואלו אסרו. אלו ואלו לא נתנו טעם לדבריהם אלא אמרו סתם, כאדם שפושט אגודלו כלפי חבירו ואומר כך דעתי, וכאדם שמלקלק את שפתיו ואומר כך אני מרגיש. מכיון שכן עמדתי למחוק שתי תיבות אלו שערער

עליהן הדקדקן. כשביקשתי למחזן באה הסוכה ועלה ריחה לפני עד שראיתי ממש שהיא מריחה, והנחתי את הדברים כמות שהם.

פרק חמישי / צדיקים מגן עדן באים לסייע את המחבר

פעם אחת בא אצלי אדם אחד לבקש ממני טובה. בתוך הדברים נגלה לי שהוא מבני בניו של רבי יעקב מליסא. מיד פניתי עצמי מכל עסקי ועשיתי לו כבוד גדול וטרחתי עמו הרבה וכיבדתי אותו בעוגת דבש ובכוס יין שרוף ועשיתי את בקשתו מתוך שמחה בשביל כבוד זקנו הגאון שאנו לומדים תורתו ומתפללים בסידורו. אחר שהלכתי ללוותו נזדמן לי תלמיד חכם אחד וספר בזרועו. שאלתי אותו מה זה בידך, סידורו של הגאון מליסא. חייך ואמר לי פעמים מחמת חריפות יתירה אדם שוכח מנהג פשוט בתפילה וצריך לעיין בסידור. אמרתי לו זו מעלה גדולה במעלות הגאון האמיתי, אחר שחיבר חידושים וביאורים בחריפות ובקיאות טרח וסידר בקצרה ענייני התפילה ושאר עניינים שום לכל נפש להלכה ולמעשה, שיהא כל אדם מוצא את הדין ואת מקורו בצירוף סדר התפילה. סידורים הרבה הנחילונו רבותינו הקדושים בנגלה ובנסתר בדקדוק ובחכמה עם כוונות ופירושים וצירופים סודות ורמזים, לעורר לבם של המתפללים בבואם אל היכל המלך. אלא אלמלא כבודם של ראשונים הייתי אומר שסידורו של הגאון מליסא יפה יפה מכולם, שרוב הסידורים אין רוב הציבור יכול לעמוד בהם מפני האורה וזה יפה לכל עין.

בעוד שאני מדבר נתעורר לבי והתחלתי מספר מקצת מאורעותיו של אותו גאון שנתפשטו הוראותיו בכל תפוצות ישראל לנהוג כדבריו. ועוד סיפרתי קצת על מדותיו הטובות מה ששמעתי מפי אנשי אמונה ומצאתי בספרים.

לסוף נפטרנו זה מזה. הוא וסידורו בידו ואני מחשבותי בלבי. לסוף חזרתי לביתי ועליתי על מטתי וישנתי שינה מתוקה. מתוך שעשיתי טובה ליהודי ושכבתי מתוך שיחות צדיקים ערבה רבה עלי שנתי.

שמעתי שמעוררים אותי. נתרשלתי ולא קמתי. חזרו ועוררו הקיצותי וראיתי זקן אחד עומד לפני וסידור דרך החיים פתוח בידו ועיניו מאירות ופניו מבהיקות ביותר. אף על פי שמימי לא ראיתי שום תמונה של ר' יעקב מליסא הכרתי אותו מיד. הוא לא היה דומה לשום איש מאנשי בית משפחתו, שגדולי ישראל אינם דומים לקרוביהם, שתורתם נותנת להם זיו פנים, שכל המשחיר עצמו על דברי תורה הקדוש ברוך הוא מבהיק זיוו ונותן לו מאור פנים.

עד שאני מציץ ומביט נסגר הסידור ונתעלם הזקן וידעתי שהוא חלום. ואף על פי שידעתי שהוא חלום אמרתי דברים בגו. נטלתי את ידי וירדתי ממטתי והלכתי אצל ארון הספרים והוצאתי את הסידור דרך החיים. מצאתי שם פיסת נייר מונחת כמין סימן. עמדתי וקראתי שם לשון זה, ומרבים במיני פרחים המריחים לשמחת יום טוב. נראה הדבר שפעם אחת קראתי באותו דף והנחתי לי שם פיסת נייר לסימן. הרהרתי בלבי, לשון זה לא כתב אותה מדעת עצמו אלא מדעת תורה. מכל מקום נטלתי סידור עמודי שמים לדודי הגאון יעב"ץ ז"ל, ואף שם מצאתי לשון זה. שמחתי שלא נכשלתי בדברי ולא פגמתי בלשוננו הקדושה, שהרי אם שני עמודי עולם כותבים

כך דין הוא שיכתב כך, והדקדקן שפטפט כנגדי עתיד ליתן את הדין.

פרק שישי / אמירת תהילים רש"י ז"ל מפרש לו למחבר פסוק בתהילים ומצהיל את רוחו

לחזור למטתי לא היה כדאי, שכבר עבר רוב הלילה ולהתפלל תפילת שחרית עדיין לא הגיע זמנה. עמדתי ונטלתי ספר תהילים. אמירת תהילים יפה בכל עת, כל שכן לעיתותי בוקר שהנפש עדיין נקיה והשפתים לא נתלכלכו בפטפוטים רעים. ישבתי וקראתי כמה מזמורים, את שהבנתי הבנתי ואת שלא הבנתי פירש לי רש"י ז"ל, עד שסיימתי כל ספר ראשון. ועדיין היתה הנפש מבקשת לומר עוד. עשיתי את רצונה וקראתי עוד מזמור ועוד מזמור, עד שהגעתי למזמור למנצח על שושנים, שהוא שיר שבח שנאמר לכבוד תלמידי חכמים שהם רכים כשושנים ונאים כשושנים, להאהיב תורתם עליהם.

יפה היתה אותה שעה של קריאת תהילים. המנורה עמדה דלוקה על השולחן ועיטרה באורה כל תיבה וכל אות וכל נקודה וכל טעם. כנגדה היה חלון פתוח לצד דרום ורוחות שלפנות בוקר נישבו בחוץ, ולא כיבו רוחות אור של המנורה ולא סיככו את הפתילה, אלא היו מכרכרים עם אילנות ושיחים שבגן וריח טוב של דפנא וטללים עלה כדבש הבר וכשמן ערב.

אור המנורה התחיל מחוויר והולך. נראה הדבר שכבר יצא לילה. ואפשר שבאותה שעה כבר תלה הקדוש ברוך הוא חמה ברקיע, כדי להאיר לפשוטי העם שאין בקיאים בתפילת שחרית ומתפללים מתוך הסידור.

מגובהו של אילן נשמע קול, קול ציפור שאומרת שירה. קול כזה יש בו כדי להפסיק אדם ממשנתו. אבל אני לא עמדתי מן הספר לשמוע קול צפור, אף על פי שהיה מתוק לאוזן וערב ללב. אמרתי, אפשר אני קורא בספר תהילים ואפסיק לשמוע שיחת עופות.

ביני ביני נשמע קול אחר, ערב מן הראשון. נתקנאה צפור בחברתה וביקשה לנצחה בניגון. או אפשר שלא נתקנאה ואף לא הרגישה בחברתה, אלא מעצמה נתעוררה לשיר לפני יוצרה והיה קולה ערב מקולה של חברתה. לסוף עשו שלום ביניהן וכל אחת סייעה את חברתה בנעימתן וחידשו שירים שלא שמעה אוזן מעולם. נעימה שכזו וקולות שכאלו יש בהם כדי להבטיל כל אדם ממשנתו. אבל אני עשיתי אזני כאילו אינה שומעת. ואין כאן שום פלא ושום שבח, שהרי ככנור של כמה נימין היה המזמור מנגן שיר ידידות שיר שכל שיר השירים בטלים כנגדו, ואני עניתי אחריו אחר כל תיבה בנעימה.

רחש לבי דבר טוב וגו' לשוני עט סופר מהיר וגו' צלח רכב על דבר אמת וענוה צדק ותורך נוראות ימינך. את שהבנתי הבנתי ואת שלא הבנתי פירש לי רש"י ז"ל. כשהגעתי לפסוק מר ואהלות כל בגדיך ולא ידעתי פירושו עיינתי בפירושו רש"י ז"ל וקראתי שם כל בגדותיך כל בגדיך מריחים כריח בשמים, ומדרשו כל בגדותיך וסרחוניך מתכפרים ומריחים ריח ערב. באותה שעה באה סוכתי ועמדה לפני והריחה ריח ערב לפני. מיד נחה דעתי עלי כאדם שמריח בפרחים המריחים.

פרק שביעי / מסיים בשבח כדרך שפתח בשבח

בוא וראה כמה גדולה לשון הקודש, שבשביל תיבה אחת הטריח עצמו צדיק גדול מישיבה של מעלה מגן עדן וגלל את ספרו לפני ונתגלגל הדבר שאקום בלילה לומר תהילים ואמצא דבר שיגעתי עליו ימים הרבה.

אורי צבי גרינברג IV

בֵּיתוֹ שֶׁל אָדָם

רַק מִי שֶׁשָּׁב אֶל הַכְּפָר לְעֵת עֶרֶב: אֶל עֵצָיו הַטּוֹבִים־בְּכָל־עֵת,
אֶל חֶלְקַת שָׂדֵהוּ שֶׁהִיא הַמְּשֻׁךְ־פּוֹרֶה לִבְשָׂרוֹ
וְאֶל בְּאֵרוֹ הַמְּקָרָה־לוֹ מֵימָיו בְּנִצְנוּץ
רַק מִי שֶׁשָּׁב בָּעֶרֶב יוֹם אֶל הַכְּפָר וְלֹא אֶל הַכְּרָךְ,
הוֹלֵךְ כְּשָׁב לְמָחוֹז חֵפֶץ וְלֹא כְהֵלֶךְ־גּוֹלֶה לְמָלוֹנוֹ;   5
הוֹלֵךְ בַּשְּׁבִיל הַנֶּאֱמָן הָרַךְ־לִצְעִידָה.. כִּי הוּא טוֹב:
מְטַל, מְשֶׁמֶשׁ, מְנֻשָּׁמַת שְׂחָקִים, מְצַעֲיֶדֶת צִפֳּרִים בּוֹ..
בְּוֶרֶד־דְּמָדֻמִּים בְּאָזְנָיו, בְּלֵב דּוֹפֵק כַּצִּפּוֹר אֶל חַלּוֹן,
קָרֵב אֶל גֶּדֶר זְרָדִים, פּוֹתֵחַ דַּלְתָּה לְבִקְתָּה לְבָנָה,
שֶׁכִּמְעַט אֶפְשָׁר לְחַבְּקָהּ.. כְּהֶמְשֵׁךְ גּוּף הִיא מִמֶּנּוּ..   10
שֶׁגַּג לָהּ מִקַּשׁ, וְהַרְבֵּה מַנְשִׁיּוֹת בָּהּ וְקַן צִפֳּרִים..
וְאֲפֵלוּלִית לַיְלָה מְבָרֶכֶת בַּחַלּוֹן הַקָּטָן;
בָּא וּפוֹתֵחַ פִּיו וְאוֹמֵר שָׁלוֹם בָּהּ לְאִשָּׁה וּלְדוֹת
וְיוֹשֵׁב לֶאֱכֹל סְעוּדַת־עֶרֶב; וְהַדְּמָמָה שָׁם: כְּאַחֲרֵי כִנּוֹרוֹת
וַחֲלִילִים שֶׁנָּדַמּוּ..   15
וְלָן שָׁם לִינַת לַיְלָה, אֲשֶׁר מֵטִיב הַרְבֵּה עֵצִים
וְצוּף הַשָּׂדוֹת בָּהּ.. וְהַיַּעַר סָמוּךְ וְהַנָּהָר – –

רַק זֶה טוֹעֵם מִיקַר הַטַּעַם שֶׁל מוֹלֶדֶת הָאָדָם הָאֲמִתִּית,
שֶׁהָיְתָה לְכָל אָדָם אֵי בִּזְמַן בְּזֶה הַיְקוּם,
בְּטֶרֶם שָׁם רַגְלוֹ בְּנַעַל וְכִסָּה אֶת כְּתֵפָיו עַד קְצוֹת גּוּפוֹ   20
וַיִּבֶן עִיר וַיִּצֹק כְּבִישׁ לְהֶעָלִים־מֵעַיִן אַדְמָה מַדְשִׁיאָה..
וַיְהִי לְגוּף מַרְבֵּה רֹגֶז.

רַק מִי שֶׁשָּׁב אֶל הַכְּפָר לְעֵת עֶרֶב, הוֹלֵךְ הַבַּיְתָה בֶּאֱמֶת:
גִּלְגֵּל מִגַּבּוֹ אֶת הַכְּרַךְ־הַגּוֹלָה, פּוֹתֵר לוֹ אֶת חִידַת הַכִּסּוּף
וְהַתּוּגָה־הַדְּאָגָה בְּשֶׁל זֶה, שֶׁאָדָם נוֹשֵׂא בְחֻבּוֹ   25
בְּכָל יְמֵי הַמָּצְאוֹ בָּעוֹלָם מִשְּׁכְלָל זֶה, הַמְאֻחָר..
מוֹלֶדֶת אָדָם הָרִאשׁוֹן, שֶׁמִּמֶּנָּה נֶעֱקַר, הִיא סִבַּת הַכִּסּוּף
וְתוּגַת הַתְּלִישׁוּת;

סוֹד כָּרֵת־הַכְּנָפַיִם וְעוֹד הֵן מַשִּׁיקוֹת..

הִיא סוֹד־רֹגֶז־הַנְּדוּד -- 30

שַׁבְתִּי לַכְּפָר, כְּשָׁב לְמוֹלֶדֶת קְדוּמָה:
לְרֵיחָהּ, לְשַׂרְפָּהּ, לְמִתְקָהּ, לְבִטְחוֹנָהּ,
לְמֵימֵי בְאֵר רִאשׁוֹנִים.

בְּשִׁיבָה לַכְּפָר - שִׁיבָה אֲשֶׁר נֵס בָּהּ.

שָׁב עֵץ הַכָּרוּת לְהִתְחַבֵּר אֶל סָדְנוֹ. 35
לָכֵן תָּמִיד כֹּה תוֹפֶסֶת תּוּגָה אֶת כָּל־בִּי לְעֵת עֶרֶב
בְּהִתְעַכֵּב רַכֶּבֶת עַל יַד תַּחֲנַת כְּפָר
וְאַחַד הַנּוֹסְעִים יוֹרֵד עִם צְרוֹרוֹ שָׁם..
אֲנִי רוֹאֵהוּ הוֹלֵךְ בְּמִשְׁעוֹל הַשָּׂדֶה הַמֻּכָּר לוֹ,
אֲנִי מֵרִיחַ אַחֲרָיו וּכְאִלּוּ גַּם לִי הוּא מֻכָּר 40
זֶה הַשְּׁבִיל: רַךְ מִטַּל וּמִצְעֲיָדַת צִפּוֹר וּבְהֵמָה בּוֹ
וּמִצֵּל עֵצִים לְאָרְכּוֹ --

מָחוֹז חֶפְצוֹ הַבִּקְעָתָה הִיא, שֶׁגַּג לָהּ מִקַּשׁ וְזֶה גֶּדֶר זְרָדִים..
וַאֲשֶׁר בִּפְנִים - זֶה הַכֹּל..

הִנֵּה נִכְנָס וְנִדְלָק לֵב זָהָב בַּחַלּוֹן הַקָּטָן.. 45
וַאֲנִי נוֹסֵעַ לִי הָלְאָה מִזֶּה אֶל הַלֵּיל, אֶל הַכְּרַךְ,
שֶׁבָּלַע אֶת חֶלְקַת שָׂדַי הַקְּדוּמָה וַיְכַסֶּנָּה כְּבִישׁ וּבָתֵּי־מִדּוֹת..
וְאֶל אֲשֶׁר אֶסַּע וְאֶל אֲשֶׁר אָבוֹא, שָׁם לֹא מְחוֹז חֵפֶץ שֶׁלִּי,
כִּי שָׁם רֹגֶז, נֵכָר.

אָדָם בַּכְּפָר לְעֵת־לַיְלָה בְּדוֹמֶה לָעֵץ הוּא מַמָּשׁ, 50
הָעוֹמֵד תּוֹהֶה בְּשַׂרְעַפָּיו עַל עַצְמוֹ: זֶה בֹטֶל וְזֶה בְּדֶמַע שֶׁלּוֹ הֶעָרֵב..
הַגּוּף מֻשְׁקֶה כַּשָּׂדֶה וְכָעֵץ בּוֹ.
הָאָדָם אֲדוֹן לְבֵיתוֹ, כִּי בֵיתוֹ בַּכְּפָר אֵינוֹ גָּבֹהַּ מִמִּצְחוֹ
וְאוּלָם אֵין אָדָם בַּכְּרַךְ אֲדוֹן לַחוֹמָה, שֶׁהִיא גְבֹהָה מִמִּצְחוֹ..

אָדָם הוֹלֵךְ בַּכְּרַךְ־מְגוּרוֹ כְּבֶן בֵּית גּוֹלָה. 55

עמליה כהנא-כרמון   V

הינומה

אש אלוהים על ילדים

אֵשׁ אֱלֹהִים עַל עָרִים
אֵשׁ אֱלֹהִים עַל בָּתִּים, אֵשׁ אֱלֹהִים עַל שָׂדוֹת
אֵשׁ אֱלֹהִים יְפֵהפִיָּה, אֱלֹהִית כַּזֹּאת.
שַׁלְהָבִים, שַׁלְהָבִים וְקוֹל שׁוֹפָר וְעֵינֵי מַלְאָכִים.
זְכוּת עֵינֵי מַלְאָכִים הַרְבֵּה יוֹתֵר מֵעֵינֵי יְלָדִים,
מַלְאֲכֵי שָׂרָף הַלְלוּיים.
יְלָדִים אֵינָם מַלְאָכִים, יְלָדִים מְלֻכְלָכִים, יְלָדִים רְשָׁעִים.
יְלָדִים צוֹוְחִים וְתוֹבְעִים, יְלָדִים רָעִים, רַק לִפְעָמִים שָׁרִים.
יְלָדִים אֵינָם מַלְאָכִים וְקוֹלָם לֹא הַלְלוּיָה.

יָבֹאוּ מַלְאָכִים וְיִבְעֲטוּ בִּילָדִים, יְגָרְשׁוּ אִמָּהוֹת מְלֻכְלָכוֹת, לֹא יָפוֹת.
אָבוֹת כְּסִילִים אֵין בָּהֶם מֵחָכְמַת אֱלֹהִים.
אָבוֹת כְּסִילִים יִזְרְעוּ רֶשַׁע, יִקְצְרוּ מָוֶת, אָבוֹת פְּגָרִים.
אָבוֹת אֲדָמָה, אָבוֹת מִזְבָּלָה, אָבוֹת אֲבָנִים.
יֶלֶד, אֵיפֹה אַבָּא, אַבָּא לֹא בַּעֲנָנִים.
מִי טָס בַּעֲנָנִים? לֹא אַבָּא כְּסִיל, רָשָׁע, פֶּגֶר.
בָּאוּ יְלָדִים, הִתְפַּלְלוּ לֵאלֹהִים אֵשׁ לְמַלְאָכִים שְׂרָפִים יְפֵהפִיִּים.
אָמַר תּוֹדָה, יֶלֶד מְלֻכְלָךְ, עָלוּב, חֲרוּמַף.
עֲנָנִים יוֹרִידוּ גֶּשֶׁם, גֶּשֶׁם טוֹב עַל כָּל אֲדָמָה.
מַלְאָכִים יַפְשִׁילוּ גְּלִימוֹת טֹהַר, יַגִּישׁוּ עֶזְרָה רִאשׁוֹנָה לָעוֹלָם.
גַּם לְךָ, יֶלֶד מְלֻכְלָךְ, בִּיסְקְוִיט מְשֻׁבָּח.
פְּרָחִים יַעֲלוּ, אַבָּא פֶּגֶר לֹא יִרְאֶה אֶת הַיֹּפִי.
אִמָּא לֹא יָפָה לֹא תִּסְתַּכֵּל, רַק תְּקַלֵּל אִמָּא.
מַלְאָכִים יְהַלְלוּ יָהּ, שׂוֹרָרוֹת יֹאמְרוּ אֲהָהּ.

מאיר ויזלטיר

25

אבא ליווה אותה וישב עמה באוטובוס של 'אגד'. עד לנסיעה. האוטובוס לפני
האחרון. כי אבא לקח אותה לקולנוע. ועתה היה קצר־רוח. כמו נרגז משום־מה.

קבוצה של חיילי־או"ם עולה היתה לאוטובוס. עלה אחד ואבא אמר: "דומה
לאנתוני פרקינס, זה". עלה אחר. דומה עוד יותר לאנתוני פרקינס, הרהרה שושנה
ולא אמרה.

שעות רבות המתינה לאבא. ערב בעיר אחרת. גן־העיר. חלקת־הילדים ריקה.
מבעד לעפאים ועלים, אורות: דיוטות־מגורים. מעונות, חלונות. בתי זרים.

עוד משעות אחר־הצהרים המוקדמות ממתינה היתה שם. הגננים עדיין יושבים
חיו לפוש בצל שיח. שני תיירים־נודדים בשיער עבות, לאחד שיער כציור־כרזה של
שמש, עולה־בלהבות במעגל של לשונות־אש שוות וחופפות, מדדו בהתרכזות רבה,
חתכו לשנים בסכין־גילוח סיגריה יחידה. ילדים וילדות קטנים החלון מגיעים. הילדים,
מהם בסיכת־ראש אוחזת שערם צד אחד. הילדות, מהן בארנק־צעצוע. או באפודה
לבנה קטנה מקופלת על זרוע. קריר לעת־ערב בעיר ההר.

אחרי־כן, ילדים חרשים־אילמים הובאו לגן. עם שתי מורות. או מדריכות. צעירות
מאד, לבושות כפרוזות.

פנו המדריכות לשבת על ספסל. הילדים האילמים פשטו על מיתקני־השעשועים.
לאכלס כל מושב. או אטומי־עין, לסובב במשנה־כוח סחרחרות, להעיף למרומים
נדנדות על יושבי בן. נפוצו בני־הטובים, אצו אל חיק הורים ומטפלות. הילדים
האילמים, כחוטפים, עלו מיד במקומות המתפנים. מאותתים זה לזה אותות תענוג
והנאה, בלא קול, תנועות־ידים והעוויות אלימות בלבד. ביניהם ילדות בוגרות רוכבות
על המושבים התינוקיים אשר בנדנדות־בשנים, בהבעת־פנים של פיגור שכלי. ילד
ארוך אחד, אפל, עיקש ביותר, וחולצתו קרועה על שכמו, ניסה כל הזמן להפריען.
הוא מתאמץ להסיר את קבקבי־הגומי שלהן, העולים ויורדים, הן מפשילות רגל,
בועטות בו בעצלתיים. בתחתית סנטרו, בבטנו, בצלעותיו, הכול לפי התנופה. וכשהוא,
בעצימת־עינים, פוער־פה בכאב נעדר־קול, רואים, השינים תותבות.

נתרוקן הגן. עוד מעט חשיכה גמורה. וכבר חשיכה גמורה. שובל קול מוקלט של
אשה נישא ובא. צלול וחי כאילו סירונית מזמרת יושבת על חוטם המכונית העוברת.
ושוב דממה. אחרי־כן, שובל קולו המוכר של קריין, במהדורת־הערב של החדשות.
ממרפסת קומה אל"ף, אשר מעבר לגזעי־הארנים, פעם או פעמים שאלות בקול־רם,
של אנשים במשפחה, לקראת לילה. ולוחות־התריסול הניצבים בפנים מקבילות
הוטו קלות, גם פנימה ופנימם חוצה, דיים כדי לאטום.

הוציאה שושנה אוכלת והחלה את אכלה, אשר נתנה לה אמה לדרך. פרוסות־
הקיבר. קצת לקרדה. קצת מישמש. קצת חלבה.

איש אחד – אשכנזי, מקריח ובעל־כרס, במכנסי־חאקי קצרים רחבים יתר על
המידה, פעם לבשו הכול בגדים כאלה, ולו תיק מהוה, כפקיד בגיל־העמידה – נכנס
היה לגן ויוצא, נכנס ויוצא. קודם, כשעובר היה על פניה, עוד יכולה היתה להבחין
באבזם המסורגל, אחוז בחור האחרון של החגורה. באגלי־זיעה על מצח ופדחת.
בעין נעוצה בה מן הצד, כעינו של תרנגול. נעוצה בה כל הזמן. אחרי־כן, רק בקושי
ניתן להבחין בשרטוטי פניו החרושות סבל. החשיכה נתעצמה מאד. שושנה גמרה

בלבה, יצאה להמתין במדרכה, ליד פנס־הרחוב. מודאגת שמא לא ימצאנה אביה, והוא אמר לה לחכות בגן, בחלקת־הילדים, כמו כל הילדים. ואם יבוא אביה לחלקת־ הילדים מן השער השני? ואם יסתלק בחזרה. אולם ככה זה. בעיר אחרת. עיר זרה.

עומדת היתה בקרן־הרחוב, מביטה בהחבא בקטע הרחוב הראשי, שם מעבר לסימטה. אנשים עוברים היו שם. אמת, פחות אנשים. אולם אנשים עוברים היו שם. ומכוניות. כל הזמן היתה טעות, נגלה לה. לא חשבה על כך, אך כנראה שיערה כי החיים בחוץ מסתיימים שעה שהולכים לישון, אחרי ארוחת־הערב. אלא אם חל יוצא מן הכלל. והנה חדש, נסתר: יש חולין של יום. ויש חולין של לילה. לחיים המשך בלילה. אבל אחרת. בלילה הכול אחרת: בתים, אנשים, מחשבות.

האוטובוס התמהמה. אבא החל מתמרמר בקול.

ממתי נוסעים חיילים של או״ם באוטובוסים, הרהרה שושנה. במושב לפניהם ישבו שנים. ושלישי עומד מעליהם, משוחח עמם.

עיני־קרח כחולות היו להם. אף שהיו בהחלט רחבי־כתפים, משהו בם כמו צר. וכמו נעשו מחמרים יבשים יותר. כאילו אנחנו, סופנו להצטמק, מגירים שלולית מתרחבת. ואחרי־כן כבר קרום דק בלבד, להתקמט, להתאדות ולא להיות. הם, סופם להתפורר, להיות לאבק, ולא להיות. ודומים הם כולם, אבל שונים. כמו גואיבות. לכולן טעם טוב, אך לכל אחת טעם גם שונה במקצת, הסבר משלה לטעם הגואיבה.

נכנס אדם נושא תיבת־כרטון גבוהה. עליה, באותיות אדומות, כמריחת־אצבע: 'חלקים – מדרגות־לללולים'. חסם בה את דלת־היציאה.

שבה שושנה ונזכרה בסיפור 'קטע' אשר במקראה 'משעולים' חלק דל״ת. אפרוח בוקע מביצתו במדגרה. אל מי יפנה את הרגש האנושי הטבעי להתקשר. שמא אל המדגרה החשמלית, כתוב היה, שמא אל הלולן המגדלו על־מנת להעבירו למשחטה החשמלית, אל מי. הרגש האנושי הטבעי, כתוב היה. הרגש האנושי לו, שאינו אנוש.

מאחד המושבים נשמע קולו של בחור, בן עדות־המזרח, מתלהב אף כי כלוחש. "תן להיות מזכיר־האגודה. לא, לא מפני שאתה אוהב אותי. כי אם מפני שתפשתי פה את העיקרון. ותראה, אם תוך ארבע שנים, אני לא הופך לך את המקום הזה למנוף פוליטי. מדרגה ראשונה. אם לא כל אחד יצטרך אותי, יחפש אותי, יבוא לבקש אותי. הנה בן־דוב. מה בן־דוב. כן, משכמו־ומעלה. היום. מה היה לפני חמש־עשרה, עשרים שנה. ימאי. והיום, אתה רואה בעיניך. ואני אפעיל לך אצלנו את כל פועלי־ הבנין. חשוב על כך: כוח. נכון, נכון, נכון. אבל את ענבי חיסלו מבחינה פוליטית משום שאיננו איש־ציבור. איננו איש חזק. נכון, ראו אותו בכל מקום, התרוצץ. אבל איננו איש חזק. זו שאלה של השפעה על אנשים. יש לדעת להפעיל. איך? לפעול במקור. חוץ־מזה אתה יודע שאצלי תקבל את הכול. מאזנים, עניינים, הכול."

האוטובוס התמהמה. קם אבא, נפרד קצרות והלך.

רק ירד אבא מן האוטובוס, עבר חייל־האו״ם העומד וישב לידה. ישיבת־אקראי, ממשיך לשוחח, מותח צוואר לעבר חבריו.

מנומש, צעיר, נאה. אולם האור כבה והוא נשתתק. תמהה שושנה על שישב לצדה. מה גם שהבחינה כי קודם שישב בחן אותה, את המושב הפנוי מעבר־למעבר,

ובההחלטה מהירה בחר לשבת לידה. ואך ישב, היה זה כאילו נתגלגלה לידה זכיה.

אף בחושך ניתן היה לראות, שפתיו עדינות, כף-היד הבשרנית, האוחזת במוט גב-המושב לפניהם, מוצקה. והוא אחד מן החבורה. מאד אחד מן החבורה.

האוטובוס החל זז. אשה גבוהה עברה בחוץ, חצתה זקופה את דרכו, והנהג קרא בחרון: "גריטה גרבו." הציצה שושנה בחייל-האו"ם, ראתהו כמחייך בתמהון. מבלי-משים, נתחייכה בלבה. אולם רצועתו של תיק-המסע – תיק 'אל-על' הכחול, בו הכביסה של אבא, אשר הניח אבא על המדף ממעל – נשמטה, כמעט ונגעה בכובעו של חייל-האו"ם היושב לפניה. להחזירה למקומה, החלה שושנה לנסות לחתרומם, לנסות לעמוד על מכסה-הגלגל לרגליה. צרה: חייל-האו"ם יושב על קצה החצאית, חצאיתה הרחבה של אמא אשר אשר ניתנה לה לכבוד הנסיעה. האוטובוס מתעקל לצאת ממפרצו אצל הרציף, מעדה שושנה ומצאה עצמה, ממתניה ומעלה, בחושך, על ברך קשה וזרה.

"סליחה," קראה עברית, תופשת בשתי ידיה, כברפסודה, במוט גב-המושב לפניה, חייל-האו"ם הנבוך אומר אנגלית: "אני מצטער. אני מצטער. זה הכול בסדר."

מנסה שוב להזדקף, חייל-האו"ם עדיין על קצה החצאית, האוטובוס מתעקל לצד שני, עפה אל ברכיו שנית. הפעם חש לעזור, להרימה כחבילה על-מנת לשימנה במקומה. אלא שהאוטובוס זז ומתיישר, הניח את ידו במקום הלא-נכון. "מצטער," נבהל והרפה מיד. מתאמצת לקום, אמרה שושנה: "זה הכול בסדר," חוזרת על דבריו אנגלית, "מצטערת." וניסתה מלה מימי בית-הספר: "שמלה." "שמלה? הו, שמלה. אני מצטער," נבהל עוד יותר והתרומם. "זה הכול בסדר," חזרה אנגלית, מבוישת. צל-החיוך נמחה מעל פניה זה כבר. עמו הכרת-הבטחון.

פעם, כשאבא עוד עבד בטבריה. מלצרית, קורצת לחברותיה, התנדבה להוכיח כושר-שיחה. הודיעה, תשאל חייל של או"ם אם נשוי הוא. לא מצאה את המלה. מצאה: "אתה, פֶּה?" "אולי, ולא יודע," צחק החייל, אולם מופתע מאד. כל המלצריות פרצו בצווחה. נשוי או לא נשוי. מה התכוון. הזמין את המלצרית לצאת עמו. "לאן," שאלה. "לרקוד לחי-אל-לחי," תרגם אבא את תשובת-החייל לכול. מה התכוון החייל. "חיילים של או"ם, כמו מלחים של אניה," הסביר לה אבא אז. לאבא שיר-זמר בצרפתית, ופעם בשבת תרגמו לנו כך, ברגש: "רואֶה אורות-נמל / רק הם סיפרו לי כי נפרדנו / אותם אורות-נמל / אותך הביאו אלי / דמעות נושרות / איך עוצרים דמעות מתנועע, כל היום נוסע, ים-הכסף / שלום לילות של גלים וחולות." ובקול עמוק: "רוצֶה אותך פה קרוב / בזרועותיך רק עוד פעם / אבל גורלי בית-הקפה על-יד נמל / וגורלך – הים." ושוב, כמקודם: "רואֶה אורות-נמל / רק הם סיפרו לי כי נפרדנו / אורות-נמל אחרים / אותך ממני כבר לוקחים."

בדרך הליילית עצים, במנוד-ראש של אנשים. אור האוטובוס הממהר נופל עליהם, מסתלק מהם. וחרמש הירח המכוסה אד מיטשטש. אולם מדוע יבש חיכה כה – הביטה שושנה דרך החלון שעה ארוכה.

נוסעת הביתה עם הכביסה של אבא, פעם ישב צעיר לידה נחמד, אולי סטודנט בטכניון, קורא ספר ספר-כיס. בשם 'זה היה רצח לאור-ירח'. משהחשיך, הכניס את הספר

לכיס ופנה לגעת בערפה באמנות כה משוכללת שעד לצומת לא ידעה אם כן או רק נדמה לה. כאז כן עתה, ברגע הראשון אותה בהלה. בהלה עיוורת. של חיית־בר. אולם שלא כאז, עתה לא היה מקום לטעות. חייל־האו״ם היושב לצדה כן, כן מצמיד מרפקו אל זרועה. הפעם הזאת לא קמה ממקומה ולא עברה למושב אחר. ישבה כפסל. ולא עשתה דבר. משקיפה מבעד לחלון.

הנה בידו האחרת מבקש הוא ליטול את כפה. וכשם שלא כדי להפעיל את שרירי־הגרון משמיעים אנשים קולות. אלא לומר דברים בעזרת מלים, הדברים עיקר. כן אף כאן. הוא מבקש לומר, אבל בדרך אחרת. מה יבקש. כן, אני יודעת. אך לא ברור מה שואל הוא כעת, עכשיו, בענין זה. ומה יצפה ממנה. קשה לדעת. מה עוד כשמבולבלים.

הציצה בו בהחבא. ונוכחה לדעת כי כבר יושב היה בסמוך מאד, סמוך מאשר שיערה. בפנים אטומות, כמו אין לו קשר אליה. מעביר את ידו להקיף אותה. חיילי־או״ם לפנינו, חיילי־או״ם אחרינו, כיצד יש לו אומץ.

בצומת הועלה אור. הזדרז החייל של או״ם, מיהר להתרחק.

חיילות עליזות עלו לאוטובוס. ״סמדר, סמדר,״ קראו לאחת עדיין למטה, קונה דבר מיל־דרוכל. יפות, מבוגרות, צוחקות. זה הסוף שלי, הרהרה שושנה. חוץ מזה, אין מנוס: אני יודעת מה יחשוב עלי עתה – לא העזה הבט לעברו. מה הוא יושב מביט קדימה, אף היא ישבה מביטה קדימה. מה הוא שלוב־ידים, שילבה־ידים אף היא.

החיילות, בהמולה, התפרסו על־פני המושבים הריקים. עלה מבקר־הכרטיסים. וחייל־האו״ם לצדה חייך לעצמו, באופן פרטי, מניף סנטרו מעט, עת חייל של או״ם במושב רחוק זרק לכולם מלה בקול, כנראה בדיחה. הוציאה שושנה מכיס חולצתה המשובצת את שני כרטיסיה. כרטיס ההלוך־וחזור עם כרטיס התוספת לשעה מאוחרת, החזיקה בידה.

ראתה: חייל־האו״ם היושב לידה דומם, הצטחק אליה. כמבקש רשות. וקודם שידעה מה רצונו, נטל את כרטיסיה מידה. מחזיקם עם כרטיסו, לגמרי יחד, הושיטם למבקר.

שמאז ומעולם עליה, הבת הבכורה, לדאוג לעצמה בכוחותיה – מהו אשר, פולח, עבר בה עתה את השיפה, חדר לכבי, ושותת הקטף. חשה את עצמה הרוסה, אינה יודעת דבר.

מחזיר לה את כרטיסיה, ניסה לקשור שיחה:

״ישראל?״ הראה עליה.

שושנה נענעה בראשה.

הראה על עצמו:

״רי״ף־רַף.״

היכן היא ריפרפיה, ניסתה להזכר.

״קנדה,״ חייך כמאשר, מגביה כתף להכניס את כרטיסו לכיס.

כל אשר ידעה אודות קנדה, הרהרה, הוא שאבא סיפר בשעתו. נכנס קנדי למטבח בית־המלון. ישב ואמר, לאבא ולשאר עוזרי־הטבחים, כי במקום ממנו בא, לפי הנוהג, האורח לטרקלין. אך אם רוצים להראות לאורח יחס חם במיוחד, מקבלים

אותו במטבח. כך אמר, ונרדם. שתוי לגמרי. רק אחר-כן מצאו שנרדם על מטחנת-
התבלינים, אותה חיפשו כל העת.

הראה החייל של או"ם באגודל לאחור. לדעת האם היא תושבת העיר אותה יצאו.
הצביעה שושנה קדימה. לאמור, העיר אליה יגיעו. הבין וצחק, כאילו הוכיחה חריפות.
הראה שוב לאחור, מנענע כף-ידו האחרת, כשאול. הצביעה שושנה על צרורו של
אבא, אמרה: "פפה." לבש החייל של או"ם ארשת של כבוד ודעתה של שושנה נחה
עליה. מאד.

נזכרה. ניסתה כוחה בכושר-שיחה:

"אתה, פפה?"

לא הבין. אולם הראה על עצמו, חייך: "לא אבא. לא אמא. לא אח. לא אחות. לא
אשה. לא ילדים. לא אף אחד," אמר. והסיר את כובעו. הניחו למעלה על תיקה: על
תיקה הניחו. עתה, בשערו האדום, יפה היה שבעתים. ואך כבה האור, חזר אליה.
פעם אחת ריקד האוטובוס. והוא, בעזרת פנים-זרועו אשר על גבה, כמו העיק עליה
אז במתכוון. כמו לחסך אותה, למנוע ממנה את הזעזוע.

כברת-דרך ממבואות העיר, אולם במרחק רב מן התחנה, היה הכביש צפוף במכוניות
ואוטובוסים עומדים. "פקק-תנועה?" אמרו האנשים, "תאונה?"

זמן רב חיכו שם. מכוניות נוספות הגיעו, עצרו. אנשים החלו יורדים. התעייפו
ועלו בחזרה. אדם בכובע 'אגד' בא. מן הוותיקים. קרתה תאונה, הסביר. יש להמשיך
ברגל. לנוסעים הלאה תומצא תחבורה. אמר וירד. הנהג תרגם לאנגלית, נטל ילקוטו
בתנועה אדישה, ירד אף הוא.

הוריד החייל של או"ם מן המדף את תיקה של שושנה, אולם אנשים נדחפו
ביניהם. בפרט אשה אחת, בשריה רוטטים, הממשיכה בשיחה תוך ירידה, כי לא
יכולה היתה להפסיק: "כעבור עשרים שנה ראיתי את זו שבגללה ויתר עלי," היאמן
כי אומרת היתה. "די דומה לי. והוא גם בה בגד. הנבל. הנקלה," אמרה. "מאין אני
יודעת? הוא בגד בה עמי," דיברה חילונית. חולין חלילה.

יורדת כמעט אחרונה, למטה ממתין היה לה החייל של או"ם.

"גוד בַּי," שמחה שושנה על שמצאה את המלה. נטלה את תיקה ממנו, בעוד הנה
אף זה חדש: השפה לא-לה בפיה. גולם מלאכותי מעשה-אדם. כמו בלחיצת-כפתור
פתאום זה פועל, חי, מבצע: חדש נסתר נוסף נגלה. פתאום העולם מלא שאלות
והפתעות. תוך כך שומעה היתה צעיר ישראלי עובר, המעיף-מבט בחייל-האו"ם,
אומר עליו עברית: "גוויה נאה." וכאילו היא אשר קיבלה מחמאה.

החייל של או"ם לא הלך. עומד היה, ידיו בחגורת מכנסיו הצרים, וממתין. הראתה
שושנה על חבריו חיילי-האו"ם המתרחקים, אשר התבדלו ועברו אל צדו השני של
הכביש. נענע בראשו לאות לאו, נטל ממנה את תיקה. מחייך ואומר "ילדה קטנה",
הורה על שעונו. לאמור, השעה מאוחרת ואינה יפה ליִלדות קטנות לבדן.

אחרונים היו עתה. ובאמרה ללכת אחרי הקהל, המתקדם בצד המכוניות העומדות,
עצרה. תופשה קלות בקצה-שרוולה. בחשאי, כבמחתרת. ומשעצרה עמו, חשה שושנה
כאילו העבירה לחלוטין לרשותו. תחת חסותו. עתה היא שלו. ממנה נדרש רק

לסמוך. ותרומתו, כמו ההשקעה שלו או ערבונות, ניתן לראותה למשל באיכות עור־
זרועותיו הפרטי שלו. הדק, שבצבע חול, זרוע־נמשים וכמו אמיץ, נכון מאד. או
שעונו, שעון־היד המרובע, אף בו היה מן הנכון והוכחה מאשרת. אף בגופייתו,
כחולצת־התעמלות לבנה, המצוה ממיפתח־החולצה. וכן הלאה.

מלאו היו הנוסעים האחרים עוד, משכה החייל של או"ם אליו, העבירה לצדו
השני, מובילה לרדת עמו לשביל – שבילים רבים היו פה – בואכה העיר. הכול
הולכים שם, ואילו הם בדרך שלהם בלבד. אף זה נכון היה. הצטרפה ללא שאלות.

מדי פעם העמיד אותה, גיפפה. פעם לש ולש אותה, אמר לתוך שערותיה, לאט,
כדי שתבין, "תראי, אני אהיה טוב," ונישקה על שערה.

המלים הדהימה. חדש נסתר: זהו שזכות לו הנערות המבוגרות. קנדיות.
מאושרות. מסתוריות, גאיונות, ראויות. וכי הן שאילפום. בערבים של שבילים בין
עפאים, ופנסים תלויים על ענפים בינות לזלזלים. שייך היה לזה גם חזהו־במדים,
אליו הצמידה בדברו. חזהו המפתיע, קרוב, ישר, כולו ריק, פנוי. ואיך זה, קן־בטחון.
אולם מה אמר. כאילו נשאלה בהשתוממות: "כל השנים הללו, ואת לא ידעת. באמת
לא ידעת כי יש, יש ים־התיכון גם בצד מזרח?" בוודאי. ים, וחוף. ולמה ההקלה
המפחידה. "לא ידעתי," אני עונה וכבר לא בטוחה: ידעתי או לא ידעתי. אולם מה
אמר. האם ביקש את ידה. ילדה קטנה. האומר הוא להמתין עד שתגדל. לקחתה עמו,
לריפריה. רוצו הימים, רוצו. עדיין לא ברור רק כיצד, בלי להכירני, מיד עמד על כי
שושנה אני מכל שושנה, על־כן בי יש לבחור.

בחצאית הפרחונית הגדולה ממידתה, מצומצמת למתניה בסיכת־בטחון. בחולצה
המשובצת הקצרה ממידתה, השרוול מכסה ולא מכסה על הכתפיה השמוטה. אותה
שושנה. ושושנה אחרת. מסתורית, ראויה. נערות יפות, נשים יפות, כמניפות יפות.
תמיד עת תראה יפות, קורת־רוח. כאילו שותפה ליפין, ממרחק. והנה שותפה,
ראויה. ועל מפתן.

כמו אז בחלום? ברחבה גדולה אני עומדת. היום מתחיל רד. אפריקנית יפה מאד,
אשת שגריר, עומדת מוקסמת מול אחת הערוגות ברחבה. פינת פרחי לוף, פרחי
ענק. מרהיבים. עקודים, נקודים וברודים, בצבעים על־טבעיים. "סוס־הררה," היא
אומרת בקול נמוך, "סוס־הררה." הקסם אוחז גם בי. "סוס־הררה?" אני שואלת.
"סוס־הררה: עֲרִימוֹת־הממתקים אצלנו בשווקים." ומישהו בא לקרוא לה. למטוס.
אל שמי־הלילה. מכוסים כבר כוכבים כפרחי יסמין. רוצו הימים, רוצו.

אוחזת כל הזמן בכפה, בסוף השביל הגיעו אל גדר נישאה, של רשת־תיל. נראית
חדשה. חזרו. ובכל פעם, בסוף כל שביל, אותה גדר. ואין ללכת לאורכה. קוצים
גבוהים, סבוכים ללא־מעבר. אין־ברירה, יש לעבור את הגדר.

השליך את צרורה אל העבר השני. אף עזר לה לעלות על הגדר. עלה גם הוא.
העביר את שתי רגליו אל העבר השני וקפץ שם. אך היא, לא יכולה היתה לרדת!
מרים ידיו לקלטה, שיחררה עצמה, נפלה לידיו.

מקבלה, מדוע לא נתן לה ללכת, מאמצה כולה אליו. ומדוע נשתנתה כה. ומדוע אין
הולכים הלאה. ומדוע פתאום שוב בבהלה של חיית־בר – ניסתה להשתחרר. אולם
גברים מה חזקים הם, נודע לה. והוא מתנשם כאחוז צמרמורות. מדוע הפילה בגסות

על האדמה. האין עוול גם בשיקוע ראשו של אדם לאחור, בעפר. מפרפרת להחלץ, חצִיה לכודה בין רגליו והוא מהדק את רגליה זו אל זו, חצִיה העליון לכוד בזרוע אחת שלו, רק רבץ עליה, קשה, בבגדיו ובנעליו, וזה הכל, בידו האחרת מפנה בכוח את פניה אל עבר פניו, מחפש את פיה, כמבקש קירבה ורצון. בעצמו נותן, מגיש, תורם את זוג־השפתיים האחד לו, האיכפת לו, מוכרח להיות, ואשר של שפתים כמטופחות. בו־בזמן מונע ממנה באכזריות מהחלץ, כאוסר לזוז, איזו מין תכנית זאת, והוא נאנח ונרגש כה. ופתאום עזב. הכל לא ברור, לא טוב. והן היינו ידידים. ואני, למענו, כבר אינני של ישראל. אני של או"ם.

יושב לצדה שאל, לאט, כדי שתבין:
"בת כמה את?"
הראתה שושנה באצבעותיה: שלש־עשרה.
צחק. כבש פניו בכתפה.
"אלהים," אמר צוחק, "סלחי לי." עתה הקיש על קדקדו, לאמור: חושב היה. ומסביר, זרק אגרופו שלוש פעמים, סגורים ופותחו, והוסיף באצבעות, לאמור: שמונה־עשרה. נענע אצבעות ידו השמאלית, לאמור: אולי. זרק אגרופו והוסיף באצבעות ידו הימנית, לאמור: שבע־עשרה. ושוב זרק ובאצבע אחת: שש־עשרה. הרהר, ורק זרק חמש־עשרה. הסתכלה שושנה ברצינות, בסבלנות, מתאמצת להבין את שפת התנועות. אולם עתה צחק, סטר לה באצבע על חטמה. נשאה שושנה את ראשה אליו, והוא חיבקה ביד אחת, מושכה אליו. עור־זרועותיו הבהיר הפרטי בכל־זאת נכון מאד. וחזהו במדים, קן־הבטחון.

"יתושים," אמר. כמובן יתושים. הוא טפח על כיס־אחורי, כבודק, הוציא חפיסה מעוכה של סיגריות־חוץ. וגפרורים, ראשם מגופם, מחוברים בשורות לפנקס קטן. הצית סיגריה. הראה על עשן הסיגריה והסביר: "היתושים," עושה בידו כמפריחם לכל עבר. עשן מבריח יתושים, למדה. הוא מלומד.
מעשן היה. מביט קדימה. פנה והציע לה את הסיגריה. נטלה שושנה את הסיגריה. צחק ותיקן את אחיזתה בסיגריה, מעודדה לעשן. אך שושנה החזירה לו את הסיגריה. וכך, זעה להישען על אמת־ידה, חשמיעה זעקה קטנה: שמה פנים פרק־ידה על שבר־זכוכית פה, ונחתכה. חיפשה, הרימה את שבר־הזכוכית, זכוכית לבנה של צואר־בקבוק. נטלו מידה, העיפו. "תני לי," ביקש לראות את החתך.
שושנה היססה. שמה את היד אחרי הגב, חייכה אליו נכלמה. חזר לעשן. מביט קדימה. הוציאה שושנה בזהירות את היד הפגועה, מצצה בחשאי. ראה, צחק. פנה אליה, בידו החפשית נטל את כל הזרוע. לא ראה מאומה בחושך. לחץ על זרועה כמבטיח, החזירה אצלה. ומסיים ממילא לעשן, תקע את זנב־הסיגריה באדמה. קם, כמעט בלי להאחז בידים, ראתה. הלך להביא את צרורה, תולהו בקלות על שכמו.
בא והקימה במשיכה: "ילדה קטנה," הורה על שעונו מחייך.
שושנה קמה כנכנעת. הוא אמר מה, לאט, כדי שתבין. והיא לא הבינה. חזר וחזר, והיא לא הבינה. "נֶווֶרמַינְד," צחק קלות.

עתה נראו כבר בבירור בתים. הכול כמו בלא־צבעים. ופנסי־הרחוב כבים שם מאליהם. וכי כך כסדרו יום אחר יום אור הולך וצח הרקיע נשטף, בפשטות ובשקט היום מתחלק מתוך הלֵיל. פתרון נכון ולא־מסובך, פתרון מלוא־עולם. ואינו צריך לעדים. אולם העינים רואות. נושא ידו, מחה החייל של או״ם בבוהן עפר מגבותיה: היה זה לה בלבה כאילו השביעה.

בין הכביש לעצי־הכביש הולכים היו. ובצפון־מזרח, בין העצים ומעבר לגגות השטוחים של הבניינים, סימן של אדמומית ראתה. מעל לסימן של כְּחול. וענני־ הכבוד. נסי האצטלוונות של דודי־השמש ולוחותיהם המשופעים, הסולמות והקיסמים הדקיקים אשר לתרני־הטלוויזיה, כולם שחורים משחור, כעל רקע של ים מואר, הולך ונדלק. מן הנגלות אשר נחלת המושבעים, המובאים בברית הסודית, להם סתרי־עולם מעשים שבכל־יום.

בחפשם דרך קודם לכן, שמעו להקת־ילדים עוברת הרחק. כנראה חניכי בית־ הספר המקצועי. אחד מהם פורט על גיטרה, אחרים מזמרים לא־ברורות. נזכרה שיום אחרון ללימודים היה זה. ״באנג־באנג,״ אף עשה אז החייל של או״ם לעבר הקולות, כמחזיק רובה בידיו. עתה, באור־השחר, נראו הילדים חוזרים. בזכר לצבעים: מכנסיים מתוחים, בזכר של תכלת; חגורה בזכר של פסים, אדומים־ושחורים; חולצה בזכר של צהוב. עדיין מזמרים, מתעכבים להריח איש את פי רעהו, חוצים את הכביש, פוסעים לרדת אל הבתים: השעה ארבע לפנות־בוקר, יעירו את כל הרחוב. ״אינני זוכר מה כתבתי בבחינה. אבל מה שכתבתי היה הנכון.״

מיהר החייל של או״ם, פנה, הדביקה אז חיש אל אחד מאילנות־האקליפטוס. ונשען אל הגזע בזרועות נטויות מעליה, עמד עליה להסתירה. השתוממה. מעצמה, לא היה עולה על דעתה. רצתה לנסות לומר דבר, אך הוא מיהר ושם שם כפו על פיה – והיא נושמת את ריח עשן הטבק הטרי החריף באצבעותיו. אחר השפיל מבטו אליה, מחייך חביבות. חייל של או״ם! – דבק לבה בו. חייל של או״ם! – עמדה כך והסתכלה בו כל העת, בראשה המוטה כלפיו, עיניה לטושות אליו, כפו על פיה. עד אשר, משלא היו הנערים עוד, ומכופף ברכיו, אחז כתפיה, הצמיד בהלצה את הלחצה אל לחיו אל לחיה. נזכר, שפשף בידו על לחיו להראות על הזיפים האדמונים אשר החלו מצמחים, עשה העוויה להצחיקה, ושיחררה. ״ילדה קטנה, ילדה טובה,״ אמר.

חייל של או״ם! – הרהיבה שושנה עוז, הושיטה ידיה, אחזה במתניו, לא אבתה ללכת. אחר הצטרפה ללכת.

משוחרר מכל תלות ידועה לי. תלויות אינן־ידועות הקנו פה קשיות ואופי, בלעדיהם אינך בן־אדם – הוא פוסע כמו ללא ניע־ראש. יתבונן לפניו כמו הכול, אבל הכול, אחד ושווה. והדיבור אינו הכרחי לו, אפשר כך ואפשר כך. רואים, המצב הטבעי לו. מין יכולת נערצה נערה פה, כמין מותרות. שאננות עולה ממאגר של כוח – ניסתה שושנה להתאים צעדיה לצעדיו. וכל הזמן פניו, זרועותיו, מדיו – כולו המוכר, ישן וחדש באור החדש.

משאית, ליילית עדיין, פנסיה דולקים עדיין, חלפה על פניהם ברעש רב. מלאה

פועלים ערבים שפופים. מעבר מזה של הכביש מגרש־הכדורגל. שני השערים, והאדמה
המנוקה משיחי־בר קשה, מוקפת מושבי־אצטדיון של עץ בשתי שורות, זו מעל זו,
כפיגומים. ותחנת־אוטובוס. לוח־המודעות. מכאן, שעדיין אינו יודע לא יוכל לדעת
כי המרובע הכהה בלוח־המודעות הוא המודעה המצוירת הגדולה של הסרט ההודי.
לנערה אפון אדום במצחה, מעל חטמה. ומחרוזת ענבר: החרוזים עבים וכמרובעים.
ואילו לגבר נטיה לפימה.

השקיף חייל־האו״ם על הכביש הבין־עירוני כתועה, מעביר כף־ידו על צווארו
האדמדם. מסתכל בה כאילו אינו בטוח ביכלתה להובילם. אולי חשב שנושאת היא
את עיניה אליו כל העת משום שתצפה לתושייתו. אולם היא צועדת ומסתכלת בו כל
העת רק משום שאינה יכולה להתיק את עיניה ממנו: למשל, לא תארתי לי אותו
בשפם, או בפיאות, או בזקן. עתה, זקוק לתגלחת, ניתן לתאר. או, הנה. על אף
החוטם המתקלף בשל שמש הארץ הזאת, רסיסיהם התכלכלים של הררי־הקרח,
רסיסים מן הארץ במרחקים שם ביתו, משמרת־התמיד אשר נקבעה בפניו במקום
עינים. פניו, בהן דרך־קבע אותה נכריות־פתאום אשר לובשות פניה של אשה משלנו,
לרגע, ברגע הראשון לענדה עגילים. כבושני זר. נכריות בה מין עידון. אף כמו רשע
דק מן הדק. רשע פרי דמיונך, פרי התבטלותך. או למשל צבעיו. צבעי אדמה אחרת,
שונה, עד סוף האופק שדות אחרים, שונים. עם עמודי־חשמל שונים, האובדים בם.
עם טרקטורים ומכונות־קציר שונים, זעירים בעברם אותם. לאנשים הנוהגים בם
סרבלים שונים. אולי סרבלי־כתפיות? כובעיהם כובעי קש פרום? כחום־היום בשדה
שותים הם כולם ויסקי ממיכלי ג׳ריקן.

שושנה עמדה. לנער גריס־אבן מתוך נעלה. ניסתה לרמוז שעמדה.

עצר, חייך הבנה.

שבה שושנה ללכת – רסיסי המרחקים, באים עם סידור של ריסים זהבוניים.
צבעיה, כל צבעיה של אדמה שונה, מנומשת, בארץ אשר מעבר להררי־הקרח: אם
תשבור בבקעה קצת קרח תפתח בגרזן, תוכל לשלות בו דג כקומת־איש. והביטו איך, מה
זה, כל אלה הגיעו, נפלו פה. פה פוסעים. כשמאחור מגרש־הכדורגל שלנו, הוא ולא
אחר, לפנינו השכונה. כל הציפורים בענפי האקליפטוס מקבלות בתזמורת את פני
הזריחה העתידה, אבל אני יודעת: גם לכבודנו, גם לכבודנו. היש כמוך בעולם, כמוך
שבדיוק נכון.

והנה השכונה.

חתול נראה עובר מגג בית אל גג מחסן. כל חבתים שקועים בשנת. קצה עגלת־
הקרשים הגדושה אבטיחים. מהראשונים העונה. אבל דומה, אף אחד מן האחים
עזרא אינו ישן בה על המזרן. אף פנס־הרוח התלוי עליה בל־יראה. בגסיסה אטית,
אשר בלא הוד־גבורה, מתפוררים שני הבתים אשר נעזבו מיושביהם. סדקים בקיר,
החצרות קוצים. אומרים, בין עמודי־יסודותיהם נחשים.

ליד הגדר האחורית של הבית עמדה. הורתה על הבית. אולם חייל־האו״ם כופף
אגודלו לאחור ותחבו אל בין שיניו, כשהוא מטה ראשו אחורנית, מדגים לשושנה
בעינים משוטטות. על חפצו לשתות. קלטה. הורתה על הברז ליד פח־הזבל.

רכב על הגדר, ועבר. קו־הכתפיים הישר כקולב, החולצה הגדולה משתלשלת על גבו דחלילית, פתח. רכן בפישוק־רגלים מעל לברז ושתה. חתול, מן־הסתם אורב שם כל העת, לפתע החליט, זינק מתוך הפח, נמלט אל חצר השכנים, והסתתר אחרי ארון־הקרח הישן המוטל שם על צדו על־פני האדמה. חייל־האו"ם מחה את פיו בפרק־ידו.

בא. עמד מולה. הרים את התיק, תלהו צוחק על שכמה, כשהוא אומר מה בשפתו. שושנה לא הלכה. הביט בה. שושנה לא הלכה. הסיט באצבעו את כובעו מוגזמות, מערפו קדימה. וממצחו לאחור. כמחקה את מי, ברוח טובה. שושנה לא הלכה.

החל מפשפש בכיסיו. הוציא את כרטיס־הנסיעה של 'אגד'. בחן את כרטיס־הנסיעה של 'אגד'. קיפלו נכונה ועוד פעם. נטל ושם את כרטיס־הנסיעה בכפה, קיפל אצבעותיה מעליו, חיזקן לאגרוף שחום סוגר על הכרטיס. "סובניר," חייך. שושנה לא הלכה. ליטף קלות את לחיה, והלך. סובב פעם אחת, נופף אליה בידו והלך.

משלא נראה עוד, הסתכלה שושנה בכרטיס־הנסיעה. איני יודעת מה שמו, עלה עתה בדעתה. אינני יודע מה שמי, הסתכלה שושנה בכרטיס־הנסיעה. קברה פניה בכרטיס־הנסיעה. אחר, היטיבה המעמסה על שכמה.

נכנסה הביתה על בהונות. עוקפת את עגלת־התינוק אצל דלת־הכניסה פנימה, עברה על פני אחיה הישנים. חגיגיים עד לבעתה, כצלובים. החליפה בגדיה בדממה. ונכנסה בזהירות לתוך המיטה, יחד עם אחותה הקטנה, המכודרת ובזרועות כסוככות על פניה וראשה.

אמה, בשערה הסתור, בחלוק האדום הנצחי מוטל עתה בחפזה על כותנתה, באה מן החדר השני, מסיטה את וילון־הפסים הצהוב ועומדת במסגרת־הפתחה: הסתכלה שושנה היישר בעיני אמה. הסתכלה אמה היישר בעיניה. ולא אמרה דבר. הלכה. ושושנה שמעה כיצד בכתה אמה חנוקות. שם, במיטתה החורקת, בחדר השני. ואחרי־כן, התינוק מתעורר. ונרדם.

מחתה עוד גרגיר־עפר אחרון, או שנים, מגבותיה הדקות, ומשורש־צווארה. ומאחורי תנוך־אזנה. רוזיטה שמי, הייתי אומרת לו. שם של מהלכים בעולם־הגדול. שם־מלידה, ועד אשר שונה במצוות חפצי־בה המורה. ילדה־קטנה ישראל שמי עכשיו. אכן, נתקטנה כדי זרת־זרתים, ובעת־ובעונה־אחת נתגדלה באמה־אמתים: סובבה המוכר והוא אחר. כמו עם הילדה עליסה, בהצגה ששלחו אלינו. לכבוד יום־האימוץ. כשאימצו אותנו ביום 'ואהבת לרעך כמוך'. והיו כל התקלות. הרמקולים לא פעלו. אחרי־כן המשאית נשברה. ואותם האורחים אשר בגורלם נפל להמתין היו מרוגזים: הביאו להם תה, הודו, וכמעט ולא שתו. אף חפצי־בה המורה ארגנה אותנו, מקהלת 'ליצנים', לזמר להם שירה־בציבור. צבי נתן את 'מחול הצביה'. במגבעת־גברת, שמלה שאולה, ארנק ולחיים לא־מגולחות, רקד ריקוד סלוני, כשהוא מחבק ומלטף בן־זוג דמיוני. אבל אחדים עצבניים התלחשו כל הזמן: משאית – מכונית־גרר – חוסר־אחריות. את מי מעניינים אלה. כבסי, אמא, כבסי הכביסה. אולי בעוד שבועיים, אולי בעוד שלושה – שם כולם יפים, כולם טובים, כולם אוהבים, ובמדי־עבודה נאים ירקרקים, בחצר־הקסרקטין, מול קמרוני־העמודים האפורים, בהנאה ובנחת כולם משקים בדליים, או מקרצפים, או מסרקים, איש את סוסו האהוב: בזה אחר זה

יעמדו מעבודתם. יחזרו להתנועע, עם סורי. עוברת מחפשת לאורך הגדר. שלום
לבן־דודי צח־ואדום: האחרון בשורה יהיה. עושה במלאכתו. באהבה. ואינו מבחין.
שם אעמוד. אחכה. עד אשר יראני. יכירני. המברשת מידו יניח. יצא אלי. יכניסני,
יביאני. וכולם יצחקו, אבל ישמחו, נערת־הגדוד. אולי בעוד שבועים, אולי בעוד
שלושה, באוטובוס של 'אגד'. עם תיק 'אל־על' כחול. אל הגורל שלי.

"אבל שמי הוא ילדה־קטנה נערת־הגדוד / וחייל של או"ם שמך / רואה אורות־
נמל..." ואולי, ואפילו בעוד עשרים־שנה. ואפילו אראה את אלו שבגללן יותרו עלי.
די דומות לי. וגם בהן יבגדו. איך אדע? – כי יבגדו בהן עמי! קברה פניה בכרטיס־
הנסיעה. בלב חלל. נדמית לה כאיש מובא לבית־דין, ובסופו של דבר מגישים לו
הפקידים לחתימה גליון־נייר נורא. והוא חותם. בין השאר, גם בשמץ של סיפוק.
סיפוק שהוא כרצון הרסנות, מושך ומפחיד כאחת. אבל האפרוח הבוקע מביצתו
במדגרה, אשר בעיות היו לו, מה עם האפרוח – החלה נרדמת. מנעה עצמה מהרהם:
כמו ללא מעצורים, איך זה, פתאום נדחף אדם להתקרב. יעניק תשומת־לב, אותות
חיבה ורצון, יפנק. לא חושש. נותן. נחשף לפני זר. עליו לחבב את אותו זר. מוכרח
להיות. אחרת למה לו כל אלה, הן מרצונו הטוב. מעצמו. ממנו. מחבב, כן, מחבב.
ושוקעת בחבלי־שינה, כאיש עושה־במאמץ המשיר לקראת סוף המסע כל משא
מיותר, זה שנותר: אדם רוצה. רוצה לקבל, לתת. אדם מעניק, מחבב, משתף, כמו לא
זרים. ואחרי־כן הולך. לא חוזר. נרדמה.

שומעת היתה את אמה קמה, עוברת למטבח. מערבבת את המזון לתרנגולות. בחום
העומד כבר בעולם, כאוויר־מכבסה, כל יגע היום הנולד: לא ברכה, לא מסווה: נולד
לא סיכוי, לא פיוס, לא חידוש. ללא־זיע עלי הצמח־המטפס: הדלועי, הקישואי,
יעטר רק את חצרות הדלים, מזמן נוכחה לדעת. משתרג שם זוקף את פרחיו הצהובים,
נלפת אל כלונס־הסוכה אשר קצהו נראה מפינתה במיטה. שומעת היתה את אמה
מחברת אל ברז־המטבח את צינור־ההשקיה. למלא במים אם שתי גיגיות־הכביסה
ודוד־החיתולים בחוץ, מתחת לחלון־המטבח. כיצד סיפרה לנו פעם. מעשה שאירע
בארץ־מולדתם. מעשה באח אשר חנק אחות נואפת והטיל את גופתה לתוך באר.
"ברוכות הידים," ברכתו אמו – סיפרה לנו בחרדת־קודש.
אולם אני, לעולם לא עוד מכאן. לעולם של או"ם.

והדבר שטפה. כמנגינה נשכחת. פרץ רעננותו של כוח המחזיר־לאחור ודַוָי, כמו
נוחם, על הנרצח כאן לרגליך כל פעם מחדש ונרמס מהו לא תדע. צדים מחדש את
אשר פס ועתה הוא רק עדנה, כל העדנה. אך משומרים בה מלוא טעמו האבוד ועומק
הצבעים – בחריפות שהיא כאגרוף בלסת. בעולם־הגדול, רק הפעם רק למעני רק
במקרה שלי, אנוכי אותך, האין־זאת, אנא – יום אחד שנית אמצא.

דליה רביקוביץ VI

רחיפה בגובה נמוך

אֲנִי לֹא כָאן.
אֲנִי עַל נְקִיקֵי הָרִים מִזְרָחִיִּים
מְנֻמָּרִים פִּסוֹת שֶׁל קֶרַח
בִּמְקוֹם שֶׁעֵשֶׂב לֹא צָמַח
5 וְצֵל רָחָב נָטוּשׁ עַל הַמּוֹרָד.
רוֹעָה קְטַנָּה עִם צֹאן עִזִּים
שְׁחוֹרוֹת
הִגִּיחָה שָׁם
מֵאֹהֶל לֹא נִרְאָה.
10 לֹא תוֹצִיא אֶת יוֹמָהּ הַיַּלְדָּה הַזֹּאת
בַּמִּרְעֶה.

אֲנִי לֹא כָאן.
בָּלַע הַר פֶּרַח כַּדּוּר אָדֹם,
עֲדַיִן לֹא חַמָּה.
15 בַּהֶרֶת כְּפוֹר סְמוּקָה וְחוֹלָנִית
מִתְהַפֶּכֶת בַּלַּע.

וְהַקְּטַנָּה הִשְׁכִּימָה כֹּה לָקוּם אֶל הַמִּרְעֶה
גְּרוֹנָהּ אֵינוֹ נָטוּי
עֵינַיִךְ לֹא קְרוּעוֹת בַּפּוּךְ, לֹא מְשֻׁקָּרוֹת
20 אֵינָהּ שׁוֹאֶלֶת, מֵאַיִן יָבוֹא עֶזְרִי.

אֲנִי לֹא כָאן.
אֲנִי כְּבָר בֶּהָרִים יָמִים רַבִּים
הָאוֹר לֹא יִצְרְבֵנִי. הַכְּפוֹר בִּי לֹא יִגַּע.
שׁוּב אֵין לִי מַה לְלְקוֹת בְּתַדְהֵמָה.
25 דְּבָרִים גְּרוּעִים מֵאֵלֶּה רָאִיתִי בְּחַיַּי.

37

אֲנִי אוֹסֶפֶת שִׂמְלָתִי וּמְרַחֶפֶת
סָמוּךְ מְאֹד אֶל הַקַּרְקַע.
מַה הִיא חָשְׁבָה לָהּ הַיַּלְדָּה הַזֹּאת?
פְּרָאִית לְמַרְאֶה, לֹא רְחוּצָה
לְרֶגַע מִשְׁתּוֹפֶפֶת בִּכְרִיעָה.   30
לְחָיֶיהָ רַכּוֹת כְּמֶשִׁי
פִּצְעֵי קֹר עַל גַּב יָדָהּ.
פּוֹזֶרֶת דַּעַת, כִּבְיָכוֹל
קַשּׁוּבָה, לַאֲמִתּוֹ שֶׁל דָּבָר.
וְעוֹד נוֹתְרוּ לָהּ כָּךְ וְכָךְ שָׁעוֹת.   35
אֲנִי לֹא בָּעִנְיָן הַזֶּה הִגַּעְתִּי.
מַחְשְׁבוֹתַי רִפְּדוּנִי בִּרְפִידָה שֶׁל מוֹךְ
מָצָאתִי לִי שִׁיטָה פְּשׁוּטָה מְאֹד,
לֹא מִדְרַךְ כַּף רֶגֶל וְלֹא מָעוֹף.
רְחִיפָה בְּגֹבַהּ נָמוּךְ.   40

אֲבָל בִּנְטוֹת צָהֳרַיִם
שָׁעוֹת רַבּוֹת
לְאַחַר הַזְּרִיחָה
עָלָה הָאִישׁ הַהוּא בָּהָר
כְּמִטַפֵּס לְפִי תֻּמּוֹ.   45
וְהַיַּלְדָּה קְרוֹבָה אֵלָיו מְאֹד.
וְאֵין אִישׁ זוּלָתָם.
וְאִם נִסְתָה לְהִתְחַבֵּא אוֹ צָעֲקָה
אֵין מִסְתּוֹר בֶּהָרִים.

אֲנִי לֹא כָּאן   50
אֲנִי מֵעַל רִכְסֵי הָרִים פְּרוּעִים וְאַיֻּמִים
בִּפְאַתֵי מִזְרָח.
עִנְיָן שֶׁאֵין צְרִיכִים לְהִתְעַכֵּב עָלָיו.
אֶפְשָׁר בְּטַלְטֵלָה עַזָּה וּבִרְחִיפָה
לָחוּג בִּמְהִירוּת הָרוּחַ.   55
אֶפְשָׁר לְהִסְתַּלֵּק וּלְדַבֵּר עַל לֵב עַצְמִי:
אֲנִי דָבָר לֹא רָאִיתִי.
וְהַקְּטַנָּה עֵינֶיהָ רַק חָרוּגִי מֵחוֹרֵיהֶן
חִכָּהּ יָבֵשׁ כַּחֶרֶס,
כְּשֶׁיַּד קָשָׁה לְפָתָה אֶת שַׂעֲרָה וְאָחֲזָה בָּהּ   60
לְלֹא קֹרְטֹב חֶמְלָה.